LEADERSHIP AT THE SPIRITUAL EDGE

This insightful book explores the intersection of spirituality and leadership, examining cutting edge research, theory, and practices that help build healthy and long-term effective leadership. Showcasing non-Western views of leadership across a range of backgrounds, the book looks at leadership styles that raise and expand consciousness to enable better problem solving when addressing the complex challenges of organizations and societies.

Across four sections, the book considers a myriad of themes from surrender to compassion, the dark and shadow side to the illuminating light of love, as well as offering a spotlight on individual leader development to highlight the role of the collective. Each chapter individually and collectively represents the essence of a profound shift in how leadership is approached in the 21st century. The volume offers a variety of viewpoints addressing this spiritual turn in leadership scholarship, and provides leadership tools to assist leaders in honing their practices to address contemporary challenges and unleash their full potential.

In a world where the challenges are immense and multifaceted, this anthology explores leadership that transcends the mundane and ventures into the extraordinary. *Leadership at the Spiritual Edge* will be of use to researchers, scholars, and students of leadership studies, particularly those interested in new ways of viewing and developing leadership.

Mohammed Raei is an independent leadership and organization development consultant, dissertation coach, and an executive coach based in Jordan.

Stacey K. Guenther is a leadership coach and consultant and affiliate faculty of the Organization Development and Knowledge Management program at George Mason University, USA.

Lisa A. Berkley is the Founding President of the Institute for Inner Economy and works at the University of California, Santa Cruz, USA, where she teaches and directs programs focusing on human thriving in the face of technology and Artificial Intelligence.

"This powerful collection brings together scholars known for pushing the boundaries of leadership inquiry beyond traditional, individually-based accounts to explore what happens if we take seriously the spiritual and collective dynamics at leadership's core. Prepare to see anew traditional theories such as adaptive and transformational leadership, and to be blown away by the possibilities enabled by recognizing leadership as an intuitive, sensory and soul-based experience emerging from the 'interspace'."

Donna Ladkin, *award-winning author of* Rethinking Leadership: A New Look at Old Leadership Questions *and Professor of Inclusive Leadership, Birmingham Business School, University of Birmingham, UK*

"I see this edited volume a most timely effort to address the rapidly increased need to better conceptualize and showcase the dynamic interplay between spirituality and leadership. Their intention to include non-Western perspectives, along with the shadow side, on this important topic, is courageous and refreshing."

Xiaoan Li, *Senior Program Manager, Fetzer Institute*

"Imagine leadership knowledge informed by the reciprocal and relational perspectives of ancient, Indigenous, and traditional wisdoms supplemented by emerging best practice and understandings. Imagine leadership oriented towards relationality and care of both others humans and other-than-humans. Imagine leadership where courage challenges existing perspectives and links reflective consciousness as spiritual practice towards building a better world for all, even while acknowledging its dark side. *Leadership at the Spiritual Edge* offers those perspectives and more in its holistic understanding of leadership is meant to be and do."

Sandra Waddock, *award-winning author of* Intellectual Shamans *and* The Difference Makers, *and Galligan Chair of Strategy, Carroll School Scholar of Corporate Responsibility, and Professor of Management, Boston College, USA*

LEADERSHIP AT THE SPIRITUAL EDGE

Emerging and Non-Western Concepts of Leadership and Spirituality

Edited by
Mohammed Raei, Stacey K. Guenther, and Lisa A. Berkley

Routledge
Taylor & Francis Group
NEW YORK AND LONDON

Cover Image: Getty Images © Kamisoka

First published 2025
by Routledge
605 Third Avenue, New York, NY 10158

and by Routledge
4 Park Square, Milton Park, Abingdon, Oxon, OX14 4RN

Routledge is an imprint of the Taylor & Francis Group, an informa business

ISBN: 978-1-032-50061-4 (hbk)
ISBN: 978-1-032-50059-1 (pbk)
ISBN: 978-1-003-39674-1 (ebk)

DOI: 10.4324/9781003396741

Typeset in Galliard
by codeMantra

CONTENTS

FIGURES

TABLES

GLOSSARY

Activism Individual and collective social activity intended to effect specific forms of change.

Acto symbolico The use of symbolic gesture, presentation, and performance in order to reflect larger themes of social discourse that are beyond practical acts. Examples include multi-layered acts of theatre, poetry, and dance.

African cosmology Refers to the way Africans perceive, conceive and contemplate their universe; the lens through which they perceive reality shaping their values and mindsets. Cosmology acts as the African's pursuit to find meaning in life and arrive at a unifying framework that offers an origin and end point. This must be understood generally, since a single philosophical view is not universally shared by all Africans, but there are common elements and characteristics found across diverse African worldviews. Fundamental questions addressed by African cosmology include: What is the essence and nature of the universe as understood in African thought? Who or what entities created and maintain the cosmic order? What is the nature of the different beings that inhabit the African cosmology (divine, human, natural, and ancestral), and what are the connections and relationships between them?

Agape "The Descending and immanent and manifesting current of the Kosmos, the principle of embodiment, and bodily incarnation, and relationship, and relational and manifest embrace, touching each and every being with perfect and equal grace, rejecting nothing, embracing all" (Wilber, 2017a, p. 232).

Ahwal The stage of states in Sufi tareeqa or path.

Amygdala The amygdala is an almond-shaped structure located deep in the brain that is considered part of the limbic system, the emotional processing center. It plays a key role in processing emotions, emotional behaviors, and motivation, including detecting threats and triggering fear and anxiety responses (Šimić et al., 2021).

Anātman (Pali : anattā) The Buddhist concept of *anātman*, or "non-self," teaches that there is no permanent, unchanging self or soul. The concept is often misconstrued as denying the existence of a self altogether. However, a more accurate understanding of anātman sees it as a way to attain detachment from the world by accepting the impermanence of everything ("Anattā," 2023).

Anitya "Anitya expresses the concept that all compounded phenomena (all things and experiences) arise due to causes and conditions and are subject to change, decline, and cessation. Hence, all phenomena are unstable, unreliable, and constantly changing" ("Anitya," n.d., para. 2).

Baqa Permanence or subsistence beyond all form in Sufism.

Brahman The unchanging ultimate reality which underlies all transient appearances (Mitra, 2020). Contrast with Maya: The illusionary and ever-changing nature of the world which underlies all transient appearances (Mitra, 2020).

Consciousness studies An interdisciplinary field exploring the nature of consciousness, encompassing various perspectives, including spirituality, quantum physics, and psychology.

Co-regulation The mutual adjustment of thinking, feeling, and acting to the ongoing and anticipated actions of one's interlocutor (Fogel, 1993)

Co-sensing Part of Scharmer's U Process (2018) designed to harness collective intelligence and to solve intractable issues by facilitating groups through a deepening experience of thinking, feeling, and then opening to future possibilities, co-sensing is a process for moving from intellect to emotional intelligence through different ways of knowing such as somatic and spiritual knowing.

Cultural capital The social assets of a person, including both material and symbolic goods, that promote trust and social status within a stratified society. Identified by Bourdieu (1977) as embodied capital, objectified capital, and institutionalized capital.

Curanderismo Based on the Spanish *curar* (to heal), *curanderismo* is a holistic system of Latin American, particularly Aztec, traditional medicine focused on sustaining overall health by creating balance between self and environment, through the integration of traditional beliefs, rituals, and practices that address the physical, spiritual, psychological, and social needs of the patient.

Duḥkha "Dukkha is often translated as suffering but it is better to consider it as unsatisfactoriness. It can be gross…or it can be subtle, such as not getting what we want exactly how and when we want it" (Huxter, 2021, para. 3).

Embodied social change Multi-faceted approach to social change that involves embodied practices that integrate spirituality, public performance, and activism.

Emptiness In Chapter 14, Leighton and Berkley describe emptiness through the Buddhist lens, quoting Sogyal Rinpoche's (2008) interpretation of *The Tibetan Book of Living and Dying:* "If everything is impermanent, then everything is what we call 'empty,' which means lacking in any lasting, stable, and inherent existence, and all things, when seen and understood in their true relation, are not independent but interdependent" (p. 37). Although emptiness may be connoted with a negative state in its general terminology, from the Buddhist perspective, emptiness is a state to be attained through spiritual practice, awakening, and realization. Emptiness is the opposite of being occupied and controlled by the lower consciousness of the ego.

Enstasis/ecstasis Greek terms found within Judeo-Christian spiritual texts denoting spiritual transcendence that is experienced "within the body" (enstasis) versus "outside of body" (ecstasis).

Entrainment Entrainment is defined according to Bluedorn (2002) "A process over time whereby two or more autonomous rhythmic processes interact with each other in such a way that they adjust towards and eventually lock-in to a common phase and/or periodicity, most often to the rhythm being more powerful or dominant. Afterwards, the processes maintain a consistent relationship" (Bluedorn, 2002, p. 149).

Eros Eros "Drives the emergence of ever higher and ever wider holons, a drive that shows up, in the interior domains, as an expansion of identity (and morals and consciousness) from matter to body to mind to soul to spirit" (Wilber, 1999, p. 130).

Fana Annihilation of self or conquering of ego.

Faqr Simplicity and voluntary poverty.

Hadith Compilations of sayings and traditions attributed to Prophet Muhammad, peace be upon him.

Hikmat Wisdom or esoteric knowledge.

Holding space/environment Concept within trauma-recovery and psychoanalytic therapy (Modell, 1976) and adaptive leadership (Heifetz et al., 2009), characterized as a liminal space that is safe enough to tolerate the discomfort of productive conflict.

Husn al-ẓann Thinking well of other people.

Idiot compassion A term coined by the Tibetan Buddhist teacher Chögyam Trungpa (1976). People exercising idiot compassion empathize with dysfunctional and maladaptive behavior no matter what and make no value judgment about the best course of action. Moreover, this involves a naive kind of selflessness that ignores one's own needs. Individuals exercising idiot compassion can be taken advantage of.

Incorporated and inscribed knowledge Two forms of social practice that allow memory to be integrated into the body, incorporating practices involving bodily communication such as a hand-shake versus inscribing practices that involve the process of archiving and the retrieval of information (Connerton, 1989).

Khidma Service.

Khushu Humility.

Kosmos The word, "Kosmos," has a rich history and variety of meanings, ranging from the scientific to the philosophical, spiritual, and artistic. In Chapter 3, Kosmos is used to describe the universe in a way that emphasizes its sacred or divine aspects and its unity and interconnection with all things. In the Bible, for example, the word Kosmos is used 188 times and its use describes all of creation (Bratcher, 1980). The Kosmos is an entity that is evolving, according to Wilber (Kornman, 1996), who explained that "the Kosmos keeps moving on. New truths emerge, new revelations unfold, new Buddhas keep popping up, it is endless" (para. 35). He elucidated the Kosmos as including "the physiosphere, or cosmos; the biosphere, or life; the noosphere, or mind, all of which are radiant manifestations of pure Emptiness, and are not other to that Emptiness" (Kornman, 1996, para. 20).

Kundalini awakening Awakening of the Kundalini energy thought to reside at the bottom of the spine. This type of awakening can involve physical and psychological side effects. It also can occasionally lead to enlightenment (Raei, 2021).

Law of correspondence Also known as the Law of Reciprocity. This "Law" is often correlated with the Golden Rule: "Do onto others, as you would have done onto you." It suggests we should treat others as we would like to be treated, because how we treat others will correspond to how we are treated in return. The Law of Correspondence is also reflected in the phrase, "as above, so below," or as reflected in the correlation between the macrocosm and the microcosm.

Maulana Title of a Muslim religious leader.

Maqamat Stations or stages in Sufi tareeqa or path.

McMindfulness A secularized and simplified form of mindfulness popular in corporate circles. Presented as a self-help technique, this approach usually divorces mindfulness from its original purpose of personal transformation and its links with societal ethics. Instead of addressing the root causes of suffering at the societal level, it reinforces negative psychological patterns (Purser & Loy, 2013).

Mohabba Love.

Murshed Spiritual guide in Sufism.

Myokines Proteins secreted by muscle contractions that are able to restore metabolic balance and overall health in the human body.

No-self No-self, in Buddhist philosophy, is the state attained through true awakening, free from the physicality of the body and the tyrannical hold of egoic consciousness. According to Buddhist monk Anam Thubten Rinpoche (2009), when awakening happens, "there is no longer any desire to become someone other than who we are. Every previous idea of who we are vanishes along with the pain, guilt, and pride associated with our body. This is the only true awakening" (p. 3).

Polyvagal theory Known as the "science of safety," Polyvagal theory is the understanding that the neurological capacity for humans to move from a sympathetic state of fight, flight or freeze (i.e. disconnection) to a parasympathetic state of rest and digest (i.e. connection and integration), requires conscious physical awareness and movement (Dana, 2018).

Received knowledge (and subjective, procedural, and constructed knowledge) Postmodern understanding that knowledge is acquired through various pathways including received knowledge (listening to the voices of others), subjective knowledge (the inner voice), procedural knowledge (evaluating knowledge), and constructed knowledge (integrating various voices) (Belenky et al., 1986).

Rida Contentment with God's will.

Sabr Patience.

Shahada Saying La ay la ha illa Allah-Arabic for there is no god but God.

Shukr Thankfulness.

Self-Cultivation The incremental life-long process of continuously perfecting the self in terms of evolving images of goodness and virtue (Gowans, 2021).

Self-forgetting Spiritual teacher and author Jeff Carreira teaches the mediation technique of self-forgetting, which he described as "your drifting awareness moves away from the memory of your earthbound identity, toward the unknown emptiness of total self-forgetting. We are drifting into the unknown" (Carreira, 2023, p. 98). In this context, self-forgetting is a means by which one who is meditating relaxes their identification with the physical human self, or earthbound self as Carreira said, in order to open to higher consciousness.

Shamanism A multi-faceted belief system that highlights the practitioners' boundary-crossing connectivity with spirit beings, the spiritual realm, and the afterlife, with the ability to restore balance and the physical and emotional well-being of the participant.

Silsilas Spiritual genealogies in Sufism.

Skandhas (Buddhist concept) "The five elements that sum up the whole of an individual's mental and physical existence. The self (or soul) cannot be identified with any one of the parts, nor is it the total of the parts" ("Skandha | Five aggregates, four noble truths," 1998). They are: (1) body; (2) feelings or sensations; (3) perceptions of sense objects; (4) mental formations; and (5) consciousness or awareness, of the other three mental aggregates ("Skandha | Five aggregates, four noble truths," 1998).

Skillful Means The Buddhist concept of skillful means refers to the ability of someone who has reached enlightenment to adjust the teachings of the Buddha based on who the audience was, that is, the teacher had the ability to teach to the student in a way that they could best understand or receive the teachings (Mitchell, 2008). In a more modern application, skillful means refer to adjusting behavior based on context with the understanding that one who has committed fully to awakening has gained deep wisdom about self, the path, and is able to bring that knowledge in a way that benefits others (Vu et al., 2018). In the context of Chapter 3, the term is used to reflect skills acquired through a dedicated journey of spiritual and personal development, wherein one can stay connected to one's inner state while also being fully aware of the nuanced experiences of others around them and being able to understand the complexities of the experience itself. It is an application of awareness, wisdom, and compassion.

Soul "A creative unit of pure awareness" (Reams, 2012, p. 104).

Soul's Knowing The intuitive and profound understanding that transcends human consciousness.

Spiritual leadership is defined as "comprising the values, attitudes, and behaviors that are necessary to intrinsically motivate oneself and others so that they have a sense of spiritual survival through calling and membership" (Fry, 2003, pp. 694–695).

Spiritual practice A spiritual practice is any practice that nurtures the qualities of the human spirit or inner life, that is "a private space for imagination and reflection which nourishes one's creative spirit and a sense of well-being" (Naiman, 2018). Practices include meditation, mindfulness, yoga, journaling, art practice, and so on.

Spiritual unfoldment The ongoing process of spiritual growth and development, often associated with practices aimed at realizing one's spiritual potential.

Spiritual ritual Intentionally repeated acts with spiritually informed meanings that connect individuals and communities to common understandings of the sacred.

Sufism Islamic mysticism.

Tamkin The stage of achievement in Sufi tareeqa or path.

Tareeqa Path of individual Sufis or approaches of Sufi orders.

Tawba Repentance and turning to God.

Tawhid God's Oneness and articulation that God is unique, incomparable, and eternal.

Tawwakul Trust in God.

Temperance The virtue of moderation; seek the golden mean; avoiding either too much or too little of a valued quality (Curzer, 1997).

Transcendence To move beyond; ascent. In the spiritual sense, to see beyond, to realize or ascend to a view of reality deeper than understood through ordinary perception. From a theistic perspective, the understanding that God is a reality that lies beyond this world. With the Buddhist realization of emptiness, the entire world is transcended or seen through. If we include a non-dual perspective, we see that "Enlightenment transcends and includes the entire manifest world." (Wilber, 2017b, p. 32).

Trauma The ongoing physical imprint and embodied experiences of the pain, fear, and emotional stress living inside an individual or community that continues to persist long after the specific event (van der Kolk, 2014).

Zikr Remembrance of God.

Zuhd Piety and indifference toward material possessions.

References

Anattā. (2023, August 2). In *Wikipedia, the free encyclopedia*. Retrieved August 14, 2023, from https://en.wikipedia.org/wiki/Anatt%C4%81

Anitya. (n.d.). In *Encyclopedia of Buddhism*. Retrieved August 14, 2023, from https://encyclopediaofbuddhism.org/wiki/Anitya

Belenky, M. F., Clinchy, B. M., Goldberger, N. R., & Tarule, J. M. (1986). *Women's ways of knowing: The development of self, voice, and mind*. Basic Books.

Bluedorn, A. C. (2002). *The human organization of time: Temporal realities and experience*. Stanford University Press.

Bourdieu, P. (1977). Cultural reproduction and social reproduction. In J. Karabel & A. H. Halsey (Eds.), *Power and ideology in education* (pp. 487–511). Oxford University Press.

Bratcher, R. G. (1980). The meaning of Kosmos, "World", in the New Testament. *The Bible Translator*, *31*(4), 430–434. https://doi.org/10.1177/026009438003100406

Carreira, J. (2023). *The soul's journey to wholeness: Illuminating the higher realms of spirit*. Emergence Education.

Connerton, P. (1989). *How societies remember.* Cambridge University Press.

Curzer, H. J. (1997). Aristotle's account of the virtue of Temperance in Nicomachean ethics III.10-11. *Journal of the History of Philosophy, 35*(1), 5–25. https://doi.org/10.1353/hph.1997.0008

Dana, D. (2018). *The Polyvagal theory in therapy: Engaging the rhythm of regulation.* W. W. Norton.

Fogel, A. (1993). *Developing through relationships.* University of Chicago Press.

Fry, L. W. (2003). Toward a theory of spiritual leadership. *The Leadership Quarterly, 14*(6), 693–727. https://doi.org/10.1016/j.leaqua.2003.09.001

Gowans, C. W. (2021). *Self-cultivation philosophies in ancient India, Greece, and China.* Oxford University Press.

Heifetz, R. A., Grashow, A., & Linsky, M. (2009). *The practice of adaptive leadership: Tools and tactics for changing your organization and the world.* Harvard Business Press.

Huxter, M. (2021, March 25). Mud and lotuses: The Buddhist meaning of Dukkha. *Insight Timer Blog.* https://insighttimer.com/blog/dukkha-meaning-buddhism/

Kornman, R. (1996, September 1). *The Kosmos according to Ken Wilber - Lion's roar.* Lions Roar. https://www.lionsroar.com/the-kosmos-according-to-ken-wilber/

Mitchell, D. W. (2008). *Buddhism: Introducing the Buddhist experience.* Oxford University Press.

Mitra, A. (2020). Maya–A conceptual history. *Prabuddha Bharata, 125*(1), 266–275.

Modell, A. H. (1976). "The holding environment" And the therapeutic action of psychoanalysis. *Journal of the American Psychoanalytic Association, 24*(2), 285–307. https://doi.org/10.1177/000306517602400202

Naiman, L. (2018, August 15). Want to be a better leader? Cultivate your inner life. *Inc.* https://inc.com/linda-naiman/want-to-be-a-better-leader-cultivate-your-inner-life.html

Purser, R., & Loy, D. (2013, August 31). Beyond McMindfulness. *HuffPost.* https://www.huffpost.com/entry/beyond-mcmindfulness_b_3519289

Raei, M. (2021). Spirituality, meditation, and kundalini: Almost everything you wanted to know but were afraid to ask.

Reams, J. (2012). Integral leadership: Opening space by leading through the heart. In C. S. Pearson (Ed.), *The transforming leader: New approaches to leadership for the twenty-first century* (pp. 102–109). Berrett-Koehler Publishers.

Rinpoche, S. (2008). *The Tibetan book of living and dying.* Random House.

Scharmer, O. (2018). *The essentials of theory U: Core principles and applications.* Berrett-Koehler Publishers.

Šimić, G., Tkalčić, M., Vukić, V., Mulc, D., Španić, E., Šagud, M., Olucha-Bordonau, F. E., Vukšić, M., & R. Hof, P. (2021). Understanding emotions: Origins and roles of the amygdala. *Biomolecules, 11*(6), 823. https://doi.org/10.3390/biom11060823

Skandha | Five aggregates, four noble truths. (1998, July 20). In *Encyclopedia Britannica.* https://www.britannica.com/topic/skandha

Thubten, A. (2009). *No self, no problem: Awakening to our true nature.* Shambhala Publications.

Trungpa, T. T. (1976). *The myth of freedom and the way of meditation.* Shambhala.

van der Kolk, B. A. (2014). *The body keeps the score: Mind, brain and body in the transformation of trauma*. Penguin UK.

Vu, M. C., Wolfgramm, R., & Spiller, C. (2018). Minding less: Exploring mindfulness and mindlessness in organizations through skillful means. *Management Learning*, *49*(5), 578–594. https://doi.org/10.1177/1350507618794810

Wilber, K. (1999). *Integral psychology*. Shambhala Publications.

Wilber, K. (2017a). *A brief history of everything (20th anniversary edition)*. Shambhala Publications.

Wilber, K. (2017b). *The religion of tomorrow: A vision for the future of the great traditions - More inclusive, more comprehensive, more complete*. Shambhala Publications.

CONTRIBUTORS

Four Arrows, PhD, Professor in Educational Leadership for Change at Fielding Graduate University, he is a member of the Lakota Medicine Horse *Tiospaye*. He has an EdD in Curriculum and Instruction with a Cognate in Indigenous Worldview. He has authored numerous publications that have been endorsed by such notables as Noam Chomsky, Vandana Shiva, Bill McKibben, Jeremy Lent, Morris Berman, and Henry Giroux. Recipient of a Martin Springer Institute Moral Courage award for his activism and of recognition from several Canadian Aboriginal organizations, his most recent book, *Restoring the Kinship Worldview*, received UC Berkeley's Science Center for the Greater Good's selection as one of the most inspiring and practice science books of 2022. On September 18, 2023, he presented on Indigenous Worldview at the 78th General Assembly of the United Nations. See fourarrowsbooks.com.

Lisa A. Berkley, PhD has dedicated her life to helping people and society thrive. As such, she has more than 30 years working at the intersection of meditation, well-being and holistic healthcare and governance, human rights, and social justice. She is the Founder and President of the Institute for Inner Economy, a non-partisan think tank dedicated to operationalizing positive peace and establishing healthy governance at the local, national, and international levels; she is the Director of Resiliency and Wellbeing at Crown College, University of California, Santa Cruz where she is both faculty and a founding Director of the Center for Applied Values and Ethics in Advancing Technologies (CAVEAT). Dr. Berkley resides in Marina, California, where she is a former elected official.

Bianca Briciu, PhD, is an Assistant Professor in the School of Leadership, Ecology and Equity, Saint Paul University, Ottawa. Her work focuses on leadership development through emotional, social, and spiritual intelligence. She is interested in the cultivation of love and its integration in knowledge, education, and policy-making. She has ten peer-reviewed publications in gender, cinema, spirituality, and transformative learning. In 2021, she published her first book, *The Revolutionary Art of Love: From Romantic Love to Global Compassion*, where she explored various definitions of love, arguing for its liberation from the romantic constraint and its revaluation as a fundamental relational human capacity.

Geoff Fitch is a coach, trainer, and facilitator of growth in individuals and organizations. He is a founder of Pacific Integral and the acclaimed Generating Transformative Change program, delivered on three continents. He researches and develops novel approaches to individual and collective growth and has been cultivating higher human potential for over 25 years, including somatic and transpersonal psychology, leadership, integral theory, and collective intelligence. Geoff also has 30 years of business leadership experience. He holds a MA degree in Transpersonal Psychology from the Institute of Transpersonal Psychology and a BS in Computer Science, magna cum laude, from Boston University.

Stacey K. Guenther, PhD, is a contemplative scholar-practitioner. Stacey's research centers on groups and how they can enter a state of deep connectedness called coherence. She is passionate about helping groups cultivate their beingness and open themselves to new forms of relating. Stacey earned her Doctoral degree in Leadership and Change from Antioch University. She is a 2023/2024 International Humanistic Management Association Fellow, and was named an MSR Fetzer Scholar in 2021 by the Academy of Management's Management, Spirituality, and Religion Division. Demonstrating her commitment to cultivating beingness, she is a certified leadership coach (PCC), an organization development consultant, and a certified meditation teacher (CMT-P). Stacey is a member of the faculty for George Mason University's Organization Development and Knowledge Management program and is affiliated with George Washington University's Center for Excellence in Public Leadership. She is the principal of a small consultancy, Awakened Impact.

Lynn M. Horan is an inter-faith theologian who specializes in women's leadership development in both secular and religious contexts. She is a PhD candidate through Antioch University where her research focuses on female clergy boundaries and psychological safety. Lynn is also a former health policy analyst for the New York State Senate and cross-cultural family counselor, having worked in homeless advocacy and domestic violence prevention in communities in upstate New York, Central Peru, and Mexico. A trained dancer and yoga practitioner, Lynn grounds her work in embodied practices that promote healing, wholeness, and reconciliation in individuals and communities. www.lynnhoran.com.

Maxinne Rhea Leighton, PhD, with two decades of leadership in design firms, merges the professional practice of engineering, architecture, and planning with the challenges of climate change. Her doctoral dissertation, "Arising," explored Hurricane Sandy's impact on design/planning professionals informs future climate-related approaches. Committed to peace, security in the built environment, Leighton served the 9/11 Ground Zero planning team, fostering collaboration between professionals and victims' families. Post-Katrina, she uncovered socio-economic and racial inequities in post-disaster recovery, shaping her advocacy in post-Sandy efforts. Recognized for her contributions, Leighton is co-leading an international working group on climate change, migration, gender, security (Women In International Security, as WIIS-NY, President), and is an Honorary Council Member for the Consortium for Sustainable Urbanization Global, and an advisory board member for a Movement in Water™.

Lizzie Linn is an Assistant Professor of Practice at Merrimack College. She has a Master's degree in Critical and Creative Thinking and is currently a PhD student in Educational Leadership at the University of Massachusetts at Lowell. Her research focuses on the post-secondary curricular inclusion of self-awareness as it relates to a reflexive sense of who one is in relation to others, of one's cognitive and affective behaviors, and of one's values and goals and capacity to act authentically in relation to them. Her research also examines how to teach eudaemonic well-being in higher education.

Abigail Lynam, PhD, is a coach at Pacific Integral and faculty for Generating Transformative Change and Emergent Leadership: Engaging the Future from Awakened Wholeness. As faculty for Fielding Graduate University's PhD program in human and organizational development, her scholarship and practice integrate interior dimensions of human knowledge and experience with interpersonal and collective change innovations. Abigail is a scorer and developmental coach with STAGES International and teaches and consults on adult development applied to education, coaching, group development, and leadership. Her work aims to support humanity's developmental unfolding for the well-being of future generations and all of life.

Amy K. MacDonald is a facilitator with Clearview Training and Consulting, with 17 years of experience in the non-profit and philanthropic sectors, helping equip organizations that address society's most pressing needs. Drawing on a diverse background in psychology, sociology, theology, leadership, and spirituality, Amy is interested in nurturing the psychospiritual development and interpersonal capabilities of individuals and groups so they can realize their full personal—and collective—potential. Amy lives in Ottawa, Ontario (Canada) with her husband David. When they're not exploring the world, they enjoy cooking and hosting gatherings for friends and family in their century home.

Michael F. Mascolo, PhD, is a Professor of Psychology at Merrimack College and the Academic Director of Compass, a year-long self-cultivation program for first-year college students. He is author, co-author, and/or editor of six books, and is currently co-editing (with Nick Shannon and Anastasia B) *The Routledge International Handbook on Dialectical Thinking.* He has published over 100 scholarly articles and book chapters. He is also the Director of *Creating Common Ground* (www.creatingcommonground.org), a nonprofit devoted to teaching people how to resolve interpersonal, social, and political conflict.

Judi Neal, PhD, is an author, scholar, and consultant. Her focus is workplace spirituality, transformation, and global consciousness. After receiving her PhD from Yale University, she served as an internal consultant to Honeywell. Judi taught management at the University of New Haven and then became the director of the Tyson Center for Faith and Spirituality in the Workplace at the University of Arkansas. She serves on the boards of Octave Institute and INDICA Academy. Author of ten books on workplace spirituality and transformation, she is the President of Edgewalkers International and the Founding Steward of the Global Consciousness Institute.

Mohammed Raei, PhD, is an independent scholar, leadership and organization development consultant, executive coach, and dissertation coach. He has consulted on strategic planning, program evaluation, and 360° feedback. Additionally, he facilitated workshops on trust, adaptive leadership, and immunity to change. He also served as the programming chair for the Pacific Northwest Organizational Development Network (PNODN). He is the co-editor of *Adaptive Leadership in a Global Economy: Perspectives for Application and Scholarship* (Routledge). He presented for a variety of professional organizations, including PNODN, Puget Sound Project Management Institute, and the International Coaching Federation (Jordan and Seattle chapters) in addition to several times at the ILA conference. In 2019, he had a Kundalini awakening that changed his life. He resides in Amman, Jordan. drraeiconsulting.com

Jonathan Reams, PhD, practices the cultivation of leadership through consulting, coaching, and action research on leadership development program design and delivery in a variety of settings. He held a position at the Norwegian University of Science and Technology (NTNU) from 2007 to 2024, and is a co-founder of the Center for Transformative Leadership. He focuses on the inner workings of human nature and developing micro-development processes to support building robust leadership capacities for today's complex challenges.

Danny Sandra, PhD, ventured into Internet startups, spearheading the launch of innovative services, before transitioning into management consulting, after completing his MBA. A deepening interest in spirituality and bodywork led him to craniosacral therapy and systemic constellations. This personal journey inspired Danny to explore spiritual leadership, entrainment, and organizational rhythms while assisting leaders and their teams through strategic transformation. His groundbreaking research culminated in a PhD from UAntwerp and notable journal publications. As an executive coach (PCC) and consultant with over 25 years of experience, Danny's vast credentials, along with his transformative approach, make him a guiding light in conscious organizational change.

S. Aqeel Tirmizi, PhD, is a Professor of Leadership and Organizational Behavior at Antioch University's Graduate School of Leadership and Change. His research and teaching focus on responsible leadership, cross-cultural leadership, well-being, and social innovation. He has developed and published multiple models of leadership. Aqeel has worked with leaders and senior managers from the private, public, and non-profit sectors. He holds a PhD in Management from the State University of New York, Binghamton and Masters in International Administration from the School for International Training.

Sharon Wamble-King, PhD, is a management consultant who possesses decades of executive leadership experience in corporate, consulting, and not-for-profit settings across the healthcare, retail, energy, entertainment, and manufacturing industry sectors. Sharon earned a doctoral degree in leadership and change from Antioch University augmenting a background in sociology and communication. A practitioner-scholar, her research has focused on decolonized examinations of culturally distinct ways that African diasporic women lead. Sharon has served in board leadership roles in higher education, public broadcasting, cultural tourism, and performing arts. She is the President of Kaleidoscope Management Consulting.

Robert Zuber, PhD, directs UN-based Global Action to Prevent War and Armed Conflict where he oversees a small team of researchers, advocates and policy interns monitoring all facets of UN work on security, gender, sustainable development, and human rights. He serves as adviser or board member to non-profit and educational organizations including Green Map System, Global Connections Television, and FIACAT (human rights). Based in Harlem, NYC with degrees in philosophy, theology, and education from Yale and Columbia Universities, he writes and speaks extensively on peacekeeping, Security Council reform, global arms issues, women's participation, servant leadership, and other human security concerns.

FOREWORD

Leadership styles have proliferated since 1970 when Robert K. Greenleaf first coined the term servant-leadership. Those aimed at promoting a social good include participative, authentic, collaborative, democratic, ethical, stakeholder, transformative, being-centered, and spiritual leadership. Yet, little has been done to enable leaders to effectively address *polycrises*—the decline of democratic institutions, social inequities, and climate change among the complex and interrelated challenges of our poly-crises. At the individual level, too many people are struggling with mental health and a sense of day-to-day survival in a world that they experience as divisive and fragmenting.

Management scholars have long proposed a variety of methods to engage leaders in promoting system change. One of the earliest efforts was Chin and Benne's 1969 paper "General Strategies for Effecting Changes in Human Systems." Change methods include rational-empirical (e.g., single use plastics are undesirable because, when discarded, they eventually enter the food stream as microparticles that can disrupt the endocrine, immune, and reproductive systems of living organisms), moral-reeducative (e.g., single use plastics cause unnecessary harm to humans and all life on earth), and power-coercive (e.g., California senate bill SB-54 requires 65 percent of all single-use plastics to be recycled by 2032).

Unfortunately, none of the three methods for affecting change have worked to tackle so-called wicked problems. None have worked, either individually or in combination, to produce a sufficient number of leaders who have the will and determination to pursue systemwide flourishing. This is true even when the economics and technology favor innovations for global good, such as in the fraught cases of BIPOC (Black, Indigenous, and other people of color) equity in the workplace or renewable energy to replace fossil fuels.

To the existing literature, this volume adds important concepts of emerging and non-Western leadership for our times. It is a "call for leadership that seeks to increase positivity and well-being and provides an undergirding for our collective consciousness." It recognizes that an increasingly diverse globalized workforce needs to draw on a variety of perspectives, including non-Western and spiritual ones. The lens of interbeing and entanglement—drawn from both cutting-edge science and perennial spiritual wisdom—challenges us to rethink what it means to be human and the nature of the world. Relational and eco-communal practices weave a fabric of oneness and connectedness that changes who leaders are *being* at a deep level of self-concept, so that they pursue flourishing at all levels (personal, organizational, and systemwide) because of who they are and not only because of what they know.

A unifying source of "all that is" can be found in the Judeo-Christian faith traditions, from Christian Gnosticism's concept of the Monad to the Kabbalah's Ein-Sof, just as it appears in the Chinese Tao, the Vedantic Brahma, the Buddhist Śūnyatā, the Zoroastrian Aša, and the inner mystical realm of Sufism. "In the beginning God created the heaven and the earth. And the earth was without form, and void; and darkness was upon the face of the deep. And the Spirit of God moved upon the face of the waters" (Genesis 1:1–2). From this spaceless and timeless void arose all the things that exist in the world. In Taoism, all things originate in the Tao and all things return to the Tao. It is both the source and destination of all things, though not directly observable or even nameable. "Tao cannot be seen by our eyes. Tao cannot be heard by our ears. Tao cannot be touched by our hands." Similarly, in Buddhism and the Vedic traditions, the manifest world of space and time as we observe it is only a surface manifestation of the deeper, beyond-space and time reality of Brahman.

In a world of such fundamental unity (oneness in pluralism), people are caring, relational, and cooperative. When they experience oneness—the wholeness, connectedness, coherence, and harmony intrinsic to the universe—they are more likely to express their essential nature as goodness and compassion for others. They instinctively see themselves as an integral part of the broader community and nature.

Readers of this volume will find a developmental path that encourages both individual and collective development as they find themselves facilitating a move toward wholeness and an opening to oneness.

Experiencing their lives as deeply connected changes how they think and act. It strengthens their ability to lead themselves and others, building their adaptive skills based on empathy and compassion. The integration of leadership and spirituality, as proposed in the pages ahead, redefines what it means to lead in service of well-being and flourishing, for a world that works for 100 percent of humanity and all life on earth.

Chris Laszlo, PhD
2021–2022 Chair of the *Management, Spirituality, and Religion* DIG at the Academy of Management
Author of *Quantum Leadership: New Consciousness in Business* (2019), Stanford University Press

INTRODUCTION

Mohammed Raei, Stacey K. Guenther, and Lisa A. Berkley

We live in a world facing the onslaught of constant, rapid change. We are grappling with the meta-crisis, the complexity of which presents no apparent path forward. We see more strife, disconnection, and difficulty within our global society. People are suffering and struggling to find meaning (Seitz, 2023).

Today's leaders face enormous challenges: the volatile impacts of the COVID-19 pandemic, climate change, and ongoing conflicts and wars, to name a few. These difficulties have profound direct and indirect effects on society (Knapp & Wong, 2020) and have contributed to the failure of multiple global social, economic, environmental, and political systems. Half of adult Americans feel lonely (Seitz, 2023), and over 700,000 people die by suicide worldwide each year, more than half of whom are under the age of 50 (Department of Mental Health and Substance Use, 2021). Pre-pandemic, nearly one billion people struggled with a diagnosable mental health condition, dying 10–20 years earlier than the general population (Kestel, 2022). The pandemic had a compounding effect, globally increasing the prevalence of depression and anxiety by 25–27 percent (Knapp & Wong, 2020).

Could we be encountering a collective dark night of the soul manifested as the meta-crisis that demands we look inward and face ourselves: mind, body, spirit, and soul? Our global challenges require a holistic approach that involves working toward both inner and outer transformation in order to heal both individually and collectively. We believe that healing and inner development are crucial to this holistic approach.

At the time that we wrote this introduction, we had multiple discussions about how best to frame this holistic approach, which is described

DOI: 10.4324/9781003396741-1

and detailed through the chapters of this book. The terms meta-crisis and poly-crisis often surfaced (Hunt, 2022; Tooze, 2022), yet despite anecdotal discourse, there appears to be little to no academic discussion about the difference between these terms. The more we reflected, the more intrigued we became. The contents of this book center around inner growth and development and the potential impact they could have on the world, given our current reality. With this in mind, we are making a clear distinction between the two terms.

In the context of this book, we elucidate that a meta-crisis denotes an overarching systemic crisis linking multiple intractable issues caused by innate flaws in current social, economic, and political structures. Addressing these societal breakdowns requires fundamentally rethinking our way of life at the individual, collective, and systemic levels. In short, a meta-crisis reflects the foundational interconnection of all systems, including the inner human landscape. In this way, we consider the root cause of the meta-crisis as the human consciousness that undergirds our thinking, decisions, behaviors, and actions, both individually and collectively. Addressing problems at a meta-crisis level requires internal changes beginning with the individual, followed by the family and community, and from there, the state, nation, and finally, the world.

Poly-crisis, on the other hand, is a term popularized by Adam Tooze (2022) and describes multiple, simultaneous crises that are distinct from each other but still interconnected and caused by external factors, such as climate change and globalization. Poly-crisis reflects a multiplicity of concurrent problems that exacerbate each other and require immediate action to mitigate their negative impacts. Addressing poly-crisis is akin to managing the symptoms rather than the cause.

In today's world, we face both the meta-crisis and poly-crisis, which require leaders' attention. We must address the immediate symptoms while simultaneously addressing the cause. It is, therefore, crucial to first transform how we think and how we have moved to view intellect, reason, and analysis as the only valued currency of intelligence while moving away from emotion, intuition, creativity, nature, and other intelligences. (See Berkley's Chapter 11 for a discussion on nine intelligences.) This book is focused on addressing the meta-crisis in its totality and calls for leaders of all kinds to tend to their inner landscapes and cultivate all of their intelligences. A clear pathway for this type of development is through spirituality.

According to Giacalone and Jurkiewicz (2015), the quest for spirituality is rising within the United States and globally. This surge in spiritual exploration may be attributed to society's evolving values, a growing sense of social disconnection, and the pursuit of purpose in an increasingly turbulent world. Severan (2021) suggested that

> just as this meta-crisis is the universally-acknowledged problem to be addressed, so is there a near universally-acknowledged component of the solution. Spirituality, for lack of a better word, is broadly recognized as a vital element of the metamodern worldview that must be cultivated if we're to succeed.
>
> *(p. 61)*

We agree with Severan. Now, more than ever, we need to begin to view the world and how we lead in a completely new way, and we believe spirituality is one of the keys to helping human beings evolve enough to meet the meta-crisis effectively. Never has spiritual exploration been so widely pursued in order to make sense of the world around us. Fortunately, we have never had more access to opportunities for spiritual development. Globally, thousands of meditation, yoga, and psychedelic retreats are on offer every year, not to mention thousands of new books and videos published on the topic. (Note: Psychedelics are legal or decriminalized in a few countries, and the editors are not recommending their illegal use.)

In an era defined by unprecedented change, complexity, and uncertainty, the quest for effective leadership has evolved beyond traditional notions of authority and command. Today, leaders face the profound challenge of guiding organizations, communities, and individuals toward a future that often seems elusive and enigmatic. In this shifting landscape, the intersection of spirituality and leadership has emerged as a vital, transformative force.

Conventional and hierarchical leadership models are facing new challenges. Leaders are now called upon to transcend mere managerial competence and cultivate qualities deeply rooted in the human spirit. Within leadership scholarship, we have witnessed a burgeoning interest in studying the intersection of leadership and spirituality. This interest is part of a more significant "spiritual turn" in organizational studies (Drive, 2007). For example, based on Google Scholar search results, the number of articles and books published yearly on this intersection increased by more than 70 percent between 2006 and 2019. Many of us whose scholarship encompasses leadership and spirituality have been moved by our awakenings and are spurred on to bring spirituality into focus. We believe this intersection's possibilities for our world to create societal healing and change are significant.

Spirituality as Embodied Direct Experience

To set a context regarding how we, the editors, are positioned, we would like to share how we view spirituality and how we came to that view. We hold spirituality as a phenomenon connected to a larger context: the Kosmos, the Universe, God, Allah, Source, or Spirit. Subjective spiritual experience originates from individual or direct experience and differs from person to person. Therefore, spirituality and what it is to engage in spirituality will vary from person to person. We each came to spirituality in our own way through a variety of experiences and journeys.

While in college and because of depression, Mohammed developed an interest in Jungian and Archetypal psychology (Hillman, 1997) before taking a detour into atheism. In 2018, he read Michael Pollan's (2018) work, in which he described studies that showed how psychedelics produced changes in the brain and the default mode network, similar to what one would see in long-term meditators. That piqued his interest, and shortly thereafter, Mohammed started meditating. Within several weeks, he experienced a Kundalini awakening (Raei, 2021) that moved spirituality to the center of his life.

Stacey is a long-time, committed spiritual seeker. Over the last 25 years, she has explored spirituality through many wisdom traditions. Over several years of daily meditation practice, Stacey began to have awakening experiences, short bursts of expansiveness. Over time, the expansiveness lasted longer and longer. She is now a certified meditation teacher who teaches mindfulness meditation and other spiritual technologies that allow for realization and opening to a different reality. She is currently finding collective awakening experiences particularly compelling.

Like Mohammed and Stacey, spirituality has always been central to Lisa's life, from profound communion with nature to high empathy for all living beings. As a meditator and healer, she has embarked on a global journey to understand how individuals and societies heal their shadow side. This exploration continues with a focus on how embracing our shadow can promote healing and create the conditions for healthy democracies so people and planet can thrive.

Our unique yet parallel backgrounds brought us together in a beautiful way. Through our hearts and minds, we, along with the other contributors, have woven together a tapestry of words, ideas, and practices that we hope will provide a guiding beacon for leaders navigating our complex and complicated world. It is our desire that you find inspiration and empowerment to integrate this work into your lives, so we may collectively lead each other into the world of which we dream.

Spirituality, Not Religiosity

Instead of trying to pinpoint a specific view of spirituality that would align nicely with leadership, we opted to provide a variety of spiritual perspectives, including emerging and non-Western viewpoints. Doing this provided a richer exploration and a more well-rounded view of the topic and avoided creating an overly dry academic volume that lacked spiritual experience. Instead, we wanted to create a book that included Spirit as an equal contributor, resulting in this dynamic compilation rich with hope and possibility.

Within the covers of this volume, spirituality is discussed through the lens of post- and trans-religious perspectives, that is, spirituality beyond the context and bounds of structured religion and religiosity. Here, spirituality has been defined in multiple ways. In some chapters, spirituality is referred to as the sacred, unitive force of life and meaning that animates all beings and things, connecting them to each other and the greater cosmos (Miller & Thoresen, 2003), the "animating essence or vital power that motivates, sustains, and directs living beings" (Oxford Dictionary of the Christian Church, 2011, p. 1501), or that part of the human psyche which "yearns for inspiration, for the transcendent, for meaning and purpose, for transcendental beauty, and for those values that connect the human to the wonder of existence itself" (Rolheiser, 2014, p. 12). Other chapters reflect cultural and philosophical perspectives of spirituality. For example, Indigenous peoples have long seen the spiritual as infused in all aspects of life and recognize "the spirituality of rocks, trees, plants, animals, places, and so on" (Deloria, 2003, p. 102). This pan-vitalism contrasts Western traditions, which have often separated the material and spiritual into opposing domains. Similarly, in many African cultures, there is no division between the sacred and the profane. All life is holy and filled with spiritual power (Mbiti, 1960). (See Chapter 7 by Wamble-King for a broader discussion on African spirituality).

All of the ways that spirituality is defined and discussed hold validity and value. Spirit's many faces—the variety and dynamism of the perspectives presented—enable us to expand our understanding of the sacred.

The Book's Dominant Themes

This volume is for practitioners, scholars, and students of leadership and spirituality who are already interested in or curious about the topic. You may seek to understand the multiple ways spirituality can impact leadership. Or you might be looking for broader perspectives than what you currently hold. You may even be a practitioner who intends to deepen your spiritual experience while widening your offerings for leaders and groups. In other words, what is offered in this volume is both provocative and applicable, and we hope the pieces will provide you with both inspiration and tools.

Broad Strokes: Themes Found in This Volume

A myriad of themes are interwoven within the four sections of this book, from surrender to compassion, from the dark and shadow side to the illuminating light of love, from a spotlight on individual leader development to highlighting the role of the collective. Each chapter individually and collectively represents the essence of a profound shift in how we approach leadership in the 21st century.

Surrender and Compassion

The concept of surrender is explored in multiple chapters as an act of relinquishing control and allowing a deeper intelligence to guide our decisions. We are invited to explore compassion for others and ourselves, recognizing that true leadership begins with a heart that beats in resonance with the suffering and aspirations of others. This compassion is rooted in wisdom and love and is the unifying force that binds us. In this way, compassion transcends superficial divisions and fosters the interconnectedness that leadership in our time desperately requires.

Wholeness

The facets of and paths to individual wholeness are integrated through the spirit, soul, mind, and body. This volume presents myriad developmental pathways and practices, all of which invite the individual leader's more profound understanding of self and the world around them. Embracing our unwanted or undesired elements is critical to the journey toward wholeness. Leaders venture into their subconscious and explore the Jungian concept of shadow work (Johnson, 2013) to become more aligned and authentic in their practices. Another critical aspect of wholeness is embodiment, and leaders who are in tune with their physical bodies and are deeply connected to the wisdom of their spiritual and emotional selves are more resilient, emotionally intelligent, and capable of navigating the complexities of the human experience (Giacalone & Jurkiewicz, 2015; Jampolsky & Cirincione, 2010). Finally, drawing on adult constructive development (Kegan, 1994), several chapters depict how evolving toward wholeness assists leaders in meeting the challenges of our complex world, the connection to which is a fundamental element of wholeness.

Collectivism

Multiple chapters within this anthology focus on the collective nature of both leadership and spirituality. A wide range of perspectives are included, from seeing collectivity as intrinsic to human existence to shifting focus from individualism toward collectivity. Shifting from individualism to collectivism often entails an awakening or moving from separateness to Oneness. Accepting collectivity involves embracing shared power-shifting from "power over" to "power with" (Follett, 1995). Leadership stems from beingness and naturally promotes the collective over the individual (Fry & Kriger, 2009).

Global Perspectives and the Importance of Decolonization

We have consciously included non-Western perspectives on leadership and spirituality, drawing from African, Sufi, and Indigenous Native American traditions. As Sosteric (2021) suggested, "The issue is that most systems of spiritual thought come to us through a white supremacist, patriarchal, social-class, and colonialist lens. Worse, most spiritual systems are specifically modified or intentionally designed as imperialist/colonial tools of suppression and oppression" (p. 2). The non-Western worldviews presented here offer unique insights that challenge our Western-centric understanding of leadership. They remind us of the importance of decolonization, inviting us to question existing power structures and explore alternative paradigms of leadership rooted in ancient wisdom.

An Overview of the Chapters

The volume is divided into four parts. *Part 1: Emerging Concepts in Leadership and Spirituality,* starts with Fitch and Lynam, who in Chapter 1 ask the question: How do we conceive of and support leadership in an emergent practice field where notions of self, other, and collective become more complex and interpenetrative? Their answer starts with two underlying premises: (1) that the ground of this emergent practice field is awakened wholeness, and (2) implicit in awakened wholeness is a non-dual ethical orientation. Based on O'Fallon's (2020) STAGES model, the chapter outlines the relationship between adult developmental stages and transpersonal states. Fitch and Lynam proceed by providing tools and practices they use in their Generating Transformative Change program for supporting individual and collective emergence or emergent leadership by engaging the future from awakened wholeness. They conclude by arguing that leadership at the spiritual edge requires realizing that we already are an expression of a deeper purpose and that spiritually enlightened service and compassionate action are the trustworthy measures of realization.

In Chapter 2, Raei uncovers the spiritual aspects of adaptive leadership and then examines how the spiritual concepts of compassion, surrender, and mindfulness can affect adaptive leadership. This examination comes from a critical stance highlighting potential misuse of these concepts in the form of idiot compassion (Trungpa, 1976), abdication, and McMindfulness (Purser, 2019). The chapter concludes with a call for using critical consciousness (Freire, 1970) to overcome some of these traps.

Chapter 3 questions the nature of reality and asks: What is it like to lead from a place of Oneness? In the chapter, Guenther argues that leadership from a place of Oneness requires letting go of outmoded forms of leadership that paint the leader as a single hero. Instead, she proposes that leadership from a place of Oneness and interbeing, a term first coined by the great Theravada Buddhist teacher Thich Nhat Hanh (2017), is better served through collective and being-centered leadership. She concludes the chapter with suggestions and ideas for individual, leadership, and collective development that support movement toward Oneness.

Mascolo and Linn introduce a model of spiritual leadership in secular organizations in Chapter 4. Spiritual organizations are animated by a moral vision, and drawing on common relational values present in many spiritual traditions (e.g., transcendence, wisdom, and morality), the model's aim is organizational problem-solving in service to the organization's moral mission. Stakeholder involvement, collegial relationships, and a spiritual ethos inform this process. The chapter provides a case study of the application of the model at Merrimack College.

Reams, author of Chapter 5, introduces a "new" conception of leadership as opening space. This conception is based on a spiritual lens drawn from the author's experience with the spiritual practices of Eckankar. After a short description of Eckankar, the chapter explores the concepts of consciousness, self, and knowing. Discussion related to adaptive, transformational, and servant leadership follows. Reams then argues that realizing the essence of being as a soul and reconceptualizing the self as a virtual entity liberates the person from the limitations of egoic consciousness and allows them to connect with the deeper purpose of existence: learning to receive and give love and serve others in doing the same. The chapter concludes with three practices from Eckankar: surrender, prayer, and signing HU.

Part 2: Non-Western Perspectives on Leadership and Spirituality provides various non-Western conceptualizations, including Indigenous views. In Chapter 6, Four Arrows (Dr. Don Trent Jacobs) outlines how a worldview based on hierarchy leads to dominance and the numerous problems that the world faces today. As an alternative narrative, Four Arrows advocates the application of Indigenous spirituality, which views everything as sacred and is non-hierarchical. He highlights several instances where assumptions around hierarchy in the natural world do not apply. The chapter concludes with a tool that might help leaders and individuals situate where they stand regarding Indigenous and Western worldviews.

Using a decolonized approach that relies on African sources, Wamble-King, in Chapter 7, explores the traditional African cosmology with its belief in the pervasiveness of Spirit and the interconnection that emerges from such a belief. She discusses this connectivity in the context of Ubuntu, collaboration, and social time. Subsequently, Wamble-King dispels the notion that having community ethos based on this African cosmology results in a sacrifice of individual needs. Instead, this view allows a balance and integration of both individual and community needs. The chapter highlights the benefits of applying the concepts emerging from this cosmology (connectivity, community, holism, time, and communication) to leadership.

In Chapter 8, Horan draws on several Indigenous examples to highlight the importance of embodied social change in shedding light on social ills and healing generational trauma resulting from colonialism and White body supremacy. One of the critical aspects of embodied social change is that it integrates spiritual ritual, social activism, and public performance to interpret and respond to communal needs. By inviting the possibility for wholeness through spiritual, physical, psychological, and emotional engagement, this embodied performance opens the door to heightened visceral consciousness and understanding, not only for the performers but also for the audience, paving the way for a collective shift and societal change. She convincingly argues that embodied social change, while presented as new in Western scholarship, has been historically a mainstay of Indigenous communities.

Tirmizi addresses how wisdom inherent in the Sufi tradition may inform leadership development in Chapter 9. He begins with an introduction to the foundational ideas of Sufism, followed by a discussion of insights from the wisdom tradition that may relate to a leader's path of growth and development. These essential understandings include the role of self-transcendence, mentoring and guidance, meditation, humility, unity, and love. The chapter concludes with reflections and caveats related to using the revered and mystic tradition of Sufism for leadership development in contemporary settings.

As mentioned earlier, our goal was to have a volume that appeals to both scholars and practitioners, and thus, we wanted to include tools that practitioners can use. *Part 3: Spiritually-Inspired Leadership Tools* contains several models and tools, some refined from previous iterations and some entirely new. In Chapter 10, Neal provides the Archetypes of Change model, which identifies five archetypes for leaders and organizations: (1) Edgewalkers, (2) Flamekeepers, (3) Hearthtenders, (4) Placeholders, and (5) Guardians based on their orientation to change. The chapter identifies the strengths and shadows of these archetypes, highlights their spiritual orientation or lack thereof, and explores enacting the model as it pertains to organizational change. The chapter concludes by providing an archetypes cycle exercise, which can help organizations use all of the archetypes to tackle organizational challenges.

In Chapter 11, Berkley introduces the inner economy framework, which defines the impact and relationship of the individual leader on society and vice versa. The framework takes the concept of the external economy and applies it as a metaphor to one's inner landscape by drawing from the law of correspondence. The model is a three-stage relational framework based on nine intelligences. The input stage focuses on absorbing information through our somatic intelligence, spiritual/perceptual intelligence, and ecological intelligence. It is followed by the processing stage, in which leaders process information through cognitive, emotional, social, cultural, and ethical intelligences. Finally, the output stage is reflected by creative intelligence. Berkley points out that these intelligences are not static but highly dynamic and influence each other. The chapter concludes with a call for consciously cultivating the nine intelligences in an integrated way, resulting in leaders growing spiritually and becoming more effective.

Sandra concludes Part 3 of the book in Chapter 12, focusing on leadership tools and introducing the concept of entrainment, which in the vernacular is described as "being in sync." He identifies four application areas along two axes using the integral entrainment matrix. The first axis determines whether the entrainment occurs within or between systems, while the second axis determines if the influence is symmetrical or asymmetrical. The chapter provides examples of each manifestation of entrainment and postulates lessons that can improve spiritual practice in service of spiritual leadership.

Many concepts promoted as beneficial are not always good. They can have a dark side, for example, innovation (Rogers, 2003), leadership (Kellerman, 2004), transformational leadership (Eisenbeiß & Boerner (2011), and knowledge (McKenna et al., 2009). Likewise, spirituality and leadership's intersectionality have their own dark side, which we explore in *Part 4: The Shadow Side of Leadership and Spirituality.* Bricui and MacDonald argue in Chapter 13 that shadow work is a complementary approach to spiritual development and leads to wholeness and interconnectedness. They identify three shadows that can hinder leader effectiveness: the shadow of hubris, the shadow of trauma, and the shadow of spirituality. To remedy and integrate these shadows, they provide five strategies that leaders can use, which include storytelling, mindfulness, and arts-based approaches. Shadow work, the authors argue, supports leaders' development of integral consciousness.

Leighton and Berkley explore the dark or shadow side of leadership in the context of climate change in Chapter 14. Through the lens of permanence and impermanence, they address the internal and external challenges leaders must face within the built environment, that is, the man-made structures that make up the environment in which humans live, when leading their communities through the post-climate disaster. In this crisis, they must choose between staying and rebuilding or leaving their homes and communities. These leaders must face their own shadow by immersing in the experiences of permanence and impermanence while holding a positive potential and navigating the personal and collective pain of an uncertain future.

The book's final chapter, Chapter 15, examines leadership and spirituality at the United Nations (UN). Berkley and Zuber argue that recent scandals emphasize a need for greater self-awareness and moral development among UN leaders. They suggest that practices like Jungian shadow work, which helps people honestly face the darker parts of themselves, could strengthen humility and integrity at the UN. Additionally, the chapter calls for the UN to evolve from rigid realpolitik frameworks focused on state power to an ethics of care paradigm prioritizing human welfare in its peacebuilding, sustainable development, climate action, and global human rights initiatives.

Our Hopes for What You Find Here

In a world where the challenges of our time are immense and multifaceted, this anthology explores leadership that transcends the mundane and ventures into the extraordinary. It takes us to a place of Oneness, where the boundaries between self and other, leader and follower, begin to dissolve. As you delve into the pages that follow, we invite you to remember that spirituality is not about escaping the world, but diving deeper into it. It is about becoming more fully human and recognizing that true leadership is a sacred endeavor and an expression of love and service. It is about balancing Heaven and Earth.

The spiritual turn in leadership is a testament to the fact that leaders must evolve beyond their traditional roles, and this evolution is inherently connected to their inner journeys. Still, despite the benefits that come from spirituality, we must make one thing clear: we are not in any way suggesting that leaders should become spiritual because it is good for the bottom line. One should not expect any benefits from their spiritual search, whether spiritual, mental, or material (Nisargadatta, 1982), the expectations of which are a form of spiritual materialism (Trungpa, 2002). By focusing on outcomes and increased benefits, the power of spirituality is diminished and becomes transactional.

During the many months of creating this book, it became evident that the most important thing we can do amid this meta-crisis is to do our inner work, genuinely engaging in our spiritual development and healing ourselves with a wholesome commitment. By developing and strengthening our spiritual, inquiry, and reflective contemplation practices and confronting our pain, wounding, and shadow material, we can all heal ourselves. Collective healing is sure to bring light to the human collective shadow. Illuminating our collective shadow and awakening together will shift consciousness and positively affect our human evolution.

Spiritual exploration is not a one-size-fits-all endeavor. Instead, it is a path we all are invited to journey in our own unique way. As individuals, walking a spiritual path, hand-in-hand and arm-in-arm with other people, is an act of union and Oneness that acknowledges we are all awakening together, whether we are aware of it or not. Paradoxically, as serious as the developmental path may feel, we must embrace playfulness and non-serious spirituality, recognizing that lightness and joy are essential aspects of our human experience and bring us to the wholeness of Oneness.

May this anthology inspire you to embark on your journey of self-discovery and leadership transformation as we collectively navigate the complex, interconnected, and ever-evolving landscape of the 21st century.

References

Deloria, V. (2003). *God is red: A native view of religion* (3rd ed.). Fulcrum Publishing.

Department of Mental Health and Substance Use. (2021, June 16). *Suicide worldwide in 2019.* World Health Organization. https://www.who.int/publications/i/item/9789240026643

Drive, M. (2007). A "spiritual turn" in organizational studies: Meaning making or meaningless? *Journal of Management, Spirituality & Religion*, *4*(1), 56–86. https://doi.org/10.1080/14766080709518646

Eisenbeiß, S. A., & Boerner, S. (2011). A double-edged sword: Transformational leadership and individual creativity. *British Journal of Management*, *24*(1), 54–68. https://doi.org/10.1111/j.1467-8551.2011.00786.x

Follet, M. P. (1995). *Mary Parker Follett prophet of management.* Beard Books.

Freire, P. (1970). *Pedagogy of the oppressed.* Herder and Herder.

Fry, L., & Kriger, M. (2009). Towards a theory of being-centered leadership: Multiple levels of being as context for effective leadership. *Human Relations*, *62*(11), 1667–1696. https://doi.org/10.1177/0018726709346380

Giacalone, R. A., & Jurkiewicz, C. L. (2015). The science of workplace spirituality. In R. A. Giacalone & C. L. Jurkiewicz (Eds.), *Handbook of workplace spirituality and organizational performance* (2nd ed., pp. 24–66). Routledge.

Hanh, T. N. (2017, August 2). The insight of interbeing. *Garrison Institute.* https://www.garrisoninstitute.org/blog/insight-of-interbeing/

Hillman, J. (1997). *The myth of analysis: Three essays in archetypal psychology.* Northwestern University Press.

Hunt, C. (2022). A tipping point? Spirituality in a time of meta crisis. *Journal for the Study of Spirituality*, *12*(1), 1–7. https://doi.org/10.1080/20440243.2022.2062149

Jampolsky, G. G., & Cirincione, D. V. (2010). *Love is the answer: Creating positive relationships.* Bantam.

Johnson, R. A. (2013). *Owning your own shadow: Understanding the dark side of the Psyche.* HarperCollins.

Kegan, R. (1994). *In over our heads: The mental demands of modern life.* Harvard University Press.

Kellerman, B. (2004). *Bad leadership: What it is, how it happens, why it matters.* Harvard Business Press.

Kestel, D. (2022, October 10). *The state of mental health globally in the wake of the COVID-19 pandemic and progress on The WHO special initiative for mental health (2019–2023)*. United Nations. https://www.un.org/en/un-chronicle/state-mental-health-globally-wake-covid-19-pandemic-and-progress-who-special-initiative
Knapp, M., & Wong, G. (2020). Economics and mental health: The current scenario. *World Psychiatry*, *19*(1), 3–14. https://doi.org/10.1002/wps.20692
Mbiti, J. S. (1960). *African religions & philosophy* (2nd ed.). Heinemann.
McKenna, B., Rooney, D., & Boal, K. B. (2009). Wisdom principles as a meta-theoretical basis for evaluating leadership. *The Leadership Quarterly*, *20*(2), 177–190. https://doi.org/10.1016/j.leaqua.2009.01.013
Miller, W. R., & Thoresen, C. E. (2003). Spirituality, religion, and health: An emerging research field. *American Psychologist*, *58*(1), 24–35. https://doi.org/10.1037/0003-066X.58.1.24
Nisargadatta, M. (1982). *I am that: Talks with Sri Nisargadatta Maharaj*. Acorn Press.
O'Fallon, T. (2020). States and STAGES: Waking up developmentally. *Integral Review: A Transdisciplinary & Transcultural Journal for New Thought, Research, & Praxis*, *16*(1), 13–38.
Oxford Dictionary of the Christian Church (2011). Spirit. In F. L. Cross & E. A. Livingstone (Eds.), *Oxford dictionary of the Christian Church* (3rd ed., p. 1501). Oxford University Press.
Pollan, M. (2018). *How to change your mind: The new science of psychedelics*. Penguin UK.
Purser, R. (2019). *McMindfulness: How mindfulness became the new capitalist spirituality*. Watkins Media.
Raei, M. (2021). *Spirituality, meditation, and kundalini: Almost everything you wanted to know but were afraid to ask*.
Rogers, E. M. (2003). *Diffusion of innovations* (5th ed.). Simon & Schuster.
Rolheiser, R. (2014). *Sacred fire: A vision for a deeper human and Christian maturity* (2nd ed.). Image.
Seitz, A. (2023, May 2). *Loneliness poses risks as deadly as smoking: surgeon general*. The Associated Press. https://apnews.com/article/surgeon-general-loneliness-334450f7bb5a77e88d8085b178340e19
Severan, A. (2021). *Metamodernism and the return of transcendence*. Palimpsest Press.
Sosteric, M. (2021). Response to Saad: The sociology of spirituality. *Academia Letters*. https://doi.org/10.20935/al4524
Suicide worldwide in 2019: Global health estimates. (2021). World Health Organization.
Tooze, A. (2022, October 22). Welcome to the world of the polycrisis. *Financial Times*.
Trungpa, C. (1976). *The myth of freedom and the way of meditation*. Shambhala Publications.
Trungpa, C. (2002). *Cutting through spiritual materialism*. Shambhala Publications.

PART I

Emerging Concepts in Leadership and Spirituality

1

LEADING THROUGH EMERGENCE

Engaging the Future from Awakened Wholeness

Geoff Fitch and Abigail Lynam

Introduction

How do we conceive of and support leadership in an emergent practice field where notions of self, other, and collective become more complex and interpenetrative? As we step into transpersonal states and stages of development, how might we orient to leadership as arising from a deeper spiritual ground? This chapter will describe the experiences, lessons learned, and essential practices of an approach to leadership that synthesizes spiritual practice, shadow work, collective intelligence, embodied awareness, and transformative change, all of which are central to the work of Pacific Integral. For twenty years, Pacific Integral has been exploring, facilitating, and researching transformative change in an integral and developmental context through its Generating Transformative Change program, the Emergent Leadership program, and through other offerings and communities of practice. We have convened, facilitated, and engaged with over 100 residential retreats and virtual courses involving over 1,000 individuals, including developmental programs lasting from nine months to several years, and offered the in-person programs on three continents.

The orientation to spirituality and leadership we describe is trans-religious and focused on practices framed in a trans-contextual way that draw on a variety of wisdom traditions: Western, Eastern, African, Indigenous, and others. The work is also based on the theory and practice of constructive adult developmental theory (Cook-Greuter, 2004, 2013; Kegan, 1994; O'Fallon, 2020; Torbert, 2004), which supports a rich, integrative approach to meaning making. As such, participants from many religious and secular

DOI: 10.4324/9781003396741-3

orientations have comfortably participated in this process. Likewise, our developmental orientation brings a complex view of leadership that transcends an orientation to individual and collective, leader and follower, insight and action, and being and doing (Lynam et al., 2022).

We originally referred to this approach as causal leadership (Ramirez et al., 2013), orienting to the movement of leadership from the ground of being. We later came to call the approach emergent leadership or simply leading through emergence. In this context, emergence carries several meanings. The experience of leadership from the causal ground is one of engaging in an emergent field, an orientation to the whole of individuals, collectives, and systems emerging into new forms. Likewise, we can say that leadership itself is part of that emergence. We recognize that the various expressions that wisdom and action take toward a more whole and just future, arise as needed in different contexts or dimensions of the whole. Whether or not we experience or refer to this movement as leadership, it carries some essential qualities we might attribute to leadership, which suggests we should include and evolve our conventional notions of leadership into new modes of human being and doing.

At its essence, our practice transcends the separation of individuals and collectives. It is an engagement with the future from awakened wholeness, by which we mean the confluence of two paths of spirituality, the ascending path of awakening and the descending path of embracing and enlightening all that is. This involves a movement toward the future in which action springs from everyone participating, from the collective as a whole, and from a ground of transpersonal awareness.

This approach is novel in that it is grounded in later-stage, transpersonal understandings. It includes an embodied experience of thinking and action that flows from a deeper ground of being and is understood to transcend the orientations of individual and collective, leader and follower, and other polarities (Gunnlaugson & Moze, 2012; Lynam et al., 2020). To support the development of these deeper dimensions of leadership, we have learned that it is profoundly important to support capacities for embodiment, relational and interpersonal agility, practical application, shadow work and ethical maturity. These capacities deepen the stable foundation for more expanded awareness and support it to be embodied and enacted in the world.

Our work is grounded in research, through an ongoing longitudinal study of the developmental growth and experience of participants, before, during, and for years after they leave the learning communities. The chapter describes our intentions, theoretical orientations, experiences, and learning.

Impact and Potential

What potential does this approach hold for the complex challenges we face today? When we originally wrote about this approach, we said:

> [We] consciously and collectively have the capacity to create new ways of being, relating, and functioning as a species. We can create new possibilities that meet the unprecedented requirements of our time, while envisioning a more elegant and generative future for humanity and for all of life. Through causal leadership, doing is done through us and by us, spontaneously, as wakeful collective intelligence. In this way, leadership is effortless, an emergence of the One seeing itself through the many, an act of grace that follows the natural order of things.
>
> *(Ramirez et al., 2013, p. 3)*

In the intervening years, we have seen this potential reflected over and over in the lives of the participants in our programs and in our own experiences. Today, we see the practice of emergent leadership as part of a larger unfolding of consciousness and action in the world, an awakening to our depths, and an evolution of our complexity, which expresses itself in countless contexts in the world today.

Background

Theoretical Orientation

The first orienting principle we hold is that the ground of this practice is awakened wholeness. This brings together a foundational polarity that may arise from perspectives of transpersonal states or of later stages of adult development. This is the polarity of transcendence and immanence.

On the one hand, awakening indicates a transcendence or emptiness of the mind's tendency to reify its own constructions and a grounding in awareness itself (an awareness that is not completely identified with the body, thoughts, emotions, and constructed sense of self). This transcendence can be accessed either as a state (a temporary experience) or as a stable stage of development (enduring or more stable). Transcendent awakening is a process, which can develop over time to deeper levels of awareness (Brown, 2006). This is recognized as at least the beginning stages of transpersonal experience. Developmentally, these capacities are reflected in O'Fallon's Metaware stages of development (in the STAGES model of adult development) starting with 5.0 (5th person perspective) also referred to as Construct Aware in ego development (O'Fallon, 2020).

Wholeness, on the other hand, indicates that what arises in awareness can be seen as whole and complete, and embraced by an immanent presence. Meaning first that our experiences are real and worthy of respect and inclusion, even while they are also inherently partial including blind spots, unconscious bias, limiting beliefs, and shadow. This draws on the recognition of holons and holarchies (Koestler, 1972; Wilber, 2001) that everything is both a whole and a part simultaneously. It is consequently important to work to surface, integrate, include, and celebrate our inner and outer diversity—the multiple dimensions of ourselves and our experiences. And to seek to integrate, heal, and include what is missing or distorted through practices such as shadow work including projection and introjection and other forms of personal, and interpersonal healing and development (for more details on Jungian shadow work, see Chapter 13). This is a movement of immanence or fullness.

We view this polarity of transcendence and immanence itself to be an interpenetrating whole, even while at a given moment one may be oriented to one dimension or another. The realization of awakened wholeness as a state or stage gives rise to a perception of a sense of completeness, beauty, and perfection of what is already the case, while paradoxically, calling or beckoning for more healing, liberation, and integration, essentially a greater wholeness.

A second orienting principle implicit in awakened wholeness is a non-dual ethical orientation (Fitch, 2012). We seek to balance, integrate, and ultimately see the unity of what divides us, not just as a spiritual ideal but as an intention to relieve ourselves (and all of life) of the suffering and confusions that arise out of the way we separate from each other and from parts of ourselves. As we grow developmentally, the divisions we attend to are more subtle. In other words, awakened wholeness is *not* an abstract ideal but an impulse to support each other to live life more awake and more whole. Doing so, we can live an existence that is more humane and en-souled and can construct a world that is more just and beautiful. In its essence, this is simply being as our spiritual nature, but the path to get there involves care, healing, restoration, grace, insight, and attention to what we are absencing or leaving out.

As we explore the relationship between spirituality and leadership, we are therefore suggesting that the ground is a spiritual realization—awakened wholeness—and that action arises from and as an expression of that ground. Next, we explore how we can make sense of spirituality and leadership from the view of awakened wholeness. Some questions we might ask are: what values is action sourced in? Whose vision influences the action, from where does this action flow, and how? These questions are fundamentally rooted in our experience of I and We, and evolve over time. We explore these questions through the perspectives of stages of consciousness and adult stages of development (our becoming), to which we turn now.

Transpersonal States and Stages

In this chapter we refer to states and stages as markers for certain capacities and orientations in consciousness. The term "states" refer to states of consciousness, largely categorized into gross (also called concrete and refers to the physical world perceived through our senses), subtle (the territory of thoughts, emotions, and subtle energies), causal (awareness itself and Witness consciousness), and non-dual (non-separation and unity of all), following the terminology used by Wilber (2000). The term "stages" refer to stages of development (described in the next section), following the frameworks of constructive adult development theory (Cook-Greuter, 2004, 2013; Kegan, 1994; O'Fallon, 2020; Torbert, 2004). We draw on the STAGES model developed by O'Fallon, which organizes stages of development into analogous tiers: concrete, subtle, Metaware, and unified. Our explorations of leadership and spirituality are informed by the capacities that arise in the more subtle states and later stages of consciousness, which open into transpersonal territory–awareness beyond the ordinary self.

Stages of Adult Development and Leadership

The STAGES model of adult development (O'Fallon, 2020) can support our understanding of leadership, because it clarifies the important ways that our conception of I and We changes as we develop, and as such, how we might conceive of the flow of leadership. Understanding developmental diversity can support individuals and groups to design structures and processes to accommodate this diversity and to maximize its creative potential. It also supports working with the misunderstanding and miscommunications that are even more common without developmental awareness. Fundamentally, it supports a deeper ethical and compassionate embrace or inclusion of human diversity.

The STAGES model describes 12 stages (four in each tier) that occur through iterating patterns over three tiers—concrete, subtle, and Metaware (Figure 1.1). These 12 stages include six important shifts in perspective

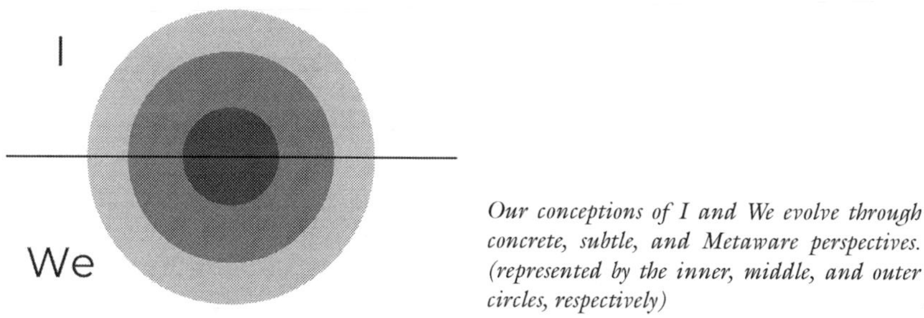

FIGURE 1.1 Concrete, Subtle, and Metaware I and We (Fitch, 2016; O'Fallon, 2020)

taking (first-person, second-person, third-person perspective taking, and so on). Each tier consists of two I-oriented stages and two We-oriented stages, although how we conceive of I and We in each tier varies in important ways. Thus, as humans move through this evolution (which spans from infancy to rarer, later stages of consciousness), we go through six unique understandings of I and We, and thus six orientations to leadership (Table 1.1). Each of these six person perspectives has two stages associated with it, an early and a late version. For example, for first-person perspective, there is the developmentally earlier, more receptive stage (1.0 or Impulsive) and the more developmentally mature and active stage (1.5 or Opportunist). Each stage transcends and eventually includes the prior experiences and meaning making.

In the first-person perspective, we are in the concrete I stages. In these stages, it is "all about me" and there is no understanding yet of a We. One can see others but does not have a truly unique identity separate from others, nor does one see others as unique in their own right. The focus is on one's concrete needs and wants. The second-person perspective stages foreground the concrete We (these stages are called 2.0 Rule-oriented and 2.5 Conformist). In this perspective, I see that others exist separate from me with their own needs and wants. These others see me and in order to satisfy my needs, I must work with them and make and follow rules together. In these We stages, the I is present and understood, but backgrounded,

TABLE 1.1 Six Distinct Understandings of I and We (Fitch, 2016; O'Fallon, 2020)

Perspective		*Foreground*	*Background*
	First person	I (concrete) body, senses	(none)
	Second person	We (concrete) groups, rules	I (concrete)
	Third Person	I (subtle) thoughts, ideas, emotions	We (concrete)
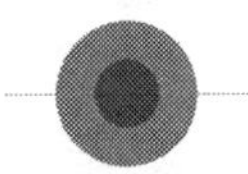	Fourth Person	We (subtle) contexts, paradigms, systems	I (subtle)
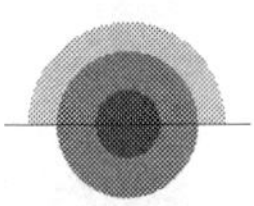	Fifth Person	I (Metaware) awareness, source, emptiness	We (subtle)
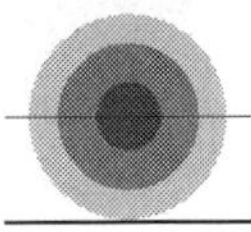	Sixth Person	We (Metaware) manifestation, Kosmos, whole	I (causal)

or deprioritized, in favor of relationships and groups. The groups here are families, groups of peers, community and cultural groups, religion, and other institutions. The sense of self and right and wrong comes from the collective and their norms and behaviors. For example, how to dress or behave is socially defined and it is important to know who is a part of your community or collective, and who is not. Leadership in the second-person perspective is hierarchical, based on the authority in the collective, which is defined by position, and tends to be rule-based, bureaucratic, authoritarian, and unchallenged.

The next perspective gives rise to subtle I stages, where we realize we have a subtle self—the thoughts, emotions, and independent mind of rational consciousness (3.0 Expert and 3.5 Achiever). We can think for ourselves and begin to think about our own and other's thinking. This is again an I-oriented space. The We that is present (but in the background), is still the concrete collective, which includes family, groups, organizations, and their norms and rituals, since no new subtle We has yet been discovered. This territory of the early subtle stages of third-person perspective comprises what we largely think of as conventional leadership. It tends to be focused on the individual leader, is goal driven, behavior-, merit-, and outcome-based, and orients from rational and abstract thought. As Torbert has suggested, in the concrete stages, power is vested in either unilateral force (Concrete I) or positional authority (Concrete We) (Torbert, 2020). In the subtle stages, power arises from the use of the subtle mind. These stages, which focus on the individual, give rise to conventional views of leadership, what Joiner and Josephs (2007) call heroic leadership, with a focus on an individual leader's behavior.

This pattern continues with the fourth-person perspective, where the individual becomes aware of more subtle dimensions of self and systems. There is a recognition of contexts and social construction. This includes a recognition of the multiple dimensions of self and self-identity, and how these identities or experiences have been shaped by context and culture. Given that there are multiple dimensions of self and systems, there is an interest in exploring who we are in relationship with others, through dialogue and other forms of reciprocity. In the fourth-person perspective, the subtle We is foregrounded. The subtle We consists of the perception of being situated in and arising out of a plurality of contexts (in the 4.0 Pluralist and 4.5 Strategist stages). The We is not, then, a specific group, but a space, and that space is complex. It consists not only of outer manifestations, such as a room, the systems in which the context is embedded, and the cultural context and form, but also inner manifestations, such as the attitudes, beliefs, assumptions, states of awareness, and ontological dispositions expressed by the group members. Here, people begin to understand that contexts shape us, and we can create contexts to support development and to experience coherence and flow with others. It is at this level that the notions of transformative learning, collaborative leadership, collective intelligence, and collective evolution begin to be of interest (O'Fallon et al., 2014; O'Fallon, 2020). These stages comprise most of what we think of as post-conventional leadership: inclusive, process-oriented, complex, adaptive, contextual, relational, and participatory. We understand that the leader's view is limited and contextual and that power is vested in our ability to bring about transformative interventions (Torbert, 2020).

As expected, newer, post-conventional forms of leadership, which arise out of these fourth-person perspective stages, have begun to acknowledge the wisdom in followers, such as servant leadership (Greenleaf, 2002) (for a discussion of leadership as opening space as it relates to servant leadership, see Chapter 5), adaptive leadership (Heifetz et al., 2009), and post-heroic leadership (Joiner & Josephs, 2007). They also recognize the wisdom and contribution of the collective and associated systems, such as network leadership (Ehrlichman, 2021), self-organizing systems (Laloux, 2014), and collaborative leadership. Post-conventional leadership models tend to focus on overcoming the pitfalls of hierarchical leadership, see leadership as socially constructed, while integrating and accounting for formal organizational hierarchies (Reams, 2020).

While spiritual insight, values, and commitments can be expressed at any stage, the next stages, at the Metaware tier open levels of awareness that are transpersonal and bring forth deeper questions about the relationship between spirituality and leadership.

At the beginning of the Metaware tier, individuals at fifth-person perspective awaken to their ever-present awareness as the ground of their own being. They begin to identify with this being as a new self, both empty and full, transcendent and immanent. In these stages (5.0 Construct Aware and 5.5 Transpersonal), the I is foregrounded, but the subtle We remains as a context for this I. The I is however not what we conventionally think of as I—our concrete bodily self or our subtle thinking or narrative self, but rather our Metaware self, the limitless open horizon of awareness that we paradoxically seem to share with everyone and everything. Knowing that transformative, adaptive, and deeply subtle collectives or relationships are possible, individuals often desire to bring in the Metaware experience by bringing the practice of witness consciousness into their collective experience (Gunnlaugson & Moze, 2012), and to provide a context in which their Metaware selves can express themselves and be recognized. In these territories, individual leadership can be seen as intense but non-demanding, sometimes in-the-moment, sometimes multigenerational in the scope or vision, outside of the conventional and postconventional constructions and pretenses, usually focused on the visionary potential expressed individually, and grounded in awareness itself.

At the sixth-person perspective, there is a shift from the I to the We. The I is backgrounded as it lets go into a much larger, Metaware or causal We. In the sixth-level stages (6.0 Universal and 6.5 Illumined), the We is all of concrete, subtle, and Metaware manifestation itself, the Kosmos, the utterly full and empty existence, eternal and beyond time, infinite and beyond space. Here one experiences themselves as this whole, with their apparent Metaware I birthed by and birthing the whole. At these stages, there is a sense of the vibrancy of the whole, of leadership as something expressed in and through all of existence, through the evolutionary unfolding and immanent embrace of all. In orienting to this, there is a deep care of each part, recognized as a microcosm of the whole and a reflection of this wholeness back through each individual. Every individual and every collective is leading and being lead, even as there are intuitions of a higher mind or divine domain that may be working through all of us, as us, and everything. In the later sixth-person stage, there is an interest in universal patterns and structures that form and shape the movement of these worlds.

There is a keen interest at the sixth-person levels in living as this larger collective, which has its own sense of We, and in allowing the intelligence of the whole, and that which births the whole, to express one's existence. In this sense, this very much reflects the interest in collective emergence at the fourth person stages, but is no longer grounded in any specific group or context but in reality itself.

As mentioned, each of these six unique perspectives (first-, second-, third-person perspectives, and so on) of I and We is further divided into two distinct stages: first, a more receptive stage, which is about awakening to a new perspective taking capacity and exploring the many dimensions of it; and second, a more active stage, in which one wants to move forward and create with these capacities. Altogether, this points to an extraordinary diversity of the constructions of human mind and deeply informs our approaches to seeing, engaging, evolving, and altogether letting go of leadership.

Leadership

As we can see from the developmental perspective, the question of leadership becomes confounded by a shifting and complex understanding of what we take to be I and We. One theorist identified over 1,500 definitions of leadership and more than 40 theories of leadership (Kellerman, 2012), but even these are largely viewed through conventional stages of development (McCauley et al., 2006; Reams, 2017). To take a developmentally informed view of leadership (or any essential distinction such as love or justice), we seek to tease out a sense of its essential qualities. Because our language and meaning making differ and evolve so profoundly, this is sometimes more of an art than a science, sometimes more poetry than prose. After exploring these essential qualities, we will return to reflect on how they are expressed from a view of awakened wholeness.

Some essential qualities of leadership that we might consider:

- Leadership is an expression of values and, considering a context of spirituality, we would expect these values to reach toward our sense of the greatest good.
- Leadership is about a transcendent vision, an immanent sense of possibility, and potential beyond what is habitual or predicted.
- Leadership is about action inspired by this vision, an evolutionary movement toward more of what is needed, and less of what causes harm or suffering.

While each stage of development would have a different view of who (or what) is leading, who is following, what values are being expressed, who (or what) determines the values and vision, and so on, these essential qualities can be seen to characterize leadership.

We should also note that in retrospect, leadership can sometimes be an expression of our worst limitations, character flaws, and blind spots. Individual leadership can be an act of narcissism. Collective leadership can be an act of group think and marginalization. Leadership can also be an expression of extraordinary human capacity and human dignity. So, we might add a fourth quality to leadership, which is that it is a process of human becoming, not one thing but a stream in the evolutionary unfolding of human being, in which each of us is a transient participant.

Engaging the Future from Awakened Wholeness

Taking a view from the ground of awakened wholeness, we find we naturally orient toward a desire for the liberation of wisdom and care in service of a more beneficial future. We understand this in a context of a complex view of I and We that includes concrete, subtle, and causal or Metaware realities, and as much of the spectrum of being that we can realize. Consequently, one experiences that there simultaneously is and is not a leader, that one is simultaneously a leader, a follower, and neither, and that the field of change is intersystemic, holistic, and complex. We are in a wider field of change and movement, not separate from it, influencing and influenced. As Barad notes,

> We are not outside observers of the world. Neither are we simply located at particular places in the world; rather we are part of the world in its ongoing intra-activity... knowing is a matter of part of the world making itself intelligible to another part.
>
> *(2007)*

We orient toward a resonance with the emergent future and with ourselves as participants in it. We do not seek agreement, but full expression of each and all in a field of coherence and wholeness, seeking to hold our conceptions lightly. Vision touches this field just as the light of the divine touches and informs all of reality. We seek to learn to trust our own knowing and sense of what is needed and to be humble in the realization that we are participating in a developmental journey that is vast and seemingly endless.

To support the development of these deeper capacities for leadership, we have learned that it is profoundly important to support the development of capacities for transpersonal awareness, embodiment, relational and interpersonal agility, practical application, shadow work, and ethical maturity. These capacities deepen the stable foundation for more expanded awareness and support it to be embodied in the world.

Principles & Practices

In this section, we share tools and practices for supporting individual and collective emergence or emergent leadership by engaging the future from awakened wholeness. The primary context of this learning arises from working with cohorts in Generating Transformative Change (GTC), Pacific Integral's nine-month program. GTC has been offered since 2004, on three continents (North America, Oceania, and Africa). The program enacts and facilitates a new way of being and action in the world, grounded in developmentally mature subtle states and stages of consciousness. GTC integrates a range of theories and practices designed to help participants not just acquire new skills but grow the inner capacities necessary for effective leadership in complex and demanding contexts. The program consists of four residential retreats and inter-session learning, coaching, and application. Cohorts include 14–16 participants with two to three faculty per cohort. Participants in GTC range in age from 20 to 75 and come from diverse cultures, countries, and professions including coaching, non- and for-profit leadership, organization development, social change, sustainability, education, the arts, and healthcare.

The principles that guide the design of GTC are that it be integral (encompassing as much of reality as possible), developmental (not merely asserting a single worldview, but situated in an ongoing, evolutionary trajectory of perspective-taking capacity), interpenetratively emergent (recognizes that individual and collective development and emergence are interpenetrative and unpredictable-meaning the development in one supports the development in the other and who or what a cohort becomes is to be discovered), and motivated by universal compassion (serving to reduce suffering and increase fulfillment in the largest span and depth imaginable). Key learning areas include adult development theory and practice (Cook-Greuter, 2004; O'Fallon 2020), Theory U and Presencing (Scharmer, 2018), dialogue (Bohm, 1996; O'Fallon & Kramer, 2008), integral theory (Wilber, 2006), integral polarity practice (Kesler, 2014), awareness and somatic practices (Brown, 2006; Pierrakos, 2005), developmental action inquiry (Torbert, 2004), paradoxes of group life (Smith & Berg, 1997), collective evolution (Gunnlaugson & Brabant, 2016) and emergence (Baeck, 2021), communication, truthfulness, and intimacy practices (Golabuk, 2012; Richo, 2014), and individual and collective shadow work (Hubl, 2020; Masters, 2018).

As designers and facilitators of GTC, it is our intent to discover the developmental unfolding in each participant and each cohort rather than to predict it or impose a particular form of development on groups or the individual as some transformative programs consciously or unconsciously tend to do. We encourage participants to continue to reveal their own implicit intentions for growth and transformation through their own responses and actions. This is a process of discovering and uncovering intentions, as well as consciously creating intentions for growth and development (Fitch, 2016). Ultimately, the provocation to emergent leadership offers a learning opportunity with the intention to expand creativity, impact, and service in the world.

GTC continues to evolve as we engage with and learn from participants and the cohorts' developmental and emergent process, and in relationship to the times we are living in. We have also engaged in longitudinal developmental research with participants, including pre- and post-developmental assessments, and ongoing assessments every two years for those that choose to participate. The results of this research, plus ongoing engagement with GTC graduates and their cohorts, have provided insights into what supports development in the context of GTC and beyond (Lynam et al., 2020). Over time, our recognition of how interpenetrative individual and collective evolution and emergence has deepened. In response to this, we developed a framework for the coemergence and coevolution of the individual and collective through a process of differentiation, embodiment, integration, and enactment.

Cultivating a Field of Awakened Wholeness

A primary orientation we practice is to cultivate a holding field that embodies awakened wholeness. This field holds the paradox/unity of the condition of openness and embrace. The field is open, in that we recognize the transparency, interconnectedness, and emptiness of what is present. We are in our experience but to some degree not purely identified with it. We recognize it is constructed and "empty" in the sense that it is in essence insubstantial. The field is embracing in that we practice acceptance of whatever is arising with compassion, love, and curiosity, recognizing it is an essential part of the whole (for a discussion of compassion as it as a component of adaptive leadership and adaptive work, see Chapter 2). This does not mean there is no discernment or boundaries toward unhealthy parts of ourselves. This too is part of the whole. When this holding field is deep and present, the experience is a sense of arriving home to our spiritual core and having parts of ourselves that we may feel shame or rejection toward welcomed unconditionally. The space is both safe in that there is a deep welcome and acceptance, and challenging in that there is less need for our defenses, which may leave us feeling more vulnerable at times. The space or field is the background and context for all our work, held by the facilitators but progressively held by the participants as they become oriented to it.

In this context, we engage in a variety of practices designed to support an integral constellation of skills and capacities. These practices cultivate awareness of awareness, complexity of sense making, embodiment, moral depth, authentic relationship, self-regulation, generative conflict, awareness and integration of individual and collective shadow, collective presencing, coherence and intelligence, creativity and play, and working with complexity and emergence.

Coming Home to Real Relationship

What often draws people to this work is the opportunity to engage with this deep practice and capacity for transformative change and development. What they initially encounter, sometimes to their surprise, is a holding field that offers a deep sense of welcome (McCauley et al., 2006). Expecting to engage in change, they find a kind of self-acceptance that paradoxically frees them to be and act in new ways. What reveals itself over time is a deeper dimension to the work; that of real relationship. One's own individual unfolding and leadership in the world takes place in the context of a collective. The quality of the collective is shaped by the unfolding and leadership of the individuals engaged with it. The I and the We interpenetrate, coshape, coevolve, and coemerge together (Lynam et al., 2022). We are inextricably bound up with each other. This understanding has led to the development of we-space practice as a core of our work (Gunnlaugson & Brabant, 2016). We have come to realize the importance of the cultivation of practices and containers that deepen our relational field. But it is not just about the quality of relating, but about real relationship. The depth of relating that is needed for our future only arises as we become friends and partners and as we work and cultivate community together. When we commit to each other, get involved in each other's lives, attend each other's wedding and funerals, work and create together all in the context of awakened depth and authenticity, we cultivate the capacities to sustain and embody our realization in the work of life and service in the world. Again, we experience this not as an instrumental benefit, but as a birthright, a sense of coming home (with and for each other), and microcosm of a more whole and integrated world.

Cultivating Emergence

All of these orienting practices are balanced by the intention to engage in emergence. We endeavor to view each individual, relationship, and collective as an unfolding mystery. How will this unfolding wholeness express itself? We cannot truly know, so we practice attuning to the subtle reality of this unfolding, supporting it as it emerges, staying present and grounded in our deepest sensing and values, while impartial toward and curious about the specific of the unfolding events. This emergence is ultimately what is leading, although we are its vehicle. Emergent leadership, the movement toward greater wholeness through us, takes many forms depending on what is needed or called for in the moment, including some of the forms of leadership that we may be familiar with. It can also be experienced as a spontaneous unfolding in the collective, as insight arising, transformations in energy, and bursts of creativity and novelty. Paradoxically, we come to embrace as part of this wholeness and even as an expression of leadership, times of confusion, stuckness, ambivalence, and "lack of leadership." The essence is to be in the space of emergence with an orientation toward love, truthfulness, depth, and wholeness. It is also to discover together what wants (and needs) to unfold and to meet each other, the moment, these times, and our challenges with humility, boldness, grace, wonder, and a commitment to a greater whole.

Conclusion

A legitimate challenge to this approach might be to call into question what we are describing as a form of leadership. Like many distinctions we hold, "leadership" comes with a mixed history and a multiplicity of meanings that we likely have to integrate and transcend should we want to become the fullest expression of human potential. What is leadership at the spiritual edge? Each spiritual tradition has pointed to enlightened service and compassionate action as the true measure of its realization. We have a true purpose here that is part of humanity's purpose expressed uniquely through us. Our spiritual path is an unfolding of that purpose in the world. The mystical understanding of this purpose is that it is not of our own making. We may be guided by this higher mind (Aurobindo & Ghose, 1993) or God's purpose or primordial wisdom (Brown, 2006). Our spiritual path is to open to that, to purify what obscures it, and to learn to move with it.

Ultimately, we suggest, this leads us to realize that we already always are an expression of this deeper purpose, that the reality we inhabit is primordially pure and complete as it is, and that this deeper wisdom has always guided us. Understanding this, it can be tempting to say there is no need for leadership. Paradoxically, the expression of this perfection is to serve the unfolding of the world, to endeavor to address our limitations and realize our potentials, and to reduce suffering and injustice. So, we make room for and honor leadership as part of this sacred mandala, and to use the distinction of leadership to describe what is happening, if it serves the unfolding that is beyond all distinctions.

References

Aurobindo, S., & Ghose, A. (1993). *The integral yoga: Sri Aurobindo's teaching and method of practice: Selected letters of Sri Aurobindo*. Lotus Press.

Baeck, R. (2021). *Collective presencing: An emerging human capacity*. https://www.collectivepresencing.org/

Barad, K. (2007). *Meeting the universe halfway: Quantum physics and the entanglement of matter and meaning*. Duke University Press.

Bohm, D. (1996). *On dialogue*. Routledge.

Brown, D. (2006). *Pointing out the great way: The stages of meditation in the Mahamudra tradition*. Wisdom Publications.

Cook-Greuter, S. (2004). Making the case for a developmental perspective. *Industrial and Commercial Training*, *36*(7), 275–281. https://doi.org/10.1108/00197850410563902

Cook-Greuter, S. (2013). *Ego development: Nine levels of increasing embrace*. [Unpublished manuscript]. http://www.cook-greuter.com/Cook-Greuter%209%20levels%20paper%20new%201.1%2714%2097p%5B1%5D.pdf

Ehrlichman, D. (2021). *Impact networks: Create connection, spark collaboration, and catalyze systemic change*. Berrett-Koehler Publishers.

Fitch, G. (2012). Evolutionary ethics. *Spanda Journal*, *3*(1), 117–122.

Fitch, G. (2016). In, as, and towards the Kosmic we. In O. Gunnlaugson & M. Brabant (Eds.), *Cohering the integral we space: Engaging collective emergence, wisdom and healing in groups* (pp. 79–94). Integral Publishing House.

Golabuk, P. (2012). *Field and fate workshop*. Unpublished manuscript.

Greenleaf, R. K. (2002). *Servant leadership: A journey into the nature of legitimate power and greatness.* Paulist Press.

Gunnlaugson, O., & Moze, M. B. G. (2012). Surrendering into witnessing. *Journal of Integral Theory & Practice, 7*(3), 105–115.

Gunnlaugson, O., & Brabant, M. (Eds.). (2016). *Cohering the integral we space: Engaging collective emergence, wisdom and healing in groups.* Integral Publishing House.

Heifetz, R. A., Grashow, A., & Linsky, M. (2009). *The practice of adaptive leadership: Tools and tactics for changing your organization and the world.* Harvard Business Press.

Hubl, T. & Avritt, J. (2020). *Healing collective trauma: A process for integrating our intergenerational and cultural wounds.* Sounds True.

Joiner, B., & Josephs, S. (2007). Leadership agility: Five levels of mastery for anticipating and initiating change. *Reflections: The SoL Journal, 8*(1), 44–51.

Kegan, R. (1994). *In over our heads: The mental demands of modern life.* Harvard University Press.

Kellerman, B. (2012). *The end of leadership.* Harper Business.

Kesler, J. (2014). *Introduction to integral polarity practice: An awareness and life practice.* Unpublished manuscript. The IPP Institute.

Koestler, A. (1972). *The roots of coincidence.* Hutchinson (2nd ed. Paperback, 1973).

Laloux, F. (2014). *Reinventing organizations: A guide to creating organizations inspired by the next stage of human consciousness.* Nelson Parker.

Lynam, A., Fitch, G., & O'Fallon, T. (2020). The aware leader: Supporting post-autonomous leadership development. In J. Reams (Ed.), *Maturing leadership: How adult development impacts leadership* (pp. 171–190). Emerald Publishing Limited.

Lynam, A., Fitch, G., Androsoff, T., & Wood, J. (2022). The interpenetration of individual and collective transformation: A framework for development, collective intelligence, and emergence. In A. Nicolaides, S. Eschenbacher, P. T. Buergelt, Y. Gilpin-Jackson, M. Welch, & M. Misawa (Eds.) *The Palgrave handbook of learning for transformation* (pp. 677–696). Springer International Publishing.

Masters, R. A. (2018). *Bringing your shadow out of the dark: Breaking free from the hidden forces that drive you.* Sounds True.

McCauley, C., Drath, W., Palus, C., O'Connor, P., & Baker, B. (2006). The use of constructive developmental theory to advance the understanding of leadership. *The Leadership Quarterly, 17*(6), 634–653. https://doi.org/10.1016/j.leaqua.2006.10.006

O'Fallon, T., & Kramer, G. (2008). *Insight dialog and insight dialog inquiry* Retrieved June 20, 2008, www.pacificintegral.com.

O'Fallon, T., Ramirez, V., & Fitch, G. (2014). Collective intelligence as a causal ground. *Spanda Journal, 2*, 91–95.

O'Fallon, T. (2020). States and STAGES: Waking up developmentally. *Integral Review: A Transdisciplinary & Transcultural Journal for New Thought*, Research, & Praxis, *16*(1), 13–38.

Pierrakos, J. C. (2005). *Core energetics: Developing the capacity to love and heal.* Core Evolution.

Ramirez, V., Fitch, G, & O'Fallon T. (2013). *Causal leadership: A natural emergence from later stages of awareness.* Paper presented at the Integral Theory Conference, San Francisco, CA.

Reams, J. (2017). An overview of adult cognitive development research and its application in the field of leadership studies. *Behavioral Development Bulletin, 22*(2), 334–348.

Reams, J. (Ed.), (2020). *Maturing leadership: How adult development impacts leadership.* Emerald Publishing.

Richo, D. (2014). *How to be an adult in love.* Shambhala Publications.

Scharmer, O. (2018). *The essentials of Theory U: Core principles and applications.* Berrett-Koehler Publishers.

Smith, K., & Berg, D. (1997). *Paradoxes of group life.* Jossey-Bass.

Torbert, W. R. (2004). *Action inquiry: The secret of timely and transforming leadership.* Berrett-Koehler Publishers.

Torbert, W. R. (2020). Warren Buffett's and your own seven transformations of leadership. *Global Leadership Associates.* https://www.gla.global/wp-content/uploads/2020/09/Warren-Buffetts-and-Your-Own-Seven-Transformations-of-Leadership.pdf

Wilber, K. (2000). *Integral psychology: Consciousness, spirit, psychology, therapy.* Shambhala Publications.

Wilber, K. (2001). *A brief history of everything.* Shambhala.

Wilber, K. (2006). *Integral spirituality: a startling new role for religion in the modern and postmodern world.* Shambhala.

2

ADAPTIVE LEADERSHIP AND SPIRITUALITY

The Inherent Spirituality of Being an Adaptive Leader

Mohammed Raei

Introduction

The adaptive leadership framework (Heifetz et al., 2009) is centered on adaptive challenges, that is, complex challenges which do not lend themselves to expert solutions. It has gained popularity as a potential solution for organizational, societal, and global intractable problems. Given the increasing number of crises in the world, adaptive leadership is needed now more than ever before (Raei & Rasmussen, 2021).

When one thinks of leadership and spirituality, often, the theories that come to mind are authentic leadership (Avolio & Gardner, 2005), transformational leadership (Bass, 1985), and servant leadership (Greenleaf, 2002). But, what of adaptive leadership? How does adaptive leadership involve spirituality, if at all? Surprisingly, adaptive leadership has a strong spiritual element; for instance, Heifetz et al. (2009) argued that the courage to engage in adaptive work requires a wholeness that involves the mind, guts, heart, and *spirit,* and advocated for drawing on multiple intelligences, including *spiritual intelligence*, as part of using the self as a leadership resource. Furthermore, they suggested that leaders should inspire people, linking the word inspire to its original meaning—to fill with spirit. Finally, for adaptive leaders to sustain themselves from the dangers and stress of adaptive work and create a personal holding environment, Heifetz et al. (2009) suggested that leaders need to create personal sanctuaries—spaces (mental or physical) where they can hear themselves think, recover from work, and feel the quieter dispositions of their spirit.

DOI: 10.4324/9781003396741-4

Besides these references in the main body of adaptive leadership writings (Heifetz et al., 2009; Heifetz & Linsky, 2002), the spirituality element has seldom been explored. However, there are exceptions. Raei (2021a) explored the application of adaptive leadership in the Chinese context and discussed how certain elements of Taoism lend themselves to adaptive leadership, specifically the concepts of Wu Wei, action without action, and the interplay between Yin and Yang when the leader alternates between action and reflection, ripening issues, intervening, and so on. Reams (2021) explored the virtuality of the self and argued that "the soul is on the balcony [observing the patterns in the social system and gaining a larger perspective] and the self is on the dance floor [acting and intervening to make progress on adaptive challenges]" (p. 85). The soul creates a field of awareness that is at the heart of a holding environment.

There is a "broadly based quest for spiritual experience and spiritual practices expressed in a variety of ways" (Sheldrake, 2012, p. 1) as evidenced in the popularity of psychedelic retreats (Kamin, 2021) and the increase of the spiritual but not religious category in the United States to more than a third of the population (Smith & Shapiro, 2021). One of the strengths of adaptive leadership is that its framework can be adapted to various contexts (Rasmussen & Raei, 2021) and can borrow from a variety of other approaches (See Raei & Rasmussen, 2021). It is therefore ripe to explore the links between spirituality and adaptive leadership that include and go beyond mindfulness. The rest of this chapter explores in detail how selected elements of spirituality can enhance adaptive leadership. It is organized into three sections: (1) a discussion of adaptive leadership highlighting some of its more spiritual aspects—aspects that have largely been ignored by practitioners and scholars alike who focused instead on more intellectual aspects like authority versus leadership and the technical/adaptive distinction; (2) an overview of selected spirituality concepts that are relevant for adaptive leadership and how they play into adaptive leadership; and (3) concluding remarks.

Adaptive Leadership

One of the key contributions of the adaptive leadership framework is Heifetz's (1994) distinction between leadership with authority (exercised from a position of power) and leadership without authority, which is leadership exercised when one lacks positional power. The focus of this chapter is the former, although some of the recommendations here apply also to leaders without authority.

As mentioned earlier, adaptive leadership deals with adaptive challenges, that is, complex challenges that do not lend themselves to expert solutions. Solutions for adaptive challenges often require losses and call for collective unlearning of behaviors, values, and assumptions as well as learning new ones (Heifetz et al., 2009). This (un)learning can be linked with double-loop learning (Rasmussen & Boyce, 2021), which involves an examination of assumptions and beliefs (Argyris & Schön, 1996).

Adaptive leadership constructs a hierarchy of values, not in terms of their ethical effects, but based on their usefulness for adaptation and what is important for the stakeholders. This hierarchy is culturally specific and not universal (Heifetz, 1994). Adaptive leaders do not create dependency and keep the distress within a tolerable range; they pace the adaptive work by giving adaptive work back to people at a rate that they can handle (Heifetz, 1994). To make progress on adaptive challenges, the leader creates a holding environment—a setting where conflict over values and (un)learning can take place—and uses interventions to keep the distress in a tolerable zone. While in this tolerable zone, progress can be made. However, if the distress in the holding environment is too high or too low, progress is impossible with adaptive work either exploding out of hand or coming to a standstill, respectively. Strengthening the holding environment allows for more progress on adaptive challenges and increases tolerance of the conflict needed for adaptive work. This can be achieved through a leader's presence and *compassion*, modifying the elements of the physical environment, creating shared values and purpose, using a shared language, and making use of lateral, vertical (Heifetz et al., 2009), and relational trust (Rasmussen & Raei, 2020).

Adaptive work is an iterative process involving making observations, interpreting the observations, and making interventions based on these observations (Heifetz et al., 2009). Heifetz (1994) used the metaphor of moving between the balcony and the dance floor to describe the movement between reflection (observing and making interpretations) and action (intervening). Adaptive leadership uses a wide range of interventions to keep attention on ripening issues and to make progress on adaptive challenges. These interventions include asking questions, silence, and quelling a diversion. Moreover, they involve strategies of provocation and evocation (Williams, 2005). Heifetz et al. (2009) discussed the importance of communicating above and below the neck—that is, communicating to reach people emotionally, *spiritually*, and intellectually as part of the framework, that is, adaptive leaders speak from the heart and express their feelings to inspire people (Heifetz et al., 2009). Importantly, it is impossible to speak from the heart, to connect with people and move them unless one is connected with one's *own* heart. Connecting with and speaking from the heart communicates what is at stake and the reasons that make it worthwhile for people to stay in the game, despite the losses. Additionally, it sustains them through the fluctuations of hope and despair that come with adaptive work. Speaking from the heart requires connecting with one's beliefs, emotions, and values and can, through a strong and calming tone, prevent things from breaking down in a tense meeting (Heifetz et al., 2009).

People resist adaptive work because it often creates stress, distress, and losses (Heifetz, 1994; Heifetz & Linsky, 2002; Heifetz et al., 2009). Moreover, it requires one to let go of cherished values and assumptions—values and assumptions that have served well in the past. Adaptive work avoidance can take many forms: using a technical solution that does not get at the real issue, scapegoating, externalizing the enemy, changing the subject, denying the problem exists, blaming or attacking the positional leader, jumping to conclusions (Heifetz et al., 2009), and silence (Heifetz & Linsky, 2002).

Heifetz and Linsky (2002) discussed some of the actions that a leader must take to mitigate the dangers of adaptive work. They recommended that leaders manage their hungers: the need for control, the need for admiration and importance, and the need for intimacy. Additionally, the authors provided tools for anchoring one's self. These tools include distinguishing the self from the role, keeping confidantes, and keeping a sanctuary. Heifetz et al. (2009) admonished leaders not to get lost in the grandiosity of their vision for change and instead to honor the tension between the grand vision that touches the leader's heart and the concrete, small transformations which they have the opportunity to make daily. Moreover, they advocated seeing one's self as a system: identifying one's loyalties, triggers, and tuning, expanding one's range of interventions, understanding the different roles that one plays, and articulating one's purpose.

Compassion is an essential element of adaptive leadership. Heifetz (1994) argued that "leadership requires compassion for the distress of adaptive change, both because compassion is its own virtue, and because it can improve one's sense of timing" (p. 241). Heifetz and Linsky (2002) wrote, "The deepest wisdom and the most profound expressions of your experience are rooted in compassion" (p. 227). They suggested that leading is an expression of one's aliveness and that the dangers of adaptive work can degrade one's compassion, *love* for people, creativity, and curiosity on a daily basis. They argued that the hardest work of leadership involves learning to feel distress without numbing one's self. They explained that "the virtue of a *sacred heart* [emphasis added] lies in the courage to maintain your innocence and wonder, your doubt and curiosity, and your compassion and love even through your darkest, most difficult moments" (p. 227). In addition to a leader's compassion, adaptive leadership recognizes that in the face of the distress accompanying adaptive change, individuals might lose their compassion for others and become cruel as a way to preserve order.

Finally, experimentation and improvisation are essential aspects of adaptive leadership. Heifetz (1994) argued that leadership demands

> an experimental mindset—the willingness to work by trial and error—where the community's reactions at each stage provide the basis for planning future actions. Research about each particular context is crucially important, but no analysis or catalogue can substitute for a leader's improvisational skills.
>
> *(pp. 242–243)*

Adaptive leaders use low-risk experiments to test the accuracy of any given interpretation in order to assuage people's fears that a certain interpretation might be incorrect (Heifetz et al., 2009).

Selected Spiritual Elements and Their Interaction with Adaptive Leadership

In this section, I explore the links between adaptive leadership and three spiritual concepts: surrender, compassion, and mindfulness. I note that compassion can be used in a relational manner and mindfulness can be used in a secular manner, in addition to being part of spirituality as I discuss below. I also note that, in addition to the three concepts discussed here, there are many other spiritual concepts that can interact with adaptive leadership; however, due to space limitations, they will not be explored here.

Surrender

Surrender is a feature of many spiritual traditions. For example, the literal meaning of Islam means to surrender to God (Nygard, 1996). It is also one of the main practices of Eckankar (See Chapter 5). Welwood (1984) suggested that "the essence of spiritual work is learning to let go and surrender" (p. 68). Surrender is one of the qualities of the sacred (Levine & Levine, 2010); it reconnects one with the source energy, and causes a different quality to flow into one's doing (Tolle, 1999). Surrender is not resignation, nor is it "defeat. It is going beyond resistance. It is the mind sinking into the heart" (Levine & Levine, 2010, p. 68). Through surrender, one can experience timelessness, dynamic immersion, improvisation, openness, limitlessness, suspension, connectedness, mutuality, receptivity, non-judgment, and mindfulness without thoughts (Moze, 2009, as cited in Gunnlaugson & Moze, 2012).

Practicing any art necessitates surrender and discipline (Wilber et al., 2008). Nachmanovitch (1991) proposed that surrender is a prerequisite of the creative process and involves "cultivating a comfortable attitude toward not-knowing, being nurtured by the mystery of moments that are dependably surprising, ever fresh" (p. 17). Integral surrender involves a consecration of energies from mind, soul, heart, will, sense, body, and life to become a vehicle for the Divine (Nandram & Bindlish, 2019). Surrender is not a weakness, but a strength (Tolle, 1999). It is perfectly compatible with initiating change, taking action, or achieving goals (1999). Moreover, it does not undermine commitment and is not to be mistaken for leaving one to drift passively through life (Wilber et al., 2008). Tolle (1999) suggested that it is not possible to have spiritual power without surrender.

Adaptive leaders (with authority) control the holding environment but are not in control of the outcome of interventions (Heifetz et al., 2009). The need for control is one of the hungers that adaptive leaders need to manage (2009); letting go of the need to control the outcome of an intervention requires surrender. Gunnlaugson and Moze (2012) suggested that surrender releases the "energy formally held in the contracted egoic state" (p. 107), something that might prevent adaptive leaders from getting lost in the grandiosity of their vision. Furthermore, refraining from intervening and allowing issues to ripen demands surrender. Adaptive leaders have to improvise (Heifetz, 1994). However, improvisation requires surrender, that is, "acceptance, in a single breath, of both transience and eternity" (Nachmanovitch, 1991, p. 17).

Instead of surrendering to the cosmos, higher being, or the universe (Nandram, & Bindlish, 2019), surrender can be co-opted by human resource development (HRD) to serve a corporate agenda (Fenwick & Lange, 1998). Fenwick and Lange (1998) argued that human resources development demands surrender without discernment.

> Workers have always been forced to surrender to organizational authority, knowledge, and values. The new HRD craving for spiritual surrender is evident in the supervision of employees' critical reflection on their belief systems. The urgent focus on workers' personal transformation or conversion, coupled with proselytizing spiritual promises of joy through systems thinking and continuous personal change, is creating a new religion.
> *(p. 76)*

Sadly, not much has changed since Fenwick and Lange wrote their article. In any event, adaptive leaders can only focus on their own surrender, but cannot force employees to surrender to a corporate agenda through spirituality or any other means. Adaptive leadership does not force solutions and protects voices of leadership without authority. In other words, it allows solutions to emerge from any level of the organization.

Compassion

Compassion is an essential element of many spiritual traditions. Kelly and Martin-Smith (2014) pointed out that "enlightenment without compassion isn't enlightenment at all" (p. 155). Compassion is one of the ways to make the sacred present (Manson, 2013). Buber (2011) made the distinction between I-It relationships in which others are treated as objects and I-Thou (you) relationships in which others are treated as subjects.

> Spirit in its human manifestation is man's response to his [Thou]. Man speaks in many tongues ….but the *spirit is one* [emphasis added]; it is response to the [Thou] that appears from the mystery and addresses us from the mystery… Spirit is not in the I but between I and [Thou]… Man lives in the spirit when he is able to respond to his [Thou]. He is able to do that when he enters into this relation with his whole being. It is solely by virtue of his power to relate that man is able to live in the spirit.
>
> *(p. 88–89)*

It is not possible to have compassion in an I–It relationship (Roberts, 2001), because in I–It relationships, others are objects. Only in I–Thou relationships can one have compassion. Compassion for others is more potent when one lives in spirit allowing us to enter into relationship with others from our whole being.

Compassion requires a grounded spirituality. Welwood (1984) wrote:

> Awakening the heart also requires grounded ness[*sic*], because without Earth [one of the three elements in the ancient Chinese system: Earth, Heaven, and man], there would be no compassion…. If our only concern is with space or spirit, then we may not be very committed to other sentient beings…. If we are only oriented toward spirit, we tend to get impatient with other people's stuckness.
>
> *(p. 70)*

This grounded spirituality is needed, not just for compassion, but for adaptive leadership in general. Adaptive leaders need to be focused on Earth—what is happening in the here and now in the social system and what is happening in their own self system—while spiritually maintaining a connection, with the transcendent (Heaven).

Sadly,

> there is an alarming tendency in spiritual circles to resort to easy answers to hard questions, to dwell in superficial compassion…but with no

> willingness to understand or confront our ecological and spiritual emergency, or the dire structural injustice that supports it.
>
> *(Patten, 2018, p. ix)*

What is often promoted as compassion is in many cases "idiot compassion"—a term coined by the Tibetan Buddhist teacher Chögyam Trungpa (1976). People exercising idiot compassion empathize with dysfunctional and maladaptive behavior no matter what and make no value judgment about the best course of action. Moreover, this involves a naive kind of selflessness that ignores one's own needs. Individuals exercising idiot compassion can be taken advantage of. Real compassion (Wilber, 2000b), on the other hand, involves "tough love" (pp. 241–242), and "includes wisdom and so it makes judgments of care and concern: It says somethings are good and somethings are bad" (p. 310).

Adaptive leadership is a step ahead of other leadership frameworks in that it advocates for real compassion instead of idiot compassion. It also recognizes that people's acting in uncompassionate ways is a resistance to distress and loss. According to Heifetz (1994),

> … compassion … is rarely soft. The respect required in leadership is often the limit-setting love that gives people little leeway for turning their eyes from difficult work. But toughness is not the same thing as the gleeful abuse of power, or vengeful delight.
>
> *(Heifetz, 1994, p. 243)*

In other words, this is a compassion that is rooted in tough love, which "means being firm but kind while setting boundaries and sticking to them" (Bhatt, 2021). This tough love is present in another aspect of adaptive leadership. The adaptive leadership framework avoids idiot compassion when it invokes a hierarchy of values. In other words, it judges values in terms of their fitness for adaptation. Wilber (2000b) pointed out that "a true holism involves levels of love, as it were in both directions: Eros reaching up and Agape reaching down. But a love that is therefore a 'tough love,' a true compassion, not an idiot compassion that avoids ranking" (pp. 241–242).

Whereas inclusion is essential in many contexts, leaders who engage in idiot compassion may have the misguided belief that they must include everyone even when it is inappropriate to do so. In other words, including others for the sake of including others. Unfortunately,

> Even the most well-crafted efforts at inclusion can rarely prevent the experience of loss by some. As a result, one often cannot shield oneself from the outrage of those parties who must face loss and are unwilling

> to change. Furthermore, from a strategic standpoint, some parties often *must be excluded* [emphasis added] from the problem-solving process. They generate more disruption than can be contained effectively by the holding environment… Sometimes one excludes people and puts aside their perspectives regardless of their validity.
>
> *(Heifetz, 1994, p. 240)*

In other words, the key consideration in inclusion/exclusion is the strength of the holding environment and how much disruption it can tolerate.

I should note, though, that the kind of strategic exclusion proposed by Heifetz might be temporary. When the adaptive capacity for the social system has increased, the leader can reintroduce the issues and include those who were excluded (Heifetz, 1994). Thus, real compassion can be thought of as strategic and requires effort, whereas it is easy for leaders to fall for idiot compassion, which only looks at the short term.

In addition to compassion for others, one can have compassion for one's self. According to Vogt (2022), if we are "compassionate with our own failures and suffering, we grow to know and accept ourselves. From being (re)active perfectionists, we gradually become reflective and creative 'imperfectionists'" (p. 322). An attitude of self-compassion involves noticing one's imperfections, even under the gravest circumstances, and accepting them as they do not go away and that it might take many tries to get things right (Patten, 2018). Adaptive leadership is generally silent on self-compassion, although it is probably as important for adaptive leaders to cultivate compassion for themselves as it is for them to cultivate compassion for others.

As a leader makes cyclical observations, interpretations, and interventions, there is a good chance that any of these will be off the mark. Self-compassion developed through spirituality can prevent the leader from getting stuck in self-pity or self-blame for mis-observing, misinterpreting, or mis-intervening. I should emphasize, though, that this self-compassion is a real compassion and not an idiot compassion that facilitates a leader letting themselves off the hook. According to Wilber (2000b), "We must *start* [emphasis in the original] to try to learn to exercise real compassion instead of idiot compassion" (p. 105). Wilber added, "We need to be gentle with ourselves, it is true, but also, we need to be firm. Treat yourself with real compassion, not idiot compassion, and therefore begin to challenge yourself, engage yourself, [and] push yourself" (p. 310). And while Wilber's writing is in the context of spiritual practice, nevertheless, the same is true in the context of adaptive leadership.

Real self-compassion is also needed when we try to manage our hungers and sometimes fail to do so. Moreover, when our triggers might be rooted in childhood trauma, they are "old hits" (Patten, 2018, p. 53) which can deplete us, overwhelm us, exhaust us, and lead us to avoid our own adaptive work. Yet,

> the hit is still a gift, but it asks us for an entirely different move. We have to find our way to a heart of compassion for ourselves. Noticing our own inseparable divinity and humanity, we can metaphorically take our inner child in our arms. Our self-care and self-compassion flow. They restore our felt connection to whatever we cared about that was attacked in the first place—and that is another source of strength.
>
> *(p. 53)*

Self-compassion can be exercised from a secular point of view, but it is significantly more potent when rooted in the recognition of our inseparable humanity and divinity.

As mentioned earlier, compassion for others is one of the ways to strengthen the holding environment. When leaders display self-compassion, they, through role modeling, allow others to have compassion for themselves, something that might increase vertical trust (trust in the authority figure) and, in the process, further strengthen the holding environment.

Because adaptive leadership can create distress, one of the ways that people avoid adaptive change is through "assassinating" the person generating the distress. Assassination can be, in rare cases, literal as in the assassination of Martin Luther King, Jr. Or, it can be figurative (Heifetz, 1994). Figurative assassination can be in the form of character or capacity assassination. A leader who is on the receiving end of a figurative assassination may begin to think of people who try to assassinate them as objects, as It(s), in the process weakening the holding environment and interfering with the leader's ability to make observations and correctly interpret the meaning of those observations. In other words, I–It thinking will cloud the leader's judgment and cause them to act in heartless ways. In these cases, the leader must have compassion for themselves.

Adult development is concerned with how one's meaning-making system changes over time (Kegan & Lahey, 2009). Adults can move through successive stages of development over their lifespans. Each succeeding stage transcends and includes the previous one (Wilber, 2000a). And although higher stages are not necessarily better (Berger, 2011), individuals at higher stages tend to have an increased capacity for perspective-taking (Kegan & Lahey, 2009), systemic thinking, and wisdom (Cook-Greuter, 2013). Moreover, they can make more distinctions (Kegan, 1982) and thus see more shades of gray (Berger, 2010) as opposed to just black or white. As adaptive leadership demands the highest stages of adult development (Kegan, 1994; Raei, 2018; Rasmussen & Raei, 2020), it might be easier for adaptive leaders to exercise compassion. According to Cook-Greuter (2013), "persons at the unitive stage [the highest stage in Cook-Greuter's model] feel tolerance, *compassion* [emphasis added], and an affiliation with all manifestations of life" (p. 89).

Nevertheless, adaptive leadership is rare (Heifetz et al., 2009), and very few individuals can make use of the various prescriptions and practices of the adaptive leadership framework, in part because of the high level of adult development required. This begs the question: how can aspiring adaptive leaders who have not yet reached the highest level of development enact compassion for others as well as for themselves? The Buddhist loving-kindness meditation (called *metta* in Pali) offers one solution (Boellinghaus et al., 2012). Additionally, a more advanced practice that further develops a leader's capacity for compassion is the Tibetan Buddhist practice of *Tonglen* (Monaghan & Viereck, 2011). In any case, the specific spiritual practice/ meditation that the person uses to foster compassion is not so important; what is important is that the person finds that practice that *works for them* (Raei, 2021b). Of course, if one does not already have strong compassion, one does not develop it overnight. There is a need for practice both in the moment (on the dance floor) and on the meditation cushion.

Mindfulness and Insight

There is a rapidly growing interest in mindfulness as a secular practice. Mindfulness is derived from Buddhist practice and is part of the eightfold path (Carmody, 2015) that leads to liberation. The most popular secular definition of mindfulness comes from Kabat-Zinn (2005), the creator of mindfulness-based stress reduction, who defines mindfulness as "paying attention in a particular way: on purpose, in the present moment, and non-judgmentally" (p. 4).

Much of the scholarship on mindfulness and leadership approaches the topic from a secular mindfulness angle. As for adaptive leadership, specifically, two articles made tenuous connections between mindfulness and adaptive leadership. Raney (2014) suggested that adaptive leadership practices complemented mindfulness and that similar to adaptive leadership, the process of mindfulness is constantly changing, reflective, and iterative in nature. Moreover, Raney suggested that both adaptive leadership and mindful administration have a "commitment to contemplation, where even present-mindedness means looking at or toward a circumstance, condition, or possibility" (p. 318). This could be true if contemplation connotes going to the balcony. Finally, she argued that mindfulness complements adaptive leadership as a means of accepting change and cultivating uncertainty.

Modern mindfulness training is focused on "acceptance of experience that is implicit in refraining from the *attempt to change* [emphasis added] the thoughts, sensations, and feelings that are noticed in the training exercises" (Carmody, 2015, p. 72). Adaptive leadership is essentially an attempt to change and thus it could be argued is incompatible with what Raney is proposing. In a related vein, McKenzie (2014) argued that the cultivation of mindfulness, with its focus on the present moment, might help adaptive leaders manage the stress of adaptive work and create the capacity to tolerate frustration, uncertainty, and pain. Moreover, McKenzie likened the concept of mindfulness to alternating between the balcony and dance floor in adaptive leadership, but provided little explanation for making such a link.

Recall that adaptive leaders go through cycles of observing, interpreting, and intervening. Being in the present moment can result in more focused observations during one-on-one and group meetings. Present-moment awareness also might help the leader to better pay attention to the level of distress in the system and the degree to which interventions keep the distress within the productive zone for disequilibrium. More importantly, there are spiritual "benefits" to being in the present moment; it allows one to realize the sacredness of all life, that is, when one enters the now, one realizes that "life is sacred. There is a sacredness to everything you perceive when you are present. The more you live in the now, the more you sense the simple yet profound joy of being and the sacredness of all life" (Tolle, 1999, p. 42). Moreover, Tolle (2003) suggested that "by giving your full attention to this moment, an intelligence far greater than the egoic mind enters your life" (p. 28). Being present is a form of surrender.

As for non-judgmentality, Kabat-Zinn's definition, mentioned earlier, deviates from canonical Buddhist definitions of mindfulness most of which do not mention non-judgment as an aspect of mindfulness (Quaglia et al., 2015). Quaglia et al. noted that "nonjudgmentality represents a 'skillful means' to enhance mindfulness rather than the thing itself" (p. 155). Even if non-judgment is not "the thing itself" and just a skillful means to get there, it can benefit an adaptive leader during the observe part of the cycle, and as a result, prevent the leader from jumping up the ladder of inference (Argyris, 1990). However, being judgmental is needed in both the interpreting and intervening parts of the cycle; the leader has to judge any observation as good or bad in relation to adaptive work. Similarly, leaders have to make judgments regarding which potential intervention is most likely to succeed in creating movement on adaptive challenges. Finally, once the intervention is underway, leaders have to make judgments about the intervention's effectiveness or lack thereof and whether it needs to be modified, abandoned midcourse, or allowed to reach completion.

Adverse Effects and Misuse of Mindfulness

Mindfulness can have some negative effects on the individual psychological and bodily levels. For example, in a recent study (Britton et al., 2021), 83 percent of the mindfulness-based intervention sample reported at least one meditation-related side effect. These side effects included, but were not limited to, derealization, insomnia, and re-experiencing trauma (Britton et al., 2021). More importantly, misuse of mindfulness can have some negative effects on adaptive work. Purser (2019) popularized the term McMindfulness—a pervasive, individualistic, apolitical form of mindfulness that serves a neoliberal agenda while ignoring systemic sources of suffering. Instead, McMindfulness provides "an expedient tool for assuaging stress without wisdom and insight about where it comes from" (pp. 19–20). It could be argued that McMindfulness is the mindfulness analog of idiot compassion. At the individual level, McMindfulness can be a form of spiritual bypassing, a "tendency to try to avoid or prematurely transcend basic human needs, feelings, and developmental tasks" (Welwood, 1984, p. 64). When this bypassing relates to larger systemic causes of suffering like racism and white supremacy, it is referred to as structural spiritual bypassing (Sherrell & Simmer-Brown, 2017). Using adaptive leadership terminology, both are forms of adaptive work avoidance.

Mindfulness and Vipassana

It should be noted that from the perspective of traditional Buddhism, that the modern operationalizations of mindfulness have a tendency to confuse the method of "paying attention with particular objects recommended for attention" (Gethin, 2015, p. 31). In other words, mindfulness is not the goal, but the method by which one gets to the desired outcome. This is partially a result of the propensity to equate mindfulness with insight practice or *vipassana* in Pali (Gethin, 2015).

> Insight meditation… refers to the practice of meditation orientated toward seeing the complex of mental and physical phenomena (comprising in Buddhist thought the five *skandhas* or collections of physical form, feeling, perception, volitional forces, and consciousness) that constitute both our selves (experiencing subjects) and the world (experienced objects) as impermanent (*anitya*), unsatisfying (*duḥkha*) and not self (*anātman*).
> (*p. 15*)

Vipassana—a more advanced practice than mindfulness—can be considered a form of double-loop learning (Argyris & Schön, 1996), which at first glance, one might think can provide the wisdom that serves as an antidote to McMindfulness's emphasis on individual causes of suffering instead of a focus on more systemic ones. However, *vipassana* is only systemic in relation to personal internal psychological structures and does not deal in any way with external ones. Still, *vipassana* can be helpful for adaptive leaders in that it might strengthen their double-loop learning muscle. Moreover, seeing things as not self, as Gethin (2015) explained, might help the leader distinguish self from their role in order to manage their hungers. Finally, realizing impermanence (*anitya*) will help the leader accept that sustainable change might be a myth (Weisbord, 2011) and avoid getting bogged down by the eventual failure of change in the long term.

Concluding Remarks

Much of the scholarship on adaptive leadership has focused on conflict and creating a holding environment. I argued (Raei, 2021a) that "adaptive leadership uniquely represents that merging of the opposites [Yin-Yang]" (p. 19). Surrender and compassion are the Yin to adaptive leadership's Yang manifest in intervention and conflict.

Meditation is not a panacea for psychological ills (Raei, 2021b), and neither is spirituality. Unfortunately, the spiritual concepts discussed in the previous section can be misconstrued and misused: surrender can become abdication and resignation, mindfulness can turn into McMindfulness, and real compassion can turn into idiot compassion. It is important for adaptive leaders to make use of the tools and capabilities of adaptive leadership in order to avoid falling into these traps. Specifically, the use of double-loop learning, systemic thinking, and the ability to think politically can prevent leaders from falling into McMindfulness. Moreover, adaptive leaders need to rely on their high level of mental complexity (adult development) in order to recognize the distinction between idiot and real compassion and accordingly, respond both compassionately and effectively to the losses inherent in adaptive work.

Purser (2019) suggested that to overcome the neoliberal agenda of McMindfulness, mindfulness needs to be coupled with critical consciousness (Freire, 1970). The benefits of critical consciousness are not limited to mindfulness and extend to surrender, compassion, and insight in addition to adaptive work. Critical consciousness can complement adaptive leadership's systemic thinking, political thinking, and double-loop learning.

Northouse (2015) suggested that adaptive leadership has a service orientation. Wilber et al. (2008) wrote, "As your devotional life becomes authentic and full, service is a way to bring that devotional spirit into action, using your *whole body* [emphasis added] to enact your communion with the beloved Kosmos" (p. 296). Adaptive work needs wholeness; this wholeness cannot just involve mind, guts, heart, and *spirit* as Heifetz et al. (2009) advocated. In order for this wholeness to be true wholeness, it has to also include the whole body and not be limited to the guts and the heart (for more details on embodied spirituality and leadership in the contexts of non-Western cultures and the role of embodiment in shadow work, see Chapters 8 and 13, respectively).

Bernstein and Linsky (2016) proposed that some find adaptive leadership wanting in excitement, fun, or inspiration as it fails to engage people in a way that provides fun, a spirit of collaboration, and observable signs of progress. Often people experience adaptive leadership as emotionally strenuous and negative in spirit. They added that it is limited in that it offers few resources for identifying the elements of an imagined future or for creating specific interventions. As mentioned earlier, adaptive leadership involves inspiring people (filling them with spirit) and communicating with them spiritually in order to reach them above and below the neck. Thus, I propose that the spirituality of the leader is a prerequisite for adaptive leadership. That said, this spirituality cannot be a serious, rigid, or uninspiring spirituality. A playful attitude and playful spirituality might be what is needed for adaptive work and keeping adaptive leaders "alive." After all, "enlightenment isn't a serious, deadly, stern affair—it's playful, fun, light, and deeply, deeply curious" (Kelly & Martin-Smith, 2014, p. 179).

References

Argyris, C. (1990). *Overcoming organizational defenses: Facilitating organizational learning*. Pearson.

Argyris, C., & Schön, D. (1996). *Organizational learning II: Theory, method, and practice*. Addison-Wesley.

Avolio, B. J., & Gardner, W. L. (2005). Authentic leadership development: Getting to the root of positive forms of leadership. *The Leadership Quarterly*, *16*(3), 315–338. https://doi.org/10.1016/j.leaqua.2005.03.001

Bass, B. M. (1985). *Leadership and performance beyond expectations*. Free Press.

Berger, J. G. (2010). Using the subject-object interview to promote and assess self-authorship. In M. B. Magolda, E. G. Creamer, & P. S. Meszaros (Eds.), *Development and assessment of self-authorship: Exploring the concept across cultures* (pp. 245–264). Stylus Publishing, LLC.

Berger, J. G. (2011). *Changing on the job: Developing leaders for a complex world*. Stanford University Press.

Bernstein, M., & Linsky, M. (2016). Leading change through adaptive design. *Stanford Social Innovation Review*, *14*(1), 48–54.

Bhatt, A. (2021, September 28). *90 tough love quotes for your relationship*. The Random Vibez. https://www.therandomvibez.com/tough-love-quotes/

Boellinghaus, I., Jones, F. W., & Hutton, J. (2012). The role of mindfulness and loving-kindness meditation in cultivating self-compassion and other-focused concern in health care professionals. *Mindfulness*, *5*(2), 129–138. https://doi.org/10.1007/s12671-012-0158-6

Britton, W. B., Lindahl, J. R., Cooper, D. J., Canby, N. K., & Palitsky, R. (2021). Defining and measuring meditation-related adverse effects in mindfulness-based programs. *Clinical Psychological Science*, *9*(6), 1185–1204. https://doi.org/10.1177/2167702621996340

Buber, M. (2011). *I and thou* (W. Kaufmann, Trans.). Scribner.

Carmody, J. (2015). Reconceptualizing mindfulness: The psychological principles of attending in mindfulness practice and their role in wellbeing. In K. W. Brown, J. D. Creswell, & R. M. Ryan (Eds.), *Handbook of mindfulness: Theory, research, and practice* (pp. 62–78). Guilford Publications.

Cook-Greuter, S. (2013). *Nine levels of increasing embrace in ego development: A full-spectrum theory of vertical growth and meaning making*. http://onesystemonevoice.com/resources/Cook-Greuter+9+levels+paper+new+1.1$2714+97p$5B1$5D.pdf

Fenwick, T., & Lange, E. (1998). Spirituality in the workplace: The new frontier of HRD. *Canadian Journal for the Study of Adult Education*, *12*(1), 63–87.

Freire, P. (1970). *Pedagogy of the oppressed*. Herder and Herder.

Gethin, R. (2015). Buddhist conceptualizations of mindfulness. In K. W. Brown, J. D. Creswell, & R. M. Ryan (Eds.), *Handbook of mindfulness: Theory, research, and practice* (pp. 9–41). Guilford Publications.

Greenleaf, R. K. (2002). *Servant leadership: A journey into the nature of legitimate power and greatness*. Paulist Press.

Gunnlaugson, O., & Moze, M. G. (2012). Surrendering into witnessing: A foundational practice for building collective intelligence capacity in groups. *Journal of Integral Theory and Practice*, *7*(3), 105–115.

Heifetz, R. A. (1994). *Leadership without easy answers*. Harvard University Press.

Heifetz, R. A., Grashow, A., & Linsky, M. (2009). *The practice of adaptive leadership: Tools and tactics for changing your organization and the world*. Harvard Business Press.

Heifetz, R. A., & Linsky, M. (2002). *Leadership on the line: Staying alive through the dangers of leading*. Harvard Business Press.

Kabat-Zinn, J. (2005). *Wherever you go, there you are: Mindfulness meditation in everyday life*. Hyperion.

Kamin, D. (2021, November 25). The rise of psychedelic retreats. *The New York Times*. https://www.nytimes.com/2021/11/25/travel/psychedelic-retreat-ayahuasca.html

Kegan, R. (1982). *The evolving self: Problem and process in human development*. Harvard University Press.

Kegan, R. (1994). *In over our heads: The mental demands of modern life*. Harvard University Press.

Kegan, R., & Lahey, L. L. (2009). *Immunity to change: How to overcome it and unlock potential in yourself and your organization*. Harvard Business Press.

Kelly, J. P., & Martin-Smith, K. (2014). *The heart of Zen: Enlightenment, emotional maturity, and what it really takes for spiritual liberation*. North Atlantic Books.

Levine, S., & Levine, O. (2010). *Embracing the beloved: Relationship as a path of awakening*. Anchor.

Manson, J. L. (2013). Acts of compassion, the sacramental imagination, and the divine reality inherent in the world of things. *Oneing: An Alternative Orthodoxy, 1*(1), 57–61.

McKenzie, B. (2014). Adaptive leadership through mindfulness-scholarship review. *Concepts & Connections, 20*(3), 21–23.

Monaghan, P., & Viereck, E. G. (2011). *Meditation, the complete guide: Techniques from east and west to calm the mind, heal the body, and enrich the spirit*. New World Library.

Nachmanovitch, S. (1991). *Free play: Improvisation in life and art*. Penguin.

Nandram, S., & Bindlish, P. (2019). Integral yoga as foundation for social entrepreneurship: Leading toward sustainable welfare (Shubh Laabh). In J. Marques (Ed.), *The Routledge companion to management and workplace spirituality* (pp. 304–317). Routledge. https://doi.org/10.4324/9781351015110-28

Northouse, P. G. (2015). *Leadership: Theory and practice* (7th ed.). SAGE Publications.

Nygard, M. (1996). The Muslim concept of surrender to God. *International Journal of Frontier Missions, 13*(3), 125–130.

Patten, T. (2018). *A new republic of the heart: An ethos for revolutionaries—a guide to inner work for holistic change*. North Atlantic Books.

Purser, R. (2019). *McMindfulness: How mindfulness became the new capitalist spirituality*. Watkins Media.

Quaglia, J. T., Brown, K. W., Lindsay, E. K., Creswell, J. D., & Goodman, R. J. (2015). From conceptualization to operationalization of mindfulness. In K. W. Brown, J. D. Creswell, & R. M. Ryan (Eds.), *Handbook of mindfulness: Theory, research, and practice*. Guilford Publications.

Raei, M. (2018). *Development and validation of the adaptive leadership with authority scale* (Publication No. 10991817). [Doctoral dissertation, Antioch University]. ProQuest Dissertations and Theses Global.

Raei, M. (2021a). Adaptive leadership in the Chinese context: Can adaptive leadership be applied in China? In M. Raei & H. T. Rasmussen (Eds.), *Adaptive leadership in a global economy: Perspectives for application and scholarship* (pp. 183–198). Routledge. https://doi.org/10.4324/9781003099109-11

Raei, M. S. (2021b). *Spirituality, meditation, and kundalini: Almost everything you wanted to know but were afraid to ask*.

Raei, M., & Rasmussen, H. T. (2021). *Adaptive leadership in a global economy: Perspective for application and scholarship*. https://doi.org/10.4324/9781003099109

Raney, A. F. (2014). Agility in adversity: Integrating mindfulness and principles of adaptive leadership in the administration of a community mental health center. *Clinical Social Work Journal, 42*(3), 312–320. https://doi.org/10.1007/s10615-014-0487-0

Rasmussen, H. T., & Raei, M. (2020). I'll only follow if I trust you: Using adult development to accelerate trust. In J. Reams (Ed.), *Maturing leadership: How adult development impacts leadership* (pp. 103–128). Emerald Publishing Limited.

Rasmussen, H. T., & Boyce, M. C. (2021). Giving credit where it's due: The theories that support adaptive leadership. In M. Raei & H. T. Rasmussen (Eds.),

Adaptive leadership in a global economy: Perspectives for application and scholarship (pp. 29–43). Routledge. https://doi.org/10.4324/9781003099109-2

Rasmussen, H. T., & Raei, M. (2021). Introduction. In M. Raei & H. T. Rasmussen (Eds.), *Adaptive leadership in a global economy: Perspectives for application and scholarship* (pp. 1–7). Routledge. https://doi.org/10.4324/9781003099109-101

Reams, J. (2021). Soul space for adaptive work. In M. Raei & H. T. Rasmussen (Eds.), *Adaptive leadership in a global economy: Perspectives for application and scholarship* (pp. 82–96). Routledge. https://doi.org/10.4324/9781003099109-5

Roberts, L. (2001). Barriers to feeling and actualizing compassion. *Philosophy in the Contemporary World*, *8*(1), 13–19. https://doi.org/10.5840/pcw2001811

Sheldrake, P. (2012). *Spirituality: A very short introduction*. Oxford University Press.

Sherrell, C., & Simmer-Brown, J. (2017). Spiritual bypassing in the contemporary mindfulness movement. *ICEA Journal*, *1*(1), 75–94.

Smith, T. W., & Shapiro, B. (2021). *Spirituality and religion in the United States, 1998–2020*. NORC at the University of Chicago. https://www.norc.org/PDFs/Center%20for%20the%20Study%20of%20Politics%20and%20Society/Spirituality%20and%20Religion%20in%20the%20United%20States,%201998-2020.pdf

Tolle, E. (1999). *The power of now: A guide to spiritual enlightenment*. New World Library.

Tolle, E. (2003). *Stillness speaks*. New World Library.

Trungpa, T. T. (1976). *The myth of freedom and the way of meditation*. Shambhala Publications.

Vogt, O. (2022). Letting go of leadership: A hopeful utopia for corporate realists. In D. Enright, J. Knights, D. Grant, & G. Young (Eds.), *Transpersonal leadership in action: How to lead beyond the ego* (pp. 301–331). Routledge.

Weisbord, M. R. (2011). *Productive workplaces: Dignity, meaning, and community in the 21st century* (3rd ed.). John Wiley & Sons.

Welwood, J. (1984). Principles of inner work: Psychological and spiritual. *Journal of Transpersonal Psychology*, *16*(1), 63–73.

Wilber, K. (2000a). *Integral psychology*. Shambhala Publications.

Wilber, K. (2000b). *One taste*. Shambhala Publications.

Wilber, K., Patten, T., Leonard, A., & Morelli, M. (2008). *Integral life practice: A 21st-Century blueprint for physical health, emotional balance, mental clarity, and spiritual awakening*. Shambhala Publications.

Williams, D. (2005). *Real leadership: Helping people and organizations face their toughest challenges*. Berrett-Koehler Publishers.

3

ENACTING LEADERSHIP FROM A PLACE OF ONENESS

Stacey K. Guenther

Introduction

In the West, particularly the United States, we are enamored with leadership. To be a leader is often held as that which is prestigious and elevated and is reinforced through hierarchy with leaders positioned above all others. Traditionally, a leader is connoted as someone possessing wisdom, expertise (Machiavelli, 2003), and a savior-like quality (Weber, 1947). But I would posit that the elevation we assign to leaders is problematic in that there is an inherent separation between leaders and followers that heightens the sense of disconnection and aloneness found in the Western world today. According to a 2021 survey on American life, for example, reports of loneliness have significantly increased, and the number of people who say they have three or fewer good friends has doubled since 1990 (Cox, 2021). This separateness is a problem of a spiritual nature.

But what is to be done about our traditional, hierarchical view of leadership that would allow for the distance and separation between leader and follower to dissolve? I suggest that we begin by examining the way we view leadership. Could it be that if we view leadership from a different vantage point, how we enact and practice leadership may also shift? By shifting away from leadership as separate and hierarchical to a view of leadership as an enactment of oneness, it may be that "leaders…evolve a new consciousness, one that is collaborative, that better balances 'I' and 'we'" (Tsao & Laszlo, 2019, p. vi).

In research that I conducted on small groups (Guenther, 2022), I found that the groups' climates, that is, their internal feel, mood, and interpersonal

DOI: 10.4324/9781003396741-5

workings, changed through experiencing and becoming aware of a deep connection and manifestation of interbeing and oneness. Through coherence, the groups awakened to a different, unified way of being. The shifting group climates that occurred in my study have implications for leadership. My research indicates that leadership focused on creating a space for the magic of interbeing and oneness to happen instead of focusing on power, hierarchy, and efficiency could completely shift the way that we work and interact with each other. My intention, through this chapter, is to explore how we may make the shift away from power, hierarchy, and a productivity focus found at the core of our current practice of leadership toward the enactment of oneness, non-duality, and interbeing.

I will begin this chapter by exploring how separation shows up in how we traditionally view leadership and then will move into a discussion regarding spirituality, non-duality, and oneness, which may be a new lens through which we view leadership. I will then introduce two leadership theories that provide an opening toward oneness. Finally, I will lay out a developmental path to support the shift toward enacting oneness. In that path, I include suggested practices and actions that a leader and followers can take to move toward leading from a place of oneness and interbeing.

The Problem with Leadership

We have a love/hate relationship with both leaders and leadership (Meindl et al., 1985). We want leaders to be without flaws and to be able to fix that which is broken. As discussed by Sinclair (2007), our love affair with the ideal of leadership has been long held. Sinclair cited as an example Bennis and Nanus's 1985 bestselling book, *Leaders: Strategies for Taking Charge*, in which they painted a glowing portrait of the transformational leader who can "invent and create institutions ... can choose purposes and visions ... can move followers to higher degrees of consciousness, such as liberty, freedom, justice, and self-actualization" (Sinclair, 2007, p. 23). The ability of leaders to fix everything has become an expectation, whether in a work setting, the political arena, or the spiritual/religious space. Not only will we most likely never express these expectations, but also we may not even be aware of them (Ladkin, 2010).

> A significant absence which always underpins leadership is the expectations of those engaged in any leadership dynamic... Followers very rarely say... I expect you to sort out the interpersonal difficulty I have with the guy who sits next to me... I expect you to notice everything I do well and always praise me for it... I expect you to make my life so much better. In fact, on a conscious level followers themselves may be unaware they hold

> such desires but such unexpressed wishes may still influence and color their own, as well as their 'leader's' experience of the relationship.
>
> *(Ladkin, 2010, p. 39)*

We love our belief that leaders can fix everything, and we hate that they rarely live up to our expectations.

Our singular focus on the person of the leader has resulted in a compounding problem. The well-known organization development consultant and author, Peter Block (2018), explained that we tend to romanticize the notion of leadership and tune our attention to leaders' actions.

> ...leaders are cause and all others are effect. All that counts is what leaders do... They are foreground, while citizens, followers, players, and anyone else not in a leadership position are background. This is a deeply patriarchal agenda, and it is this love of leaders that limits our capacity to create an alternative future.
>
> *(p. 41)*

A consequence of this cause-and-effect view of leadership is that it also lets everyone else, that is, everyone else not in a leadership position, off the hook (Block, 2018). Absolving everyone else of responsibility and the part they play results in a decrease in and loss of engagement, interest, awareness of individual agency, and innovation. In short, when we remove ourselves from being interested parties and participants in whatever leadership action is happening, we all lose.

There is an inherent duality baked into this view of leadership that is apparent through simply viewing the common dichotomy of leader and follower. In this context, I refer to duality as a manifestation of separation (Taylor, 2017). There is a separateness that exists between the leader and everyone else. Not only is the duality clear, but also the hierarchy involved in our elevation of leaders results in a caste system of sorts, with leaders at the top of the food chain and all others below. While a hierarchy itself is neither a positive nor negative structure, it presents a differentiation between leaders and everyone else. Hierarchies, in this sense, can be "structures where certain people have more power or influence than others, forcing us into dominance and aggression and conflict" (Greer, 2020, para. 1).

This separateness is at the very heart of the problem with leadership and reflects a wound at the center of Western life and culture. Modern-day philosopher Charles Eisenstein (2013) called the experience of this duality the "wound of separation, the pain of the world" (p. 20). He explained that this "wound of separation" is a story that has us all believing that we are separate from each other.

> Who are you? You are a separate individual among other separate individuals in a universe that is separate from you as well. You are a Cartesian mote of consciousness looking out through the eyes of a flesh robot, programmed by its genes to maximize reproductive self-interest. You are a bubble of psychology, a mind (whether brain-based or not) separate from other minds and separate from matter. Or you are a soul encased in flesh, separate from the world and separate from other souls. Or you are a mass, a conglomeration of particles operating according to the impersonal forces of physics.
>
> *(Eisenstein, 2013, p. 4)*

Similarly, Taylor (2023) explained that most of us experience some degree of separation, that we are people with our individual, separate interiorities, experiencing life, thoughts, emotions, and sensations. He argued that this separateness "can be uncomfortable, bringing a sense of isolation and incompleteness" (p. 18). Simply stated, the separation and duality between leader and follower is built upon a false belief that we are disengaged, disconnected, and alone and is a reflection of the false story that tells us we are not connected.

There is another story of reality that centers around connectedness, is relational, and the experience of which is expansiveness, creative, and rich with potentiality. Eisenstein (2013) called this story the story of interbeing, and among the principles he associated with this story are the ideas that our state of being is relational, and therefore, "what we do to one another, we do to ourselves" (p. 14). Additionally, each of us is a unique gift whose life purpose is to express that gift, and "humanity is meant to join fully the tribe of all life on Earth, offering our unique human gifts toward the well-being and development of the whole" (p. 14).

If we accept Eisenstein's story of interbeing as true, the possibility of our connectedness must change the way we view leadership. It must influence how we interact in all the systems of which we are a part. In the next section, I will explore the concept of oneness, provide an overview of my research, and then revisit the concept of reality.

Spirituality, Interbeing, and Oneness

Through my own spiritual path, my research, and in my work as a mindfulness and meditation teacher, leadership coach, and consultant, my experience as a human in the world and how I view that experience has shifted. I believe I have awakened to a different reality. This awakened reality is what Taylor (2017) described as being "awestruck by is-ness and the beauty of your surroundings" (p. 185) and being part of a Kosmos that is fueled by divine love and in which all things are parts of a greater–the ultimate–whole. (For more on awakening, see Chapter 1).

This all-encompassing connectedness has been called oneness. Brought into focus by Ivanhoe (2017), and discussed by Aşkun (2019), the Oneness hypothesis brought together a number of theories and perspectives on oneness.

> [Oneness] is defined as a view about the nature of the world, the nature of the relationship between self and others including not only people but also other creatures, plants, animals, and all sorts of beings. The main claim of the Oneness hypothesis is that we all are interrelated with other beings around us. The main argument is not more about how oneness comes about per se, but more of how it serves the deep need of all beings to belong to larger wholes.
>
> *(Aşkun, 2019, p. 155)*

The Oneness hypothesis (Ivanhoe, 2017) presents a world deeply connected and interrelated, and this is a very different perspective from the one mainstream media and culture have depicted. The Western, and particularly the United States, media, television shows, and movies have most of us believing that we have much to be fearful of, that we are indeed separate and alone, and that our incessantly chattering minds are in fact who we are.

Through my awakening experiences, my type A self has become softer, more compassionate, more aware that we are all connected. Along the path of my awakening process, I began to wonder what it would be like for us, as a collective human species, to awaken as I had begun to do. How would we relate to each other and the planet if we knew that we were all simply parts of a whole? How would our behaviors and perceptions of "the other" shift if we began to realize that, as Ramana Maharshi said, "There are no others" (Osborne, 2002, p. 79)?

This wondering about the impact of widespread awakening experiences led me to study collective awakening and then, later, a group phenomenon called coherence (Guenther, 2022). I chose to inquire into coherence, theorizing that it is a moment of awakening that occurs in the collective. It is through engaging in the study and then the findings that emerged that I could see that acting from a unified whole could be revolutionary for groups, teams, organizations, communities, and social systems of all kinds.

In the next section, I provide a brief overview of my research on coherence, the findings related to oneness, and the implications that should be considered related to leadership. The section includes several quotes by participants, all of whom are referred to by a pseudonym.

Direct Experiences of Interbeing

Through my research (Guenther, 2022), it became clear that we are much more connected than we can possibly know. And because we are so deeply connected and interwoven, it seems that our interconnectedness comes from a reality that is connected, unified, and one. As one of my research participants, Monica, explained, "That is the very core of deeper connections: an authentic love for the human experience shared by each of us" (Guenther, 2022, p. 129).

Through an interpretive phenomenological investigation, I sought to understand the following research question: What is the lived experience of coherence in the intersubjective field? The study (Guenther, 2022) was conducted primarily through two day-long, facilitated sessions that were designed to move two small groups toward coherence using various meditative and dialogic practices and activities. From the study, I was able to develop an empirically-derived definition of coherence.

> Coherence is a group-level phenomenon wherein members experience a collective shift into a heightened state of connectedness marked by a quieting, slowing, and calming of the group climate, an activation of an enlivened intersubjective field, and a calling forth for members' best selves resulting in an acceptance and celebration of differences among members. The shift is aided by [the Buddhist concept of] skillful means, and members can process and make sense of the experience through somatic, emotional, spiritual, and creative ways of knowing. Coherence experiences are often accompanied by individual and collective awakenings.
>
> *(p. 169)*

Through an analysis of the data, 18 themes in four categories emerged as the primary findings (Guenther, 2022). Among the themes that emerged was a profound sense of connection among group members; an awareness of each member's best self-coming forward, seen, and celebrated; and an enlivened energetic field pulsating through the groups. The connectedness was explained by one research participant, Ginger, "I felt a level of wholeness and a deep level of connection that felt very good in my heart," and by another, Monica, as, "We are souls connected" (p. 129). As the groups grew the deep roots of connection, they started to notice how accepting of each other's differences they were. Participant Dina said she "felt drawn to the field as an equal and valued person" (p. 132). And another participant, Katie, explained her experience:

> This is probably one of the first groups where I felt that everyone in the group was very accepting of all our differences. That's an awesome

> experience. We were all different. And I wasn't feeling like, for the first time, that one of us doesn't belong, and it's me. I felt like, wow, we're all different, and it's okay. This is my dream world.
>
> *(p. 132)*

The connected and accepting group climate was supported by an energetic field around the participants that felt alive. Dina explained, "The energy was strong—I could feel that network, the weaving, happening" (p. 136). One of the two study groups described the energy as a "pulsing of this common heartbeat" (p. 137), while the second group described the energy of the experience as a "mesmerizing vortex of our collective reality [that was] moving… circulating… vibrating" (p. 137).

As the group members discussed their experiences with each other, I could feel their understanding and the threads of coherence tighten and deepen. To investigate my felt sense of the experience, I analyzed approximately 12 pages of the transcript from one of the sessions and found that the group was making meaning of their experience together. They were discussing "something" that happened within their group as a result of the facilitated session, and through this collective sensemaking, or co-sensing (Scharmer, 2016), using different ways of knowing, such as emotions, somatic intelligence, intuition, and spiritual knowing, the members of this group began to understand what the "something" was. Research participant Alex described the "something" as

> I don't fully understand all the magic that happened, whether it was biological, spiritual, energy flow, or a combination, but I believe the experience of it opened me up to understanding there are beautiful and deep ways of connecting that I had not experienced quite like before.
>
> *(Guenther, 2022, p. 131)*

The experience of coherence launched the groups into "something" that they all reported feeling, sensing, and encountering.

I named the "something" a "direct experience of interbeing" (Guenther, 2022, p. 173). First and foremost, the data indicated that it was a direct experience in which participants made contact with "something." The phenomenon seems to have been transpersonal in nature and to have coalesced through collective consciousness. Therefore, it is related to a consciousness of connectedness (Tsao & Laszlo, 2019). Through the experience, it may be that participants made contact with an experience of interbeing (Hanh, 2017) that brought about degrees of awakening (Taylor, 2017) on a collective level. According to Taylor (2017), awakening is "fundamentally an experiential state" (p. 158), which formed the basis of the phenomenon—direct experience.

A consciousness of connectedness closely relates to Buddhist monk Thich Nhat Hanh's conceptualization of interbeing. "Interbeing is the order coined by Thich Nhat Hanh that reveals the interconnectedness of all things, connected through our actions, feelings, thoughts, and basically everything else" (Scult, n.d.). Again, the root is deep connectedness. According to Hanh (2017), "To inter-be and the action of interbeing reflects reality more accurately. We inter-are with one another and with all life" (para. 2). In some cases, interbeing could also be considered an experience of oneness, where there is no separation of subject and object. Instead, subject and object reveal themselves as one and the same. "My experience is subjective and mediated because I share it within my context, including my intersubjective social context and my participation in nature and cosmos—the field of interbeing" (Heron, 1998, p. 15). One of the participants, Monica, summarized her experience: "We levitated in a graduated form of exchanging and experiencing each other" (p. 176). This participant's statement reveals an interconnectedness that goes beyond relational interaction and seems to embrace the mystery of interbeing.

What Is the Nature of Reality?

The experiences that I witnessed in my research study led me to wonder what our true collective nature is as a human species. Was our true nature revealed through these sessions: deeply connected, joyful, safe, fully accepting, peaceful, and heart-centered, where our best selves naturally come forward? Or is our true nature the space we typically occupy that often involves fear, limitations, and doubt and is heavily cognitive? In the movie, *The Matrix* (Wachowski & Wachowski, 1999), one of the three main characters, Morpheus, discussed how humans determine reality, explaining that we view what is real as that which we can derive through our senses but questioned if senses alone could actually determine reality. Our society tends to favor that which can be measured and proven and thus holds concrete sensory experiences and thought as the purveyors of reality and truth.

I have come to realize that the thinking mind is not the essence of who I am and who other people are. As Taylor (2017) discussed, "Because of our ego-isolation and the thought-chatter that almost constantly runs through our minds, we spend much of our time in a state of *abstraction*. Rather than live in the world, we live in our minds" (p. 15, emphasis in original). We have succumbed to a story that is small, rigid, and steeped in fear and error.

According to Bohm (1996), our thoughts are derived from our collective experience, are manufactured, and deviate from the truth through filtering and censoring. With fellow meditation practitioners, we often urge each other to not believe everything we think, because the many stories that we have developed over a lifetime may seem true but are subjective and filtered. Is it possible that our collective reliance on intellectual and analytical knowing has made our experiences in the world smaller than they actually are? Could reality be much more expansive and communal than we know? Could it be as the Buddhist wisdom tradition has suggested, that reality is fuller, richer, and even emptier than we choose to perceive? (For more on the nature of reality, see Chapter 1). Based on the findings of this study and my own awakening experiences, the answers to those questions are not as clear-cut as our society would lead us to believe.

Oneness and Interbeing

According to the Oneness hypothesis, we are all connected to each other, to nature, and to the Kosmos itself (Aşkun, 2019). Oneness is closely related to the experience of interbeing. In Eisenstein's (2013) story of interbeing, he presented human life as relational: what we do has effects on other people. We all have unique gifts and taken together, the collectiveness of our unique gifts is meant to be offered toward the greatest good.

The experience of interbeing is devoid of suspicion, competition, and not-enoughness. Instead, as I found in small windows during my research study, interbeing is appreciative, connected, celebratory of difference, and open to the greater reality of Kosmos. If we believe that reality is steeped in interbeing, then how can that reality be reflected through leadership practice?

Leadership as an Enactment of Oneness and Interbeing

If reality is connected, coherent, and whole, how might leaders cultivate these qualities in the systems in which they lead? As I discussed earlier, one of the problems with how we traditionally view leadership is the inherent duality found in hierarchy, wherein the leader is elevated above and separated from followers. Based on this problematic duality, I posit that one way to move closer to enactment of oneness is by de-centering the leader and instead focusing on the collective.

The mainstream depiction of leadership generally focused on a single person, the leader, who is most often male and acts heroically (Crevani & Endrissat, 2016). This is a misrepresentation of what leadership is. In this chapter, I approach leadership from the perspective that leadership is a practice.

> The foundation of the leadership-as-practice approach is its underlying belief that leadership occurs as a practice rather than from the traits

> or behaviors of individuals. A practice is a coordinative effort among participants who choose through their own rules to achieve a distinctive outcome. Accordingly, leadership-as-practice is less about what one person thinks or does and more about what people may accomplish together.
> *(Raelin, 2016, p. 3)*

In other words, the core of leadership is collective action found through leadership practice. In this way, who the leader is could be considered irrelevant. The collective body enacting leadership is of most interest.

If leadership is a practice, how might a leadership practice focused on oneness be represented through behaviors and actions? In the next section, I introduce two leadership theories and one leadership perspective that may inform oneness-based leadership practice.

Leadership Theories, Perspectives Embodying Oneness

In 1993, Thich Nhat Hanh (1994) told a crowd assembled at Spirit Rock retreat center that the next Buddha may be a sangha (a community of spiritual practitioners). If Hanh was correct, then collectively enacted leadership may be what we are naturally evolving toward. Two leadership theories, collective leadership and being-centered leadership, hold perspectives that could elucidate what a leadership practice grounded in oneness could look like. Additionally, the notion of power over versus power with (Follett, 1995) further develops the idea of leading together from a place of oneness and why that is something we should care about.

Collective Leadership

Conceptually and in practice, collective leadership provides guideposts for how a leadership practice can depart from viewing the leader as de facto polestar to a collective sharing of leadership responsibilities and duties with no one actor dominating the limelight (Hiller et al., 2006). In the collective leadership model, an emphasis is placed on cooperation, in-group harmony, and group goals over personal goals and achievement. Mentoring and development also hold an important focus. The process and structure of self-management, a similar concept to collective leadership, wherein a team shares management and leadership responsibilities, was listed by Laloux (2014) as one of the practices of highly-evolved organizations, which he termed teal organizations. The teal worldview focuses on the world as a place for individual and collective unfolding and wholeness.

Being-Centered Leadership

Non-duality and collective leadership enactment are explored in another theory of leadership, being-centered leadership (Fry & Kriger, 2009). In the theory, the authors outline five levels of leadership, with level 1 leadership being "leadership from the non-dual" (p. 1682).

> The most inclusive level of being is the non-dual, in which there is only a Transcendent Unity that is beyond all qualification. This level is beyond all dualities and sense of otherness. The non-dual thus embraces both pure being as well as pure emptiness.
>
> *(p. 1683)*

Non-dual leaders, according to Fry and Kriger, manifest unconditional regard for themselves and others and can understand the needs of their team quickly. Additionally, "a leader at the level of the non-dual (level 1) fosters equality and makes less of a distinction between leader and follower" (Fry & Kriger, 2009, p. 1685).

Power Over versus Power With

By shifting the focus of leadership from the person of the leader to inspired collective action both collective and being-center leadership called for, leadership becomes a shared practice spread among the social system instead of limited to one person. In this way, power is distributed and shared. No longer does one leader hold power over the social system, but instead, power is a shared commodity. In the words of Mary Parker Follett (1995), "power usually means power-over, the power of some person or group over some other person or group, [and] it is possible to develop the conception of power-with, a jointly developed power, a co-active, not a coercive power" (Follett, 1995, p. 103). In other words, instead of leveraging power as a means to control and manipulate, power can be a shared resource passed among a group of people in order to move toward a collective goal. In this way, power is not connected to a position or a person.

Why Enacting Oneness Matters

Taken together, collective leadership, being-centered leadership, and the concept of shared or collective power begin to piece together a new leadership practice and structure that may allow for a shift toward enacted oneness. Through collective leadership, it is possible to elevate the collective and de-center the individual leader, thereby dissolving the separateness of leader and follower. Non-dual leaders are able to further this dissolution of separateness by fostering equity and de-emphasizing the distinction between leader and follower.

If we are moving toward an awareness of oneness through a heightened sense of collectivity, how is it that leaders can shift their practices and behaviors to enhance interbeing and awareness of oneness? How can we all develop toward an easy awareness and embodiment of something that we may understand intellectually but perhaps struggle with in our day-to-day experience of the world?

Shifting into Oneness

It is well and good to discuss oneness and a focus on collectivity from a theoretical perspective. Viewing leadership through the lens of practice, we may begin to wonder how such a practice is enacted and how it varies from mainstream leadership practice. Before discussing developing toward oneness, we must first become grounded in beingness.

Beingness is "who we are in the world" (Studdert, 2016). From a Buddhist perspective, beingness "reflects the unconditioned, the unmanifest nature of mind…It indicates a supramundane, timeless is-ness" (Amaro, 2003, p. 24). It is both being and doing, but beingness is that from which doing originates. Therefore, it is "not about the doing which a human does; it is about the doing which a human is" (Kegan, 1982, p. 8). It is an activity of existence (Wheeler, 2020).

To focus on beingness requires a keen awareness of and engagement with wholeness. This wholeness invites the different parts of the self, such as the professional self that we often see at work, to integrate the emotional, intuitive, and spiritual parts of the self (Laloux, 2014). A focus on beingness results in

> …a deep yearning for wholeness—bringing together the ego and the deeper parts of the self; integrating mind, body, and soul; cultivating both the feminine and the masculine parts within; being whole in relation to others; and repairing our broken relationship with life and nature. Often the shift…comes with an opening to a transcendent spiritual realm and a profound sense that at some level, we are all connected and part of one big whole.
>
> *(Laloux, 2014, p. 48)*

Through an integration toward wholeness, we can begin to know and experience that we are indeed deeply connected. When we stop focusing on the constant doing and achieving, we begin to shift into a different way of being in and seeing the world. And this seems to be more significant if it occurs with other people.

Developing Toward Oneness and Interbeing

The developmental path that supports a shift from duality to an awareness of oneness and interbeing can be cultivated and engaged through a committed, sustained contemplative practice as well as intentional growth and learning activities that move toward transpersonal leadership (Knights et al., 2018). Both of these enriching activities create conditions for a leader to build self-awareness, self-management, and cultivate compassion toward self and others (Smalley & Winston, 2010).

According to Fry and Kriger (2009), leadership development when focusing on beingness and collectivity may differ from the typical developmental path for leaders focused on developing leadership efficacy through self-awareness, self-regulation, and self-motivation. For a leader to cultivate an awareness of beingness and oneness, they must also cultivate what they value, particularly

> ...honesty, open-mindedness, and willingness to seek and embody higher levels of being. Leaders need to be able to engage in other-centered values and attitudes that build the competence needed to form accurate self-assessments and to use these self-understandings to effectively perform in increasingly complex leadership roles.
>
> *(Fry & Kriger, 2009, p. 1688)*

The authors continued to explain that non-dual leadership should be focused on spiritual development through awareness-centered and consciousness-raising practices. Such development should hold an intention for creating a gateway for dynamic spiritual experience with the ultimate reality.

One such practice is mindfulness meditation, which is thought to foster "leadership presence by cultivating focus, clarity, creativity, and compassion in the service to others" (Marturano, 2014, p. 11). This type of meditation nurtures mindfulness, a way of being in the world that focuses on present-moment, non-judgmental awareness (Greiser & Martini, 2018). As a mindfulness meditation teacher, I would suggest that mindfulness could be an appropriate and accessible practice to begin with. Additionally, anyone beginning a mindfulness meditation practice should also be aware of the transactional use and the oversimplification of the wisdom tradition that has shown up as McMindfulness in our current reality (For more on McMindfulness, see Chapter 2, which provides an expanded discussion). Over time, the practitioner will most likely engage with other wisdom traditions and spiritual practices that allow them to continue to grow and develop beyond a simple state of mindfulness. For example, any advanced practice that allows the practitioner to perceive a reality larger than themself may open the practitioner to higher states of consciousness. In a longitudinal study of awakened and enlightened people, Martin (2019) suggested that many "finders", as he named this cohort of people whose seeking has ended, engaged in practices that facilitated an awareness of emptiness (*Śūnyatā*), no-self (Thubten, 2009), or self-forgetting (Carreira, 2023). Additional practices may include prayer, chanting, yoga, qigong, tai chi, kundalini practices, labyrinth walking, and others. There is no one right practice; instead, each practitioner must find what works best for them. Regardless of the practice or practices chosen, a commitment to practicing regularly (as close to daily as possible) and consistently provides leaders with a pathway toward an awareness of oneness and interbeing.

Cultivation of the inner world through spiritual practice and development enhances the leader's awareness of their internal processing resulting in enhanced situational awareness and connectedness. Spiritual development builds upon rational intelligence and traditional leadership skills, such as strategic thinking, vision, and direction. Amplified self-awareness allows for greater emotional intelligence, values, and ethics, resulting in the ability to shape a pro-social culture and to orient toward the greater good and an evolutionary, ethical purpose (Knights et al., 2018). In this way, becoming aware of and connecting to a larger reality shifts how a leader engages in traditional leadership development. (See Chapter 11 for information on the development of a leader's other intelligences).

The Paradox of Development as Doorways to Oneness and Interbeing

Oneness and an experience of interbeing are gifts of the Kosmos and cannot be made to happen or forced (Carreira, 2022; Martineau & Martineau, 2016). The paradox of these types of experiences is this: the harder we try, the more likely they will not happen. Efforting is antithetical to the process of just being. Likewise, enacting leadership from a place of oneness does not just happen because a leader believes it is a nice idea. Intentional development is needed for that shift. Even so, there are ways that leaders can open themselves to oneness and experiences of interbeing, and that is through two types of development: individual leader development and intersubjective or collective development. Through development, leaders are able to de-center themselves as the center of the social system, tune into the collective, and create a space for collective magic to happen.

To expound on this paradox of trying and not trying, many spiritual leaders would probably say that we are already interbeing (Hanh, 2017). We are already awakening collectively. We are already one. The developmental process, then, can be viewed as a process for helping us to become aware of what already is by helping us to open our consciousness and to experience the universe beyond our limited story of reality. Only through development can we build an awareness of reality as a coherent, interconnected whole instead of one that is separate and alone.

Discussion

To enact leadership from a place of oneness, we must begin by revisiting the construct of leadership as it is inherently dual, dichotomous, and bears a separateness between leaders and followers. This separateness may be a reflection of the separateness we largely experience in Western society (Eisenstein, 2013).

If a leader embraces the possibility that reality is a unified whole and that manifesting oneness and interbeing is possible, then how does a leader shift their leadership practice in order to reflect wholeness? I have proposed in this chapter that through a developmental process that includes both individual and collective practices and activities, a leader can open their awareness to a larger reality while also attuning to the collective social system.

And while oneness and experiences of interbeing cannot be forced to happen, one may build the awareness and the capacity to both embrace the Kosmos and at the same time let go and allow the infinite's presence to be known. Through this process of both growing, opening, and expanding while also relaxing, allowing, and just being, we develop toward a greater reality. I believe this polarity of developing and allowing is an important nuance to embrace and get comfortable with. Additionally, this developmental process need not be overly serious. At a recent shamanic gathering, I and other participants were invited to sing, dance, and tell jokes to attract Spirits and the ancestors to join our gathering. Over the next hour and a half, we did just that. We were silly. We laughed. We played. We danced—hard. And then, there was a palpable shift in the energy, and it was clear to all of us that those to whom we called were present. We need to have fun on this path, play and be silly, and celebrate life. It is in that lightness of being, I believe, that we are closest to God and able to experience our oneness with the Kosmos.

References

Amaro, B. (2003). *Small boat, great mountain*. Abhayagiri Monastic Foundation.

Aşkun, D. (2019). Organizational oneness: A possible vision or an inescapable reality? In Marques, J. (Ed.) *The Routledge companion to management and workplace spirituality*, pp. 154–167. Routledge.

Block, P. (2018). *Community: The structure of belonging* (2nd Ed.). Berrett-Koehler Publishers.

Bohm, D. (1996). *On dialogue*. Routledge. https://doi.org/10.4324/9780203822906

Carreira, J. (2022). *The mystery of collective awakening: Questioning identity and connecting in oneness*. Emergence Education.

Carreira, J. (2023). *The soul's journey to wholeness*. https://bookstore.jeffcarreira.com/

Cox, D. (2021, June 8). The state of American friendship: Change, challenges, and loss – Findings from the May 2021 American perspectives survey. Survey Center on American Life. https://www.americansurveycenter.org/research/the-state-of-american-friendship-change-challenges-and-loss/

Crevani, L., & Endrissat, N. (2016). Mapping the leadership-as-practice terrain: Comparative elements. In Raelin, J.A. (Ed.) *Leadership-as-practice: Theory and application*, pp. 21–49. Routledge.

Eisenstein, C. (2013). *The more beautiful world our hearts know is possible*. North Atlantic Books.

Follett, M. P. (1995). *Mary Parker Follett–Prophet of management*. Beard Books.

Fry, L., & Kriger, M. (2009). Towards a theory of being-centered leadership: Multiple levels of being as a context for effective leadership. *Human Relations, 62*(11), 1667–1696. https//doi.org/10.1177/0018726709346380

Greer, L. (2020, September 29). Four keys to a healthy workplace hierarchy. *Greater Good Magazine*. https://greatergood.berkeley.edu/article/item/four_keys_to_a_healthy_workplace_hierarchy

Greiser, C., & Martini, J. P. (2018, April 19). *How companies can instill mindfulness*. Knowledge@Wharton. https://knowledge.wharton.upenn.edu/article/how-companies-can-instill-mindfulness/

Guenther, S. K. (2022). *From me to we: A phenomenological inquiry into group beingness* (Publication No. 29028032). [Doctoral Dissertation, Antioch University]. ProQuest Dissertations and Theses Global.

Hanh, T. N. (1994). The next Buddha may be a sangha. *The Inquiring Mind: Storytelling, 10*(2), [blog]. https://www.inquiringmind.com/article/1002_41_thich-nhat_hanh/

Hanh, T. N. (2017). *The insight of interbeing* [blog]. Garrison institute. https://www.garrisoninstitute.org/blog/insight-of-interbeing/

Heron, J. (1998). *Sacred science: Person-centered inquiry into the spiritual and the subtle*. PCCS Books.

Hiller, N. J., Day, D. V., & Vance, R. J. (2006). Collective enactment of leadership roles and team effectiveness: A field study. *Leadership Quarterly, 17*(4), 387–397. https://doi.org/10.1016/j.leaqua.2006.04.004

Ivanhoe, P. J. (2017). *Oneness: East Asian conceptions of virtue, happiness, & how we are all connected*. Oxford University Press.

Kegan, R. (1982). *The evolving self: Problem and process in human development*. Harvard University Press.

Knights, J., Grant, D., & Young, G. (2018). *Leading beyond the ego: How to become a transpersonal leader*. Routledge. https://doi.org/10.4324/9781315178806

Ladkin, D. (2010). *Rethinking leadership: A new look at old leadership questions*. Edward Elgar.

Laloux, F. (2014). *Reinventing organizations: A guide to creating organizations inspired by the next stage to human consciousness*. Nelson Parker. https://doi.org/10.15358/9783800649143

Machiavelli, N. (2003). *The prince* (G. Bull, Trans.). Penguin Classics. (Original work published 1532)

Martin, J. A. (2019). *The finders.* Integration Press.

Martineau, M. M., & Martineau, S. (2016). Evolving the we: A journey and inquiry. In Gunnlaugson, O. & Brabant, B. (Eds.) *Cohering the integral we space: Engaging collective emergence, wisdom, and healing in groups,* pp. 157–176. Integral Publishing House.

Marturano, J. (January 2014). Finding the space to lead. *Mindful.* https://www.mindful.org/finding-the-space-to-lead-3/

Meindl, J. R., Ehrlich, S. B., & Dukerich, J. M. (1985). The romance of leadership. *Administrative Science Quarterly, 30*(1), 78–102. https://doi.org/10.2307/2392813

Osborne, A. (Ed.) (2002). *The teachings of Ramana Maharshi in his own words* (8th Ed.). Messrs. Rider & Company.

Raelin, J. A. (2016). Introduction to leadership-as-practice: Theory and application. In Raelin, J.A. (Ed.), *Leadership-as-practice: Theory and application,* pp. 1–17. Routledge.

Scharmer, C. O. (2016). *Theory U: Leading from the future as it emerges* (2nd ed.). Berrett-Koehler Publishers.

Scult, J. (n.d.). *Interbeing: The interconnectedness of you to the nature of all things* [blog]. One Golden Thread. https://onegoldenthread.com/blogs/news/the-greatest-lie-was-the-illusion-of-separation

Sinclair, A. (2007). *Leadership for the disillusioned: Moving beyond the myths and heroes to leading that liberates.* Allen & Unwin.

Smalley, S., & Winston, D. (2010). *Fully present: The science, art, and practice of mindfulness.* Da Capo Press.

Studdert, D. (2016). Sociality and a proposed analytic for investigating communal beingness. *The Sociological Review, 64*(4), 622–638. https://doi.org/10.1111/1467954X.12430

Taylor, S. (2017). *The leap: The psychology of spiritual awakening.* New World Library.

Taylor, S. (2023). *DisConnected: The roots of human cruelty and how connections can heal the world.* Iff Books.

Thubten, A. (2009). *No self, no problem.* Shambhala Press.

Tsao, F., & Laszlo, C. (2019). *Quantum leadership: A new consciousness in business.* Stanford Business Books.

Wachowski, L., & Wachowski, L. (1999). *The matrix* [film]. Warner Bros.

Weber, M. (1947). *The theory of social and economic organisations* (T. Parsons, Trans.). Free Press.

Wheeler, M. (2020). Martin Heidegger. In Zalta, E. N. (Ed.), *The Stanford encyclopedia of philosophy* (Fall 2020 Edition). https://plato.stanford.edu/archives/fall2020/entries/heidegger/

4

BEYOND THE SELF

Spiritual-Relational Leadership for Secular Organizations

Michael F. Mascolo and Lizzie Linn

Traditional organizations are organized as hierarchies where higher-level individuals have authority over lower-level employees (Leavitt, 2003). The task of the leader is to find ways to mobilize the activity of employees toward goals set primarily by leaders (Maak & Pless, 2006). Many such organizations are structured around business values: productivity and efficiency, profit and reward, authority and fear (Goldman, 1980; Lam & Xu, 2019). However, within the traditional business framework, people have become increasingly unfulfilled. Beginning with the COVID pandemic, people have left their positions in record numbers in what is referred to as the great resignation (Miller & Jhamb, 2022). People seek more than the pay and benefits (Spartz, 2022). They seek meaning, purpose, and genuine belonging (Duffy et al., 2015; Pargament, 2013). They want to matter, to feel their work is meaningful, and that they are part of an organization where worth is defined by something beyond mere productivity (Peters & Waterman, 1982).

A spiritually structured organization provides an alternative to traditional enterprises. It organizes its mission in terms of the goal ***contributing to something beyond itself*** (Allen & Fry, 2023). While traditional organizations are motivated to pursue profit, spiritual organizations are animated by a ***moral vision***. The goals of spiritually infused organizations are ***morally defined*** (Cropanzano & Walumbwa, 2010; Mea & Sims, 2019) even if those goals involve providing everyday products and services. Any institution requires income to support its goals. However, spiritually driven organizations seek profits to provide services rather than provide services to procure profits.

DOI: 10.4324/9781003396741-6

People are viewed not as mere resources to be used, but as ends unto themselves—partners who walk together to advance moral ends.

Spiritual Leadership

At a fundamental level, we maintain that leadership consists of the *capacity to mobilize people toward a shared vision or purpose.* Scholars have proposed a variety of leadership styles—autocratic, transactional, transformational, democratic, servant leadership, laissez-faire, and many more (Janićijević, 2017; Mintzberg, 1979). There are, of course, no pure types of leadership; leaders likely embrace different leadership styles in different contexts. Spiritual organizations, however, identify with modes of being that extend beyond the self. We ordinarily think of leadership as the province of an individual leader (see Wood & Dibben, 2015). However, we regard spiritual leadership as a process that is distributed throughout the organizational system itself. From this viewpoint, spiritual leadership is the process, animated and inspired through identification with a shared moral mission, of mobilizing shared problem-solving.

In what follows, we elaborate on the concept of spirituality as it relates to leadership within secular organizations. We examine the need for the cultivation of a moral ethos with which leaders and colleagues alike can identify. Drawing on these ideas, we then propose a spiritual-relational model of leadership. We illustrate the process as it operates within the context of higher education. In doing so, we show how one program, through spiritual-relational leadership, is countering the trend toward corporatization and commodification in higher education (Giroux, 2009) even as it functions within a broader hierarchical organizational system.

A Secular Concept of Spirituality

To understand how spiritual leadership can function even in secular enterprises (Udani & Lorenzo-Molo, 2017), it is helpful to differentiate between spirituality and religion (Niekerk, 2018). Although religion and spirituality are distinct, they are not independent. Religion refers to a system of ideas and practices structured with reference to spirituality or the divine. Spirituality is a form of experience defined in terms of transcendent connection to something beyond the self (Bouckaert & Zsolnai, 2012). Spirituality thus includes a quest for *inspiration* and *transcendence*. To inspire is to *breathe into* (Ramli, 2016). Maslow (1969) included in his exploration of transcendence the ideas of moving beyond the ego and the fusion that takes place with another person or the whole cosmos (p. 58). We see transcendence as moving toward identification with a greater whole or sense of oneness.

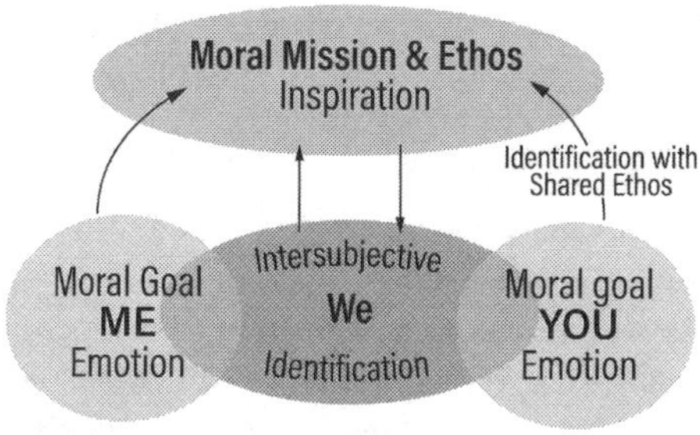

FIGURE 4.1 Spirituality as Intersubjective Identification with a Transcendent Ethos

This involves connecting with that which inspires-God, the universe, art, community, and so on. This transcendence can be manifested through intersubjective experiences that occur among people.

An intersubjective model of spirituality is provided in Figure 4.1. We define morality in terms of what Taylor (1989) refers to as *strong evaluation*. Moral judgments are those defined in terms of worthiness, goodness, or standards of right and wrong. In advancing this conception, we define moral life not in terms of extraordinary issues viewed as somehow separate and distinct from everyday life, but instead as everyday judgments that function as part of everyday relationships (Mascolo & DiBianca Fasoli, 2020). Morality is not something that "hovers over" human experience; it is part of the everyday process of relating to others.

As shown in Figure 4.1, a spiritually led enterprise is organized around some (1) moral conception of the *good*. Because it is not organized with reference to a divine order, a secular perspective raises the question of the origins of the moral values that structure it. Our conception of secular spirituality is organized by the spirit of *moral relationalism* (Mascolo & DiBianca Fasoli, 2020; Mascolo et al., 2021), the idea that strong evaluations are emergent values that arise from human relationships. Any moral ethos evolves as individuals and societies seek to respond to the demands of living in relationship (Donahue, 1977). Thus, judgments of moral goodness have relational origins; are constrained by material, psychological, and sociocultural circumstances; and evolve over time.

In this context, the concept of (2) *intersubjectivity* becomes especially important. Intersubjectivity refers to the capacity to share, coordinate, and mutually incorporate experience and meaning between people (Cipolletta et al., 2022). Intersubjectivity is not a property of individual persons. It is not simply the process by which one individual takes the perspective of another. Instead, intersubjectivity is a dynamic property of *relational activity itself*. In continuous face-to-face experience—whether that takes place in person or online—each person contributes directly to the moment-by-moment experience of the other. Each adjusts their experiences and actions to the ongoing and anticipated actions of the other. As a result, individuals (3) *co-regulate* each other's action in the process of relating (Fogel, 1993). When this happens, novel experiences are created that neither individual would be capable of producing alone. Intersubjective exchanges occur against the backdrop of a broader form of intersubjectivity that operates at the level of small groups or *community*. We act with reference to symbolically shared and contested meanings, values, beliefs, and practices that define our life-world (Rivera, 2019). In this way, my experience—my selfhood—develops through my relationship with you within a larger community. Over time, we become persons through other people. This is the hallmark of the South African concept of Ubuntu (Ncube, 2010).

In its secular form, transcendence cannot be understood as something divine or other worldly. We suggest transcendence include one's identification with the shared experience of *community*. As such, spirituality is not simply the *having* of shared experience, but also the (4) *identification* of the self as an integral part of a valued and unified whole. When we identify with a system of moral goals, our (5) selves become defined in terms of moral ideals organized around (5) strong emotion. To illustrate this point, consider the following example taken from a transformational learning program, The Compass Program at Merrimack College, to which each of this chapter's authors contribute and will be discussed further on in this chapter. The leader of the program described a spiritual connection to a colleague as follows:

> When a new professor was hired, we'll call her Molly, she was already quite competent, but she didn't yet understand the philosophy and methods we used. She worked hard to learn the ropes. Five years later I was moved by how she talked about her students–her understanding that they needed both compassion and direction. When I observed Molly working 1-1 with students, I experienced a sense of marveling at the effort, love, and devotion she put into helping her students learn. It was at that point that I experienced something that I would call spiritual–a deep communion with Molly. I experienced a feeling of *being with her* as she cared for her students. I felt proud because I was part of the process that brought her there; but mostly I felt a grateful sense of being part of something good, something bigger than me.

In this situation, the leader not only experienced a sense of communion with the teacher, but also with the broader communal whole—a valued unity of which both colleagues were a part.

Moral Foundations of Spiritual Leadership

Dahlsgaard et al. (2005) identified a series of virtues and values associated with a variety of cultures and religious traditions (Table 4.1). They proposed six dimensions of meaning and value that were present in some form in most of the major religious traditions they examined. These include courage, justice, humanity, temperance, wisdom, and transcendence. These categories of virtue provide guideposts for living a good and moral life. When applied to organizations, these spiritual values inform leadership toward relational leadership practices that encourage a shared power as opposed to a more hierarchical model. Table 4.1 identifies a series of moral values that cut across religious traditions which can undergird a spiritual leadership with secular organizations.

Transcendence and Wisdom

According to Nozick (1989), "wisdom is what you need to understand in order to live well and cope with the central problems and avoid the dangers in the predicament(s) human beings find themselves in" (p. 269). We are not born wise beings. We can become wise through moral self-cultivation (Mascolo, in press). Wisdom embraces movement in the direction of Aristotle's definition of well-being—*eudaimonia*—the flourishing that comes from cultivating virtue (Crespo & Mesurado, 2015). In spiritually inspired organizations, wisdom becomes an ideal to be attained—the belief that it is important to cultivate an evolving moral code to live by. Sustained efforts to cultivate relational virtue over time lead not only to wisdom but also a sense of transcendence—the sense of being part of something good that extends *beyond the self.*

Morality

Mascolo and Greenway (2022) proposed a tripartite moral framework for understanding the moral structure of enterprises. These include three core values: *justice*, *virtue*, and *care*. A concern for justice recognizes the importance of individual rights, responsibilities, and self-determination. A mainstay of Western conceptions of morality, justice is a necessary but not sufficient value for fostering moral relations. Justice must co-occur along with virtue and care. Virtues are principles of moral goodness. While care is one of the many virtues, its status is sufficient to warrant elevation to a core moral principle in itself. We act out of care when we act out of concern for the well-being of the other. In an ethos of care, justice extends to responsivity to the demands of right relationships (Donahue, 1977).

TABLE 4.1 Common Relational Values

Transcendence	*Wisdom*	*Morality*	*Courage*	*Humanity*	*Temperance*
Identification with a unity beyond self. A spiritual mission is defined in terms of a moral purpose organized around connection to a broader whole.	***Purposive moral meaning.*** Moral purpose gives life meaning; virtue fosters well-being	***Rights, virtue, and care.*** Self-cultivation toward virtue; rising to proper demands of relationship	***Character and perseverance.*** Developing a proper attitude toward pleasure, pain, struggle, and suffering.	***Developing through others.*** People first; compassion; collaboration; conflict management	***Moderation.*** Coordinating diverse moral goods: virtue, social life, wealth, pleasure, self-care.

Humanity

The Ubuntu motto "I am because we are" emphasizes the interconnectivity of all beings (Tshivhase, 2018). The Ubuntu philosophy recognizes people as fundamentally social beings, who thrive through strong relationships. This contrasts with individualistic models of self that fail to recognize how individuals are constituted within interconnected social relations. Hindu and Buddhist traditions share the philosophy of relational selves. Vital to this relational moral framework is the role of *virtue*—and particularly the virtue of love. Love is a form of valuing; to love something or someone is to bestow value on it or them. In love, individuals are motivated to care for each other. In doing so, they can come to identify the needs and interests of the other as part of their own (Mascolo & Greenway, 2022).

Courage

Spiritual leadership is not only organized around "soft" virtues—compassion, care, and so forth (Sharma & Singh, 2019). It also embraces strong virtues such as *courage* (Pury & Glennon, 2014), *persistence* (Veilleux et al., 2018), *self-regulation* (McCullough & Carter, 2013), and *resilience* (Shelton et al., 2020). Consistent with many spiritual traditions, strong virtues foster psychological well-being by helping people cope with suffering (Wright et al., 2020).

Temperance

Temperance is not only recognized as a virtue; it provides a principle that helps to determine how to use virtues in the service of a good life. There are many virtues. We are continuously faced with the task of identifying which virtues are relevant to any given context. This task is made even more difficult when we realize how virtues can conflict with each other or vary from culture to culture. In everyday life, temperance is the principle that stipulates the need for moderation in all things. Aristotle maintained a central role for moderation in the virtues (Kaptein, 2017). A virtue consists of the midpoint between two vices. Too little courage is cowardice; too much is foolhardiness. Many major religions including Christianity and Sikhism hold temperance in high regard (Chan & Ananthram, 2019).

While we do not claim that the above mentioned values are universal, they are nonetheless common to many cultures and religious traditions (Tenzin, 2010). Each represents a principle that individuals can follow to lead an ethical life of depth and flourishing. However, these values can also be mirrored on an organizational level to foster the collective well-being of the organization and the society in which it functions (Dahlsgaard et al., 2005).

A Spiritual Model of Secular Leadership

Drawing on these principles, we suggest that a spiritual model of leadership for a secular organization includes three basic propositions: (a) cultivation of a shared *moral ethos* informed by a relational-moral mission; (b) *guided collaboration* among leaders and colleagues; and (c) *continuous collaborative problem-solving* as a mode of operation. Figure 4.2 provides a sketch of this spiritual-relational model of leadership for secular organizations. As we have already elaborated upon the moral basis of a spiritual mission, in what follows, we focus primarily on the latter two principles.

Spiller et al. (2010) argued that organizations should base decisions upon an ethic of care that focuses on "multidimensional well-being" achieved through improved relationships (both interpersonal and with the natural world) (p. 153). This idea immediately raises questions of how members of an organization relate to each other. Organizations structured primarily around concerns for efficiency and profit may indeed value ethical treatment of people, mainly for practical purposes, because treating people poorly impacts the bottom line. However, to the extent that an organization embraces

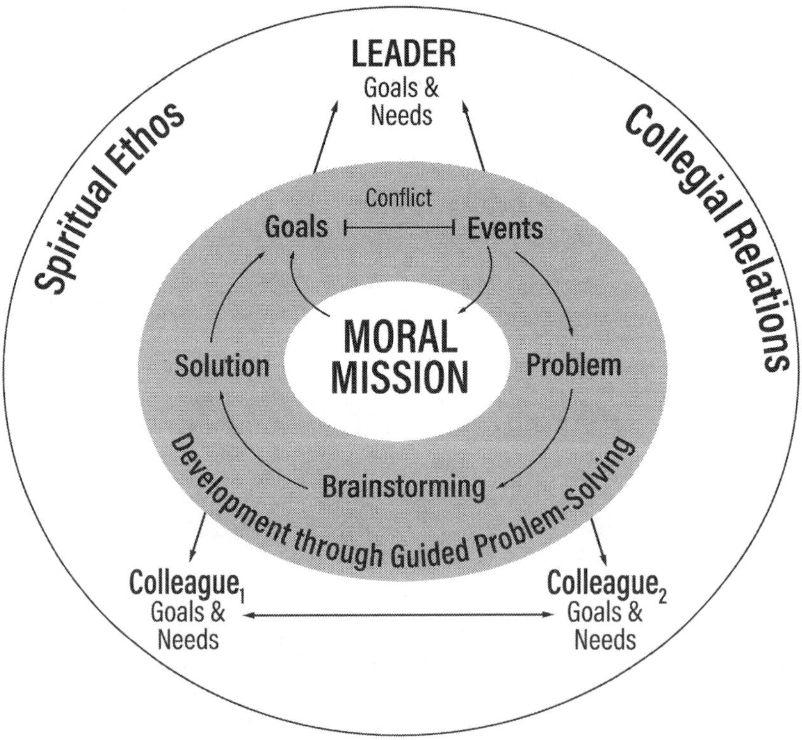

FIGURE 4.2 A Relational Model of Spiritual Leadership

a moral identity, then its relation to the full range of its stakeholders is *part of its very mission*. Spiller et al. (2010) explained that the concept of wealth originated from the old English word "welth," which means "to be well." If fostering well-being is a high-level good, the good of the organization relies upon fostering the integrity and well-being of all stakeholders. This means treating each person as an end unto themselves, seeking to promote individual and collective development, and including stakeholders as meaningful parts of organizational decision-making processes. We suggest one way to meet these goals is to adopt a collaborative approach to decision-making—albeit one that is guided and constrained by leaders.

In a spiritual-relational organization, decision-making is not the prerogative of any individual leader. Instead, it is a collaborative process informed by the organization's evolving moral mission. Moral mission is indicated in the center circle of Figure 4.2. The middle circle constitutes the heart of the guided collaboration process. To solve any problem, large or small, stakeholders come together to (a) identify the full range of the problem; (b) to articulate the needs, obstacles, concerns, and challenges experienced by each stakeholder in the problem; and then (c) brainstorm strategies for meeting the full range of needs and concerns identified by the stakeholders in question at the same time. In this way, a spiritual organization avoids the pitfalls of either top-down or bottom-up leadership (Parker, 2001). Even though the process is organized by responsible leaders, the process is designed to operate so that no single person will ordinarily be charged with making decisions.

It would be easy to think of the spiritual leader as someone who relinquishes authority to the group—someone who leads primarily by inspiration or mere facilitation. However, full decentralization of authority risks aimlessness and unstable decision-making (see Ågotnes et al., 2018; Diebig & Bormann, 2020). Informed by the moral mission of the organization and a collaborative, relational ethos, a spiritual leader must have the capacity to consolidate a vision, orient action, and exert control over decision-making commensurate with their responsibilities as leader. It is helpful to think of spiritual leadership as a form of *guided collaboration*. Guided collaboration seeks joint decision-making through a continuous process of collaborative problem-solving (see below), it nonetheless preserves a role for leaders as individuals charged with the responsibility for the process of advancing and orienting action defined in terms of a moral mission.

Spiritual Leadership in a Corporate System: An Example from Higher Education

In recent decades, higher education has faced deep challenges (Mascolo & Castillo, 2015). As the cost of education has increased, many smaller colleges have gone out of business (Baker et al., 2020; Toner, 2015).

To increase efficiency and financial viability, colleges have transitioned from collaborative modes of governance toward more corporate and hierarchical ones. Despite being a, mostly, non-profit endeavor, higher education is comparable to for-profit corporations. Its "product" is often to create a student capable of securing employment in the workplace. While students do seek college for purposes of self-improvement, instrumental motives figure prominently in reasons to attend college (economic success, credential seeking, etc.) (Kennett et al., 2011). Colleges tend to adjust their offerings to meet student and family demands (Love, 2008; Tomlinson & Watermeyer, 2022).

Currently, the very structure of education is organized in a way that promotes this consumer mindset. Students take courses to obtain grades—an instrumental reward that confers status and worth. As students satisfy requirements, they are rewarded with a diploma. The desire for grades and instrumental rewards focuses the student's attention away from learning or the cultivation of self, and instead on the acquisition of credentials and social status (Forsythe & Jellicoe, 2018; Gaudet, 2021; Pittinsky, 2015). Higher education thus becomes a place where students can earn credentials (Tomlinson, 2017), rather than a milieu in which they can cultivate the skills, knowledge, and values necessary to become worthy selves and members of a community.

Against this backdrop, it is easy to see how higher education would adopt the business model of seeking to accommodate student demand for credentials instead of inviting students to participate in the more noble process of self-cultivation through learning. When this happens, the moral mission of the university gives way to the need for economic survival. It is true, of course, that one cannot pursue a moral mission without a reliable financial base. However, when finances eclipse missions, an institution loses its reason for being. This raises a perennial question: how can moral mission be reconciled with the need for a stable income?

Cultivating Moral Selves in Higher Education: The Process is the Product

One way to monetize a mission is to develop programs that meet the actual moral and spiritual needs of the community. The Compass Program at Merrimack College developed into such a program. It was founded from a desire to raise the skills and knowledge of underperforming students so that they could enjoy success in college and in life. Compass is organized around the idea—common to Ubuntu, Confucianism, Greek philosophy, and other traditions—that people develop through relationships. This principle was applied not only to the cultivation of learning in students, but also to the structure of leadership within the program itself. In this way,

Compass embodies the spiritual-moral ethos described in this chapter. Both the process and the product of the program are people-centered: it consists of moral self-cultivation to foster development of the person, whether they are a student, teacher, leader, or follower.

The founders of the program believed that the goal of raising the skill levels of struggling students could not be achieved in the piecemeal fashion typical of programs that seek to "remediate" struggling students. Instead, they developed a program not simply to foster academic skills, that is, reading, writing, and critical thinking, but also the *non-cognitive* skills necessary for academic development. These include the need to develop *purpose*, a *growth mindset,* and the capacity to *persevere through struggle*, *self-compassion*, and a willingness to identify with the *values* of a challenging yet compassionate learning community (for a discussion of compassion and self-compassion in the context of adaptive leadership, see Chapter 2).

As such, the goal of Compass is to foster *self-cultivation* through academic, socio-emotional, and moral development. This is done by adopting a developmental approach to the cultivation of student selves through academic content. Student work is subject to continuous feedback and revision. Their work is evaluated not by assigning grades for individual tasks, but instead by charting progress in the incremental development of both cognitive and noncognitive skills en route to achieving degrees of mastery. This is done through the formation of relationships with students defined by high levels of demandingness, emotional responsiveness, and support for the growth of student autonomy over time.

Compass is led collaboratively by a program director and an academic director. Problem-solving occurs through the process of guided collaboration. Meetings are organized with reference to how emergent problems relate to the mission of the program. Issues are solved through guided collaborative problem-solving. For any given issue, the group (a) seeks to identify the needs and goals of each stakeholder relative to the larger problem at hand; (b) solicits ideas intended to meet the full range of needs that have been identified; and (c) drawing on these ideas, synthesizes a systemic solution that can meet as many needs as possible in the circumstances presented. The goal is to engage in shared decision-making while keeping the overall vision in mind. In this way, Compass functions as a deliberately developing organization (Kegan et al., 2016).

Spiritual-Relational Leadership: Three Examples

In Compass, the process of spiritual-relational leadership is a collaborative one. The founding directors of the program established its initial core values, which function as a set of evolving standards that ensure programmatic integrity. Guided by those values, the team works together to address programmatic issues and exigencies. Thus, while guided, leadership is distributed within the relationships that exist between and among faculty, coaches, and administrators. We describe three areas in the execution of spiritual-relational leadership in the Compass program. In what follows, we provide comments provided by students and faculty as they reflected upon various aspects of the process of teaching and learning within the program. All names indicated in the following examples are pseudonyms.

Caring and Collaborative Change During the COVID

One way to illustrate the process of spiritual-relational leadership in the program is to examine how members of the program responded collectively to a novel crisis. The COVID-19 crisis caused a precipitous disruption in college operations in March of 2022. The pandemic forced Compass to transform its operations in a single week. Beyond the provisions made by the college, the Compass team adopted a "people first" approach to the transition. They put the physical and emotional needs of students, faculty, and staff before any particular set of formal procedures. Mutual care was seen as an intrinsic value for academic and professional progress.

One faculty member explained care in action.

> The most important thing was the way we supported each other. We had beers at four o'clock over Zoom. We purposefully had informal meetings to check in with each other. We invited former staff who were sad to join us in informal Zoom sessions to combat isolation and keep up our morale. Our community was held together under extreme duress.

This faculty member indicated the role of deep collaboration rather than top-down direction in responding to exigencies:

> We had to talk to each other a lot. All this shit's going on in Zoom class. I'd try something, someone else tried something in a different way. What are you seeing? The kid on Zoom is sleeping. He has his shirt off. Are they engaged? No. What do we do? I did it this way. It helped them get engaged. I'll try that tomorrow. Everyone was open to suggestions.

One faculty member held that faculty and academic coaches were able to work well together not only because they had mutual values, but also because they had mutual knowledge of each other's strengths, challenges, and skills. They worked hard to collaborate and support each other.

> Jackie [an academic coach] [and I] had complementary skills. The fact that we saw eye to eye on a lot of issues made it seamless...There was no sense of competition, that this is my student, this is my turf. It's more how do we help this student...There was collegiality and mutual support. Jackie would say to me, "this is hard, but it is going to get easier".

One faculty member commented on how her focus on the student's emotional and academic needs led her to articulate a set of values that could give students hope and a sense of community:

> It's like Maslow's need hierarchy. You can't study if you're hungry or afraid. So many of the students felt like, "Oh my god, the whole world is going to shit." They had to study and focus with that in the background. But studying presupposes a precondition of hope. You must have hope that what you are learning can lead to something...people were losing hope...That's when I decided to put the values that guide us on the syllabus: fairness and trust; courage and perseverance; responsibility and accountability; compassion and community.

To address concerns about hope and community, in collaboration with the campus ministry, the team organized a Zoom retreat on Fridays over four weeks. Reflecting on the collaborative effort that structured the retreat, one administrator remarked, "This was meaningful for our students. It was a bright spot at a hard time."

These examples highlight the key principles of caring, collaboration, community, and shared values in spiritual-relational leadership.

Fostering Self-cultivation in Students

There are many ways in which students underwent self-cultivation over the course of their experience in Compass. The most obvious ways involved the slow, incremental development of academic skills over the course of the year. There were, of course, large differences in the shapes of moral self-cultivation as it occurred (or did not occur) in different students with different instructors. Students made meaningful and measurable progress in their reading, writing, and note-taking skills over the course of the year.

The most dramatic transformations that occured are self-transformations—qualitative changes in the student's *identity* and *purpose*. Such transformations typically emerged as a result of "aha" moments preceded by long periods of slow changes. These transformations typically arose within face-to-face interactions involving three basic properties. In particular, students:

- Come to understand that they are not who they think they are
- Begin to see a possible way to move toward becoming who they want to become
- Confront these feelings in emotionally supportive contexts that mitigate experiences of shame

One student, Thomas, a 19-year-old White male in his first year of college, experienced a sense of self-transformation midway through his second semester in the program. Prior to that point, he described himself as

> going with the wind and didn't care at all about my school work and about my future. I wasn't there yet, so why should I care? I was lost and I didn't know I was…all I wanted to do was play my Playstation and do anything except my schoolwork. I would get it done–except not good. But I was lying to myself that it was good.

The turning point came with a conversation initiated by his professor about Thomas' goals in life. When asked about his goals, Thomas explained:

> I had zero answer. That was the weakest I've ever felt…I felt stupid…I didn't have anything–why am I here? As soon as I realized that, it changed me. It was the best thing ever that happened to me.

The professor gave Thomas an assignment. Thomas was asked to imagine that he was "the king of the world" where money and ability were no object. If you had a carte blanche, what would you do to make the world a better place? In addition, beyond sports, list anything that comes to mind that you would regard as important, interesting or meaningful in life. The next day, to his surprise, Thomas had produced a list of 50 things that he found meaningful and important. He said:

> If I didn't write that thing, I don't think I would have even graduated. It was life altering. Now I care…I have a goal. I'm switching my major from marketing – I don't know why I was doing marketing – to get money, I guess. But now it's history. I don't know what to do with history, but I guess that's what it's about. I'm excited to find out. The difference between who I was then and now is just flat out caring.

These experiences highlight the necessity of moral self-cultivation that focuses on identity, meaning, and purpose in relational-spiritual leadership. This student's experience illustrates the transformative effect this type of leadership has on individuals.

Experiences of New Team Members

A sense of the relational spirit of Compass can be gleaned from the experiences of new members of the Compass team. One new faculty member commented on the connection between the *values* of the program and the curriculum: "We encourage an underlying understanding of people as a whole–individually and collectively." She explained how the curriculum fosters *curiosity* about the needs and motivations of individuals, which leads to a deeper understanding of the self and others.

Another staff member expressed how he felt a sense of close collaboration and care among the faculty and staff. He commented, "*Collaborative* effort is a central focus point of Compass staff and faculty. All ideas are valued. Although opinions may be challenged, a professional discourse brimmed with *compassion* is at the heart of the daily work we do." This reflects how Compass values compassion and dialogue as a way of developing through others.

And still, another faculty member reflected on the shared sense of *purpose* within the program. She explained, "From the very first day, I felt a sense of community and common purpose." She explained the various ways the faculty and staff model and encourage the shared goal of self-cultivation, "Students see faculty and staff trusting and encouraging each other in their pursuit of *common goals*." She added, "It is beneficial for them to see when different instructors have a shared message and common goals but individual ways of communicating and getting to these goals."

Toward a Spiritual-Relational Ethos in Organizations

Spiritual leadership reconciles the goals of self-interest and concern for others into a common relational ethos and seeks to bring people together in terms of a purpose that exists beyond any individual self. By identifying with a moral mission, colleagues in a successful spiritual organization can experience a sense of belonging and transcendence that comes from pursuing a shared moral mission. People are not mere means for the pursuit of profit; instead, the well-being of people is part of the organization's moral mission.

Any approach to spiritual-relational leadership must confront the perennial tension between hierarchy and equality (for an Indigenous view on non-hierarchy and its application to leadership, see Chapter 6), self-interest and care for others, and the problems of operating within broader social systems that do not embrace relational values. Whereas spiritual-relational leadership embraces collaborative values, it does not eliminate the need for some degree of hierarchy. Although it may sometimes be possible to organize decision-making in a fully egalitarian way, as organizations increase in size and scope, there is typically a need for some members of a collaborative to assume a degree of responsibility for the direction and operation of any given unit or whole (Gruenfeld & Tiedens, 2010). The relationship between direction and collaboration within an organization is an issue that requires sustained reflexivity.

Spiritual-relational leadership is difficult. Hierarchical decision-making is arguably easier in the sense that it does not require the level of coordination among stakeholders that is characteristic of relational forms of leadership. Spiritual-relational leadership becomes easier, however, as relationships coalesce around an ethos of collaboration. The more competent and collaborative the team, the more the demands of spiritual leadership can become distributed through interactions and relations among people. Thus, while cultivating relational systems of leadership may be difficult, once relationships are formed, they not only operate synergistically to create novel ways of solving problems, they also provide the checks and balances needed to reduce the likelihood of bad decisions by any single individual.

References

Ågotnes, K. W., Einarsen, S. V., Hetland, J., & Skogstad, A. (2018). The moderating effect of laissez-faire leadership on the relationship between co-worker conflicts and new cases of workplace bullying: A true prospective design. *Human Resource Management Journal*, *28*(4), 555–568. https://doi.org/10.1111/1748-8583.12200

Allen, S., & Fry, L. W. (2023). A framework for leader, spiritual, and moral development. *Journal of Business Ethics*, *184*(3), 649–663. https://doi.org/10.1007/s10551-022-05116-y

Baker, P., Moore, P. H., Byars, K. P., & Aden, C. G. (2020). Covid closing down colleges: How the Covid-19 pandemic has accelerated nonprofit college closings. *Brigham Young University Education & Law Journal*, *2020*(2), 101–113. https://scholarsarchive.byu.edu/byu_elj/vol2020/iss2/4

Bouckaert, L., & Zsolnai, L. (2012). Spirituality and business: An interdisciplinary overview. *Society and Economy*, *34*(3), 489–514. https://www.jstor.org/stable/90002270

Chan, C., & Ananthram, S. (2019). Religion-based decision making in Indian multinationals: A multi-faith study of ethical virtues and mindsets. *Journal of Business Ethics*, *156*, 651–677. https://doi.org/10.1007/s10551-017-3558-7

Cipolletta, S., Mascolo, M. F., & Procter, H. (2022). Intersubjectivity, joint action and sociality. *Journal of Constructivist Psychology*, *35*(3), 904–929. https://doi.org/10.1080/10720537.2020.1805066

Crespo, R. F. & Mesurado, B. (2015). Happiness economics, eudaimonia and positive psychology: From happiness economics to flourishing economics. *Journal of Happiness Studies*, *16*, 931–946. https://doi.org/10.1007/s10902-014-9541-4

Cropanzano, R., & Walumbwa, F. O. (2010). Moral leadership: A short primer on competing perspectives. In M. Schminke (Ed.), *Managerial ethics: Managing the psychology of morality*. (pp. 21–52). Routledge.

Dahlsgaard, K., Peterson, C., & Seligman, M. E. P. (2005). Shared virtue: The convergence of valued human strengths across culture and history. *Review of General Psychology*, *9*(3), 203–213. https://doi.org/10.1037/1089-2680.9.3.203

Diebig, M., & Bormann, K. C. (2020). The dynamic relationship between laissez-faire leadership and day-level stress: A role theory perspective. *German Journal of Human Resource Management, 34*(3), 324–344. https://doi.org/10.1177/2397002219900177

Donahue, J. R. (1977). Biblical perspectives on justice. In J. C. Haughey (Ed.), *The faith that does justice: Examining the Christian Sources for social change* (pp. 68–112). Wipf & Stock.

Duffy, R. D., Autin, K. L., & Bott, E. M. (2015). Work volition and job satisfaction: Examining the role of work meaning and person–environment fit. *The Career Development Quarterly*, *63*(2), 126–140. https://doi.org/10.1002/cdq.12009

Fogel, A. (1993). *Developing through relationships*. University of Chicago Press.

Forsythe, A., & Jellicoe, M. (2018). Predicting gainful learning in higher education: A goal-orientation approach. *Higher Education Pedagogies*, *3*(1), 103–117. https://doi.org/10.1080/23752696.2018.1435298

Gaudet, M. (2021). The two types of grades and why they matter to ethics education. *Teaching Ethics*, *20*(1/2), 75–90. https://doi.org/10.5840/tej20214992

Giroux, H. A. (2009). Democracy's nemesis: The rise of the corporate university. *Cultural Studies? Critical Methodologies*, *9*(5), 669–695. https://doi.org/10.1177/1532708609341169

Goldman, A. H. (1980). Business ethics: Profits, utilities, and moral rights. *Philosophy and Public Affairs, 9(3)*, 260–286. https://www.jstor.org/stable/2265117

Gruenfeld, D. H., & Tiedens, L. Z. (2010). Organizational preferences and their consequences. In S. Fiske, D. T. Gilbert, & G. Lindzey (Eds.), *Handbook of social psychology*, (Vol. 2, 5th ed., pp. 1252–1287). John Wiley & Sons, Inc. https://psycnet.apa.org/doi/10.1002/9780470561119.socpsy002033

Janićijević, N. (2017). Organizational models as configurations of structure, culture, control and change strategy. *Economic Annals*, *62*(213), 69–71. https://doi.org/10.2298/EKA1713067J

Kaptein, M. (2017). When organizations are too good: Applying Aristotle's doctrine of the mean to the corporate ethical virtues model. *Business Ethics: A European Review*, *26*(3), 300–311. https://doi.org/10.1111/beer.12147

Kegan, R., Lahey, L., Miller, M., Fleming, A., & Hesling, D. (2016). *An everyone culture: Becoming a deliberately developing organization*. Harvard Business Review Press.

Kennett, D. J., Reed, M. J., & Lam, D. (2011). The importance of directly asking students their reasons for attending higher education. *Issues in Educational Research*, *21*(1), 65–74. http://www.iier.org.au/iier21/kennett.html

Lam, L. W., & Xu, A. J. (2019). Power imbalance and employee silence: The role of abusive leadership, power distance orientation, and perceived organisational politics. *Applied Psychology: An International Review*, *68*(3), 513–546. https://doi.org/10.1111/apps.12170

Leavitt, H. J. (2003). Why hierarchies thrive. *Harvard Business Review*, *81*(3), 96–102. https://hbr.org/2003/03/why-hierarchies-thrive

Love, K. (2008). Higher education, pedagogy and the "customerisation" of teaching and learning. *Journal of Philosophy of Education*, *42*(1), 15–34. https://doi.org/10.1111/j.1467-9752.2008.00600.x

Maak, T., & Pless, N. M. (2006). Responsible leadership in a stakeholder society—a relational perspective. *Journal of business ethics*, *66*(1), 99–115. https://www.jstor.org/stable/25123815

Mascolo, M. F. (in press). The development of wise decision-making across adulthood: An intersubjective analysis. In J. Stevens-Long & E. Kallio (Eds.), *International handbook of adult development*. Oxford University Press.

Mascolo, M. F. & Castillo, J. (2015). On the origins of underperformance in higher education: Proximal influences. *Pedagogy and the Human Sciences*, *4*, 1–40. https://scholarworks.merrimack.edu/phs/vol5/iss1/1?utm_source=scholarworks.merrimack.edu%2Fphs%2Fvol5%2Fiss1%2F1&utm_medium=PDF&utm_campaign=PDFCoverPages

Mascolo, M. F., & DiBianca Fasoli, A. (2020). The relational origins of morality and its development. In M. F. Mascolo & T. Bidell (Eds.) *Handbook of integrative psychological development* (pp. 392–421). Routledge.

Mascolo, M. F., DiBianca Fasoli, A., & Greenway, D. (2021). A relational model of moral development in societies, organizations and individuals. *Integral Review*, *17*, 37–68. https://integral-review.org/a-relational-approach-to-moral-development-in-societies-organizations-and-individuals/

Mascolo, M. F., & Greenway, D. (2022). Love and the moral structure of business: Toward a tripartite economic ethos. In M. Pirson (Ed.). *Love and organization: Lessons in love for human dignity, leadership and motivation* (pp. 90–111). Routledge.

Maslow, A. H. (1969). Various meanings of transcendence. *Journal of Transpersonal Psychology*, *1*(1), 56–66.

McCullough, M. E., & Carter, E. C. (2013). Religion, self-control, and self-regulation: How and why are they related? In K. I. Pargament, J. J. Exline, & J. W. Jones (Eds.), *APA handbook of psychology, religion, and spirituality (Vol 1): Context, theory, and research* (pp. 123–138). American Psychological Association. https://psycnet.apa.org/doi/10.1037/14045-006

Mea, W. J., & Sims, R. R. (2019). Human dignity-centered business ethics: A conceptual framework for business leaders. *Journal of Business Ethics*, *160*(1), 53–69. https://doi.Org/10.1007/s10551-018-3929-8

Miller, A. L., & Jhamb, S. (2022). A comprehensive programmatic investigation of the antecedents and consequences related with the great resignation of individuals and organizations – A COVID-19 strategic review and research agenda. *Journal of Management Policy & Practice*, *23*(2), 48–57. https://doi.org/10.33423/jmpp.v23i2.5264

Mintzberg, H. (1979). *The structuring of organizations*. Prentice Hall.

Ncube, L. B. (2010). Ubuntu: A transformative leadership philosophy. *Journal of Leadership Studies*, *4*(3), 77–82. https://doi.org/10.1002/jls.20182

Niekerk, B. (2018). Religion and spirituality: What are the fundamental differences? *HTS Teologiese Studies/Theological Studies*, *74*(3). http://dx.doi.org/10.4102/hts.v74i3.4933

Nozick, R. (1989). *The examined life*. Touchstone Press.

Pargament, K. I. (2013). Spirituality as an irreducible human motivation and process. *International Journal for the Psychology of Religion*, *23*(4), 271–281. https://doi.org/10.1080/10508619.2013.795815

Parker, P. (2001). Local-global partnerships for high-tech development: Integrating top-down and bottom-up models. *Economic Development Quarterly*, *15*(2), 149. https://doi-org.proxy3.noblenet.org/10.1177/089124240101500204

Peters, T. J., & Waterman, R. H. (1982). *In search of excellence: Lessons from America's best-run companies*. Harper & Row.

Pittinsky, M. (2015). Credentialing in higher education. *Educause Review*, *50*(2), 35–42. https://er.educause.edu/articles/2015/3/credentialing-in-higher-education-current-challenges-and-innovative-trends

Pury, C. L. S., & Glennon, K. N. (2014). Psychological and spiritual aspects of courage for self-renewal. In R. J. Wicks & E. A. Maynard (Eds.), *Clinician's guide to self-renewal: Essential advice from the field*. (pp. 251–262). John Wiley & Sons, Inc.

Ramli, A. M. (2016). Imagination and intuition in the poetic philosophies of Samuel Taylor Coleridge and Muhammad Iqbal. *World Literature Studies*, *1*(8), 98–111.

Rivera, J. (2019). We-synthesis: Husserl and Henry on empathy and shared life. *Research in Phenomenology*, *49*(2), 183–206. https://doi.org/10.1163/15691640-12341418

Sharma, S., & Singh, K. (2019). Religion and well-being: The mediating role of positive virtues. *Journal of Religion and Health*, *58*(1), 119–131. https://doi.org/10.1007/s10943-018-0559-5

Shelton, C. D., Hein, S., & Phipps, K. A. (2020). Resilience and spirituality: A mixed methods exploration of executive stress. *International Journal of Organizational Analysis*, *28*(2), 399–416. https://doi.org/10.1108/IJOA-08–2019-1848

Spartz, A. (2022). Five creative ways to attract and retain talent amid the great resignation. *HR News Magazine*, *88*(4), 12–13. https://doi.org/10.1108/IJOA-08–2019-1848

Spiller, C., Erakovic, L., Henare, M., & Pio, E. (2010). Relational well-being and wealth: Māori business and an ethic of care. *Journal of Business Ethics*, *98*(1), 153–169. https://doi.org/10.1007/s10551-010-0540-z

Taylor, C. (1989). *Sources of the self*. Harvard.

Tenzin, G. (Dalai Lama XIV) (2010). *Toward a true kinship of faiths: How the world's religions can come together*. Doubleday.

Tomlinson, M. (2017). Student perceptions of themselves as 'consumers' of higher education. *British Journal of Sociology of Education*, *38*(4), 450–467. https://doi.org/10.1080/01425692.2015.1113856

Tomlinson, M., & Watermeyer, R. (2022). When masses meet markets: credentialism and commodification in twenty-first century higher education. *Discourse: Studies in the Cultural Politics of Education*, *43*(2), 173–187. https://doi.org/10.1080/01596306.2020.1814996

Toner, M. (2015). The highly endangered higher education business model (and how to fix it). *Presidency*, *18*(3), 15–18.

Tshivhase, M. (2018). Love as the foundation of Ubuntu. *Synthesis Philosophica*, *33:1*(65), 197–208. http://hdl.handle.net/2263/71139

Udani, Z. A. S., & Lorenzo-Molo, C. F. (2017). The utility of virtue: Management spirituality and ethics for a secular business world. *Asian Journal of Business Ethics*, *6*(1), 21–39. https://doi.org/10.1007/s13520-016-0067-1

Veilleux, J. C., Hill, M. A., Skinner, K. D., Pollert, G. A., Baker, D. E., & Spero, K. D. (2018). The dynamics of persisting through distress: Development of a Momentary Distress Intolerance Scale using ecological momentary assessment. *Psychological Assessment*, *30*(11), 1468–1478. https://doi-org.proxy3.noblenet.org/10.1037/pas0000593

Wood, M., & Dibben, M. (2015). Leadership as relational process. *Process Studies*, *44*(1), 24–47.

Wright, J., Snow, N., & Warren, M. T. (2020). Suffering, virtue, and character: Why the science of virtue matters. *Acta Philosophica: Pontificia Universita Della Santa Croce*, *29*(1), 55–72. https://doi.org/10.19272/202000701004

5

THE SOUL OF LEADERSHIP AS OPENING SPACE

Eckankar Principles Applied to Leadership

Jonathan Reams

Conceptions of leadership abound. In this chapter, I introduce yet another one, leadership as opening space. This approach to understanding the phenomenon of leadership is based on a spiritual lens drawn from my experience with the spiritual practices of Eckankar. In essence, this view says that we are soul, and through our embodiment in human experience, create spaces, or environments which can either enable or constrain the growth of others. Applied to leadership, this conception can bring a more holistic and integrative understanding to the purpose and practice of leadership.

These opening comments likely raise more questions than answers. I have spent decades attempting to develop and clearly articulate this approach. Taking insights gained from experiences with an emerging, non-Western spiritual practice and connecting them to relevant research is challenging enough. To then also integrate this with the rich and diverse set of constructs used to describe the phenomenon of leadership is even more challenging. This chapter will introduce some threads that, woven together, can bring this conception of leadership as opening space to life and offer simple practices to use for enhancing one's leadership practice.

I begin with some personal context, where I situate my own journey that brought me to investigating this intersection of spirituality and leadership. I then present the non-Western spiritual practice that has shaped my view, Eckankar. This will provide the reader with a brief overview of key elements of this practice that will then be woven through the rest of the chapter. The next section on related perspectives provides a bridge, describing some of the research I have found that aligns with my understanding of Eckankar and can illuminate assumptions about the world underlying approaches to

DOI: 10.4324/9781003396741-7

leadership. The following section uses the views from Eckankar and these bridging concepts to reframe three major leadership theories: transformational, adaptive, and servant leadership. The section ends by drawing forward these threads to further elaborate on my conception of leadership as opening space. To close, I introduce three practices emerging from this view and make some concluding remarks.

Personal Context

My journey to this conception of leadership as opening space began as early as I can remember, with experiences that awakened a deep curiosity to cultivate ongoing spiritual unfoldment. Later, I found myself wondering where I could find bridges between my understanding of spirituality and the diversity of perspectives I encountered in the world, which led to discovering the field of leadership studies. In this section, I describe a bit of this journey.

My earliest memories are about dream experiences of shrinking beingness to almost nothing, then expanding to encompass the universe. Later, when I was about ten years old, I experienced images of time as the movement of attention and awareness across a panorama of the physical universe spread out in parallel in each momentary configuration. I recall hearing a high-pitched sound current even when isolating myself from all possible man-made sources. Brought up Christian, at 12 years of age I recall attending an evangelical church's vacation bible school and having one of the leaders come and ask me if I had accepted Jesus Christ as my lord and savior. In that moment, time stood still, and I searched around inside myself, examining every nook and cranny to find some sense of meaning or connection to what I had been brought up with, only to find a terrifying emptiness. This planted a seed that took seven years to germinate.

At the age of 19, I was having a conversation one evening about esoteric topics with a friend, who stated that he wanted the power to psychically bend spoons like Uri Geller (at the time, a famous psychic). While I thought this was interesting, the response that came out of my mouth was that I wanted the power to change consciousness. That unanticipated pronouncement was a signal from my future, beckoning me into a journey of discovery. Soon after that evening, I came across Eckankar, the spiritual practice I present in this chapter. It resonated profoundly with everything I had experienced, yet not understood.

At about this time, I dropped out of university where my study of physics and philosophy were leaving me empty and wanting a more direct and explicit path for learning something spiritual rather than just intellectual. After 12 years of practicing Eckankar, I went back to university, looking for a bridge from my experience of this spiritual practice into the mainstream world. I took up studying the humanities and social sciences, and early in this journey experienced a "call" (literally a booming voice in my head at a pivotal moment) to take up the study of leadership. Through the next seven years of graduate study of leadership at a Jesuit university, I was exposed to theories such as transformational leadership (Burns, 1978), adaptive leadership (Heifetz, 1994), and servant leadership (Greenleaf, 1970). The thread running through my study of these, and other leadership theories, was my underlying interest in how they related to changing consciousness. For this, I pursued parallel work in the emerging field of consciousness studies. My doctoral dissertation research on *The Consciousness of Transpersonal Leadership* (Reams, 2002) integrated what I had learned from my spiritual practice in Eckankar with what I learned about consciousness development, and applied it to leadership.

The essence of this spiritual view is that we *are* soul, and *have* a mind, emotions, and physical body, in other words, egoic human experiences. There is a logical incoherence in thinking that a finite, limited and mortal egoic human self could "have" an inherently infinite, unlimited and immortal soul. This lays a foundation for a larger question: If we are souls having human experiences, and the purpose of our lives is to realize our divine nature and serve this process in others, then how do we understand leadership? This chapter is an attempt to answer this question.

Eckankar

Eckankar (www.eckankar.org) is known today as the path of spiritual freedom. The term comes from Sanskrit and translates as coworker with God. The term ECK (all capitals) is another word for spirit, or the Holy Spirit and also an abbreviation for Eckankar. Divine energy, or ECK, is known primarily through its twin manifestations of light and sound, as well as through the experience of divine love. The practice is based on direct personal experience of contacting the light, sound, and love of God, thus transcending philosophy and orthodox religion. As an individual path, it recognizes the uniqueness of each soul and its journey. Spiritual freedom is a central tenet and members are not required to step away from their traditional faith.

Eckankar is an ever-evolving, dynamic teaching, understood as a direct path for people to reach God. It has been on earth since the dawn of human history and is considered to be the original source of all true religions. Paul Twitchell, the modern-day founder, gathered elements of the teachings from a wide variety of sources, such as Sufism, Gnosticism, and Sant Mat, and updated them from their cultural associations and language, fitting them to the modern consciousness. He brought the teachings out into the modern world in 1965 when he became the spiritual leader of Eckankar.

Eckankar always has a living teacher, known as the Living ECK Master. They serve to guide all souls, from whatever path or religion, who wish progress on their journey to God. They are also responsible for continually evolving the Eckankar teachings to keep up with the evolution of consciousness. Harold Klemp serves as the current Living ECK Master.

A key facet of the teaching is that while serving in the physical realm, the Living ECK Master also serves soul's unfoldment in the inner worlds, for example, in the dream state or through soul travel. This enables the teachings to be customized for each individual. The inner master is known in Eckankar as the Mahanta.

Eckankar teaches that we are soul. Soul is eternal and exists because God loves it. Soul's journey is to realize itself and God and as part of that journey, in this physical world, soul takes on a mind, emotions, and material body to gain experience. Soul unfolds spiritually through karma and reincarnation.

As a spiritual practice, Eckankar is deeply individual, giving each person the spiritual freedom to creatively learn how to make contact with the Holy Spirit, or the ECK. Eckankar provides a set of active, contemplative spiritual exercises that an individual can adapt to their own needs. A central practice is singing the word HU (pronounced like the word "hue"). Practicing these spiritual exercises for twenty minutes each day is recommended to help speed up spiritual unfoldment, expanding soul's consciousness through means such as dream experiences, soul travel, and direct contact with God's love (Eckankar, 2023).

This brief overview of Eckankar and its main teachings serves as a basis for exploring links to related perspectives and as a foundation for reframing conceptions of leadership.

Related Perspectives

"Reality is One, though religions call it by various names" according to Twitchell (1987, p. 27). This sentiment could also be applied to the field of leadership. My experience of searching for leadership literature dates back to the mid-1990s, and the state of the field can be characterized as a proverbial Tower of Babel. (See Chapter 3 for a more elaborated discussion of oneness). What I have noticed is that these diverse perspectives on what leadership is are generally the result of the diversity of underlying conceptualizations, worldviews, and assumptions people hold about the nature of reality. In this section, I explore some key aspects of how Eckankar's view connects to three topics that touch on these underlying foundations behind conceptions of leadership: consciousness, self, and knowing.

Consciousness

A place to begin is with consciousness. Klemp (2002) noted that "... Soul is the thinker of thoughts. The consciousness responds when directed by Soul" (p. 9). He also stated that "a state of consciousness is the level of acceptance that one has to changes in conditions" (Klemp, 2009, p. 13). To better understand consciousness from this view, I briefly explore related conceptions, to distinguish it from our everyday associations with the term.

I start with some philosophy. Chalmers (1996) defined the hard problem of consciousness as: "Why is all this processing accompanied by an experienced inner life?" (p. xii). He notes that this question is "seen as a Great Divide in the study of consciousness" (p. xiii). This divide correlates with underlying philosophical views of materialism, in contrast to idealism. Many neuroscientists as well as philosophers view consciousness as epiphenomenal, or an emergent property of neural processes in the brain (e.g., Dennett, 1993; Robinson, 2010). However, Chalmers goes on to say that "if a physicist or cognitive scientist suggests that consciousness can be explained in physical terms, this is merely a hope ungrounded in current theory" (p. xii). Thus, there are serious questions to be addressed requiring a non-materialist understanding of consciousness.

Quantum physicist Goswami (1989, 1993) inquired into the equations of quantum physics and found that in order to resolve issues in understanding these equations, it was necessary to identify consciousness as a key component of these equations. From this, he saw consciousness as the causal force in the creation of material reality. He found that matter does not have an independent existence of its own, but is given existence and form through consciousness, although not the everyday, pre-frontal cortex, intellectual, abstract thinking, consciousness we normally think about.

The causal effect of consciousness has been explored by Hagelin et al. (1994), who documented research undertaken by the Institute of Science, Technology and Public Policy on the effects of large groups of Transcendental Meditation (TM) practitioners on crime rates and other relevant indicators. This study considered numerous variables and used multivariate statistical analyses of the data, which showed a reduction of up to 18 percent in the violent crime rate during the period in which the largest group practiced TM. This finding was shown to be statistically significant, and not able to be explained by any other means.

From this brief tour of perspectives on consciousness, it is apparent that it is possible to see it having a central role, not only in reflecting on experience, but also in creating experience. "We each choose our own state of consciousness. ... We make our own worlds" (Klemp, 2002, p. 9). Considering the view of being soul and having human experiences, my own inquiry (Reams,

1999) came to see consciousness as "soul's relationship with embodiment" (p. 318). The greater our consciousness, the greater our capacity to enable soul to be present in our human experience.

Self

Central to our human experience is the self. Klemp (2002) noted that "each must understand and act to solve the mystery of their little self before they can solve the mystery of God" (p. 43). The self is described as soul's vehicle for experience in this world, "the place where Soul begins its journey home to God" (p. 43). What are the implications for the self when we say that we are soul? What does this imply for our sense of identity?

Non-materialist views of consciousness enable us to transform our core understanding of identity. Deikman (1996) equated the essence of our being, or the "I" of subjective experience with pure awareness and Klemp (2002) described the creative nature of soul. These views help describe the characteristics of viewing ourselves as soul having human experiences and led to my own definition. "We can thus define soul as a *creative unit of pure awareness*" (Reams, 2012, p. 104, emphasis in original).

But then what about self? Constructive developmental theory conceptualizes an "evolving self" (Kegan, 1982) as something that is always being constructed. Bohm (1992) describes how the system of thought constructs an image of self as an object. Identifying with this self "may be very close to the source of the major block" (p. 170) to the coherence of thought. From this, Bohm saw that the "point is to have a notion of creative being, rather than of an identified being" (p. 169). The definition of soul given above is grounded in this creative sense of being. If the self is not our source of being, yet we have an ongoing subjective experience of it, how can we reconceive the self?

Rowson (2008) addressed this with the notion of the self being a *virtual* entity. "The idea, in essence, is the traditional Buddhist claim that selfhood is a powerful and functional illusion, but is ultimately groundless" (p. 4). Bohm (1992) described how the system of thought deceptively inserts the perception of a "self" into our consciousness, which then incorrectly gives an ontological status to this self, creating a fundamentally incoherent assumption. Rowson indicates that it is in becoming aware of this process that we gain freedom from such assumptions. Conceptualizing the self as a virtual entity, much like how we can relate to an online game avatar, or a character we identify with in a good movie, provides us with a mental image that can help us give the self a functional role in our everyday lives.

By acknowledging the self as virtual, we can perceive it as a vehicle for soul to gain experience through. We can question the limiting assumptions tied to having an identified sense of being. This process opens up a different consciousness from which we can reflect on experience, giving us a different kind of knowing.

Knowing

"Knowing is the highest form of working with the Mahanta" (Klemp, 2002, p. 154). The experience of self-realization as soul "gets us to the state of seeing, knowing, and being" (Klemp, 2002, p. 161). In this section, I explore how knowing as soul is distinct from the everyday mental knowing of the human consciousness and how these can work together through the concept of the virtuality of self.

The knowing of the self tends to be focused on what can be called the human consciousness, mind, or in materialist terms, the brain. Gidley (2007) noted that "humans have become *brain bound* during the establishment of the intellectual-mental-rational mode" (p. 110, emphasis in original) of consciousness. She proposes a "postformal-integral-planetary consciousness" (p. 110), drawing on Gebser's work on an "integral-aperspectival consciousness" (p. 111) that "involves an actual re-experiencing, re-embodying, and conscious re-integration of the living vitality of magic-interweaving, the imagination at the heart of mythic-feeling and the purposefulness of mental conceptual thinking, their presence raised to a higher resonance" (p. 111). This integral consciousness can be conceived as the knowing of soul (Reams, 2012).

There are numerous references to knowing beyond the human consciousness. Senge et al. (2004) discussed how "some things are beyond human comprehension ... something larger than your mind can encompass" (pp. 225–226). The implication of this is captured by Twitchell (1987), who noted that the mind makes a good servant but a poor master. If we base our perception and judgment primarily from the mind, we are relying on a partial, derivative, or secondary picture of reality and experience (Palmer, 1969).

On the other hand, soul's mode of knowing was noted above as a "state of seeing, knowing, and being" (Klemp, 2002, p. 161), a direct perception unmediated by mental conceptions. What makes the mind a poor master is the inherent incoherence of thought (Bohm, 1992). The remedy for this incoherence is a realization of soul's presence infusing the mind, emotions, and bodily organs of perception.

Having defined soul as a creative unit of pure awareness, I was later able to take Deikman's (1996) conception of "I" being pure awareness and connect it with the description of the virtuality of self to define awareness as "*the experiential realization of the virtuality of self*" (Reams, 2016, p. 81, emphasis in original). This helps distinguish that soul, as pure awareness, is not a product of the system of thought. The realization of soul brings an awareness that is "ontologically different from perceptual knowledge" (Deikman, 1996, p. 355). This experiential realization can infuse the mind, emotions, and body (the virtuality of self) with what Bohm (1992) called insight from outside the system of thought. Thus, the knowing of soul enables the "re-experiencing, re-embodying, and conscious re-integration" (Gidley, 2007, p. 111) of experience gained through the virtuality of self in the world.

The field of neurocardiology can provide insights into how soul's knowing can be accessed while bringing greater coherence to human consciousness. McCraty and Shaffer (2015) use the term "*physiological coherence* to describe the degree of order, harmony, and stability in the various rhythmic activities within living systems over a given period of time" (p. 55, emphasis in original), which can be measured through heart rate variability (HRV). This coherence is orchestrated through the "little brain" of approximately 40,000 neurons in the heart. McCraty et al. (1995) provided evidence indicating that positive emotions such as appreciation have a measurable and significantly positive effect on functioning in numerous areas of health and wellbeing. McCraty et al. (2009) also established a direct link between coherence and positive effects on cognitive functioning resulting from coherent psychophysiological states. From their research, it becomes clear that the coherent state is a desirable one to access. Soul, infusing the mind, emotions, and body, enhances coherence.

Yet McCraty (2004) also showed how the actual impact of the heart goes well beyond these psychophysiological phenomena, into the realm of electromagnetic fields. He noted that the electromagnetic field generated by the heart is 5000 times stronger than the electromagnetic field produced by the brain, and "can be measured several feet away from the body with sensitive magnetometers" (McCraty et al., 2009, p. 55) which provides "a plausible mechanism for how we can 'feel' or sense another person's presence and even their emotional state, independent of body language and other signals" (McCraty et al., 2009, p. 55). From this, it is clear that our heart states, being coherent or incoherent, will not only have a significant impact on the body and brain, but also generate a field that can be detected by other people. While the awareness of soul's presence enhances coherence, incoherence results from self-deception (The Arbinger Institute, 2000). This has immense relevance for our conception of leadership.

Reframing Leadership

Klemp (1992) proposed "three mainstays of leadership: responsibility, accountability, and delegation" (p. 146). These align with principles of spiritual unfoldment, in that as creators of our own world, we are responsible for our actions. The law of karma provides accountability. (This is also known as the principle of karma or universal justice (Larson, 2020). Put more simply, it is cause and effect, meaning that our actions return to us and thus we are responsible and held accountable for them). We also need to involve others, as no one can do it all alone, thus we need to delegate and collaborate. These principles show up in various ways throughout the many theories of leadership. In this section, I examine the implications of the concepts described above for theories of transformational, adaptive, and servant leadership and close by exploring a view of leadership as opening space (Reams, 2002, 2012).

Transformational Leadership

Burns (1978) introduced the concept of transformational leadership, a process where leaders and followers go beyond transactional interactions to engage in a mutual process of raising one another to higher levels of morality and motivation. (See more on morality in relation to spirituality in Chapter 4). What is implied by higher levels has been explored through a number of researchers who have built on Burns' work. Kuhnert and colleagues (Kuhnert & Lewis, 1987; Lucius & Kuhnert, 1999) applied Kegan's (1982) model of the evolution of self to transformational leadership. This highlighted the importance of consciousness in transformational leadership, both in terms of capacities needed by the leader, as well as how it relates to moving followers to higher levels.

Carey's (1992) inquiry into transformational leadership describes a fundamental option we have for self-transcendence. This is a choice we make deep inside for which direction we are going with our life, either toward self-embeddedness or self-transcendence. Self-embeddedness comes from identification with and attachment to the egoic self. Self-transcendence is inevitably going to be easier if we are detached from this identification and realize self as a virtual entity.

This theme of self-transcendence can also be found in a quote from Gandhi. "There comes a time when an individual becomes irresistible, and his action becomes all pervasive in its effect. This comes when he reduces himself to zero" (in Chatterjee, 1998, p. 51). This can be seen as allowing soul to be present and infuse the self, so that spirit can flow through.

There are further implications to be explored here. While Burns' original focus was on political leadership, the direction taken by Kuhnert, Carey, and Gandhi implies a teleological stance. The aim of transformation might begin with changing the human level of egoic consciousness, but it also has the seeds of recontextualizing and purifying the self. The shift to being soul and having a virtual self places the transformations of the egoic self in a larger context. Part of this larger context is the concept of karma. "The Law of Karma, yet another facet of the Law of Love, purifies people by holding them responsible for their thoughts and deeds, both to themselves and others" (Klemp, 2002, p. 103). (The Law of Love is a phrase used in Eckankar to emphasize the essential and impartial nature of love, similar to karma). This conception of transformational leadership is aligned with this purification process, enabling more love to shine through soul, through the self, and into the world.

Adaptive Leadership

Enabling this transformation requires a leader to create an environment that supports this process. Heifetz's (1994) concept of adaptive leadership highlights the principle of responsibility and the personal challenges this brings for leaders, "those who lead take responsibility for the holding environment of the enterprise" (p. 250). The concept of a holding environment can be understood as the spaces leaders create to enable adaptive work. In this section, I focus on how the view outlined above reframes the creation of this holding environment and the nature of adaptive work. (See Chapter 2 for a more extensive discussion of how spirituality shows up in relation to Heifetz's conception of adaptive leadership).

Heifetz (1994) lists three key principles involved in adaptive leadership: regulating distress, directing disciplined attention to the issues, and giving the work back to the people at a rate they can handle. The key process for leaders here is learning to get up on the balcony, taking a step back from immediate involvement in action. This is essentially enabling perspective taking and reflection, also described elsewhere as meta-cognition, or the witness self. My inquiry into this (Reams, 2022) focused on reframing who is on the balcony. "Thus, soul is on the balcony, and the self on the dance floor" (p. 85). Soul can observe large patterns in activity and inform the interventions of the self on the dance floor.

Regulating distress is made easier by seeing stress inducing experiences from a more detached perspective. If we use the virtual self as the experiencing self, we will not experience an existential threat to our beingness as soul. Our ability to direct attention is also enhanced, when attention is not so subject to emotional triggers, biases, and limiting assumptions. As soul, we can have a greater ability to have empathy and understanding for where others are at. We can come from a stance of compassion, realizing that the nature of spiritual unfoldment operating through karma and reincarnation means that we too have once been in the others' shoes. This allows us to listen carefully for the next step they can handle in their own adaptive journey of transformation.

While these components of reframing adaptive leadership from the view of soul on the balcony are important, I also wish to go deeper into how the holding environment is created by the presence of soul as the leader. For this, the concept of field theory (Lewin, 1951) is useful. Wheatley (1992) described how organizations appear from a field perspective, noting that leaders become "broadcasters, tall radio beacons of information, pulsing out messages everywhere.... If we do that, fields develop, and with them, their wonderful capacity to bring energy to form" (p. 56). Harung (1999) also explored the concept of fields in relation to leadership and organizations, where he studied how individual leaders, or relatively small groups of individuals, can have an impact on the collective consciousness of an organization, or even an entire city (Hagelin et al., 1994). The theoretical foundations for this research included an understanding of fields of consciousness as having a causal relationship with individual human actions, similar to how it is understood in Eckankar. Thus, the quality and nature of these fields of consciousness is critical to the effectiveness of leadership. Part of this effectiveness comes from the purification of self, enhancing the quality of the field of consciousness, noted above in relation to transformational leadership.

However, there is more to how fields create a holding environment than information and messages. There is an energetic component to this as well. Above, I described McCraty and colleagues' work that showed that the heart creates an electromagnetic field that can be measured. Bradley et al. (2010) noted that the energy of this field "is a measure of the means–the fuel–for maintaining order in the face of challenge (novelty) or changing an order in the face of inertia" (p. 7). In examining the forces that shape such fields of energy, they described the impact of various bio-emotional energetic frequencies such as love, appreciation, and respect versus frequencies of anger, frustration, and resentment. The former set lead to a coherent field of energy, while the latter produce incoherence and a resulting lack of capacity in such a field. Bradley et al.'s (2010) conception further supports this by noting that "to the degree to which a coherent order of positive affective attachment interconnects all members, this is communicated throughout the collective by a quantum-holographic process, thereby giving shape to the group's action on a moment-to-moment basis" (p. 10). On the other hand, "incoherent groups, involving relations of predominantly negative affect, the wave field of collective energy is too disorganized for energetic resonance" (p. 12). This connects back to the above description of the importance of coherence and how this is better enabled by realizing our being as soul and the human self as virtual. (A further elaboration of coherence, especially in relation to its effect on a deep connection in groups, can be found in Chapter 3).

Servant Leadership

In the above reframing of transformational and adaptive leadership, the principle of being soul and the virtuality of self has provided a powerful way of understanding what is implicitly at the heart of these approaches. Another key principle in Eckankar for spiritual unfoldment is service. "The outflow that comes from giving of oneself opens the door to spiritual unfoldment … when one gives without ever thinking of rewards, he is in the first stage of immortality. … Soul lives forever by giving" (Klemp, 1986, p. 56). The connection between this principle of Eckankar and servant leadership is clearly visible. In this section, I will explore this connection, related perspectives and link it to purpose.

Greenleaf (1970) introduced the concept of servant leadership as putting the needs and interests of others first, rather than the leader's own interests. A person starts with the impulse to serve, and from there, is motivated to lead. While inspirational and influential, Van Dierendonck and Patterson (2015) have noted a need to unpack the "mystery of what happens in-between the impetus to serve and the outcomes of serving" (p. 120). They propose compassionate love as a cornerstone of servant leadership that leads to virtues, further enabling behaviors that contribute to optimal human functioning. "A leader's compassionate love is related to a stronger virtuous attitude in terms of humility, gratitude, forgiveness, and altruism" (p. 126). (Note that this conception of compassion and love is also noted in Heifetz's adaptive leadership. See Chapter 2). While service and love are shown to provide optimal end results, there is still a question of results for what? What is the purpose behind servant leadership?

Ray (2004) described connecting people with a sense of their purpose, or "Work" (with a capital "W" to signify it as not simply our job, but a deep sense of why we are here in this world) and "Self" beyond the ego constructed sense of everyday identity. This aligns naturally with the principle of being soul. Ray pointed to success resulting from people shifting "their priorities in life toward the highest goal" (p. 137). The secret of sustaining this connection to Self, source, and the highest goal is to "participate in the flow of giving and receiving" (p. 142). Taking this notion one step further, Klemp (2002) described the purpose of life here on earth as "to learn to give and receive love" (p. 177). This can provide a powerful context for understanding the deeper motivations behind wanting to serve by leading.

To reframe servant leadership in this context, the impulse to serve is grounded in the purpose of life. When a person realizes themselves as soul, this awareness brings the understanding of the human egoic self as a virtual entity. This self can be seen as a vehicle for serving soul's purpose in this world, to learn how to give and receive love. In this way, servant leadership is serving spiritual unfoldment. The challenge is how to see this in action, in the daily details of our lives. This brings me to exploring the act of leadership as opening space.

Leadership as Opening Space

My dissertation research led me to conceive of *leadership as opening space* (Reams, 2002). In this section, I unpack how our quality of character and presence as soul can inform the understanding of leadership as opening space.

The concept of *opening space* comes from one of the principles in Eckankar, that is, that soul is a distributor of spirit in this world.

> This Spirit, ... has one great quality and that is to create effect. As It flows down through the worlds, from Its fountainhead in the center of all creation, far above the earth world, It needs distributors, and It works through Souls.
>
> *(Klemp, 2002, p. 47)*

As soul, we utilize our minds, emotions, and bodies to distribute spirit and create effects in this world. These effects open spaces, or holding environments, which influence others. The nature of these spaces and outcomes of the effect on others begin with our quality of character.

How we show up in any given context begins with the subtle energetic qualities soul brings. These are then filtered through the self, which shows up as character, or what we do with the self we have in this life. Twitchell (1990) described space making in terms of psychic space: "You can mock up space for yourself which will give you plenty of room in which to have freedom of thought and physical motion. On the other hand, you can smother someone by cutting his space ..." (p. 67). If a leader's character constricts the spiritual, mental, emotional, and physical space others (or themselves) have to work in, they create what Owen (2000) characterizes as "soul pollution" (p. 1). On the other hand, Carey's (1992) "fundamental option for self-transcendence" (p. 217) points to character that opens these spaces.

In addition to how character shapes space, so does our quality of presence, through the space soul creates through the electromagnetic fields generated by the heart. While subtle, it is essential. Bill O'Brian observed, during years of studying and practicing organizational learning efforts, that the "success of the intervention depends on the *interior condition* of the intervener" (Scharmer, 2007, p. 7, emphasis in original). Leadership is enacted through our presence as soul, which distributes spirit and generates spaces, the holding environments necessary for the adaptive work of spiritual unfoldment.

Scharmer (2007) describes the blind spot of leadership as the inner place from which leaders lead. He invites us to shift attention from the what and how of doing to the self as source. (See Chapter 1 for a related description of leadership from transpersonal perspectives, or the causal ground of being). Building on this, realizing the essence of our being as soul and reconceptualizing self as a virtual entity as described above liberates us from the limitations of the egoic human consciousness. This allows us to connect with the deeper purpose of our existence, learning to give and receive love and serve others in doing the same.

To enhance our capacity to lead with character and presence as soul, I introduce three practices from Eckankar.

Practice

This final section focuses on practices that can align our leadership with the view presented in this chapter. Whereas the focus has so far been on reframing our conception of leadership, applying key practices from Eckankar can help us make progress on the journey of living this conception of leadership. I present three simple practices: surrender, prayer, and singing the HU.

Surrender is not a giving up, but a giving over. (For more on surrender, see Chapter 2). In the context described in this chapter, it is giving over direction of the self to soul. In turn, soul gives itself over to the inner master, or Mahanta. "Surrender of the little self to the Mahanta is the only way to gain love and wisdom" (Klemp, 1992, p. 7). This allows us to lead through serving the highest purpose. As a practice, this is similar to what Scharmer (2007) described as having an open will, or "the capacity to let go of old identities and intentions and tune in to an emerging future field of possibility" (p. 244). Letting go of identifying with the human egoic self and realizing soul allows us to truly lead by distributing the flow of spirit into the world.

Yet this process of surrender requires more than human will. The second practice, prayer, can aid us in this process. Prayer can be framed as a contemplative mode of listening with an appreciative heart, focused with an attitude of open will. Klemp (2009) describes it this way:

> Correct prayer is listening to God. If a person is going to err in prayer, it's through too much telling or talking to God. There's nothing wrong with talking to God. But after you've asked your question, listen. Be quiet and listen.
>
> *(p. 25)*

When we want to surrender and use prayer as a contemplative spiritual exercise, it can help if we can align our vibrations with spirit. The use of mantras, chanting, or singing are long-established practices in most traditions. In Eckankar, the use of HU is suggested for this purpose. "HU, the secret name for God, … Sing HU every day. You will begin to vibrate in tune with the sound current" (Klemp, 2009, pp. 29–31). Singing HU, listening for the voice of God as the sound current, and surrendering egoic will, can enhance our leadership.

Conclusion

My understanding at 19 years of age of the words about wanting the power to change consciousness, while containing a glimpse of the future, was primarily an egoic understanding. Now, decades later, I can begin to articulate this through the conception of leadership as opening space as a means that enables changing consciousness. This is done in a manner of invitation, always giving the freedom and space to others to make choices that fit their journey.

Using the practices described above for over 40 years has helped me distinguish leadership from many other activities used in the diverse situations we encounter, such as power, management, tyranny, influence, and so on. It has also provided me with a more holistic and integrative context for understanding how to reframe approaches like transformational, adaptive, and servant leadership to bring a deeper sense of purpose and meaning to them.

At the heart of any endeavor, when we look behind the details of situations, this fundamental purpose comes through. To lead is to open space for spiritual unfoldment, the ever-increasing capacity to give and receive love. While we can be faced with all manner of challenges in this world, learning to realize and enact this, is truly leadership.

References

Bohm, D. (1992). *Thought as a system*. Routledge.

Bradley, R. T., Gillin, M., & Tomasino, D. (2010). Transformational dynamics of entrepreneurial systems: The organizational basis of intuitive action. *Regional Frontiers of Entrepreneurial Research*, 1–15. https://doi.org/10.1504/IJESB.2010.034958

Burns, J. M. (1978). *Leadership*. Harper & Row.

Carey, M. (1992). Transformational leadership and the fundamental option for self-transcendence. *Leadership Quarterly*, *3*(3), 217–236. https://doi.org/10.1016/1048-9843(92)90013-6

Chalmers, D. (1996). *The conscious mind: In search of a fundamental theory*. Oxford University Press.

Chatterjee, D. (1998). *Leading consciously. A pilgrimage toward self mastery*. Butterworth-Heinemann.

Deikman, A. (1996). 'I' = awareness. *Journal of Consciousness Studies*, 350–356.

Dennett, D. (1993). *Consciousness explained*. Penguin UK.

Eckankar. (2023). *Frequently asked questions.* Eckankar. Retrieved 07.07 from https://www.eckankar.org/explore/faqs/

Gidley, J. (2007). The evolution of consciousness as a planetary imperative: An integration of integral views. *Integral Review, 5*, 4–226.

Goswami, A. (1989). Idealist interpretation of quantum mechanics. *Physics Essays, 2*(4), 385–400. https://doi.org/10.4006/1.3035899

Goswami, A. (1993). *The self aware universe: How consciousness creates the material world.* Penguin.

Greenleaf, R. K. (1970). *The servant as leader.* Greenleaf Center, Indianapolis, IN, 1–37.

Hagelin, J., Ormre-Johnson, D., Rainforth, M., Cavenaugh, K., & Alexander, C. (1994). *Results of the national demonstration project to reduce violent crime and improve governmental effectiveness in Washington D.C.* (ITR-94:1).

Harung, H. (1999). *Invincible leadership. Building peak performance organizations by harnessing the unlimited power of consciousness.* Maharishi University of Management Press.

Heifetz, R. (1994). *Leadership without easy answers.* Harvard University Press. https://doi.org/10.4159/9780674038479

Kegan, R. (1982). *The evolving self. Problem and process in human development.* Harvard University Press. https://doi.org/10.4159/9780674039414

Klemp, H. (1986). *The book of ECK wisdom.* Eckankar.

Klemp, H. (1992). *Wisdom of the heart.* Eckankar.

Klemp, H. (2002). *The spiritual laws of life.* Eckankar.

Klemp, H. (2009). *The call of soul.* Eckankar.

Kuhnert, K. W., & Lewis, P. (1987). Transactional and transformational leadership: A constructive/developmental analysis. *Academy of Management review, 12*(4), 648–657. https://doi.org/10.2307/258070

Larson, P. (2020). Karma. In D.A. Leeming, (Ed.), *Encyclopedia of psychology and religion.* Springer, Cham. 1318. https://doi.org/10.1007/978-3-030-24348-7_373

Lewin, K. (1951). *Field theory in social science; selected theoretical papers.* Harper & Row.

Lucius, R. H., & Kuhnert, K. (1999). Adult development and transformational leader. *Journal of Leadership Studies, 6*(1–2), 73–85. https://doi.org/10.1177/107179199900600105

McCraty, R. (2004). The energetic heart: Bioelectromagnetic communication within and between people. In P. J. Rosch & M. S. Markov (Eds.), *Bioelectromagnetic Medicine* (pp. 541–562). Marcel Dekker.

McCraty, R., Atkinson, M., Tiller, W. A., Rein, G., & Watkins, A. D. (1995). The effects of emotions on short-term power spectrum analysis of heart rate variability. *The American Journal of Cardiology, 76*(14), 1089–1093. https://doi.org/10.1016/S0002-9149(99)80309-9

McCraty, R., Atkinson, M., Tomasino, B., & Bradley, R. (2009). The coherent heart: Heart-brain interactions, psychophysiological coherence, and the emergence of system wide order. *Integral Review, 5*(2), 4–107.

McCraty, R., & Shaffer, F. (2015). Heart rate variability: new perspectives on physiological mechanisms, assessment of self-regulatory capacity, and health risk. *Global*

Advances in Health and Medicine, *4*(1), 46–61. https://doi.org/10.7453/gahmj.2014.073
Owen, H. (2000). *The power of spirit. How organizations transform*. Berrett-Koehler.
Palmer, R. E. (1969). *Hermeneutics: Interpretation theory in Schleiermacher, Dilthey, Heidegger, and Gadamer*. Northwestern University Press.
Ray, M. (2004). *The highest goal. The secret that sustains you in every moment*. Berrett-Koehler.
Reams, J. (1999). Consciousness and identity: Who do we think we are? *New Ideas in Psychology*, *17*(3), 309–320. https://doi.org/10.1016/S0732-118X(99)00030-6
Reams, J. (2002). *The consciousness of transpersonal leadership* (Publication Number 3053701) [Doctoral dissertation, Gonzaga University]. ProQuest.
Reams, J. (2012). Integral leadership. Opening space by leading through the heart. In C. Pearson (Ed.), *The transforming leader* (pp. 102–109). Berrett Koehler.
Reams, J. (2016). Immunity to change revisited: Theoretical foundations for awareness based practices for leadership development. *Integral Review*, *12*(1), 65–110.
Reams, J. (2022). Soul space for adaptive work. In M. Raei & H. T. Rasmussen (Eds.), *Adaptive leadership in a global economy: Perspectives for application and scholarship* (pp. 82–96). Routledge.
Robinson, W. S. (2010). Epiphenomenalism. *Interdisciplinary Reviews: Cognitive Science*, *1*(4), 539–547.
Rowson, J. (2008). *From wisdom-related knowledge to wise acts: Refashioning the conception of wisdom to improve our chances of becoming wiser.* (Publication Number uk.bl.ethos.659116) [Doctoral dissertation, University of Bristol]. British Library EThOS.
Scharmer, O. (2007). *Theory U. Leading from the future as it emerges. The social technology of presencing*. The Society for Organizational Learning, Inc.
Senge, P., Jaworski, J., Scharmer, C. O., & Flowers, B. S. (2004). *Presence: Exploring profound change in people, organizations and society*. Society for Organizational Learning Inc.
The Arbinger Institute (2000). *Leadership and self-deception*. Berrett Koehler.
Twitchell, P. (1987). *The Shariat-ki-Sugmad*. Eckankar.
Twitchell, P. (1990). *Letters to Gail III*. Eckankar.
Van Dierendonck, D., & Patterson, K. (2015). Compassionate love as a cornerstone of servant leadership: An integration of previous theorizing and research. *Journal of Business Ethics*, *128*, 119–131. https://doi.org/10.1007/s10551-014-2085-z
Wheatley, M. (1992). *Leadership and the new science: Learning about organization from an orderly universe*. Berrett-Koehler.

PART II

Non-Western Perspectives on Leadership and Spirituality

6

NONHIERARCHY AS SPIRITUAL RECIPROCITY

An Indigenous Approach to Leaderless Leadership

Wahinkpe Topa (Four Arrows), aka Don Trent Jacobs

Introduction

Hierarchy is about ranking humans over humans, humans over nonhumans, and nonhumans over other nonhumans. It conveys relationships that subordinate one to another. Hierarchy is a concept crucial to how the social organization of humans and our relationship to other life forms can lead us toward or away from the mass extinction that threatens us. This chapter asserts that most precolonial cultures practiced a nonhierarchical way of being that encouraged respect and equality between all life forms. In essence, giving such respectful significance to all life forms describes Indigenous spirituality. According to Indigenous worldviews, understanding the role of hierarchy in leadership studies is a spiritual undertaking.

As we face mass extinction, we must consider the Indigenous perspective on hierarchy. First Nations peoples who still embrace this perspective comprise the 20 percent of the Earth that holds 80 percent of its biodiversity (Raygorodetsky, 2018). Indigenous peoples do not view humans as superior to one another, trees, plants, insects, birds, fish, reptiles, mammals, or mountains. The path most hierarchical human societies are on today has been the root of inequality, oppression, and genocide. When we began to see ourselves as superior and dominating over other than human life, we set the stage for intraspecies domination in our mainstream institutions, including science, religion, education, business enterprise, sports, entertainment, and media.

DOI: 10.4324/9781003396741-9

Indigenous Social Structure

Indigenous nonhierarchical societies reveal themselves in diverse ways but are all based on trust. A "leader" uses dialogue, stories, and good sense to move an idea or a policy forward. In "Indigenous Anarchic Hierarchy," Eepa (2020) suggested that leadership does not have to derive from coercive power; on the contrary, it may be earned from the space of respect and cooperation. For example, respect-based leaders serve in select roles in the Kwapas (also spelled Quapaw) Nation. The chief serves as the uniter and coordinator for the entire tribe, responsible for gathering people for funerals, deliberations of justice, trade, and diplomatic discussions with foreign emissaries. Unlike the Western hierarchical model of leadership, the Indigenous model lacks a mechanism to enforce obedience or observance. Under the traditional Indigenous leadership model, the chief is upheld by the collective—the tribe—based on their respect for the leader and his wisdom. The leader has preferential authority to guide and suggest actions, but he has no authority to compel it. If the people lose respect for their chief, he is demoted from his position without ceremony (Eepa, 2020). The Western hierarchical structure has much to learn from this. We must be ready to build such systems in our societies to root out self-serving people who use acts of domination to achieve their goals.

An Indigenous system of hierarchy has some exceptions. For example, as Rick Two Dogs (personal communication, 2000) once told me, the Oglala Lakota, who generally had nonauthoritarian matriarchies, would select someone to be in command during a buffalo hunt. Having one expert guide, the hunt proved safer and more efficient. After the event, the community would return to its more egalitarian routines, with a different leader likely chosen for the next hunt. Although infrequent before the colonial invasion (Demeo, 2006), war was another exception to nonhierarchical systems. Some Indigenous nations took hostages and enslaved them. Such practices, as terribly hierarchical as they were, differed from European chattel slavery in that the members of the tribe eventually adopted the hostages or allowed them to marry into the tribe and become a full member of the nation.

Nonhierarchical models work especially well under matriarchal systems. They also appear in some patriarchal cultures when people understand the true power of women and their important role in decision-making. Lakota women who Sun Dance do not have to pierce themselves because they know how to bleed, suffer labor, nurture, raise children, settle arguments, handle suffering, and lead with the heart. We men keep forgetting. A Lakota Sun Dance sister told me how the delicate power hierarchy balance with an emphasis on women worked in preconquest days. She shared,

> When postconquest warfare increased for the Lakota, the men believed it was spiritually important to wear new deerskin moccasins into battle. The women made them and wove designs with chewed porcupine quills. When a decision about going to battle was on the table, the men would do *inipi* (to live again) ceremony in the *initi* (purification lodge). In between prayer rounds, they would discuss the pros and cons and share spiritual insights. The women did the same in their own initi. When each group finished their four rounds of praying, a spokesperson from each lodge would meet. If the men made the decision to attack the fort, they would tell this to the woman. If the women had decided it was not a good idea, the spokeswoman would say something like, "I understand. We deeply respect the wisdom of those who have made this choice. We have gratitude for the work that was done in making such a decision. However, we have decided not to make the moccasins." The men would then probably not go into battle.
>
> *(personal communication, 2006)*

Indigenous Relationship with Nonhuman Life

The social hierarchies of Indigenous people stem from their close observation of Nature and their inseparability from, and reciprocity with, all life forms. Robin Kimmerer, who, in October 2022, became the first Indigenous woman to receive a MacArthur grant, said in an interview with *The Washington Post*, "In return for the spectacular gifts of the Earth, say to yourself: What am I going to do about that? What is my accountability in return for everything I've been given?" (Heller, 2022). In her presentation at the conference Sustainable Wisdom: Integrating Indigenous Knowhow for Global Flourishing, Kimmerer referred to Western science as a fortress that has separated us from Nature (Kimmerer, 2016). Indeed, many dictionaries exclude humans from the definition of nature. The *Oxford Dictionary of Phrase and Fable* defines "nature" as "the phenomena of the physical world collectively, including plants, animals, the landscape and other features and produces of the Earth, as opposed to humans or human creations" (2005, p. 242).

Kimmerer (2017) put Indigenous languages in the context of a historical colonizer framework, discussing how the languages were forbidden because they threatened Western culture. Western culture and the English language reflect the structure of domination, or "power-over," in which the natural world is purely for humans' use and exploitation. She stated,

> Indigenous languages challenge the fundamental tenets of Western thinking—Those whom my ancestors called relatives were renamed *natural resources.* In contrast to verb-based Potawatomi [language of

the Potawatomi people], the English language is made up primarily of nouns, somehow appropriate for a culture so obsessed with things.

(para 7)

The Indigenous ways of communication, however, are rooted in interdependency, expressing that we are all one family. There is no separation between humans and Nature. Birds, bugs, berries, and boulders are spoken of with the same respectful grammar as humans. Living beings—regardless of their form—are referred to as subjects, never as objects. Personhood is extended to all animate and inanimate beings.

The nonhierarchical eco-centered emphasis of the "kinship worldview" (Four Arrows & Narvaez, 2023) leads to reciprocal engagement with our more-than-human relationships. Through the nonhierarchical emphasis, we come to realize the sentience and intelligence of nonhuman life forms. We better learn how our lives depend on our four-leggeds, two-leggeds, winged ones, swimmers, crawlers, and rooted relatives. We find ourselves bringing ecological considerations into discussions about otherwise human-centered issues. Ultimately, we participate in helping the rest of Nature rebalance life systems. Perhaps we can prevent the worst-case scenario. If not, it is important for future generations to rebuild with our original kinship-based, nonhierarchical worldview. Instead of polarization, the Indigenous nonhierarchical worldview seeks complementarity between the precolonial and postcolonial ways of being in the world. As Seneca scholar Barbara Alice Mann (2021) stated, "The whole point of the Twinned Cosmos is to achieve balance, not the victor of one over the other" (p. 137).

Origin Myths and Nonhierarchy

It may be helpful to consider one's uninvestigated cultural or religious myths when attempting to break the spell of hierarchy that continues policies like the Doctrine of Christian Discovery (Newcomb, 2008). Christel Loar (2010) opened her article titled "The Meaning of Life: Joseph Campbell on the Power of Myth with Bill Moyers" with a quote from Campbell: "Myths are clues to the spiritual potentialities of the human life" (para.1). Many Indigenous origin stories offer such clues as relate to our relationship with nonhuman creatures. For example, in the Haudenosaunee tale about Sky Woman and the creation of Earth, note how essential the animals are to our existence. As the story goes, before the Earth was created, there was a place in the sky where the sky people lived. The Great Spirit gently dropped his daughter down through a hole to the lower world so as to bring light to the darkness. The animals looked up and saw the light emanating from her. They worried that she would be hurt when she landed in the sea.

Many different animals dove down to get mud. A muskrat managed to get some but died from the effort. A large turtle was summoned and quickly the animals pounded the mud onto the turtle's back. The swans watched the woman, they now called Sky Woman, continue to fall and gathered to gently lay her on the newly formed earth (George, n.d.).

In addition to the inclusion of animals and women in Indigenous origin stories, twins are also common. Twins represent complementarity between opposites and work collaboratively despite their differences to maintain balance in the world (Wilkinson, 2009). They possess solar and lunar characteristics: the solar twin represents directness, strength, and dominance, whereas the lunar twin's power comes from reflection, passivity, and collaboration. Despite their opposing traits, Indigenous twins work as complementary partners. They demonstrate a nonhierarchical model of apparent opposites and exemplify the egalitarian interconnectedness of life on Earth. They see all life forms as having equal value. Egalitarian twins are in stark contrast to what occurred after the rise of civilization and humanity's anthropocentric separation from Nature, as Greek and Roman twin stories began to promote solar dominance over lunar. Teich (2012) suggested that origin myths supported a change of consciousness that promotes hierarchy. In some cases, the solar twin subordinates, or even murders, the lunar one. Romulus and Remis, Jacob and Esau, Cain and Able, Appolo and Artemus, Hercules and Iphicles—all represent this hierarchical relationship.

Most dominant worldview institutions ignore or dismiss nondualistic thinking. Unfortunately, the rejection may be especially prominent in education, where hierarchy rules. Dr. Walter Block, a professor of economics at Loyola University, believes hierarchy is natural and necessary. Because I disagreed with all his books and knew he disagreed with mine, I convinced him to coauthor a book with me. My goal was for the two of us—he, a "Jewish, atheist libertarian, [and I], a mixed blood American Indian" (Brill, n.d., para. 1)—to use cooperative argumentation, not debate, to see if our opposing views could find some complementarity relating to social and ecological justice and sustainability education. The journey of our book, *Differing Worldviews in Higher Education: Two Scholars Argue Cooperatively About Justice Education* (Four Arrows & Block, 2011), was best described by our publisher as "an entertaining and enlightening journey that reveals surprising connections and previously misunderstood rationales that may be at the root of a world too polarized to function sanely" (Brill, n.d., para. 1).

The two of us became friends during the writing, strange bedfellows that we are. Our friendship may seem remarkable, considering the extent of our disagreement. For example, Walter says in the book and video posted on YouTube (*Social Justice Night Part 1 - Walter Block and Four Arrows aka Don Trent Jacobs*: https://www.youtube.com/watch?v=uiCrC08_7eo&t=3s)

that only humans have intrinsic value; everything else on Earth is utilitarian for the benefit of human beings. We never came to agree on this particular notion, but I learned from it. I realized that his position was exactly that which is behind most, if not all, of our ways of being in the world. His position helped me better understand our predicament and supported my emphasis on a nonhierarchical worldview. Not everyone agrees with me about my partnership with Walter. Not everyone is pleased that I wrote this book as a way to practice nondualistic, complementary-seeking truths. I gave a copy to my friend, Alice Walker, the well-known activist, poet, and author of many books, including *The Color Purple*. She threw it in the waste can and told me I was in bed with the devil. She was concerned I had given more attention to his dangerous libertarian philosophy. Still, I stand by what we did. Also, many of his fans have contacted me over the years and expressed a change of opinion after reading the book.

Perhaps the biggest challenge to restoring a relatively nonhierarchical world is recognizing that science, media, superficial observations, and folklore support the idea of humans at the top of a pyramid. A counter-hegemonic awareness is crucial if we are to succeed in transformation. As long as people believe Nature is fundamentally hierarchical, they will see this goal as a romantic fantasy. The most open-minded, liberal, and well-intentioned individuals will note how one creature or another is at the "top of the food chain" in support of the belief that domination hierarchy is natural.

Although traditional Indigenous wisdom has always known otherwise, more and more scientists are challenging the worldviews and science that try to support this idea. In *Control Without Hierarchy*, Deborah M. Gordon (2014) showed how ants are not hierarchical and biological systems operate without central control. In their article "Hierarchy Is Detrimental for Human Cooperation" Cronin et al. (2015) noted that studies of animal behavior consistently demonstrate how cooperation is key to thriving. When hierarchies do occasionally emerge in primates, they are detrimental to all group members' well-being. Primates, wild dogs, hyenas, rooks, parrots, and elephants all fare better in nonhierarchical social groups. Hierarchies in wild animal groups do emerge, but only amid constant threats or abnormally limited resources (Cronin et al., 2015).

One might blame the neo-Darwinists who popularized the phrase "survival of the fittest" to describe the naturalist's complex theory. However, it is not Darwin's writings per se, but rather interpretations of them that support a "dog-eat-dog" mentality or rationalization. Although Darwin wrote about competition, he came to believe that survival of the fittest was more about cooperation, symbiosis, and reciprocity (Rifkin, 2009). An impressive group of contributing scholars in the book *Cooperative Evolution: Reclaiming Darwin's Vision* support this perspective (Bryant & Brown, 2021).

One of the early biologists to interpret Darwin correctly was the Russian revolutionary biologist and nobleman-turned-anarchist Peter Kropotkin. His research in Siberia laid the groundwork for modern biological studies of cooperation and altruism. In *Mutual Aid: A Factor of Evolution*, Kropotkin (1902) wrote,

> Wherever I saw animal life in abundance…I saw mutual aid and mutual support carried on to an extent which made me suspect in it a feature of the greatest importance for the maintenance of life, the preservation of each species, and its further evolution…when my attention was drawn to the relations between Darwinism and sociology, I could agree with none of the works that had been written upon this important subject…that every animal against all its congeners, and of every man against all other men was "a law of Nature." [This position lacked confirmation from direct observation]. On the contrary, a lecture ... "On the Law of Mutual Aid," which was delivered at a Russian Congress of Naturalists in January 1880, the well-known zoologist, Professor Kessler, struck me as throwing a new light on the whole subject. Kessler's idea was that besides the law of mutual struggle, there is in Nature the law of mutual aid, which, for the success of the struggle for life, and especially for the progressive evolution of the species, is far more important than the law of mutual contest. This suggestion—which was, in reality, nothing but a further development of the ideas expressed by Darwin himself in *The Descent of Man*—seemed to me so correct and of so great importance, that since I became acquainted with it (in 1883) I began to collect materials for further developing the idea.
>
> *(p. viii)*

Our Indigenous ancestors already knew all of this (Lopes, 2016). Taking care of one another is how humans survived for 99 percent of human history before we decided to claim the top of the pyramid. The act of hunting and killing an animal for food was deeply understood in terms of the animals participating in this mutual aid. Paul Nadasy (2007), a professor of anthropology and American Indian Studies at Cornell University, offered persuasive scholarship to support this notion of a nonhierarchical "reciprocal exchange" in his article "The Gift of the Animal." From his field studies and references, Nadasy concluded that the Indigenous hunters studied believed the act of hunting was about reciprocity. The hunters believed that the animals gift themselves to the hunter in the right circumstances, such as when hunters treat the animals appropriately. If hunters overtax the animals' generosity, the animals can become angry and not give themselves anymore. Recognizing this compels the receiver to provide a gift to reciprocate, seeing the relationship as relating to the spirits or souls of both the hunter and the animal.

Western science and education scholars continue their denial of such beliefs—or they know better but are afraid to take a stand against the overwhelming opposition of their peers. Abraham Maslow, author of the well-known hierarchy of needs, is one such scholar. In placing self-actualization at the top of the pyramid, Maslow contradicted what he learned in a 1930s internship on the Blackfoot Nation reservation. From the Indigenous perspective, he learned that people are born with self-actualization, which he witnessed in the people. Due to concerns that his academic peers would reject what he had seen, however, Maslow (1943) did not refer to what he had learned (Safir, 2020). How different sociology and psychology might be if Maslow had shared what he learned from the Blackfoot: Self-actualization is with us from birth instead of at the top of a hierarchical pyramid that few ever reach.

Horses and the Myth of Hierarchy

I close this chapter with my personal experiences with wild horses to support the nonhierarchical notion of animal–human relationships. Although I was well known for having "trained" mustangs, I prefer to say I entered a reciprocal, nonhierarchical relationship with them. The result was that the horses, often within a few months, allowed novice riders and children to mount and ride them. When a syndicated television show, *Evening Magazine,* learned about my work, they asked me to demonstrate with a recently adopted wild horse. Readers can watch the seven-minute episode on YouTube (*Four Arrows Wild Horse Hypnotist*: https://youtu.be/vxzAm08731c?si=ai_bByXGat9M-SpTF) where I mount a horse just brought into captivity shortly after it rears and falls fearfully and dangerously for the camera (*Evening Magazine*, 1984).

Most equestrian books and journals present horses as herd animals with a clear hierarchy. Equestrian authorities claim that this hierarchy prevents confrontation in the group, resulting in fewer injuries. I will admit to drawing the same conclusion from my early observations of horses in corrals. However, most of the support for ranking among horses came from observations of horses in confined areas versus the open range. I have observed horses in the wild, and they are very differently motivated than when in the process of being captured or when they are domesticated and have too little space for their instinctual readiness to escape from a predator. Although even wild horses will nip or kick at one another, if one watches long enough, one sees this behavior as more about relational acceptance and cooperation than domination. (The same goes for flocks of vultures on the ocean beach, taking turns to eat a dead fish).

I consider horses the ultimate biofeedback machines for humans who work with them. Horses' sensitivity to people's thoughts and body language indicates that trust is critical to the human–horse relationship. Telepathic communication creates a communication channel between a person and a horse. Although I initially perceived my success in terms of having the horse see me as "dominant," I eventually learned that domination attitudes and practices did not create an optimum relationship between the horse and me. Trust and cooperation were vital, and only when they were established did the magic happen. Not only could I mount a Mustang within days of captivity, but I could also find one only three months out of the wild, let her free in a remote mountain, and call her back to get in the horse trailer.

A few horse experts agree with the nonhierarchy descriptor of wild horse herds, and Leslie Skipper is one of them. She has written at least five books on horsemanship. Skipper (n.d.) opened an article for the Equine Behaviour and Training Association titled "The Myth of Dominance" with a quote from Daniel Goleman: "Leadership is not domination, but the art of persuading people to work toward a common goal" (para 1). She challenged the *dominance hierarchy* language of ethologists, whose lens starts with the assumption that hierarchy guides everything. She spoke about how observers of wild horses have switched from talking about a dominant stallion to a dominant mare, but they do not go far enough. The full story is that a kind of cultural knowledge emerges to orchestrate a more complex way to encourage group cohesion. Skipper supported a you-scratch-my-back-and-I'll-scratch-yours kind of reciprocity as the hallmark of a stable, happy group of horses, even domestic ones. She concluded the piece by writing, "So long as we are not seduced by some feeble vision of 'boss and subordinate,' and instead think of the relationship [between human and horse and between horses] as more of a partnership…, we shall not go far wrong" (Skipper, n.d., para. 65).

If precontact Indigenous cultures, wild animals, and domestic horses thrive in nonhierarchical environments, perhaps we should rethink the hierarchical nature of contemporary leadership and religion. From an Indigenous perspective, spirituality is ultimately about giving significance and reverence to all life forms, emphasizing respect, responsibility, and reciprocity. One way to practice moving into more egalitarian, nonhierarchical ways of being is with metacognitive worldview reflection, which you can do using the 40 contrasting dominant and Indigenous worldview precepts I have made available online (Four Arrows, 2022; see Appendix). Looking at the precepts and seeking complementarity between them in ways that locate one's thinking and behaviors related to the pairs of beliefs could help bring a sense of balance and equality where it may be missing. Society's emphasis on "leadership" and the usual hierarchical ways we tend to define it must shift into a more collaborative "leaderless leadership" approach.

As you study the chart in the Appendix, consider how moving closer to Indigenous worldview precepts like the following might bring forth a less-hierarchical world.

- Precept 8. Inseparability of heart over head (right-brained)
- Precept 11. Animistic and biocentric (nonanthropocentric)
- Precept 14. Flexible boundaries and interconnectedness (not rigid or fragmented)
- Precept 20. Intolerance of injustice (prevention and resistance)
- Precept 34. Laws of Nature are primary (as opposed to laws of man)
- Precept 36. Autonomy on behalf of group and future generations (instead of self-gain as a priority)
- Precept 39. High respect for women (with many nations having matriarchy)

Concluding Reflections

In this chapter, I have outlined how a worldview based in hierarchy leads to dominance and the myriad problems that the world faces today. I have showed how Indigenous spirituality, which views everything as sacred, or equal and is nonhierarchical in nature provides an alternative to Western narratives. I have also highlighted several instances where assumptions around hierarchy in nature do not hold true. Finally, I shared my experience with horses and how this could be an inspiration for a nonhierarchical leadership practice. Finally, I included a tool in the appendix that might help leaders and individual alike situate where they stand in terms of Indigenous and Western worldviews.

As we consider new paths forward, it is my hope that we have the courage to challenge assumptions of hierarchy within ourselves and our institutions. When leaders have the wisdom to, with openness and humility, honor the sacredness and wisdom of all beings, we can walk together into a more just, equitable and sustainable world. By looking to Nature as our guide, and resting in the truth that none stand above the rest, we take steps on the journey toward right relationship so that we all may thrive.

References

Brill. (n.d.). *Differing worldviews in higher education: Two scholars argue cooperatively about justice education*. https://brill.com/display/title/36860?language=en&contents=editorial-content

Bryant, C., & Brown, V. A. (2021). *Cooperative evolution: Reclaiming Darwin's vision*. ANU Press. https://doi.org/10.2307/j.ctv1j9mjjf

Cronin, K. A., Acheson, D. J., Hernández, P., & Sánchez, A. (2015). Hierarchy is detrimental for human cooperation. *Scientific Reports*, *5*(1), Article 18634. https://doi.org/10.1038/srep18634

Demeo, J. (2006). Peaceful and warrior societies in pre-Columbian America: What anthropology and archeology tell us. In Four Arrows (Ed.), *Unlearning the language of conquest: Scholars expose anti-Indianism in America* (pp. 135–151). University of Texas Press.

Eepa. (2020, November 2). *Indigenous anarchic hierarchy*. The Anarchist Library. https://theanarchistlibrary.org/library/eepa-indigenous-anarchic-hierarchy

Evening Magazine. (1984). *The horse hypnotist* [YouTube video]. https://www.youtube.com/watch?v=vxzAm08731c&t=13s

Four Arrows. (2022, October 9). *The essential worldview reflection approach to rebalancing life systems on Earth*. Kindred. https://kindredmedia.org/2022/10/the-essential-worldview-reflection-approach-to-re-balancing-life-systems-on-earth/

Four Arrows & Block, W. (2011). *Differing worldviews in higher education: Two scholars argue cooperatively about justice education*. Sense Publishers.

Four Arrows & Narvaez, D. (2022). *Restoring the kinship worldview: Indigenous voices introduce 28 precepts for rebalancing life systems on planet Earth*. North Atlantic Books.

Four Arrows & Narvaez, D. (2023, September 18). *Connection to the land and to one another* [Panel presentation]. Science Summit at the 78 United Nation General Assembly.

George, K. (n.d.) "The Haudenosaunee creation story." Oneida Indian Nation. https://www.oneidaindiannation.com/the-haudenosaunee-creation-story/

Gordon, D. M. (2014). *Control without hierarchy*. Harvard University Press.

Heller, K. (2022, October 16). 'Braiding Sweetgrass' has gone from surprise hit to juggernaut bestseller. *The Washington Post*. https://www.washingtonpost.com/books/2022/10/12/braiding-sweetgrass-robin-wall-kimmerer/

Kimmerer, R. (2016, September 12). *The fortress, the river and the garden: New metaphors for knowledge symbiosis* [YouTube video]. https://www.youtube.com/watch?v=BSnJzvGDMVw

Kimmerer, R. (2017, June). Speaking of Nature: Finding language that affirms our kinship with the natural world. *Orion Magazine*. https://orionmagazine.org/article/speaking-of-nature/

Kropotkin, P. (1902). *Mutual aid: A factor in volution*. The Anarchist Library. https://theanarchistlibrary.org/library/petr-kropotkin-mutual-aid-a-factor-of-evolution

Loar, C. (2010, October 28). *The meaning of life: 'Joseph Campbell on the power of myth with Bill Moyers.'* Pop Matters. https://www.popmatters.com/132546-joseph-campbell-on-the-power-of-myth-with-bill-moyers-2496120081.html

Lopes, M. B. (2016). Nonhierarchical social structures in Indigenous societies. *Cadermos de Campo*, *25*(25), 29–42.

Mann, B. A. (2021). Complementary duality. In Four Arrows & D. Narvaez (Eds.), *Restoring the kinship worldview: Indigenous voices introduce 28 precepts for rebalancing life* (p. 137). North Atlantic Books.

Maslow, A. H. (1943). A theory of human motivation. Psychological Review, *50*(4), 370–396.

Nadasy, P. (2007). The gift in the animal: The ontology of hunting and human-animal sociality. *American Ethnologist*, *34*(1), 25–43. https://doi.org/10.1525/ae.2007.34.1.25

Newcomb, S. T. (2008). *Pagans in the promised land: Decoding the doctrine of Christian discovery*. Chicago Review Press.

Nature. (2005). *The Oxford dictionary of phrase and fable* (2nd ed.). Oxford University Press. p. 242.

Raygorodetsky, G. (2018, November 16). Indigenous peoples defend Earth's biodiversity—but they're in danger. *National Geographic*. https://www.nationalgeographic.com/environment/article/can-indigenous-land-stewardship-protect-biodiversity-

Rifkin, J. (2009). *The empathetic civilization: The race to global consciousness in a world in crises* (1st ed.). Penguin.

Safir, S. (2020, December 2). *Before Maslow's hierarchy: The whitewashing of Indigenous knowledge*. https://shanesafir.com/2020/12/before-maslows-hierarchy-the-whitewashing-of-indigenous-knowledge/

Skipper, L. (n.d.). The myth of dominance. *Equine Behavior*. http://www.ebta.co.uk/dominance-ls.html

Teich, H. (2012). *Solar light, lunar light: Perspectives in human consciousness*. Green House.

Wilkinson, M. (2009). The cosmology of twin heroes: An exploration of Native American mythology. In S. I. Johnson (Ed.), *Religions of the ancient world: A guide* (pp. 95–104). Harvard University Press.

APPENDIX

Chart for Nonbinary Metacognitive Reflection to Rebalance Life Systems on Planet Earth

Instructions: Consider this chart as complementary pairs, the left column being the left-brain hemisphere and the right column the right-brain hemisphere. The idea is that we are out of balance, with too much emphasis or inaccuracies relating to the left side.

Common Indigenous Worldview Manifestations	#	*Common Dominant Worldview Manifestations*
Egalitarian	1	Rigid hierarchy
Courage and fearless trust in the universe	2	Fear-based thoughts and behaviors
Socially purposeful life	3	Living without strong social purpose
Emphasis on community welfare	4	Focus on self and personal gain
Respect for various gender roles and fluidity	5	Rigid and discriminatory gender stereotypes
Self-transcendent	6	Materialistic
Earth and all systems as living and loving	7	Earth as an unloving "it"
Emphasis on heart over head	8	More head than heart
Competition to develop positive potential	9	Competition to feel superior
Empathetic	10	Lacking empathy
Animistic and biocentric	11	Anthropocentric
Words as sacred, truthfulness as essential	12	Words used to deceive self or others
Truth seen as multifaceted, accepting the mysterious	13	Truth claims as absolute
Flexible boundaries and interconnected systems	14	Rigid boundaries and fragmented systems
Regular use of alternative consciousness	15	Unfamiliarity with alternative consciousness
Recognition of spiritual energies	16	Disbelief in spiritual energies
Emphasis on holistic interconnectedness	17	Disregard for holistic interconnectedness
High interpersonal engagement, touching	18	Minimal contact with others
Inseparability of knowledge and action	19	Emphasis on theory and rhetoric
Resistance to authoritarianism	20	Acceptance of authoritarianism
Time as cyclical	21	Time as linear

(*Continued*)

Common Indigenous Worldview Manifestations	#	*Common Dominant Worldview Manifestations*
Seeking complementary duality	22	Dualistic thinking
Intolerance of injustice	23	Acceptance of injustice
Emphasis on responsibility	24	Emphasis on rights
Generosity as highest expression of courage	25	Aggression as highest expression of courage
Ceremony as life-sustaining	26	Ceremony as rote formality
Learning as experiential and collaborative	27	Learning as didactic
Trance-based learning as helpful and natural	28	Trance as dangerous or stemming from evil
Human Nature as good but malleable	29	Human Nature as corrupt or evil
Humor as essential tool for coping	30	Humor used for put downs
Conflict resolution as return to community	31	Conflict mitigated via revenge, punishment
Learning is holistic and place based	32	Learning is fragmented and theoretical
Personal vitality is essential	33	Personal vitality minimized
Laws of Nature are primary	34	Social laws of society are primary
Holistic Self-knowledge is most important	35	Self-knowledge not prioritized
Autonomy for group and future generations	36	Autonomy for self
Nature as benevolent and relational	37	Nature as dangerous or utilitarian only
All lifeforms are sentient	38	Other-than-human beings are not sentient
High respect for women	39	Low respect for women
Honors diversity	40	Little realization of the importance of diversity

Note: ©2020 Wahinkpe Topa (Four Arrows). Shared at the UNGA78 Science Summit at the 78th United Nation General Assembly.

7

AFRICAN SPIRITUALLY INFORMED LEADERSHIP

Galvanizing and Mobilizing for the Common Good and Human Flourishing

Sharon Wamble-King

Introduction

Exploring African spirituality and how it informs leaders and leadership provides an opportunity to examine a human phenomenon within a specific cultural context and to conceptualize alternative approaches to engaging, mobilizing, and organizing people collectively. According to Mbigi (2007), African spirituality focuses on people and their inherent dignity, underscoring an ideology of "human-ness" that engages the heart and spirit. This contrasts with Western-oriented spirituality which is rooted in individualism, rationalism, and materialism (Akbar, 1984; Mamman & Zakaria, 2016).

As the bedrock of the traditional African worldview, precolonial spirituality is described as *permeating* the lifeways of African people and institutions (Mbiti, 1960) shaping the African cultural ambiance (Paris, 1995) as collective, communal, and holistic (Lutz, 2009; Ndlovu, 2016). In contrast, the Western perspective regards spirituality as a personal search for meaning through connections to self-chosen beliefs, values, and practices that inspire optimal being (Allen & Fry, 2022). Western-oriented spirituality ultimately manifests outwardly shaping characteristics parallel to those inherent in African spirituality including mutual vision, increased collective social responsibility, and feelings of connection (Tourish & Tourish, 2010).

Given the far-reaching nature of spirituality across many aspects of African life (Mbiti, 1960), the core belief system holds the potential to inform leader practices, leadership processes, and performances. African spirituality promotes leadership approaches that embrace holism, community, and human dignity while prioritizing people over profits (Malunga, 2009). This

DOI: 10.4324/9781003396741-10

predisposes leadership toward holistic, relational, creative, and harmonious practices that shape the collective nature of the phenomenon (Ojo & Olomu, 2022). Western-oriented spirituality, on the other hand, is often characterized as emanating from an individual who eventually impacts others and their communities. Normative Western dualisms of leader-follower, individual-group, and hierarchy-egalitarian (for more on the dualism of leadership, see Guenther's Chapter 3) are not germane to understanding leadership within an African spiritually distinct cultural context (Dent et al., 2005; Fernando, 2011). African spiritually permeated leadership is perceived to facilitate change and transformation and to promote collaborative problem-solving. This leadership creates trusting environments that encourage consensus decision-making, foster collective responsibility, and galvanize people to reach beyond self-interest to pursue fairness, justice, and well-being; thus, achieving the common good and human flourishing together (Mangaliso, 2001; Mbigi, 2007). These contrasts fundamentally differentiate the nature of leadership informed by ancient African spirituality from that which is grounded in a Euro-Western orientation.

This chapter is organized into three sections. The first section examines African spirituality focusing on the cosmological foundations that undergird its widespread influence across Africa (Viriri & Mungwini, 2010). The discussion utilizes a worldview framework as the basis for analysis (Dixon, 1977). The second section highlights the key dimensions of African spirituality and how they shape leader practices, values, and leadership processes. The chapter concludes with a focus on application, outlining key tenets and values of African spirituality, and how they may be expressed within organizations and manifested through leader characteristics and values.

Positionality

As an Afrocentric practitioner-scholar, it is important to share how my life experiences shape my perspectives and approaches toward examining African spirituality and leadership. I am an African American cisgender woman born and raised in the western United States. Due to my lifelong diasporic location and African-American bi-cultural lenses, I acknowledge the complexities inherent in adeptly interpreting traditional African philosophies and lifeways. I was socialized into African-oriented thought by a plethora of African diasporic women—my mother, grandmothers, aunts, cousins, "play aunties," Godmothers, teachers, friends, colleagues, and other women who mothered me in my communities, churches, schools, media, and social organizations—some of whom were born a generation from enslavement in the United States.

I have studied traditional African spirituality and written this scholarship from the position of outsider-insider: I am not a native-born African whose life has been ensconced in the lifeways and societal ambiance of the continental motherland. I am, however, an African diasporic insider, a daughter of the adaptive, resilient, traditional African worldview, who has been tacitly socialized into its mores, beliefs, and spirituality derived from that acculturation.

I recently presented my research in South Africa. My Afrocentric scholarship focused on African American women's leadership perceived through the traditional African philosophical orientation and worldview framework. Concluding the presentation, I was challenged by some South African students regarding my interpretation of the African worldview, which they perceived as flawed because of my geographic/cultural dislocation. They shared concerns regarding my inability to ably tease out the cultural/tribal nuances of the African worldview that would be second nature if I were native-born and had resided on the continent. We had a robust dialogue about the nature of worldviews and their implicit and pervasive influence on all peoples of African descent despite their geographic/cultural location. This was not the first time I have been exposed to those who are suspicious of mis- and disinformation based on Indigenous distance and cultural dislocation. I am sensitive to this criticism and understand the basis of the perceptions. It is for that reason that I aimed to *primarily* use African scholars (rather than those of the diaspora) as the sources for this examination, my interpretations, and my conclusions. I am cognizant of, and committed to, decolonizing my scholarly assumptions, perspectives, and approaches to inquiry and presentation of the content regarding African worldview and culture, its subtleties, diverse interpretations, and manifestations. As a diasporic African woman, I approach this subject humbly and critically, being dedicated to questioning my assumptions, continually learning from my global African family, and seeking accuracy throughout the research and writing process. Dislocated from the continent, I embrace my identity as an Africana daughter committed to the sharing of scholarship with integrity, embodying the life force and spiritual connectivity empowered by Spirit, the wellspring of our truth.

Difficulties in Applying African Spirituality as a Lens of Examination

There are a number of challenges that inhibit a universal grasp of the concept of African spirituality. Its metaphysical, transcendent nature makes it hard to define which is further complicated by its history and strong religious association (Mamman & Zakaria, 2016). Depending on scholars' reasoning, the definition of African spirituality in the literature spans from secular experiences in the search for meaning and purpose, to a quest for freedom, empowerment, human dignity, and genuine community (Bigger, 2008; Paris, 1995).

Distinguishing African spirituality from religion presents a particular challenge in that they are intrinsically linked but distinct, and many scholars including the noted African theologian Mbiti (1960) use the terms interchangeably. Spirituality has been described as beliefs in the sacred and the supernatural that spring from a holistic notion of interconnection with all things, and a journey for peace, harmony, goodness, and justice (Alkebulan, 2013; Paris, 1995); it is essential to being human (Bigger, 2008). Religion, on the other hand, is described as the systematized manifestation of those beliefs and values through practices, rituals, and symbols designed to facilitate intimacy with the sacred (Marumo & Chakale, 2018).

The diversity of religious expressions and beliefs stemming from the traditional worldview and belief systems presents another challenge to comprehensively grasping the concept of African spirituality. The concept of African spirituality expressed within a religious context comprises dogmas across 54 countries, encompassing more than 1,000 linguistic groups and dialects, and religious expressions of hundreds of tribal cultures and ethnic groups (Ayanga, 2007; Viriri & Mungwini, 2010). Christianity and Islam are each practiced by approximately 40percent of the African population according to Jacob Olupona, professor of Indigenous African religions at Harvard Divinity School and professor of African and African-American studies (Chiorazzi, 2015). Christianity dominates the southern part of the continent, Islam the northern portion, and Indigenous African practices are predominant across the center of Africa. Olupona reports that traditionally oriented Indigenous practices and beliefs are also evident across most of the continent (Ojo & Olomu, 2022). Because of the inherent linkages, the term spirituality often sparks notions of religions and religious practices.

The diversity of religious/cultural life as well as diverse perceptions of spirituality also presents challenges in establishing a single definition of African spirituality that encompasses the sentiment of the continent. Africans increasingly are defining their primary identities as Muslim or Christian, prioritizing religious selfhood over traditional cultural legacies. This shift is suggested to diminish their innate bond to a distinctive African belief system that has been perceived as unifying all things, connecting peoples to their land and the place where their clan, lineage, and people were birthed (Ojo & Olomu, 2022). African scholars indicate that despite these changes, there remains a persistent, widespread traditional belief across the continent in the supremacy of Spirit, described variably as life force, God, creator, supreme being, preserver, and cosmic orchestrator underscoring all reality (Adofo, 2016; Ayanga, 2007). This commonality fosters a collective bond among African peoples, explaining the universal essence of spiritual consciousness. Such harmony appears fundamentally rooted in and configured by the pre-colonial African worldview paradigm, which scaffolds Indigenous African spirituality and many religious traditions. The worldview framing provides access to a broad set of concepts that characterize African spirituality, thereby conferring an interpretive structure to examine leadership and leader practices.

Traditional African Cosmology: Framing an Examination of Leadership

Pre-colonial African cosmology is the *core* of the traditional African worldview and culture (Ayanga, 2007; Nyang, 1980). This philosophical orientation transcends the nuances and complexities of the myriad African religious systems, revealing an interlocking set of concepts through which to perceive traditional African spirituality and its socio-cultural expressions. Some scholars argue that the two are so closely intertwined that it is difficult to understand one without considering the other, as one serves as the foundation for the manifestations of the other (Marumo & Chakale, 2018). The cosmological view differentiates African spirituality from its cultural artifact, African religion.

Examining broad themes and concepts derived from the traditional African philosophical orientation offers a conceptual framework through which to understand shared elements of African spirituality across diverse belief systems and religious expressions. The following section describes African spirituality through the lens of its philosophical foundation. Furthermore, it examines the primary themes from the traditional African worldview that undergirds and defines African spirituality and informs leader behaviors and attitudes, leadership processes, and lifeways of African peoples.

African Spirituality Described Through a Worldview Lens

According to Kambon (2004), the traditional African belief system describes the interconnection of humanity, nature, and the universe, which emerges from being one with Spirit. It is "the lens through which [Africans] see reality … the underlining thought link that holds together the African value system, philosophy of life, social conduct, morality, folklores, myths, rites, rituals, norms, rules, ideas, cognitive mappings and theologies" (Kanu, 2013, p. 533). Broadly, the traditional African viewpoint begins and ends with Spirit—*everything* in African thought reveals God or Spirit

(Mbiti, 1960). In contrast to the Western worldview which emphasizes detachment and discounts the influence of Spirit, African thought is grounded in the belief that Spirit and all matter are one (Schiele, 1996). Spirit gives life force and energy to matter, and people are perceived as spiritual beings since they contain this essence. With Spirit as the eternal starting point, humanity is joined to Spirit and consequently linked in a continuum across time and space to ancestors, those unborn, all communities, and nature (Nyang, 1980). Paris (1995) asserted that the "primary cohesive power in every African cosmology is the power that unites the realms of nature, history, and spirit" (p. 28). Africans' view of reality, therefore, is that the physical and spiritual worlds are separated by one degree of visibility; one is imperceptible but no less palpable and discernable. "African people are concerned about the invisible more than they are about the visible ... That is the nature of the spiritual orientation ... more concerned about the infinite than they are about the finite" (Harris, 2003, p. 115).

This belief in the interconnection emerging from Spirit formed the basis for much Indigenous thought.

Scholars have surmised, for example, that the foundational belief in a supreme deity and the primacy of Spirit created fertile ground for the colonial evangelizing of Africans into Christianity. "The Christian message to Africa through the Western missionaries did not find a *Tabula Rasa*... It is the awareness of God and religious disposition that made the evangelization of Africa possible and provided a basis for it" (Paris, 1995, as cited in Setiloane, 1986, p. 30, emphasis in original). According to Olupona, African cosmology, which is grounded in notions of Spirit and the holism and connectivity that stem from it, comprises tenets that persist despite the diversity of religious expressions evident throughout the continent. For example, he described respecting but not personally participating in Yoruba traditions in his native Nigeria while still affirming the importance of connection with members of the community (Chiorazzi, 2015). His behavior highlighted his cultural alignment with the worldview tenet of interconnectedness even without adhering to specific African religious practices.

Traditional African Spirituality

Traditional African principles are characterized by notions of "inclusiveness and synthesis, cooperation and collective responsibility, groupness, sameness, and commonality, and at the core of it all, of course, is spirituality" (Kambon, 2004). These notions, moored in the tenets of harmony and balance, engender beliefs in an interdependent continuum comprised of ancestors, the unborn, animals, land, flora, and cosmic elements united and define community. The cosmic interconnectivity across all realms of the universe promotes a perspective that damaging one part of this cosmic web will destroy the whole (Mbiti, 1960). This viewpoint recognizes the spiritual essence permeating all elements and emphasizes the interdependence between humanity and the natural world, situated within an overarching spiritual framework. According to Marumo and Chakale (2018), "African spirituality is about having harmony and peace with [the] intention of protecting the environment for survival" (p. 11701). The universal cohesion fosters a harmoniously holistic view of embodiment in which spirit, soul, and body are perceived as united and describes embodied balance as the physical realization of spirituality (Alkebulan, 2013).

Rooted in spiritual connectivity, personal identity, for example, is not perceived individually, but as part of *community*. The individual is not recognized nor understood as distinct from the *collective*. An African's individual identity is perceived as a collective identity; the interconnectedness, however, does not thwart the uniqueness of the individual within the community nor does it minimize their distinct contribution to the whole (Akbar, 1984). "The communal character of African culture does not mean that the good of the individual person is subordinated to that of the group… the individual… pursues his or her own good through pursuing the common good" (Lutz, 2009, p. 314).

The individual's knowledge of self emanates from a perpetual connection with the indwelling power resulting in a union with Spirit, nature, and the collective, yet individually expresses a distinct manifestation of infinite consciousness. Baldwin (1984) described this embodied communal extension as "innate (biogenetically determined), unconscious, and operationally defined by the concept of 'Spirituality'—a dynamic energy that allows the self to merge (extend) in the totality of phenomenal experience" (p. 180). An individual is, therefore, an extension of the collective, simultaneously individual and collective.

Traditional African spirituality fosters human interactions characterized by connectivity, collectivity, and community. These elements are interdependent and appear imbricated; they emulate a fluidity, sphericity, and unified beingness that mirrors the rhythm and endless synchronicity of the universe (Myers, 1988). When viewed through the paradigm of traditional African spirituality, leadership practices incorporate a cosmic whole—ancestors, present and future generations, nature, and the universe—and leadership manifests as relational (Uhl-Bien, 2006), holistic, communal processes that strive to promote harmony and balance.

The following section is a discussion of some of the key tenets of African spirituality which fashion a set of leadership dimensions and characteristics.

Connectivity

The tenet of connectivity is key to understanding the mystical amalgam that knits all peoples together, creating an innate collective sense of personhood manifested through shared values and mission. This cornerstone belief promotes the concept of extended self-orientation (Baldwin, 1984), which manifests in relational leadership approaches centering collective responsibilities and mutual accountabilities. Connectivity and collective identity shape leaders as communal stewards of the group processes and their leadership as crucial to catalyzing group trust and cooperation.

Ubuntu: I am Human Because I Belong

One of the primary expressions of spiritual connectivity is characterized by Ubuntu, which is often described as the heart of African spirituality and whose philosophy reflects the collective nature of the traditional worldview (Ncube, 2010). This South African Bantu phrase is conveyed in many languages and tribes across the continent (Mnyaka & Motlhabi, 2005) and is perceived as a spiritual paradigm (Masango, 2006; Ngunjiri, 2016). Ubuntu reflects African peoples' understanding of the essence of collective personhood and morality (Ndlovu, 2016). Tutu (1999) contended that this South African concept is not easily translated into Western language. He posited that an English equivalent of Ubuntu translates to "'My humanity is caught up, is inextricably bound up in yours.' We belong in a bundle of life… 'I am human because I belong. I participate, I share'" (p. 30).

The perception of interconnectivity shapes relationships and is supported by a number of values including compassion, generosity, and unity (Murove, 2014; Ndlovu, 2016). It encourages leaders to communicate transparently, promoting group collaboration and unity (Ncube, 2010; Sulamayo, 2010). From a leadership perspective, Ubuntu, demonstrated by treating people well, may lead to improved performance and increased productivity (Mangaliso, 2001; Ojo & Olomu, 2022). Connectivity shapes a leader's focus toward advancing collective well-being and communal thriving.

Connectivity Fosters Collaboration and Cooperation

Ubuntu philosophy propagates commitment to organizational objectives (Mangaliso, 2001), and leaders embodying Ubuntu tend to demonstrate transparency and promote accessibility (Ojo & Olomu, 2022). They support the goals and aspirations of group members and are not deterred by criticism or intimidation. Organizational cultures aligned with Ubuntu emphasize inclusivity accepting diverse ways of knowing in order to build and maintain community. Core values include altruism, peacemaking, and social justice (Booysen, 2015).

Ubuntu also engenders a deep sense of connectivity that cultivates relationships characterized by shared agency which emphasizes the concept of power with others rather than power over others (Ojo & Olomu, 2022). It fosters leaders who empower others and encourage them to act. In this communal setting, group members tend to make assumptions regarding leader behavior. They expect leaders to prioritize the group's needs and the common good (Ngunriji, 2016). Based on the notion of self-extension (Baldwin, 1984), leaders most likely perceive themselves as part of the collective effort, not detached from it. This is integral to collective responsibility and accountability. (For more on the collective aspect of leadership from a Western perspective, see Guenther's Chapter 3).

Connectivity Expressed Through Social Time: Potential Impact on Productivity

Connectivity shapes how people use time, which impacts leadership practice and group efficiency (Mpofu, 2016). There are many misconceptions and misunderstandings regarding how Africans regard time, sometimes characterized by the phrase "African time" (Nnajiofor, 2016, p. 253). Time is often viewed as a socialized activity through the lens of connectivity; communal obligations and human relationships are seemingly prioritized over rectilinear-time punctuality. This behavior is characterized by the expression, "It is not the clock that rules the day… but the relationship. It is being a human being instead of human doing" (Nnajiofor, 2016, p. 268). Africans do value punctuality; relational leaders, however, must balance implicit communal notions of time with Western expectations. These unspoken expectations can cause conflicts if not managed well. Leaders can explore the meanings of time with the group to uncover interpretations. Subsequently, they can consider how worldviews may influence organizational efficiency and productivity (Mangaliso, 2001). The decision-making process, for example, aims to consider all voices and promote harmony. Reaching collective objectives may require more time, planning, and managing expectations than autocratic decision-making.

In summary, African spirituality, as manifested through the principle of connectivity, fosters leadership with a communal orientation. The principle of connectivity promotes organizational culture centered around communal bonds, which can cultivate robust loyalty and dedication to collective goals. This ethos of interconnectedness fosters shared vision, mission, and group cohesion, mitigating fractures and facilitating the resolution of misunderstandings and conflict. The communal emphasis minimizes individualism which can inhibit collaboration and accountability. Building on the communal values evident in the principle of connectivity, the following section explores how African spirituality is expressed through the encompassing concept of community.

Community

The principle of community shapes organizations into being akin to an extended family with kinship deriving from Spirit rather than biological ties. This holistic perspective conceptualizes an organization as an integrated whole rather than simply an assemblage of individuals (Lutz, 2009). The pervasive notion of community fosters social relations characterized by egalitarianism, democracy, and equity (Ncube, 2010), shifting the focus away from an individual leader to the group. Mbigi (2007) described community as the "cradle of the individual" (p. 300) a safe, nurturing space for teaming that enhances the performance of everyone in the group, promoting creativity and innovation. Group, team, and organizational interests are perceived as more important than personal ones through the lens of community.

Balancing Individual and Community Goal Achievement

Prioritizing community does not mean that the ambitions of individuals are sacrificed. Rather, it fosters recognition that achieving goals for the collective good is integral to pursuing individual objectives (Lutz, 2009). Community reinforces that individuals need not pursue either their own interests *or* the common good separately. Instead, an individual's interests can be advanced through working toward shared goals and collective well-being. Social relations are structured for community, not just for individuals. Leaders concentrate on fostering common goals with team rewards having primacy over individual ones as the enterprise functions communally (Mnyaka & Motlhabi, 2005). Performers, even the outstanding ones, benefit from group/team rewards as it reinforces their perception that their success is inextricably related to the success of others, especially their fellow team members. Community extols the holism of the group cultivating leaders focused on reciprocity and pursuing goals that achieve mutual purposes.

Community Nurtures Leader Identity and Development

The communal orientation of African spirituality profoundly shapes leader development. Community provides the setting for collective gifts to emerge that move collectives toward mutuality and well-being (Bolden & Kirk, 2009). The communal context molds leadership as a collective process rather than an individualistic endeavor with leaders arising organically and relying on group support (Ncube, 2010).

Within an African spirituality context, leaders are socialized into cultural values of cooperation, service, ethics, and social responsibility that guide leadership praxis (Msila, 2014). Storytelling, proverbs, rituals, and traditions teach important leadership lessons, which strengthen leader skills grounded in ancestral wisdom (Mbigi, 2000). Leaders gain legitimacy through their moral character and upholding cultural norms—not from formal titles, roles, or authority (Mbiti, 1960). Communal accountability spurns selfishness while encouraging ethical leadership focused on the collective good (Mangaliso, 2001; Mbigi, 2007). In summary, the African spiritual perspective frames community as the setting for leaders' gifts to emerge and grow centered in cultural values and communal well-being.

Spiritually Activated Communication Shaped in Community

Traditional African perspectives conceive existence as communal, with individuals expressing reality and recognizing their worth *in relationship to* Spirit and community. As the locus of spiritual development (Masango, 2006), community serves as the cultural incubator where self-identities are nurtured, abilities are honed, and epistemologies are modeled and shared (Akbar, 1984; Myers, 1988). Individuals are seen as conveying these spiritually oriented, communal ways of knowing through symbolic imagery like words, gestures, tones, rituals, and rhythm to articulate collective perceptions of reality (Pasteur & Toldson, 1982). This holistic, embodied knowledge emanates from within and is often described as heart or soul and expressed with the dynamism and fluidity of the cosmos. "Africans think with their soul–I would even say with their heart…formed intuitively in the style of feeling-thinking subject, that is to say, in feeling, sensitivity is thought" (Senghor, 1971, p. 44, as cited in Pasteur and Toldson, 1982, p. 21).

Communication, a key leadership process informed by African spirituality, is perceived to be infused with *Nommo* (Nyang, 1980), a Dogon (ethnic group indigenous to Mali, West Africa) concept of the metaphysical, transformative power that brings words to life (Asante, 1998; Richards, 1981). Jahn (1961) characterized *Nommo* as the "driving power…that gives life and efficacy to all things [expressed through] the spoken word" (p. xxi). Thus, traditional African perspectives conceive communication as spiritually potent with orality fueled by the moral character of the speaker (Knowles-Borishade, 1991).

Leader communication within the ubiquitous reality of community is characterized by dialogue and discussion. Its focus is on activating a unified purpose rather than simply disseminating information (Karsten & Illa, 2005). Communication appears to "enlighten and stir the audience into some productive action" (Alkebulan, 2013, p. 32). Within this relational process, unity and understanding among the collective are valued above the efficiency and accuracy of language. "The pervasive axiom is that to talk and to name is to create experience, to construct reality" (Mangaliso, 2001, p. 26). As such, leaders are spiritually oriented to serve as skillful change agents and instruments of social justice and transformation.

In summary, the concept of community represents a fundamental component of African spirituality with profound implications for leaders and leadership. Community engenders egalitarian, transparent, and democratic social relations that balance individual and collective goals (Ncube, 2010). As the cradle of individual identity (Mbigi, 2007), community creates a secure space for collaborative teaming and enhanced performance (Mbiti, 1960; Msila, 2014). Leaders emerge through developmental nurturing within communal life, internalizing spiritual values of service, ethics, and responsibility (Bolden & Kirk, 2009). Community shapes spiritually activated communication practices used by leaders to engage and mobilize groups and communities (Karsten & Illa, 2005). African spirituality positions community as the essential backdrop conferring meaning, purpose, and cultural grounding to leadership processes to advance the common good.

Leadership grounded in community fosters equity and inclusion shaping safe places to give voice and agency to all, prioritizing collective over individual interests. It draws on collective wisdom which in turn nurtures the creativity and innovation generated by the group. The leader, perceived as extending from the group, is expected to galvanize members to architect collaborative pathways to achieve common goals. Communal engagement fosters the type of solidarity that facilitates organizational adaptability, building the capacity to thrive in rapidly changing environments.

Connectivity and community shape leadership that prioritizes shared humanity, elevating "we-ness" over "I-ness" and eliminating power differentials based on roles, positions, or status. This opens access to diverse contributions from everyone involved and collaborative action fueled by a common purpose. Tapping into communal intelligence provides myriad sources of knowledge to inform organizational productivity and effectiveness. Supported by values of group solidarity, harmony, and social and ecological justice, leadership anchored in these elements accelerates efforts to define and achieve the common good.

This section has offered a discussion regarding how traditional African spirituality experienced through connectivity and community shapes leader behavior and leadership as well as values that emanate from those cosmological elements. Connectivity and community as well as other African spiritual elements shape leader behavior, leadership processes, and values. These are outlined in Table 7.1 along with a summary of how they may be expressed in organizations. The table's content is based on a compilation of the work of several scholars as well as my own.

TABLE 7.1 Applying Traditional African Spirituality to Leadership

Traditional African Spiritual Tenets	*Leader Values and Characteristics*	*Description in Organization*
Connectivity	Ubuntu: human-ness, one is truly human as a member of community. Scaffolded by dignity, respect, compassion, reciprocity, hospitality, generosity, empathy patience, and diplomacy. Leaders supportive of others' goals and aspirations tend not to be intimated by the expertise and performance of others.	Open, transparent, accessible communication to build shared goals and vision. Leaders empower others, facilitate shared agency, and power *with* not power *over* others. Centering people may lead to stronger loyalty and commitment to organizational goals. Collective responsibility, accountability, and participation to achieve shared goals.
Community	Relationships reflect kinship: connected through Spirit, not necessarily blood. Organization as one body, not an assemblage of individuals.	Organization nurtures creativity and innovation, building what is best for everyone. Leader perceived as an extension of the group; connection assumed/unstated. Group interests are assumed to take priority over individual interests. Mission and vision are shaped to benefit the collective including internal and external constituents.
Collectivity	Interests of the group are prioritized over the individual. Individual pursues their good by pursuing the common good. Galvanizing people to reach beyond self-interest to pursue justice, fairness, well-being, and human flourishing.	Trusting environments that encourage teaming, group solidarity, consensus decision-making, and participatory problem-solving.
Continuum	Recognizing the influence of ancestral wisdom and that gained from nature and the cosmos, metaphysical knowing, knowledge produced across all segments of community. Age is perceived as a process of maturing providing sage insights.	Inclusive organizational cultures, integrating and valuing the diversity of learning working styles, balanced acceptance of different ways of knowing, being, and doing. Older workers are sought out for their knowledge, understanding, and wisdom. Leverage proverbs, fables, folklore, cultural metaphors, and storytelling.

(*Continued*)

TABLE 7.1 (Continued)

Traditional African Spiritual Tenets	*Leader Values and Characteristics*	*Description in Organization*
Continuum—Nature	Leaders facilitate policy development that supports ecological efforts, and learn from patterns evident in nature.	Organization goals stretch beyond internal constituents to support ecological and sustainability efforts.
Dignity and respect	Valuing the inherent worth of each person based on their connection to Spirit and every member of the collective. Fostering an environment characterized by generosity, mutuality, caring, support, and empathy.	Respecting the diversity within the group perceiving it as a tapestry of productivity.
Wholism	Recognition that no one exists in isolation all are interconnected and part of a matrix of relationships and interactions.	Undergirds implementation of systems thinking and ways to aim for group synergy. Empowering others to act in an emotionally safe, trusting environment.
Time	Understand the meaning of time through a communal lens as a socialized activity that prioritizes communal obligations and human relationships over rectilinear-time punctuality circularity in conversations and decision-making. Value allocation of time-based on relational notions of connectivity. Expectations regarding time are usually unspoken, especially in Western normative settings.	Explore meanings of time in various contexts; consider how diverse worldviews regarding time may impact constituent engagement productivity and conflict resolution. Allow time for consensus building and group bonding. Diversity and listening to all voices may take more time but strengthen loyalty and organizational commitment.
Teamwork—collective responsibility and accountability	Demonstrate partnership, shared goal and vision setting; group solidarity, cooperation, and collaboration supported by team rewards and performance management.	Achieving goals together fosters the belief that none of us is greater than all of us. The whole is greater than the sum of its parts; the needs of the group and group process considered are prioritized.

Decision-making	Inclusive facilitation in which all voices are encouraged and accepted. Dissenting voices are protected. Curiosity and questioning are normative, and dialogue may be circuitous to reach a conclusion.	Consensus-oriented, adaptive group processes support collective solidarity and fidelity to organizational aims. The preservation of group harmony and unity takes precedence over expedient problem identification and resolution; balance characterizes the critical underpinning for effective group decision-making.
Communication	Process is perceived as engagement and is enhanced by leader listening to ensure mutual understanding of diverse positions; use of persuasion rather than manipulation, and focus on conversation and dialogue to involve.	Facilitates shared goals and vision, group solidarity, ownership of solutions and programs, transformation, learning, and growth.

Note: Sources used for preparation of this table included Bolden and Kirk (2009), Booysen (2015), Mangaliso (2001), Masango (2006), Mbigi (2007), Mnyaka and Motlhabi (2005), Mpofu (2016), Msila (2014), Murove (2014), Ncube (2010), Ndlovu (2016), Nnajiofor (2016), Ojo and Olomu (2022), and Sulamayo (2010).

Conclusion

This chapter has explored fundamental dimensions of African spirituality as viewed through the framework of the traditional, pre-colonial African worldview. It outlined the underpinnings of African spirituality and its universal influence on the lifeways of African peoples. Core tenets of connectivity and community grounded in spirituality were explored and applied to leader practices and values, including how these could shape organizational leadership processes.

Fundamentally, African spirituality as elucidated through the traditional cosmological framework instills leadership with profound meaning, purpose, and cultural grounding focused on communal well-being and human and ecological thriving. Connectivity, community, and collectivity derive from a spiritual construct that shapes leader identity formation and development processes (Akbar, 1984; Ncube, 2010). Rather than individualistic endeavors, leaders and leadership derive meaning, purpose, and validation through community and fidelity to cultural principles at the heart of the spiritual worldview, as opposed to formal positions or titles (Bolden & Kirk, 2009).

The African continent faces numerous systemic challenges including poverty, lack of infrastructure, political instability, corruption, health crises, and the lingering effects of colonialism. Some scholars have proposed that applying the core principles of African spirituality to leadership could help address some of these persistent problems (Mbigi, 2007; Sulamayo, 2010). While not aiming to replace Western leadership approaches completely, proponents argue that communally focused, spiritually anchored leadership that prioritizes inclusion, the pursuit of justice and equity for the common good, and promotes human and ecological flourishing holds promise as an alternative way forward for the region. However, it remains aspirational as some leaders have not embraced this approach despite its potential (Mabovula, 2011; Ncube, 2010).

African spirituality provides a holistic framework through which to develop leaders and leadership practices focused on human development and ecological well-being. Some African scholars see spirituality, especially as expressed through Ubuntu, as promoting values such as empathy and communalism that can inform ways to engage in diverse contexts. It seems that this is an opportune time to reimagine notions of leadership by integrating the spiritually grounded epistemologies, ontologies, and axiologies found throughout Africa. As Joseph (1991) suggested, future leaders will likely have diverse backgrounds but share a commitment to advancing civil society.

There are a number of benefits to applying this spiritually anchored framework to leadership as it:

- Promotes an interconnected, communal view of organizations rather than focusing solely on individuals.
- Encourages inclusive, participative decision-making processes that value all voices.
- Fosters social relations based on egalitarianism, transparency, and equity.
- Aligns with ethical values like reciprocity and generosity.
- Shapes communication focused on dialogue, relationship-building, and activation.
- Provides purpose and meaning by linking organizational goals to those of the community and greater society.
- Fosters emphasis on ecological survival and human well-being.

Given the complexity of today's global challenges, African spiritual perspectives may offer timely wisdom to those desiring to perform leadership that is ethical, holistic, and focused on individual, community, and societal well-being. While comprehensive adoption of this ancient wisdom may encounter impediments, integrating even facets of this spiritually rooted paradigm could stimulate profound transformation to meet the challenges of our times.

References

Adofo, D. Y. (2016). *Ancestral voices: Spirit is eternal / Dalian Y. Adofo* ; foreword by Robin Walker. www.ancestralvoices.co.uk.

Akbar, N. (1984). Africentric social sciences for human liberation. *Journal of Black Studies, 14*(4), 395–414. https://doi.org/10.1177/002193478401400401

Alkebulan, A. A. (2013). The spiritual and philosophical foundation for African languages. *Journal of Black Studies, 44*(1), 50–62. https://doi.org/10.1177/0021934712465183

Allen, S., & Fry, L. W. (2022). A Framework for leader, spiritual, and moral development. *Journal of Business Ethics, 184*(3), 649–663. https://doi.org/10.1007/s10551-022-05116-y

Asante, M. F. (1998). *The Afrocentric Idea: Revised and Expanded*. Temple University Press.

Ayanga, H. (2007). African cosmologies past and present. In A. Eisen, & G. Laderman (Eds.), *Science, Religion, and Society: An Encyclopedia of History, Culture and Controversy* (Vol. I), pp. 325–331. Routledge.

Baldwin, J. A. (1984). African self-consciousness and the mental health of African-Americans. *Journal of Black Studies, 15*(2), 177–194. https://doi.org/10.1177/002193478401500203

Bigger, S. (2008). Secular spiritual education. *Educational Futures, 1*(1), 60–70.

Bolden, R., & Kirk, P. (2009). African leadership: Surfacing new understandings through leadership development. *International Journal of Cross Cultural Management, 9*(1), 69–86.

Booysen, L. A. E. (2015). The two faces of ubuntu: An inclusive positive or exclusive parochial leadership perspective? In L. M. Roberts, L.P. Wooten, & M.N. Davidson (Eds.), *Positive organizing in a Global Society: Understanding and Engaging Differences for Capacity Building and Inclusion*, pp. 135–140. Routledge.

Chiorazzi, A. (2015). The spirituality of Africa. *The Harvard Gazette*. https://news.harvard.edu/gazette/story/2015/10/the-spirituality-of-africa/

Dent, E. B., Higgins, M. E., & Wharff, D. M. (2005). Spirituality and leadership: An empirical review of definitions, distinctions, and embedded assumptions. *The Leadership Quarterly, 16*(5), 625–653. https://doi.org/10.1016/j.leaqua.2005.07.002

Dixon, V. J. (1977). African-oriented and Euro-American-oriented worldviews: Research methodologies and economics. *Review of Black Political Economy, 7*(2), 119–156. https://doi.org/10.1007/BF02689392

Fernando, M. (2011). Spirituality and leadership. In A. Bryman, D. Collinson, K Grint, B. Jackson, & M. Uhl-Bien (Eds.), *The SAGE Handbook of Leadership*, pp. 483–494. SAGE.

Harris, N. (2003). A philosophical basis for an Afrocentric orientation. In A. Mazama (Ed.), *The Afrocentric Paradigm*, pp.111–120. Africa World Press.

Jahn, J. (1961). *Muntu: African Culture and the Western world*. Faber and Faber.

Joseph, J. A. (1991). Leadership for America's third century. *National Forum, 71*(5), 5–8.

Kambon, K. K. (2004). The worldviews paradigm as the conceptual framework for African/Black psychology. In R. I. Jones (Ed.), *Black Psychology* (4th ed.), pp. 73–92. Cobb & Henry.

Kanu, I. A. (2013). The dimensions of African cosmology. *Filosofia Theoretica: Journal of African Philosophy. Culture and Religions, 2*(2), 533–555.

Karsten, L., & Illa, H. (2005) Ubuntu as a key African management concept: Contextual background and practical insights for knowledge application. *Journal of Managerial Psychology, 20*(7), 607–620.

Knowles-Borishade, A. F. (1991). Paradigm for classical African orature. *Journal of Black Studies, 21*(4), 488–500. https://doi.org/10.1177/002193479102100408

Lutz, D. W. (2009). African Ubuntu philosophy and global management. *Journal of Business Ethics, 84*(S3), 313–328. https://doi.org/10.1007/s10551-009-0204-z

Mabovula, N. N. (2011). The erosion of African communal values: A reappraisal of the African Ubuntu philosophy. *Inkanyiso: Journal of Humanities and Social Sciences, 3*(1), 38–47.

Malunga, C. (2009). *Understanding organizational leadership through Ubuntu*. Adonis & Abbey.

Mamman, A., & Zakaria, H. (2016). Spirituality and Ubuntu as foundation for building African institutions, organizations and leaders. *Journal of Management, Spirituality & Religion, 13*(3), 246–265. https://doi.org/10.1080/14766086/2016.1159976

Mangaliso, M. P. (2001). Building competitive advantage from Ubuntu: Management lessons from South Africa. *Academy of Management Executive, 15*(3), 23–33.

Marumo, P. O., & Chakale, M. V. (2018). Understanding African philosophy and African spirituality: Challenges and prospects. *Gender and Behaviour, 16*(2), 11695–11704.

Masango, M. J. (2006). African spirituality that shapes the concept of Ubuntu. *Verbum et Ecclesia, 27*(3), 930–943.

Mbigi, L. (2000). *In Search of the African Business Renaissance: An African Cultural Perspective*. Knowledge Resources.

Mbigi, L. (2007). Spirit of African leadership: A comparative African Perspective. In K. April, & M. Shockley (Eds.), *Diversity: New Realities in a Changing World*, pp. 294–303. Palgrave MacMillan. https://doi.org/10.1057/9780230627529_19

Mbiti, J. S. (1960). *African Religions & Philosophy* (2nd Ed.). Heinemann.

Mnyaka, M., & Motlhabi, M. (2005). The African concept of Ubuntu/botho and its socio-moral significance. *Black Theology, 3*(2), 215–237. https://doi.org/10.1558/blth.3.2.215.65725

Mpofu, V. (2016). Time. In G. Emeagwali, & E Shizha (Eds.), *African Indigenous Knowledge and the Sciences. Anti-colonial Educational Perspectives for Transformative Change*. SensePublishers, pp. 65–78. https://doi.org/10.1007/978-94-6300-515-9_5

Msila, V. (2014). Ubuntu: Shaping the current work place with African wisdom. *Mediterranean Journal of Social Sciences, 5*(4), 609–616.

Murove, M. F. (2014). Ubuntu. *Diogenes, 59*(3–4), 36–47. https://doi.org/10.1177/0392192113493737

Myers, L. J. (1988). *Understanding an Afrocentric Worldview: Introduction to an Optimal Psychology*. Kendall/Hunt.

Ncube, L. B. (2010). Ubuntu: A transformative leadership philosophy. *Journal of Leadership Studies, 4*(3), 77–82.

Ndlovu, P. M. (2016). *Discovering the Spirit of Ubuntu Leadership: Compassion, Community, and Respect*. Palgrave Macmillan. https://doi.org/10.1057/9781137526854

Ngunjiri, F. W. (2016). "I am because we are": Exploring women's leadership under Ubuntu worldview. *Advances in Developing Human Resources, 18*(2), 223–242. https://doi.org/10.1177/1523422316641416t

Nnajiofor, O. G. (2016). Justification of the concept of time in Africa. *OGIRISI: A New Journal of African Studies, 12*(1), 253–281. http://dx.doi.org/10.4314/og.v12is1.16

Nyang, S. (1980). Reflections on traditional African cosmology. *New Directions, 8*(1), 28–32. https://dh.howard.edu/newdirections/vol18/iss1/8

Ojo, T., & Olomu, D. (2022). *Leading through African Ubuntu*. Infomediaworks Ltd.

Paris, P. J. (1995). *The Spirituality of African Peoples: The Search for a Common Moral Discourse*. Fortress Press.

Pasteur, A. B., & Toldson, I. L. (1982). *Roots of Soul: The Psychology of Black Expressiveness*. Anchor Press/Doubleday.

Richards, D. (1981). Let the circle be unbroken: The implications of African-American spirituality. *Présence Africaine, 117/118*(1), 247–292. https://doi.org/10.3917/presa.117.0247

Schiele, J. H. (1996). Afrocentricity: An emerging paradigm in social work practice. *Social Work, 41*(3), 284–294. https://doi.org/10.1093/sw/41.3.284

Senghor, L. S. (1971). *The Foundations of "Africanité,"* (Mercer Cook, Trans.). Présence Africaine.

Setiloane, G. (1986). *African Theology: An Introduction*. Skotaville Publishers.
Sulamayo, D. (2010). "I am because we are": Ubuntu as a cultural strategy of OD and change. *Organization Development Journal*, *4*(28), 41–51.
Tourish, D., & Tourish, N. (2010). Spirituality at work, and its implications for leadership and followership: A post-structuralist perspective. *Leadership*, *6*(2), 207–224. https://doi.org/10.1177/1742715010363210
Tutu, D. (1999). *No Future without Forgiveness*. Doubleday.
Uhl-Bien, M. (2006). Relational leadership theory: Exploring the social processes of leadership and organizing. *Leadership Quarterly*, *17*(6), 654–676. https://doi.org/10.1016/j.leaqua.2006.10.007
Viriri, A., & Mungwini, P. (2010). African cosmology and the duality of Western hegemony: The search for an African identity. *The Journal of Pan African Studies*, *3*(6), 27–42.

8

ACTIVISM, PERFORMANCE, AND SPIRITUAL RITUAL

Honoring the Indigenous Roots of Embodied Leadership and Social Change

Lynn M. Horan

Introduction

In the bustling Andean community of Huánuco, Peru, enveloped by a ridge of majestic mountains and the rushing current of the Huallaga River, a huddled mass of no more than 50 people gathered by candlelight at dusk in the *Plaza de Santa Domingo*. The thin wavering flames reflected off the aluminum storefronts, now closed for the day, that surrounded the small courtyard. The decaying façade of a colonial church presided over the small gathering of people, who were at once prayerful and desperate. Those present had come to honor and mourn the children and families who had been affected by sexual violence in their community. The candlelight vigil was an act of remembrance and healing just as it was a call for justice. There was a deeply spiritual quality to the gathering, a soul-level engagement felt through the unintelligible moans of despair and muffled prayers in both Spanish and Quechuan, in which Indigenous, Christian, and non-religious spiritual sensibilities intermingled in a common need for wholeness (For an analysis of the transformational capacity of oneness and interbeing, see Chapter 3).

Bowed heads suddenly lifted with alertness, transfixed by the choreographed movements taking place before them. Four figures entered the public space, sharing the same stretch of cracked cement as those observing. The figures carefully lowered themselves to the ground, each covered with a tattered potato sack. An eerie religious aria played from a dusty stereo as the four heaps of tangled bodies came to utter stillness. One of the figures began to make subtle shifts beneath the sackcloth. He slowly emerged out

DOI: 10.4324/9781003396741-11

of the tattered bag, leaving the remains behind like a discarded cocoon. Dressed in rags, each figure rose from the rubble to re-enact an image of violence and abuse. With dirt-smeared faces and limbs, the figures slowly crawled back into their own crumpled covering. As the four bodies returned to stillness, they revealed a chilly resemblance to lifeless body bags waiting in a darkened morgue.

The tone suddenly changed as four other figures dressed in white entered the space, each carrying a candle and a cardboard placard with an inscribed name. The first name was "Yuri," an eight-year-old girl who was raped and murdered by the owners of a local dance club. Another card read "Lilia," an adolescent survivor of incest who was raising her infant son at a nearby dairy farm, safely removed from abusive relatives. The cards were placed in front of the covered bodies, before the cluster of deeply moved observers. After a lengthy pause, the seemingly lifeless figures emerged from the bags in unison, somehow transformed. Each kneeled reverently before the written name, with head hung low, honoring each victim or survivor. While this transition to repentance may seem oversimplified, there was a visible change in the demeanor of the perpetrator, the violator, and the aggressor. In the minds of some observers, the performance might have appeared to be an idealized resolution to a painful and ongoing reality. Yet, for those present, a cathartic exhale seemed to have taken place at a deeply existential level, which created a new space in which to metabolize paralyzing grief into communal power and action. It was clear that something revelatory had happened, a visceral awareness within a newly mobilized community where spiritual ritual, public performance, and activism had galvanized a broken community through embodied social change.

I open with this vignette in order to illustrate the multiple layers of human interaction involved within this act of embodied social change including activism, performance, and spiritual ritual. These elements have often been compartmentalized into discrete categories within Western social science research (Wong & Clammer, 2017). However, the *acto symbolico* in Huánuco reflected Indigenous and non-Western approaches to embodied social change, in which there is continuity between performance, spiritual ritual, and activism. In her exploration of the socio-cultural impact of Peruvian folkloric dance, Mendoza (2000) pointed out that anthropological study of cultural ritual and performance has inaccurately assumed that such acts are "essentially an unchanging conservative force and a redressive mechanism of the "order' of society" (p. 31). As the above-described acto symbolico illustrates, there is a much more complex and integrative process at play that is not merely a "reenactment of a preexisting script," but a means of radical and discursive social change that challenges prevailing norms, beliefs, and practices (Fabian, 1990, p. 13).

The following discussion seeks to highlight the multi-dimensional nature of embodied social change as a means of grassroots and spiritually-oriented leadership, grounded in non-Western and decolonizing practices. This discussion applies a non-binary approach to questions of healing and wholeness within individuals and communities by asking how communities heal and reconcile amidst diverse spiritual understandings, while simultaneously challenging oppressive social structures. A core objective is to destabilize any assumed "newness" to this line of inquiry and instead firmly acknowledge the already existing landscapes of embodied spirituality and social change within Indigenous and non-Western leadership models. As these embodied approaches emerge within Western academic and therapeutic fields, there is an opportunity for meaningful cross-pollination between incorporated (embodied) and inscribed (cognitive) epistemologies, which together point to an evolving era of embodied spiritual leadership and social change.

Social Context and Author Positionality

Despite its idyllic surroundings, Huánuco is an under-resourced community in Central Peru, with the majority of its residents struggling to survive well below the poverty line (Valdivia, 2021). This reality is exacerbated by the fact that the larger department of Huánuco holds the highest rate of child sexual abuse in Peru (Valdivia, 2021). Based on these extreme levels of economic deprivation and social turmoil, the performance at the Plaza de Santa Domingo could have easily passed unnoticed. However, the student organizers, supported by the faith-based human rights organization Paz y Esperanza (Peace and Hope International), were aware of the importance of recording their act of resistance, protest, and healing. As a result, the performance was documented by a team of photographers, filmmakers, and journalists, in order to inform local newspapers, alert legal authorities, and galvanize the support of local and international human rights organizations around the issue of child sexual abuse.

My engagement with embodied social change in Huánuco was not in the capacity of a researcher, but as an American volunteer working with Paz y Esperanza, from 2008 to 2009. My work was financially supported by the Young Adult Volunteer program through the Presbyterian Church (United States), which prioritized local spirituality and leadership practices in a conscious departure from Western hegemonic notions of colonizing missionary work. Paz y Esperanza staff is comprised of local lawyers, psychologists, and spiritual leaders who together address the systemic socio-religious issues related to domestic violence and child sexual abuse. As I entered this community, I approached my work with a posture of humility through the process of "becoming, unlearning, and relearning" (Datta, 2018, p. 2), which enabled my purpose to evolve organically based on the needs of the local community, rather than maintaining pre-conceived notions of my own expertise and agency. Formal research was never part of my work or identity, which enabled my integration within the community and reinforced the process of decolonization. Drawing upon the work of Indigenous scholars Denzin et al. (2008), Datta (2018) defined decolonization as "a continuous process of anti-colonial struggle that honors Indigenous approaches to knowing the world, recognizing Indigenous land, Indigenous peoples, and Indigenous sovereignty–including sovereignty over the decolonization process" (p. 2). If my work with Paz y Esperanza had been in the form of data collection and analysis, conscious and unconscious power differentials would have presented significant ethical issues related to Indigenous sovereignty, as well as barriers to upholding the knowledge, agency, and dignity of individual participants.

After an initial period of observation and relationship-building, it became evident that my background in creative movement and dance met a critical need within a support group of survivors of child sexual abuse. This led to my primary work as a creative arts therapist specializing in embodied expression as a means to therapeutic self-discovery and intrinsic human worth. Beyond my work as a movement-based therapist, the most observable aspects of identity pointed to my race and economic status as a White, well-resourced foreigner. My privileged social status was evident in my ability to leave my previous career as a legislative policy analyst, forgo consistent income for a year, travel from the United States to Peru, offer fair payment for room and board with a local host family, and allow myself a monthly stipend from my previously raised funds. My identity as a White foreigner was generally accepted within the work community of Paz y Esperanza, due to its ongoing partnership with American and European volunteers. However, my physical presence was often viewed with suspicion and at times fear among the local Indigenous population, whose long history of oppression at the hands of colonial powers continues to leave a mark of deep distrust of White foreigners. I deferred to my Peruvian colleagues as to whether I would be welcomed during our community outreach efforts, and at times was asked to remain at the Huánuco office. At each level of engagement, I continually placed my trust in my Peruvian collogues to determine when my presence was of value or a hindrance. I am grateful for the many spaces in which I was invited to be present, including homes, hospital rooms, churches, classrooms, community-building and advocacy events, police departments, and prisons. I never took for granted the opportunity to be included, even as an obvious outsider, in this deeply sacred and essential work of human rights advocacy and embodied social change.

Embodied Expression as a Form of Social Change

It is difficult to categorize a symbolic act, such as the one performed on the streets of Huánuco, Peru. Is it theater or dance? Social activism, protest, or public education? Liturgy, ceremony, or ritual? One cannot easily label such a complex work of physical, psychological, spiritual, and cultural expression. The performers themselves could have been dancers, actors, clergy, teachers, or others who might be accustomed to symbolic presentation in the public sphere. Yet, unbeknownst to the majority of the observers, the performers who presented the acto symbolico in Huánuco were psychology students from a local university. They created various works of public performance art to demonstrate the effects of sexual violence in their community. Their embodied approach to consciousness-raising had the unique ability to integrate the often-separate Indigenous Quechua and Spanish-speaking communities of Huánuco around the common purpose of upholding human dignity and addressing the prevalence of widespread child sexual abuse. This multi-layered practice of embodied leadership and social change reveals the potential to integrate diverse cultural and linguistic communities through symbolic physical movement in a way that addresses the painful injustices of daily life.

Whether embodied social change takes place on the streets, in the academy, within places of communal worship, or in a clinical therapy setting, meaning can be found in and through the body in ways that offer transformation and healing within the individual and the larger community. Embodied social change is a lived approach that resists the one-dimensionality of feel-good spirituality and the limited scope of exclusively policy-oriented human rights activism. Instead, embodied social change prioritizes the integration of self and community, body and spirit, trauma and transformation, in ways that promote wholeness and restoration to broken and severed communities. It is an integrative approach that challenges dualistic approaches to healing and wholeness, which situate mind, body, and spirit as discrete categories. Instead, embodied social change is enacted at the intersection of activism, performance, and spirituality, in which the relationship between self, community, performer, observer, and existential meaning are intertwined, as shown in Figure 8.1. Embodied social change invites individuals and communities into a place of healing and reconciliation amidst diverse spiritual understandings, while simultaneously challenging oppressive and colonizing social structures. Like the vigil's burning candles themselves, this work has the capacity to both soothe and restore the soul and at the same time create the flames of desire needed for change to occur.

The first challenge in exploring the nature of embodied social change is whether to categorize it at all. What was presented on the gritty concrete

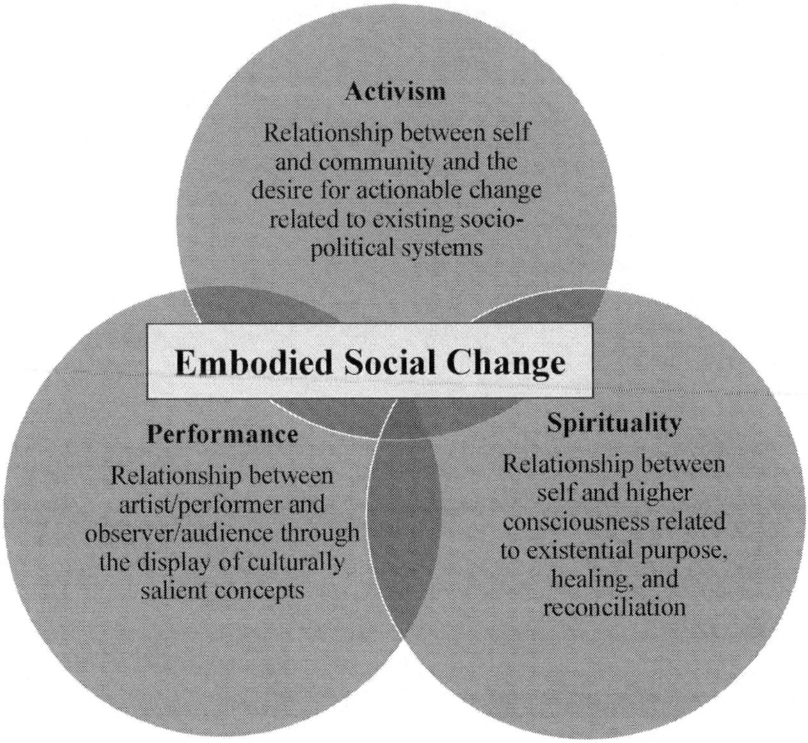

FIGURE 8.1 Elements of Embodied Social Change

of the Plaza de Santa Domingo was an intervention by individuals troubled by repeated abuses in their community, but what does this intervention mean? Rather than attempt to compartmentalize the event as a form of public protest, a spiritual act of remembrance, or an example of adaptive leadership (Heifetz et al., 2009), one must instead be open to the ineffability of embodied performance. Taylor (2003) defined performance as a "process, a praxis, an episteme, a mode of transmission, an accomplishment, and a means of intervening in the world" (p. 15). As Taylor noted, discourse around art and academia has been conditioned by the "unidirectionality of meaning-making and communication," which has prioritized written over embodied knowledge. Moreover, Taylor argued that this one-dimensional approach to interpreting our world is embedded with colonial practices in which a privileged "us" defines and critiques a disempowered "them" (p. 8). Performance studies aim to break down the reliance on distinct genres, which seek to organize and limit the intended effect of a given performance experience. By not limiting the embodied acts performed in Huánuco to one particular mode of expression, one can appreciate the multi-layered impact of embodied social change. Whether it was a spiritual ritual, an act of healing or memorial, a platform for public education, or a call to activism, the importance of this particular embodied performance was its ability to viscerally affect those who experienced it, leading to spiritual and actionable transformation within individuals as well as in the larger community.

The transformative space created by embodied social change contains elements of the "holding environment" of trauma-recovery and psychoanalytic therapy (Modell, 1976) and its more recent application within adaptive leadership (Heifetz et al., 2009). This liminal space enables a psychological context that is safe enough to tolerate the discomfort of productive conflict. The adaptive leadership framework seeks to equip stakeholders to tolerate a productive zone of disequilibrium, and strives for an "optimal range of distress within which the urgency in the system motivates people to engage in adaptive work" (p. 306–307). However, unlike the "pressure cooker" dynamics encouraged within adaptive leadership, embodied social change involves a deeply spiritual component, including contemplative and sacred rituals, which offer a deeper level of both stability and transformation. In the case of the acto symbolico in Huánuco, the corresponding candlelight vigil was equally, if not more, palpable than the elements of embodied performance and social activism. Therefore, embodied social change offers both a form of adaptive leadership grounded in artist-activist sensibilities, as well as integrating a highly-nuanced layer of sacred meaning-making, drawing predominantly from Indigenous and non-Western models of social change (For a detailed analysis of the inherent spirituality of adaptive leadership, see Chapter 2). It is this non-Western spiritual and existential context that makes embodied social change such a deeply transformational human endeavor.

In addition to the spiritually salient holding environment created by the symbolic act in Huánuco, the vigil also functioned as an act of collective remembrance and consciousness-raising. Tismaneanu and Iacob (2016) illustrated the interplay between the public use of history, the politics of memory, and the work of transitional justice, highlighting the fact that remembrance is not merely a private or spiritual endeavor but one that viscerally compels individuals and communities to act. In the case of the vigil in Huánuco, the act of remembrance was both a communal act of public resistance as well as a private space of spiritual grief and healing, with the lines between these categories blurred and integrated. In his research on how societies remember, Connerton (1989) addressed the bodily practices that enrich acts of remembrance and also make them possible. He described two forms of social practice that allow memory to be integrated into the body, which he denoted as *incorporating* and *inscribing* practice. Incorporating practice speaks to moment-by-moment bodily communication such as a smile or a handshake, which is limited to a physically prescribed time and place. Inscribing practice, on the other hand, is the capacity to store and retrieve information, through writing, film, libraries, and other forms of media. According to Connerton, "The transition from an oral culture to a literate culture is a transition from incorporating practices to inscribing practices" (p. 73). Whereas some may view this transition as an example of cultural progress, the prioritization of inscribed practices can ultimately devalue and marginalize incorporated or embodied expressions of knowledge, particularly within Indigenous and minoritized communities.

The tension between inscribed and incorporated knowledge highlights inequalities in various communities' capacity to preserve and pass down spiritual and transformative practices, within and beyond their particular community. Taylor (2003) was concerned about the inherent transience or "ephemerality" of embodied performance as she posited the question, "Whose memories, traditions, and claims to history disappear if performance practices lack the staying power to transmit vital knowledge?" Taylor was particularly interested in Indigenous and marginalized communities who may not have access to the means in which to inscribe their embodied practice. Without the opportunity to record in some way their embodied expressions, such individuals are denied the opportunity to make known their "memories, traditions, and claims to history" (p. 5) in a lasting way. As a result, communities that thrive on oral traditions and embodied practices of social change, yet who may have limited access to media technology and financial resourcing to preserve and/or inscribe their practices, face significant challenges in sustaining their embodied acts for future generations. If we consider the symbolic act on the streets of Huánuco, both the observers and performers represented the marginalized individuals that Taylor addressed in her research. As noted above, the artists, activists, and community members of Huánuco could not afford to let their acts of embodied social change go unnoticed and unrecorded and made every effort to inscribe the knowledge of their incorporated practice through various forms of media.

Cognitive versus Embodied Epistemologies in Western Academia

While incorporated (embodied) and inscribed (cognitive) knowledge were equally endorsed by the psychology professors and students at the Universidad de Huánuco, if one considers the Western academic sector, the dissemination of knowledge is predominantly through inscribed practices. With its emphasis on more cognitive epistemologies, the academic environment has the potential to undermine, neglect, and even reject knowledge and practices that are located within our distinct bodily experiences. In order to explore this phenomenon, Belenky et al. (1986) identified various forms of epistemology as expressed by 135 female students in the American colleges and universities where the authors taught. Through their research, the authors explored the sociology of knowledge production and differentiated between four epistemologies utilized by the student participants, including received knowledge, subjective knowledge, procedural knowledge, and constructed knowledge. What was challenging for many of the students interviewed was the extent to which their collegiate learning environments emphasized received and procedural knowledge, or the external "voice of reason" (p. 95), as opposed to more internal modes of epistemology based on embodied experience, and the intuitive or perhaps spiritual voice (For a thorough discussion on the importance of somatics and psychospiritual practices in knowledge development, see Chapter 13).

This more holistic and postmodernist understanding of the sociology of knowledge production has its roots in Paulo Freire's (1970) seminal work on decolonizing pedagogy, which argues for liberative education systems that prioritize the experiences, knowledge, and identities of oppressed peoples. As Ollis (2015) noted, Freire's approach to education resisted expressions of "naïve activism," in which reflection and practice are disconnected from action. Instead, Freire promoted an embodied pedagogy that "connected the importance of epistemology to emotions and action" (p. 522). As embodied epistemologies gain greater acceptance within Western academia, there is the opportunity for meaningful integration between incorporated (embodied) and inscribed (cognitive) approaches to leadership and social change. This non-dualistic and multi-layered approach was evident within the work of embodied social change on the streets of Huánuco, through the collaborative engagement between university students, social justice activists, and the surrounding community affected by the traumas of child sexual abuse.

Re-centering Indigenous Models of Embodied Social Change

Scholarship surrounding the theory and practice of embodied leadership and social change has recently emerged in a variety of contexts including business (Mansour, 2023), education (Schwartz, 2019), healthcare (Koya et al., 2017), and religious leadership (Shoop, 2010). However, as Western academic research and practice draw upon methodologies of embodied social change, it is important to underscore that this is not a new way of learning, knowing, and/or being. One must destabilize any sense of "newness" to this form of social engagement and instead honor the Indigenous roots, ancient practices, and deeply-held beliefs surrounding embodied knowledge and social change that are particularly present in Indigenous and historically marginalized communities. Any exploration of embodied social change and its accompanying research must firmly acknowledge its already existing landscapes within

Indigenous and non-Western models of social change (for a discussion on non-hierarchical leadership within pre-colonial cultures, see Chapter 6). As Lorde (2017) urged in her seminal piece *The Master's Tools Will Never Dismantle the Master's House,* we must "become more in touch with our ancient, non-European consciousness of living as a situation to be experienced and interacted with... [and] to respect those hidden sources of our power from where true knowledge, and therefore, lasting action comes" (p. 2).

While the practice of embodied social change has been active in Indigenous communities for centuries, its formal exploration within the context of Western academic and leadership studies has only recently emerged through the field of embodied leadership. Ladkin (2012) outlined this trajectory in leadership studies noting, "From the end of the 1990s to the present, a growing shift can be seen in the leadership literature away from predominantly cognitively-based accounts to those which recognize the emotional, affective, and aesthetic aspects of leadership" (p. 1). Through this lens, focus is placed on the interactions between sensing and perceiving bodies in the context of leadership and social change. Sinclair (2005) noted that historically there has been a tendency for "bodies to disappear under the weight of theorizing" (p. 387), which has led to an overall lack of scholarship on embodied social change until recently. Referred to by Sheets-Johnstone (2009) as the "corporeal turn," the expanding scholarship around embodiment and the role it plays in learning, cognition, and perception is a "matter of not only attending to something heretofore simply assumed and largely ignored, but of correcting something misrepresented for centuries" (p. 2).

By addressing the Cartesian legacy of Western epistemologies, theologies, and social practices, which prioritize the mind as the center of cognition and reason, approaches to embodied leadership and social change offer the opportunity to draw upon Indigenous models of leadership and spirituality as well as embodied resistance and resilience among marginalized communities. Overall, Indigenous spirituality is a more embodied practice than Western religion and philosophy. However, such embodied practices, traditions, and epistemological vantage points have been historically suppressed due to the Cartesian belief in the "hyperseparation of knower from the known and subject from the object, leaving the free-flowing 'understanding' ideally uncontaminated by bodily particulars of sensation or emotion" (Hawkins, 1998, p. 162). Embodied leadership practices appear to emerge from communities of resistance and resilience, whereas more disembodied leadership approaches are central to communities of power and privilege. Communities that have experienced significant racial, gender, and/or economic oppression have not had the luxury of dissociating themselves from their corporeal experiences, as one's own body is the target of such oppressive structures as slavery, discrimination, and abuse. In light of these oppressive regimes and histories, embodied leadership practices have become even more essential to the survival, resistance, and resilience among oppressed and marginalized populations.

Drawing upon the work of Bessel van der Kolk (2014), psychologist and cultural somatics educator Resmaa Menakem (2017) noted, "Contrary to what many people believe, trauma is not primarily an emotional response. Trauma always happens *in the body*... a wordless story our body tells itself about what is safe and what is a threat" (pp. 7–8, emphasis in original). As Menakem revealed, the primary catalyst for such lack of safety and its manifestation within the body is the widespread phenomenon of White-body supremacy. Menakem noted, "We've tried to teach our brains to think better about race. But White-body supremacy doesn't live in our thinking brains. It lives and breathes in our bodies" (p. 5). This is reinforced by Yancy (2018) and his work on Black embodied wounds, in which he argued that the experience of trauma points to the connectedness between bodies as opposed to a "metaphysics of enclosure" in which human beings are considered separate and distinct entities (p. 142). The phenomenon whereby racial supremacy has been viscerally justified within White bodies and racial oppression viscerally absorbed in non-White bodies is precisely why embodied leadership practices are so essential to the sustainability and survival of Indigenous and minoritized communities.

Approaches to embodied social change that recognize and incorporate our living, moving bodies, offer a pathway for individuals and communities to return to a sense of safety, equilibrium, and sustainability when such wholeness is threatened or compromised. In her research on physical movement and resilience, McGonigal (2019) noted,

> Physical activity helps us tap into instincts that have allowed humans to survive for millennia: the abilities to persist, cooperate, and form communities of mutual support, to invest in the future, overcome obstacles, and endure hardships; to defend and protect the vulnerable, to sense ourselves connected to other people and the world we live in.
>
> *(p. 213)*

This research is reinforced by the development of polyvagal theory, which posits that the neurological capacity for humans to move from a sympathetic state of fight, flight, or freeze (i.e., disconnection) to a parasympathetic state of rest and digest (i.e., connection and integration), requires conscious physical awareness and movement (Dana, 2018). Known as the "science of safety," polyvagal theory reinforces the importance of embodied social change as it situates our physical being and embodied knowing at the center of our ability to problem solve, develop connections, and ultimately heal from trauma and discord in our individual lives and communities. This newly outlined neurochemistry of resilience offers important scientific justification for long-held practices of embodied leadership and social change within Indigenous and marginalized communities.

Examples of Indigenous Models of Embodied Social Change

Current leadership scholarship often presents embodied leadership as an emerging field, and while it may be new within the context of formal Western academic literature, it is certainly not a new phenomenon within the course of human experience. Instead, embodied leadership and social change is a deeply engrained practice prevalent in Indigenous communities, where it is both endemic to certain Indigenous world views and spirituality, and also a proactive response to colonialism and its imposition of disembodied practices of leadership, power, and oppression. Spirituality is an essential component of embodied social change as it points to the process of individual and communal transformation. Penman (2021) noted that encounters with the sacred involve a change in both vertical relationships (self and higher power) and horizontal relationships (self and other). It is this multi-dimensional dynamic of spirituality, involving self, community, and higher consciousness, that enables human beings to extend meaning "beyond the limits of ordinary experiences" (p. 4085). This spiritual awareness provides the foundation for the following examples of Indigenous models of embodied social change, each of which reflects a highly nuanced and sophisticated approach to community-based and spiritually-engaged leadership.

Aztec Curanderismo

In her research and personal experience of the Aztec healing arts of *curanderismo,* Avila (1999) identified several components of the Indigenous roots and development of embodied social change in contrast to colonial practices of conquest and control. Practiced throughout various Indigenous regions of Mexico, curanderismo involves distinctly embodied practices in which the emotional, physical, mental, and spiritual are involved in the healing process. As Avila noted, "There is no separation between the nature of humans and their environments. In curanderismo, the healing takes place under one roof, with earth as the foundation and God as the source" (p. 17). Despite its widespread practice throughout Mexico, Avila observed a lack of formal research and academic attention, noting "In curanderismo, it is taught that insight is strengthened by climbing the mountain of one's own humility… The curandera is not a vehement seeker of limelight, but rather in solitude, in [their] own community bounded by the heart" (p.12). Similarly, Joyce (2011) described curanderismo as "a spiritual orientation that supports a deeper and more direct connection to the earth and Indigenous traditions of healing; to the spiritual values of humility, loving-kindness, and service; and to an embodied knowledge of spiritual realities" (p. ix). Both Joyce's (2011) and Avila's (1999) research sought to protect the intentionally private practice of curanderismo, yet at the same time included it within the realm of formal academic inquiry, thereby expanding its exposure as a methodology of embodied social change and healing relevant to other cultures and leadership practices.

The exploration of Aztec curanderismo is an important lens through which one is able to see both the Indigenous development of embodied social change as well as its response to the imposition of colonial power. Avila (1999) noted that curanderismo is the confluence of three cultural lineages of holistic healing arts including Aztec *Wewepahtli* (Greatest Medicine), traditional Spanish medicine, and African healing modalities. Racial integration throughout Latin America resulted in a layered approach to spirituality and healing, "a system that was deeply rooted in practical observation, in the thousand-year-old traditions of three continents, and in the personal style, creativity, intuition, and spiritual strength of the healer" (p. 16). Therefore, it is evident that the embodied practices of curanderismo are a combination of local Indigenous practices as well as interactions with other marginalized communities devastated by oppressive colonial regimes. Avila noted that curanderismo did not develop out of a purely symbiotic relationship between these three cultural identities. To the contrary, Avila stated, "There was a need to develop a medicine that could heal the pain and the immense *susto*, [or] soul loss, that resulted from the cultural destruction, enslavement, and rape that occurred during the Spanish conquest of the Americas" (p. 28). Ortiz et al. (2008) described further how the use of spiritual ritual within curanderismo enables the patient to "integrate the meaning of the loss of her soul," as well as the traumatizing event(s) into one's own personal narrative (p. 287). Much like the spiritual ritual embedded within the acto symbolico in Huánuco, the transcendent capacity of curanderismo does not seek to erase or minimize the trauma, but empowers survivors to proactively engage in their own healing process.

Cross-Cultural Shamanism

Like Aztec curanderismo, cross-cultural shamanism involves the interplay of ancient embodied healing practices, which can provide the foundation for contemporary examples of embodied social change. As Waddock (2016) noted, "It is the shaman's capacity for breaking down boundaries and seeing things holistically, or at least from a different perspective than usual, that makes the leader's work as shaman particularly crucial today" (pp. 58–59). Waddock lifts up shamanism as an important metaphor for contemporary leadership and social change, by emphasizing healing, connecting, and sensemaking within both corporate and communal contexts. However, it is important that Western leadership scholars do not idealize, romanticize or oversimplify the shamanic tradition, as it too has reflected prevailing gender inequalities within its own historical and social contexts. In her research on reclaiming the feminine in religion and healing practices, Tedlock (2005) observed the historical centrality of women in medicine and spiritual leadership, and the systematic shift toward male-dominated leadership in such fields. In her research, Tedlock uncovered the original primacy of the embodied leadership of female shamans, noting that overarching sexism within shamanic communities led to the erasure of female embodied leadership. An archeological discovery led by Bohuslav Klima in 1952 in the Pavlov Hills of the Czech Republic revealed a sixty-thousand-year-old burial site of the oldest skeletal remains of a shaman. The fact that the remains were of a woman immediately shifted the exclusive male focus of shamanic leadership within prior research. As Tedlock (2005) argued, research on shamanism and other embodied modalities must involve a careful exploration of biographies and ethnographic depictions of female leaders, as well as new field research that uncovers what has been systematically diminished by prevailing research interests. The widespread silencing of female shamans in both practice and research reinforces the importance of embodied practices of social change in acts of resistance and resilience amid not only racial and political oppression, but also gender oppression.

North American Indigenous and African-American Perspectives

In order to recover the early understandings of embodied social change, important insights can be drawn from Indigenous leadership models in North America and New Zealand. For example, Gutiérrez (2012) highlighted Indigenous models of embodied social change and spiritual activism from across the United States that are at the "forefront of transforming the culture of social justice leadership" (p. 108). She described her own evolving consciousness as an Indigenous being and leader noting, "I recognize that all moments are connected together and influence how we see, hear, and feel the moments that reveal our self-truths and capacity for growing" (p. 109). Gutiérrez co-designed and co-facilitated an important leadership convention titled "Spiritual activism: Claiming the power and ideology of a liberation spirituality," held in 2005 at the

Garrison Institute, a Capuchin monastery now used for non-sectarian gatherings in upstate New York. The purpose statement of the gathering reveals a deeply intentional model of embodied social change that challenges Westerns concepts of male leader-centric, disembodied models of social change:

> We are moving towards a doing that grows more deliberately out of being: an understanding that freedom from external systems of oppression is dynamically related to liberation from our internal mechanisms of suffering… instead of being limited by the reactions of fight or flight, we encounter a path that finds fullness in presence… We recognize the pervasive beauty of paradox, the dynamic tension between two simultaneous truths that seem contradictory. We enlarge our capacity to hold contradictions and to be informed by them. And our movements for change are transformed as a result.
>
> *(pp. 109–110)*

This description of liberative spirituality involves a deeply embodied approach as evidenced by the prioritization of being over doing as the primary catalyst for change, as well as the desire to address "internal mechanisms of suffering" (p. 110) alongside the external systems of oppression which cause such suffering. Within this Indigenous leadership context, the process of addressing unhealed trauma becomes a core aspect of embodied social change.

Gutiérrez's perspective resonates with the work of Menakem (2017), who described the impact of unhealed trauma as it is passed down through generations noting:

> Unhealed trauma acts like a rock thrown into a pond; it causes ripples that move outward, affecting many other bodies over time… if it gets transmitted and compounded through multiple families and generations, it can start to look like culture.
>
> *(p. 39)*

Menakem described this traumatic retention through the lived experiences of Black Americans, including his own encounters with the generational impact of slavery through the lived experiences of his grandmother. The kind of liberative spirituality that Gutiérrez described within Indigenous consciousness reflects the embodied consciousness that Menakem promoted in order to liberate Black- and Brown-skinned bodies from the generational impact of White-body supremacy. These liberative leadership models integrate lived corporeal experiences as the basis of leadership development and practices of social change.

Māori Embodied Performance in New Zealand

Fraser (2012) offered additional insights into the embodied emphasis of Indigenous leadership as she described the importance of *Kapa haka* (performing groups) within Māori culture of New Zealand. Female elders and grandmothers often guide the Haka groups, incorporating stories, histories, and instruction of social responsibility into dance and song. Historical knowledge, including experiences of oppression and colonial violence, are passed down to younger generations as the performers "tell and relive stories through [their] entire body" (p. 123). The representation of these experiences involves a wide range of emotions including "aggressive display [of] the abhorrent treatment of the Maori by the Crown," or tearful representations of an ancestors' passing" (p. 122). Fraser also noted the importance of not restricting this kind of embodied leadership and education to the *marae,* or communal meeting space, which highlights the importance of school teachers and tutors trained in Kapa haka practices. By bringing these embodied leadership practices into everyday life, Fraser noted that this gives access to embodied leadership spaces for all community members, in particular, Māori women.

Embodied Cultural Capital in Samoan Leadership

In his ethnographic research on Samoan leadership, Peterson (2018) built a theoretical context for the importance of Indigenous models of embodied leadership rooted in postcolonial thinking. He drew upon the work of French sociologist Pierre Bourdieu (1977) as it relates to cultural capital, or the non-economic bonds of social and familial groups, which reflect one's relational power in society. Bourdieu described cultural capital in three different states: the embodied state, the objectified state, and the institutionalized state. For Bourdieu, both objectified and institutionalized cultural capital serve to maximize an individual's positional power and social status, through the acquisition of specific skills, credentials, and formal education. Embodied cultural capital, on the other hand, involves the individual participating in the meaning-making process of their social context, thereby ensuring a more co-creative process of building one's understanding of reality. The development of embodied cultural capital is a foundational element of Indigenous models of embodied social change, in contrast to the objectified and institutionalized forms of cultural capital historically utilized by Western and industrialized leadership and social change practices. Through this research, Peterson sought to highlight the embodied cultural capital of Indigenous models of social change, which can be transferred to other contexts in an effort to decolonize more capitalistic leadership structures.

Indigenous Folkloric Dance in Peru

The above examples of Indigenous models of embodied social change highlight and support the powerful work with which I was engaged in Huánuco, Peru. The acto symbolico and candlelight vigil for victims and survivors of child sexual abuse resonated with the gathered community because an ethos of embodied social change was already deeply embedded within Indigenous cultural self-understanding. Similarly, my work as a creative movement therapist with young survivors was generally embraced by both the participants and Pay y Esperanza staff, because it resonated with an already existing epistemological framework that situated notions of cultural identity and agency within the embodied practice of movement and dance. This proclivity toward embodied social change through movement and dance is illustrated by the widespread practice of Indigenous folkloric dance throughout Peru. Each regional *danza folklorica* is a "major vehicle through which its members [can] locally explore, create, and/or reshape relevant categories of their everyday lives" (Mendoza, 2000, p. 34). With this already existing multi-layered use of embodied expression as a form of spiritual ritual, activism, and performance, it seems there is nothing unique or surprising about the acto symbolico that served to mobilize the Huánuco community around the human rights issue of child sexual abuse. It was entirely consistent with and derivative of long-held practices of embodied social change evident within Quechuan history, culture, and communal meaning-making.

Conclusion

Embodied social change is not a new phenomenon, despite its recent emergence within Western religious and academic communities who inaccurately identify these practices as ground-breaking or cutting-edge. Instead, this multi-faceted approach to communal transformation and holistic healing is grounded in the ancient beliefs and practices of Indigenous and socially-marginalized communities, who continue to integrate spiritual ritual, social activism, and public performance in order to interpret and respond to the needs of their communities. As illustrated above, such embodied approaches to social change are expressed within Aztec curanderismo and cross-cultural shamanism, with their ability to integrate the physical and spiritual realms, as well as the liberative action-oriented social change promoted within Native American, Samoan, and African-American communities. Alongside these spiritual and activist components of embodied social change, is the communal engagement of public performance, illustrated by the embodied story-telling of Māori of New Zealand and Indigenous folkloric dance throughout Peru. While these examples are just a few of the many expressions of embodied social change within both ancient and contemporary practice, each reflects the integration of spiritual ritual, activism, and public performance, which are the basis for embodied social change.

If we recall the candlelight vigil on the streets of Huánuco, what was so apparent within this acto symbolico was its expression of *enstasis,* literally "standing within," in which healing is found within and not apart from the body. Rather than strive for a state of transcendence or *ecstasis* in which those present were transported or elevated beyond their corporeal experiences of grief and mourning, this embodied performance infused a sense of incarnational (in-the-flesh) humanity amidst the brutal realities of this particular community. Rather than utilize merely technical skills of education, instruction, preaching, or protest, this experience was saturated with the metaskills that Mindell (1995) described, in which moods, feelings, and attitudes are in conversation with one another. By inviting the possibility for wholeness, through physical, emotional, psychological, and spiritual engagement, this embodied performance created the opportunity for greater visceral awareness and insight both on the part of the performers as well as the observers, creating a pathway for collective social change. Having demonstrated the profound impact of embodied social change on a dusty candlelit street in central Peru, this form of embodied knowledge and expression can provide significant possibilities for further transformation if applied to Western academic and leadership spaces.

Rather than identify embodied expression as ungrounded or unscientific, both academic and leadership sectors have an opportunity to recognize and embrace embodied epistemologies as a means through which we understand and reflect on the world around us. However, it is important that socially-conscious leaders and communities who implement forms of embodied social change, do so in ways that do not merely co-opt embodied practices that seem appealing, attractive, or trendy, without fully appreciating and understanding the vulnerabilities that exist when applying such practices. When incorporating elements of embodied social change, through spiritual ritual, activism, and/or public performance, one must be extremely conscious of the ways in which spiritual leadership can intentionally and unintentionally promote abuse, re-victimization, and manipulation of power dynamics (Purcell, 1998). With a posture of humility and a deep awareness of the needs and vulnerabilities of the surrounding community, the practice of embodied social change can be developed and nurtured in all areas of life, whether in the streets, schools, clinical therapy, or collective worship, as well as in a variety of corporate and grass-roots leadership spaces. As we find deeper awareness in and through our bodies within these various contexts, we have a greater ability to restore the broken aspects of ourselves as well as heal the wounds within our communities.

References

Avila, E. (1999). *Woman who glows in the dark: A curandera reveals traditional Aztec secrets of physical and spiritual health.* Tarcher and Putnam.

Belenky, M.F., Clinchy, B.M., Goldberger, N.R., & Tarule, J.M. (1986). *Women's ways of knowing: The development of self, voice and mind.* Basic Books.

Bourdieu, P. (1977). Cultural reproduction and social reproduction. In J. Karabel & A.H. Halsey (Eds.), *Power and ideology in education* (pp. 487–511). Oxford University Press.

Connerton, P. (1989). *How societies remember.* Cambridge University Press.

Dana, D. (2018). *The polyvagal theory in therapy: Engaging the rhythm of regulation.* W. W. Norton & Company. https://doi.org/10.1177/174701611773329

Datta, R. (2018). Decolonizing both researcher and research and its effectiveness in Indigenous research. *Research Ethics, 14*(2), 1–24.

Denzin, N.K., Lincoln, Y.S., & Smith, L.T. (Eds.). (2008). *Handbook of critical and Indigenous methodologies.* SAGE.

Fabian, J. (1990). *Power and performance: Ethnographic explorations through proverbial wisdom and theater in Shaba, Zaire.* The University of Wisconsin Press.

Fraser, T.N. (2012). The legacy of leadership: From grandmothers' stories to kapa haka. In Kenny, C., & Fraser, T.N. (Eds.), *Living indigenous leadership: Native narratives on building strong communities* (pp. 114–124). UBC Press.

Freire, P. (1970). *Pedagogy of the oppressed.* Penguin Classics.

Gutiérrez, R. (2012). Indigenous grandmas and the social justice movement. In Kenny, C., & Fraser, T.N (Eds.), *Living indigenous leadership: Native narratives on building strong communities* (pp. 97–113). UBC Press.

Hawkins, R.Z. (1998). Ecofeminism and nonhumans: Continuity, difference, dualism, and domination. *Hypatia, 13*(1), 158–197. https://doi.org/10.1111/j.1527-2001.1998.tb01356.x

Heifetz, R.A, Grashow, A., & Linsky, M. (2009). *The practice of adaptive leadership: Tools and tactics for changing your organization and the world.* Harvard Business Press.

Joyce, A. (2011) *The sixth sun: The spiritual path and practice of Mexican-American curanderismo* (Publication No. 3489676) [Doctoral dissertation, California Institute of Integral Studies] ProQuest Dissertations Publishing.

Koya, K., Anderson, J., & Sice, P. (2017). The embodied nurse: Interdisciplinary knowledge exchange between compassionate nursing and recent developments in embodied leadership studies. *Journal of Advanced Nursing, 73*(12), 3028–3040. https://doi.org/10.1111/jan.13363

Ladkin, D. (2012) Perception, reversibility, "flesh": Merleau-Ponty's phenomenology and leadership as embodied practice. *Integral Leadership Review, 12*(1), 1–13. https://doi.org/10.1177/17427150134858

Lorde, A. (2017). *The master's tools will never dismantle the master's house.* Penguin.

Mansour, R. (2023). *Cultivating embodied leadership: Why embodied leadership is a sustainable and empowering management style.* https://coachingfederation.org/blog/cultivating-embodied-leadership

Mendoza, Z.S. (2000). *Shaping society through dance: Mestizo ritual performance in the peruvian andes.* University of Chicago Press.

McGonigal, K. (2019). *The joy of movement: how exercise helps us find happiness, hope, connection, and courage.* Avery.

Menakem, R. (2017). *My grandmother's hands: Racialized trauma and the pathway to mending our hearts and bodies.* Central Recovery Press.

Mindell, A. (1995). *Metaskills: The spiritual art of therapy.* New Falcon.

Modell, A.H. (1976). "The holding environment" and the therapeutic action of psychoanalysis. *Journal of the American Psychoanalytic Association, 24*(2), 285–307. https://doi.org/10.1177/000306517602400202

Ollis, T. (2015). Activism, reflection, and Paulo Freire: An embodied pedagogy. *Counterpoints, 500*, 517–527.

Ortiz, F.A., Davis, K.G., & McNeill, B.W. (2008). Curanderismo: Religious and spiritual worldviews and indigenous healing traditions. In McNeill, B.W., & Cervantes, J.M. (Eds.), *Latina/o healing practices: Mestizo and indigenous perspectives* (pp. 271–300). Routledge/Taylor & Francis Group.

Penman, J. (2021). Cognitive and behavioral changes arising from spirituality. *Journal of Religion and Health, 60*(6), 4082–4096. https://doi.org/10.1007/s10943-021-01321-7

Peterson, L. (2018). *Uncovering indigenous models of leadership: An ethnographic case study of Samoa's Talavou clan.* Rowman.

Purcell, B.C. (1998). Spiritual abuse. *American Journal of Hospital Palliative Care, 15*(4), 227–231. https://doi.org/10.1177/104990919801500409

Schwartz, H.L. (2019). *Connected teaching: Relationship, power, and mattering in higher education.* Stylus Publishing, LLC.

Sheets-Johnstone, M. (2009). *The corporeal turn: An interdisciplinary reader.* Imprint Academic.

Shoop, M. (2010). *Let the bones dance: Embodiment and the body of Christ.* Westminster John Knox Press.

Sinclair, A. (2005). Body possibilities in leadership. *Leadership, 1*(4), 387–406.

Taylor, D. (2003). *The archive and the repertoire: Performing cultural memory in the Americas.* Duke University.

Tedlock, B. (2005). *The woman in the shaman's body: Reclaiming the feminine in religion and medicine.* Bantam.

Tismaneanu, V., & Iacob, B. (Eds.). (2016). *Remembrance, history, and justice: Coming to terms with traumatic pasts in democratic societies.* Central European University Press.

Valdivia, M.R.R. (2021) *Reinserciones de niñas, niños y adolescentes afectadas por el abuso sexual después de la salida del albergue casa del buen trato hovde de huánuco en el periodo 2010–2014.* (Publication No. 28449718) [Doctoral dissertation, Pontificia Universidad Catolica del Peru]. ProQuest Dissertations Publishing.

Van der Kolk, B.A. (2014). *The body keeps the score: Brain, mind, and body in the healing of trauma.* Penguin Publishing Group.

Waddock, S. (2016). Leaders as shamans working to heal a troubled world. *Journal of Management for Global Sustainability, 4*(1), 57–73. https://doi.org/10.13185/JM2016.04102

Wong, P., & Clammer, J. (2017). Performance and development: Theatre for social change. In: Clammer, J., & Giri, A. (Eds.), *The aesthetics of development.* Palgrave Macmillan. https://doi.org/10.1057/978-1-349-95248-9_14

Yancy, G. (2018). Black embodied wounds and the traumatic impact of the White imaginary. In Boynton, E., & & Capretto, P. (Eds.), *Trauma and transcendence: Suffering and the limits of theory* (pp. 142–162). Fordham University Press. https://doi.org/10.5422/fordham/9780823280261.003.0008

9

PERSPECTIVES ON SELF AND LEADERSHIP DEVELOPMENT FROM THE TRADITION OF SUFISM

S. Aqeel Tirmizi

Introduction

"I am the drop that contains the ocean" is a line from a poem by Yunus Emre, a Turkish Sufi (Helminski & Algan, 1989, p. 36). I share this verse from Emre to set the stage for this chapter in terms of how I understand Sufism given my positionality. My curiosity about Sufism is connected to both my professional and personal interests and background. My professional work as an academic includes a focus on pathways and approaches that facilitate well-being and happiness. The science of happiness recognizes the role of faith and spirituality in happiness and well-being. This correlation has intrigued me to consider linkages between spirituality and other organizational phenomena. And this intrigue is at the foundation of exploring the linkages between Sufism and leadership development. Personally, my spiritual practice is connected to ideas of Sufism as well. Over the years, this has also led to certain curiosities. For instance, the importance of humility within Sufi thinking has made me wonder about its relevance to authentic (Avolio & Gardner, 2005) and inclusive leadership (Korkmaz et al., 2022). In particular, the relational developmental dynamic between a Sufi as *murshed* (Sufi spiritual guide) and their followers has been a part of my emerging interest. Finally, the increasing interest in the works of the great Sufi Maulana Rumi, in the United States, and perhaps more globally as well, has made me wonder about the relevance of Sufi teachings in our contemporary lives.

With this background outlined above, this chapter addresses the question of how wisdom and insights inherent in the grand Sufi tradition may

DOI: 10.4324/9781003396741-12

inform leadership development. The chapter is divided into the following sections: (a) an introduction to the foundational ideas of Sufism; (b) a discussion of ideas and insights from Sufism that may relate to leadership development; and (c) some reflections and caveats related to using the revered and mystic tradition of Sufism for leadership development in contemporary settings.

A few considerations are important to note before proceeding with our discussion. Sufism, as a philosophy and practice, is full of rich history, sacred traditions, rituals, and complex doctrines that are not readily visible or understandable. Given the scope and thematic focus of this chapter, it is important to note that it will only provide a basic introduction to Sufism considering its epistemic depth and breadth. This grounding in epistemic humility extends to the main inquiry focus on the relevance of Sufi wisdom to leadership development. In other words, while the prospects that this inquiry offers are rich and intriguing, the relevant insights must be approached with a humble orientation. In that sense, it is also a caution against approaching the Sufi teachings and ways from a reductionist perspective.

Origins and Presence of Sufism

The roots of the term mysticism go back to the mystery cults of the Greeks. These cults included small groups of devotees who were thought to possess divine knowledge through revelation (Nizamie et al., 2013). Mysticism has been a part of numerous religious and spiritual traditions. It is present in prominent faith systems including Buddhism, Christianity, Judaism, and Islam. In the Islamic tradition, mysticism is primarily anchored in the Sufi tradition (Anjum, 2006) and its roots are traced all the way back to Prophet Muhammad, peace be upon him (PBUH), and his cousin and close follower Imam Ali Ibne Abi Talib. While numerous definitions are available to introduce the ideas of Sufism, I have chosen Küçük's (2008) language to introduce it. This choice was motivated by the need for brevity and concision given the limited scope of this chapter. Küçük notes that Sufism is a particular type of mysticism that originated in Islam. She explains that the essential tenets of Sufism:

> ...are that nothing really exists but God, that the human soul emanates from His essence, and though separated from its 'heavenly source' for a time when it is on this earth, it will finally be reunited with it, and the highest possible happiness will arise from this reunion.
>
> *(Küçük, p. 292)*

Interest in Sufism and Sufi practice remains relevant in different parts of the world including many Muslim countries. For instance, Saeed and

Batool (2021) conducted an empirical study to understand the spiritual and social experiences and practices of contemporary Sufis in Pakistan. These researchers engaged with Sufis representing different *silsilas* (spiritual genealogies) and their work demonstrates the continuing and widespread occurrence of Sufism in the fifth most populated country in the world. Khumidovich et al. (2021) traced a rich history and evolution of Sufism in the Northern Caucuses over the past several centuries. In their review of Sufi leaders and their movements in West Africa, Seesemann (2010) observed, "...Sufism articulated itself in a variety of ways over the past three centuries, and that it continues to be a formidable spiritual, intellectual, and social force in many countries in the Western parts of the African continent" (p. 606). The presence and interest in Sufism is not limited to the Muslim world. Rawlinson (2009) observed how Sufism is taking root in the West. He argued this Western Sufism has innovatively borrowed from multiple Eastern traditions and developed a view of the human condition that may be synthesized into the following principles (Rawlinson, 2009, p. 37):

- human beings are best understood in terms of consciousness and its modification,
- consciousness can be transformed by spiritual practice,
- there are gurus/masters/teachers who have done this,
- and they can help others to do the same by some form of transmission.

Küçük (2008) provided an important overview of Sufi leaders and different Sufi schools and movements in the West over the last century. She concluded this review with an important reminder:

> Western Sufis do not always emphasize their relationship to Islam, Sufism can still be considered as the 'beautiful face of Islam' in the West; peaceful, tolerant, and culturally adaptive. So, we see in Western Sufism a situation which can be called eclecticism and appropriation, or adaptation.
>
> *(p. 316)*

Sufi Doctrines

With a rich history of traditions spanning over fourteen centuries, Sufism teachings, philosophy, and practices have developed an extensive set of principles and guidelines. In this section, I have attempted to provide a short introduction to what are considered key Sufi doctrines. As noted above, it is simply not possible to convey all the wealth of wisdom and details about the themes being explored here in relation to Sufism. The purpose is to provide a glimpse into the complex world of Sufism, its beauty, and its relevance in a somewhat accessible and useful fashion. Whereas some of the ideas anchored in the Sufi doctrines and ways may not be directly relevant to contemporary organizational practices, it is nonetheless important to briefly share them here to provide a meaningful introduction.

Anjum (2006) provided the following summary of the key doctrines of Sufism. The concept of *hikmat* or gnosis consists of intuitive knowledge or esoteric knowledge. It may be understood as a spiritual vehicle to comprehend God. The author goes on to compare this inner knowledge with exoteric knowledge gained through and connected with logic and the senses. Thus, esoteric knowledge is concerned with inner meaning and exoteric knowledge relates more to outer meaning. For instance, collective faith-based rituals, which are public in nature are anchored around exoteric dimensions of one's faith. Whereas esoteric knowledge is connected to individual prayer, inner meaning, and deeper levels of consciousness. The doctrine of *fana* (annihilation of the self) emphasizes the abolition of self-will and self-consciousness. In other words, in pursuance of one's spirituality and devotion, the separation between the self and the other blurs. The concept of fana may be understood in relation to the doctrine of *baqa* (permanence). In pursuing fana, a Sufi hopes to experience renewal through devotion to God. Thus, the doctrine of baqa denotes permanence or a stage when one is immersed in the attributes of the Real and achieves a vision of God himself. Some Sufi schools consider fana and baqa as different progressive stages or stations in terms of spiritual development (Murata, 2011). The annihilation of self is not the end of the journey or the absence of self-awareness in this developmental process. Murata (2011) goes on to observe that the highest stage of closeness toward God consists of maintaining self-awareness and at the same time being aware of Divine presence. Returning to Anjum's summary of Sufi doctrines, the doctrine of *tawhid* (oneness) articulates that God is unique, incomparable, and eternal. Tawhid is the most significant doctrine within Sufism and Islam. One of the additional doctrines Sufism emphasizes is called *Faqr* and it focuses on simplicity and voluntary poverty. It is concerned with the refutation of worldly pleasures and material attachments.

The Sufi Way–Tareeqa

Bilqies (2014) observed that "Tariqah literally means the path in the desert that the Bedouin would follow to travel from oasis to oasis" (p. 66) and it focuses on the inner practices of Sufism. Sufi *tareeqa* or pathway may be understood in two different but related ways according to Encyclopedia Britannica (n.d.). Firstly, until the 11th century, tareeqa was primarily the spiritual path or way of individual Sufis. Secondly, as Sufism grew and disciples committed to associating themselves with particular Sufis, these Sufis' tareeqas developed into ritualistic systems and various Sufi orders began to emerge around these systems (Encyclopedia Britannica, n.d.). In that sense tareeqa is both the individual way a Sufi may follow, and it also represents different Sufi orders that disciples may adhere to. Begum and Awan (2015) summarize the prominent Sufi orders as *Suhrawardiyya*, named after Shihab Al-Din Suhrawardi, *Qadiriyya* is associated with a famous Sufi known as Abdul Qadir al-Jilani, *Chishtiyya* is associated with Moinuddin Chishti, *Mawlawiyya*—a Turkish order which took prominence following the fame of Jalaluddin Rumi, and *Naqshabandiyya* is associated with Shah Baha Al-Din Naqshband.

According to Nizamie et al. (2013), the Sufi tareeqa consists of three stages–the stage of stations (*maqamat*), the stage of states (*ahwal*), and finally the stage of achievement (*tamkin*). The first stage symbolizes the Sufi's efforts toward God and is gained through self-discipline and self-denial. These efforts entail going through the stations of repentance *(tawba)*, piety (*zuhd*), trust in God (*tawwakul)*, poverty (faqr*)*, remembrance of God (*zikr*), patience *(sabr),* thankfulness (*shukr)*, and contentment (*rida*) to reach the ultimate station love *(mohabba*).

Nizamie et al. (2013) further noted that the stage of states (*ahwal*) is understood to be a consequence of the divine graces (*tajalli*) and occurs during or after the first stage. The final stage of achievement (tamkin) denotes the end of the pursuit when a Sufi is understood to achieve gnosis (*marifa*), the divine knowledge. In pursuing tareeqa, the Sufi is first supposed to annihilate himself in his mentor *(fana-fi-shaykh),* then in Muhammad PBUH (*fana-fi-rasul*), and finally in God (*fana-fi-Allah*) before he achieves eternal existence in his God (baqa) (Nizamie et al., 2013). This brief introduction is obviously not fully representative of the thorough and diverse Sufi tareeqas that individual Sufis and Sufi orders have practiced and promulgated, but is meant to provide a basic overview.

Before moving to the next section which relates ideas based on Sufi doctrines to contemporary organizational life and more specifically self and leadership development, a couple of points in relation to the preceding sections are important. Firstly, as evident from the discussion on Sufi origins, doctrines, and ways, Sufism is anchored in Quranic and *Hadith* teachings and guidelines. Hadith collection are compilations of sayings and traditions attributed to Prophet Muhammad (PBUH). However, individual Sufis and Sufi orders have offered their interpretations of these teachings both in spiritual and worldly practices. For instance, the notion of zikr (remembering God) is consistent across many orders, but the actual zikr practice may be different. Given this chapter's scope and aim, I have focused on the broad ideas, instead of a deep analysis of the Sufi insights, in examining their relevance. Secondly, this chapter is based on the premise that these faith-based notions and their Sufi manifestations offer important ideas which have relevance for contemporary and secular settings.

Sufism and Self and Leadership Development

In this section, I attempt to relate some of the tenets of Sufi teachings, beliefs, and practices, to individual self and leadership development. As noted above, I again emphasize that the purpose and scope of this chapter necessitate that the Sufi wisdom shared here only represents a limited and narrow set of insights given its rich, sacred, and complex philosophy and practice. The relevance of Sufism to self and leadership development discussion starts with the idea of annihilating or conquering the self. Some of the barriers to change and transformation are a lack of self-awareness, insecurity, heroic expectations, and egoistic tendencies (Schweiger et al., 2020; Kegan & Lahey, 2001).

Fana and Self-transcendence

At the foundation of the Sufi idea of annihilating (fana) and conquering the self is the assumption that a deep inward examination and letting go of the ego is the first crucial step that one must take before starting the journey of self-transformation. This and other Sufi practices are designed to help one surrender and realize one's existence relates to something beyond the horizon of the mind and ego (Vaughan-Lee, 2012). Emphasis on this self-examination is closely aligned with some of the classic and contemporary change and leadership development models in social systems and settings. For instance, Kurt Lewin, who is considered one of the founders of American Social Psychology, offered the notion of unfreezing as an integral element of change dynamics (Cummings et al., 2016). The unfreezing entails getting the individual or the social system to recognize the need for change and commit to it. It involves letting go of existing assumptions through focused unlearning.

The idea of self-annihilation allows this unlearning of assumptions about the existing self-image. It implies awareness of what needs to change and committing and taking steps toward that change. This dynamic also involves letting go of existing habits and trying and practicing new ways of doing things. To meaningfully elevate one's level of leadership practice, the Sufi ideas that lead to self-transcendence offer important reinforcement in that regard.

Murshed, Murids, and Mentoring

In the Sufism context, once a commitment to change is in place, the next step is to access guidance on the best ways to move forward with one's spiritual journey. Sufi teachings make it clear that the developmental journey is best facilitated by a murshed when they accept someone as a *murid* (Sufi disciple). Hill (2021) summarizes some of the key dynamics of the relationship between a murshed and a murid. The relationship is characterized by a mutual obligation between the guide and the disciple. Initiation may involve a declaration of allegiance to the murshed. The spirit behind the murshed-murid practice of Sufism offers some important linkages to self and leadership development.

For instance, Roupnel et al. (2019) examined the role of coaching, mentoring, and action learning in leadership development. Their review and reflections align with the spirit of the Sufi principle of sustained effort to self-development with the help of a guide. Further, the authors emphasized the importance of approaching the work of leadership development from a holistic and sustained perspective. Roupnel et al. note, "By way of conclusion, leadership development should not be considered as a once-off measure or an optional expense item for organizations. Quite to the contrary, it should be made an organizational priority" (p. 137).

In his best-selling book, Malcolm Gladwell (2008) proposed the "10,000-hour rule." His basic argument was that it takes about ten thousand hours to master a particular field. He provided relevance of the rule with examples from fields ranging from music to technology. While the rule's length of time needed to develop expertise has been debated in recent years, the basic advice that a disciplined and sustained effort is needed to develop deep expertise is closely aligned with the Sufi idea that one needs to fully commit oneself to be successful in a transformational journey and seek mentors to facilitate that development. In fact, Young (2020) observed that the original research on which Gladwell based his argument, clearly emphasized the role of a teacher as a significant force in achieving deep expertise.

Zikr and Meditation

Meditation has received increasing attention as a vehicle for meaningfulness and well-being in contemporary organizational settings. Frizzell et al. (2016) emphasized the importance of meditation and contemplative practices for leadership development and effectiveness and organizational investments in that regard. In this section, I briefly introduce the Sufi practice of zikr, or dhikr, and its potential implications for self and leadership development. According to Bashir (2013), "the term …'dhikr' [is] the Islamic concept most likely to come to mind when we seek an equivalent for the English term meditation" (p. 201). Zikr or remembrance has been an important part of Sufi thinking and practice over the centuries. In fact, Bashir (2013) observed that doing zikr regularly in some form is part of being a Sufi.

The practice of zikr entails the repetition of a sacred word or phrase, such as the Shahada–La ay la ha illa Allah (there is no god but God) and often it is an attribute or a name of God. Zikr may be conducted silently or vocally (Vaughan-Lee, 2012). Bashir (2013) goes on to argue that zikr, unlike other forms of meditation, has an interpersonal orientation to it in terms of murshed-murid relations where a murid (at least in the early stages of initiation) performs zikr under a murshed's guidance and in many cases, it is performed communally. Despite some of zikr's differences with what are considered contemporary forms of meditation, its focus on attention and awareness, awakening of inner focus, and renewed connections to one's surroundings, overlap with modern and classic meditation practices. In that sense, zikr-inspired approaches to meditation, whether with an individual or collective focus, may play a role in self and leadership development. Two specific implications are (a) meditation in contemporary organizational settings for leadership development must be a regular or sustained practice (see Chapter 12 on how to use entrainment to enhance spiritual practice) and (b) guidance of a coach or guide is important in learning and practicing contemplative practices to fully understand them and benefit from them.

Khushu–The Limits of Humility

Another important dimension of Sufi thinking and practice is humility (*Khushu* and *tawadu*). The notion of humility is approached in a nuanced and careful fashion in Sufi thinking and practice. According to Khalil (2020), Sufi philosophy, among other ways, sees humility as "self-lowering" and places it between vices of pride and self-denigration. Following his detailed discussion of humility's spiritual and symbolic meanings in Sufism, he observes, "From this 'higher' perspective, we come to an understanding of humility that moves well beyond the parameters of the debates we usually find in modern Western virtue theory" (p. 248). Citing Chodkiewicz (1993), he continues, "Here humility is no longer a quality placed somewhere in between pride and self-loathing, but beyond them both, in a subject who effaced of all traces of selfhood, stands at 'the station of no station'" (Khalil, 2020, p. 248).

While humility is a virtue of the heart, it is its interpersonal manifestations that offer important implications for self and leadership development. As Khalil (2020) observed, humility "…requires above all service (*khidma*), thinking well of people (*ḥusn al-ẓann*), a certain openness of mind, as well as an absence of feelings of entitlement, and no desire to be treated as if one were special and unique" (p. 246).

Most Western conceptions of leadership have placed explicit or implicit value on leaders as individuals who exhibit confidence through their vision and their interpersonal demeanor. For instance, Bobbio and Manganelli (2009) developed a leadership self-efficacy scale to measure and assess leadership confidence. Borrowing from Sufi conceptions of humility, the challenge for leaders and leadership development is to combine their confidence with humility in a way that creates humbleness within but equally importantly, manifests that humbleness in relation to others in ways that respect their dignity and focus on their best selves. In addition, as noted above, developmental efforts should not mistake equating humility with self-denigration.

Unity and Love

Sufism is well known for its deep connection to love and unity. According to Andrabi (2015), "The only message of Sufism is unity and love. It implies that the truth is attained when aspirant abandons his lower self (nafs) and develops his pure self. Pure self is a mirror which reveals the glory to God" (p. 35). While divine love is at the center of the Sufi journey, love for fellow human beings is a significant part of Sufism. Maulana Rumi was an extraordinary scholar and poet, and his writing is deeply anchored in deep knowledge of Islam and devotion to God. The Americans in particular, and the world in general, admire Maulana Rumi for his message of love. Rumi has been well known in the Eastern world for a long time, but it was access to his translated works by Coleman Barks in the 1990s, which made him a best-selling poet in North America (Gray, 2020). Additionally, as Gray (2020) further noted, in 1996 UNESCO's declaration that 2007 would be international "Rumi year," has led to widespread interest in Rumi's work during the last couple of decades. This interest in Rumi and Sufism clearly demonstrates the hunger being felt for the expression of love in the Western societal context and beyond and emphasizes the relevance of Sufi ideas in contemporary society (Dressler et al., 2009).

In terms of its relevance to leadership and organizations, the *Humanistic Management Journal* devoted space to the topic of love in a recent special issue. In introducing this special issue, Pirson et al. (2021) noted, "in this issue, we create space for the topics of love, dignity, and the common good in the frame of family firms and beyond" (p. 1). This publication is a rare but timely step in the right direction and paves the way to study the relevance of love to self-development, self-fulfillment, leadership, and leadership development.

Final Reflections

Over the last three decades, an important aspect of self and leadership development has been connected to the concept of emotional intelligence

(Goleman & Boyatzis, 2017) (see Chapter 11's discussion of emotional intelligence as one of nine intelligences that can be used for leadership development). The premise is that emotional intelligence is an important competency at the individual, interpersonal, and leadership levels. This in turn implies that it is important to invest in cultivating emotional intelligence and the literature has seen numerous efforts in this regard (e.g., Suciu et al., 2010; Batool, 2013). Suciu et al. (2010) list overcoming emotions, compulsions, ability to empathize, social flexibility, adaptability to change, as important emotional competencies for individual and leadership success.

As noted above, a significant emphasis is put on the Sufi practices that focus on self-awareness and self-regulation–two foundational elements of emotional intelligence. The expected level of effort that murids must exert in relation to different practices may spread over months and years. Similarly, a significant focus is placed on empathy–understanding and caring for fellow human beings. This aspect also closely aligns with the relational aspects of emotional intelligence. In summary, what we are learning under the emotional intelligence umbrella has been a part of Sufi thinking and practices. In that sense, it is appropriate to argue that whether it is emotional intelligence or other human development pathways, Sufi insights bring wisdom to augment the ways we may approach these learning and development endeavors with more authenticity.

Our hyper-consumer and capitalistic orientations have put tremendous pressure on the planetary eco-systems. The emerging consequences of these pressures are devastating for humanity on a global scale. Leadership theory and practice have put forward ideas under the umbrella of social responsibility and sustainability leadership to help organizations meet the existential challenges through these leadership approaches. Following two decades of efforts toward sustainability leadership, we have made little progress on this front. For instance, Bendell and Little (2015) noted that, "The challenge for professionals in sustainability and corporate responsibility, therefore, is now to move beyond their existing expertise in social or environmental content, and explore the fundamentals of leadership and its development from a critical perspective" (p. 24).

Clearly, more urgent and radical changes are needed in how organizations should be led toward sustainability. Embracing simplicity in how we live and lead is a good starting point and Sufism offers important guidance in that regard. Along with other commentators, Begum and Awan (2015) observed that according to some interpretations, "the word Sufi is...derived from Arabic word Suf, which means a woolen cloth. Sufis were supposed to wear that woolen garment to avoid the worldly luxuries and to show simplicity" (p. 240). This emphasis on simplicity and distance from materialism has remained important aspects of Sufi thinking and practice. We need to develop and support leaders everywhere so that they become role models and advocates of simplicity as we wrestle with increasing forever plastics at the depth of our oceans and polluted cities across the world due to unsustainable consumerism and growth.

In terms of this chapter's limitations, I have noted above that the discussion of Sufi philosophy and practices does not capture the vastness, diversity, depth, and full beauty of its extensive wisdom. Similarly, given the divine anchoring of Sufi thinking, I have attempted to approach its application and relevance with care and caution. This care and caution are also driven by the sacred orientation of the focal phenomena and the exploratory nature of this review.

Additionally, it is important that given the aim and scope of this chapter, I have not offered critical reflections on how some aspects of Sufism are being approached, attacked, or appropriated in the Eastern and Western hemispheres. There have been some terrorist attacks on Sufi institutions in Pakistan and Egypt in recent years. Regarding the commercialization and appropriation of Sufism, Gray (2020) noted, "Rumi's success as a pop-culture icon in the United States can partly be explained by the various and gradual processes of domestication, appropriation, and Americanization of the Rumi narrative" (p. 128). In addition, this popularity is linked to considerable efforts aimed at presenting Sufism as an alternative to the religious extremism that dominated the post 9/11 Islamophobic discourses (Gray, 2020).

Finally, due to the chapter's scope and space limitations, there are aspects of Sufism which were not covered. For instance, the popular and highly regarded Sufi musical and poetry form of *qawali,* famous in South Asia was not discussed. Similarly, the discussion does not cover some other music and poetry focused aspects such as whirling dervishes and *sama*. Andrabi (2015 notes, "The Sama means listening to the Sufi poetry for the enlightenment of soul. For Sufis Sama is an act of devotion, devised to draw the attention of God…[it] acts as a way of bringing illumination into one's consciousness" (p. 35). I share the preceding quote to recognize the importance of some of these aspects that were not covered in detail and of course invite the reader to explore these aspects of Sufism as their interest dictates. Our world today and its institutions face unprecedented divisions and uncertainties and require humanistic and courageous leadership. I hope some of the ideas anchored in Sufism shared in this chapter offer humble but bold possibilities to develop and encourage leadership approaches that we need urgently.

References

Andrabi, S. D. A. (2015). Sufism: Origin and basic concepts. *International Journal of Culture and History, 2*(1), 30–36. https://doi.org/10.5296/ijch.v2i1.7597

Anjum, T. (2006). Sufism in history and its relationship with power. *Islamic Studies, 45*(2), 221–268.

Avolio, B. J., & Gardner, W. L. (2005). Authentic leadership development: Getting to the root of positive forms of leadership. *The Leadership Quarterly, 16*(3), 315–338.

Bashir, S. (2013). Movement and stillness: The practice of Sufi dhikr in fourteenth-century Central Asia. In H. Eifring (Ed.), *Meditation in Judaism, Christianity, and Islam: Cultural histories* (pp. 201–211). Bloomsbury Academic.

Batool, B. F. (2013). Emotional intelligence and effective leadership. *Journal of Business Studies Quarterly, 4*(3), 84–94.

Begum, S., & Awan, A. B. (2015). A brief account of Sufism and its socio-moral relevance. *The Dialogue, 10*(1), 23–34.

Bendell, J., & Little, R. (2015). Seeking sustainability leadership. *Journal of Corporate Citizenship, 60*, 13–26. http://dx.doi.org/10.9774/GLEAF.4700.2015.de.00004

Bilqies, S. (2014). Understanding the concept of Islamic Sufism. *Journal of Education & Social Policy, 1*(1), 55–72.

Bobbio, A., & Manganelli, A. M. (2009). Leadership self-efficacy scale: A new multidimensional instrument. *TPM-Testing, Psychometrics, Methodology in Applied Psychology, 16*(1), 3–24.

Britannica, T. Editors of Encyclopedia (n.d.). tariqa. Encyclopedia Britannica. https://www.britannica.com/topic/tariqa

Chodkiewicz, M. (1993). *Seal of the saints: Prophethood and sainthood in the doctrine of Ibn ʿArabī*. Islamic Texts Society.

Cummings, S., Bridgman, T., & Brown, K. G. (2016). Unfreezing change as three steps: Rethinking Kurt Lewin's legacy for change management. *Human Relations, 69*(1), 33–60.

Dressler, M., Geaves, R., & Klinkhammer, G. (Eds.). (2009). *Sufis in western society: Global networking and locality*. Routledge.

Frizzell, D. A., Hoon, S., & Banner, D. K. (2016). A phenomenological investigation of leader development and mindfulness meditation. *Journal of Sustainable Social Change, 8*(1), 14–253. https://doi.org/10.5590/josc.2016.08.1.02

Gladwell, M. (2008). *Outliers: The story of success*. Little, Brown and Co.

Goleman, D., & Boyatzis, R. (2017). Emotional intelligence has 12 elements. Which do you need to work on. *Harvard Business Review, 84*(2), 1–5.

Gray, B. (2020). Rumi, Sufi spirituality and Western Sufism in Elif Shafak's The Forty Rules of Love. *Scripta Instituti Donneriani Aboensis, 29*(1), 124–146. https://doi.org/10.30674/scripta.84280

Helminski, K., & Algan, R. (1989). *The drop that became the sea: Lyric poems of Yunus Emre*. The Threshold Books.

Hill, J. (2021). Sufism between past and modernity. In R. Lukens- Bull & M. Woodward (Eds.), *Handbook of contemporary Islam and Muslim lives* (pp. 55–80). Springer.

Kegan, R., & Lahey, L. L. (2001). The real reason people won't change (p. 75). Boston, MA: *Harvard Business Review, 79*(10) 84–92.

Khalil, A. (2020). Humility in Islamic contemplative ethics. *Journal of Islamic Ethics, 4*(1–2), 223–252.

Khumidovich, A. V., Dikalovich, S. M., & Lemovich, E. G. (2021). Sufism in spiritual culture of the peoples of The North Caucasus. In D. K. Bataev, S. A.

Gapurov, A. D. Osmaev, V. K. Akaev, L. M. Idigova, M. R. Ovhadov, A. R. Salgiriev, & M. M. Betilmerzaeva (Eds.), *Social and cultural transformations in the context of modern globalism*, vol 117. European Proceedings of Social and Behavioural Sciences (pp. 45–51). European Publisher. https://doi.org/10.15405/epsbs.2021.11.7

Korkmaz, A. V., Van Engen, M. L., Knappert, L., & Schalk, R. (2022). About and beyond leading uniqueness and belongingness: A systematic review of inclusive leadership research. *Human Resource Management Review*, *32*(4), 100894. https://doi.org/10.1016/j.hrmr.2022.100894

Küçük, H. (2008). A brief history of Western Sufism. *Asian Journal of Social Science*, *36*(2), 292–320.

Murata, K. (2011). Fana and Baqa. *Middle Eastern Studies*, *38*(1), 95–118.

Nizamie, S. H., Katshu, M. Z. U. H., & Uvais, N. A. (2013). Sufism and mental health. *Indian Journal of Psychiatry*, *55*(Suppl 2), S215. https://doi.org/10.4103/0019-5545.105535

Pirson, M., Dessi, C., Floris, M., & Giudici, E. (2021). Humanistic management: What has love got to do with it? *Humanistic Management Journal*, *6*(1), 1–4.

Rawlinson, A. (2009). Sufism in the Western history: A primary outline. *Falsafeh*, *37*(2), 37–64.

Roupnel, S., Rinfre, N., & Grenier, J. (2019). Leadership development: Three programs that maximize learning over time. *Journal of Leadership Education*, *18*(2). 126–143. https://doi.org/10.12806/v18/i2/t1

Saeed, B., & Batool, S. (2021). Experiences and practices of contemporary Sufis in Pakistan. *NUST Journal of Social Sciences and Humanities*, *7*(1), 99–119. https://doi.org/10.51732/njssh.v7i1.69

Schweiger, S., Müller, B., & Güttel, W. H. (2020). Barriers to leadership development: Why is it so difficult to abandon the hero? *Leadership*, *16*(4), 411–433. https://doi.org/10.1177/1742715020935742

Seesemann, R. (2010). Sufism in West Africa. *Religion Compass*, *4*(10), 606–614. https://doi.org/10.1111/j.1749-8171.2010.00241.x

Suciu, S., Petcu, D., & Gherhes, V. (2010). Emotional intelligence and leadership. *Annual Economic Science Series*, *16*, 549–554.

Vaughan-Lee, L. (2012). *Sufism: The transformation of the heart*. The Golden Sufi Center.

Young, R. (2020, May 5). Researcher behind '10,000-hour rule' says good teaching matters, not just practice. Edsurge, https://www.edsurge.com/news/2020-05-05-researcher-behind-10-000-hour-rule-says-good-teaching-matters-not-just-practice

PART III

Spiritually Inspired Leadership Tools

10

LEADING TRANSFORMATION IN TURBULENT TIMES

Judi Neal

Introduction

Growing numbers of us have a dream of a world without war, where all living things flourish in harmony, and where all children can grow up feeling safe and cherished. We have a long way to go to realize this dream, and there are many challenges facing humanity. There are also many opportunities. Old leadership paradigms do not serve the world that is emerging now. In turbulent times, we have been hard-wired to focus on problems rather than dreams, but it will be dreams that save us.

Amid unprecedented and unpredictable change globally, new kinds of leaders are emerging at the spiritual edge. The challenges facing humanity are so immense and so systemically interconnected that to respond effectively, we must evolve to a higher level of consciousness. Together, these entangled challenges are referred to as the meta-crisis—a crisis of overlapping crises—and they require metamodern solutions that include spirituality and higher states of consciousness (Freinacht, 2017). Freinacht described "metamodern" as the mindset that is evolving out of the modernist and post-modernist mindsets. In these times of ecological disaster, increasing authoritarianism, and growing social injustice, we are called to move beyond the traditional modernist and capitalist mindsets and beyond the post-modern critique of modernism and capitalism to a worldview that transcends and includes the realities that have gone before, and this movement must include spirituality. Modernism and post-modernism have been materialistic

DOI: 10.4324/9781003396741-14

and ego-centric movements, and have neglected the spiritual consciousness that includes compassion, interconnection, and altruism.

Evolution is a natural force for growth, and we are naturally expanding our human capacities and potential not just individually but collectively. We can intentionally expand our capacities and potential through spiritual awakening and spiritual practices. We are in these turbulent times together. While humanity is faced with the challenges of the meta-crisis, people are coming together with new visions, methods, and models to create a flourishing world. New initiatives, groups, and organizations are committed to a new era of well-being and flourishing for all life (Tsao, 2023). These initiatives and groups do not make headlines. They are below the radar, a quiet revolution. And they constitute a growing and interconnected movement that incorporates full human potential, spirituality, and the evolution of higher consciousness. They are at the leading edge of collective transformation.

The field of leadership is coming to include a more holistic view of the qualities and skills for responding to the meta-crisis and beginning to envision and manifest new ways of being and new systemic approaches to building a flourishing world. It is important to remember that not everyone comes to leadership at the spiritual edge at the same time and in the same way. Therefore, how do metamodern leaders understand and work with transforming the meta-crisis into a more conscious way of being that is both proactive and responsive in the face of change?

The Archetypes of Change model, originally called the Organizational Orientation model (Neal, 2006), is one approach that helps leaders and organizations to understand and work with five common worldviews about change and transformation. The five archetypes are: (1) Edgewalkers, (2) Flamekeepers, (3) Hearthtenders, (4) Placeholders, and (5) Guardians.

The Archetypes of Change model helps leaders to assess their teams and their overall organizational culture. The model provides insights into openness to spiritual-based or human values-based language and approaches within the culture. With this understanding, leaders can develop strategies and programs that support the healthiest and most effective responses to changes in their environment, including the proactive creation of a spiritual-centered culture. The model helps leaders to assess which of the five archetypes is their predominant default mode as well as which archetypes can be called upon in different contexts and situations.

This chapter describes the development of the Archetypes of Change model and provides detailed descriptions of each of the five archetypes at the organizational level. The chapter concludes with practical applications of the model applied to organizations for leading from the spiritual edge.

The Development of The Model

I began conducting research on workplace spirituality in 1992 with a focus on the ways individuals and leaders were integrating their personal spiritual journeys with their career journeys. I came to see these leaders as having a foot in the material world and a foot in the spiritual world. I refer to those who integrate these two worlds as *Edgewalkers*. Patterns began to emerge in peoples' responses to my questions about what helped them to navigate the terrain between these two seemingly very different worlds. Using grounded theory, I identified five qualities of an Edgewalker: (1) self-awareness, (2) passion, (3) integrity, (4) vision, and (5) playfulness. Five skills emerged from an analysis of their interviews and stories: (1) knowing the future, (2) risk-taking, (3) manifesting, (4) focusing, and (5) connecting (Neal, 2006).

An instrument measuring these five qualities and skills was developed and was tested for reliability and validity. A strong correlation was found between measuring high on Edgewalker qualities and skills and being high on the seven factors of personal resilience to change (Neal & Hoopes, 2013). The seven factors of personal resilience to change are: (1) positive: the world, (2) positive: yourself, (3) focused, (4) flexible: thoughts, (5) flexible: social, (6) organized, and (7) proactive (p. 438).

For more than 20 years, my colleagues and I have been offering Edgewalker workshops and retreats during which we share a checklist (Neal 2006, p. 20) titled, Are You an Edgewalker? (Box 1). Participants are told that, while this checklist is not scientific, if they checked 12 or more items on the checklist, they were more than likely an Edgewalker. A question that frequently arose after completing the checklist was, "What if I'm not an Edgewalker? I don't relate to most of the items in this list. What is my value to the organization and to the changes we are experiencing?" As an organization development consultant, I realized that my view of how people relate to change was narrow and biased towards a spiritual view. I expected people to be excited about potential changes and want to dive right in, but upon reflection on the organizational changes I have been involved in, this is not how most people respond. I started thinking about the most common responses to change that I have observed and developed what was originally called the organizational orientations model (Neal, 2011) and is now more accurately called the Archetypes of Change model. Each of the five Archetypes has a spiritual aspect to it that can be enhanced through leadership development approaches that align with that particular archetype.

BOX 10.1 ARE YOU AN EDGEWALKER? CHECKLIST

- I have a strong spiritual life.
- I frequently feel different from most people.
- I seem to have the ability to sense coming trends before they emerge.
- I have an unusual combination of interests and passions
- I have had mystical or spiritual experiences that have provided guidance in my everyday life and/or work.
- I speak more than one language or have deep familiarity with more than one culture.
- I have made, or am contemplating, a major career shift that no one would have predicted.
- I often find myself being a bridge or "translator" for people from very different backgrounds.
- I have this feeling that I was called to do something very special and important in the world.
- I find myself attracted to and wanting to learn from people who are very different from me.
- I am strongly aware of the problems of the whole planet (global warming, destruction of rain forests, overpopulation, exploitation of people in poorer countries) and want to see some more action on them.
- People often see me as a leader, even though I am different from most of the people who have been leaders in that organization.
- I have the ability to listen beyond the words that are spoken.
- I consciously tune into something higher than myself for guidance and inspiration.
- It is extremely important to me that my work be aligned with my deepest values.
- I have artistic abilities or unusual gifts that I combine with down-to-earth practical skills.
- I tend to bend the rules if I think it is for a higher purpose.
- People often see me as a risk-taker, but the things I do don't seem risky to me. Somehow, I just know they will work out.
- I have a strong sense of adventure.
- I find myself exploring new ideas and wondering about what the next new thing is in my field or area of interest.

The Archetypes of Change Model

There are two primary dimensions to the Archetypes of Change model: (1) orientation to time and (2) orientation to change. These orientations can vary in different circumstances or contexts. In healthy leaders, they are not rigid personality constructs, and in healthy organizations, they are not a rigid part of the culture.

Orientation to Time

For simplification, orientation to time is defined as a continuum with three variables: (1) focused on the past, (2) focused on the present, and (3) focused on the future.

Focused on the Past

We all know people who love to talk about the "good ol' days" and the way things used to be. They are the keepers of the memories, and in the best of circumstances, they are the ones who can tell stories of the past that carry universal messages or guiding principles for today's world. Their focus on the past can be a longing for a real or imagined past that was better than the current times and can be healthy or unhealthy. This focus becomes unhealthy when an individual or an organization becomes stuck and unable to consider options for moving forward into the future. Humans, as living systems, must be able to adapt to changes in our internal states as well as to the world around us.

Organizations that are focused on the past need to make a choice. Is the focus on the past helpful because it guides the organization to stay in alignment with the founding vision and purpose? Or does the focus on the past keep the organization from adapting to a world that is rapidly changing? There is always something valuable from the past. Two key questions are: what to keep, and what to let go of. If an organization is in a very stable environment, then a focus on the past is beneficial, particularly a focus on what has worked over the years. Organizations that have a monopoly or organizations that have very little interaction with the outside world, like a monastery or a prison, may function very well with a time orientation towards the past. However, the reality is that very few organizations fit that profile.

Focused on the Future

Let us look at the other end of the time orientation continuum: a focus on the future.

There are three primary ways that future-oriented leaders anticipate what will be unfolding:

> First, there is the rational, data-gathering, mathematical-modeling method of understanding the future. This is the "Traditional" method of knowing the future. The key skill is being able to gather and analyze concrete data.
>
> The second approach is the gut-level, shamanic, divination approach to embracing the future. The key skill is being able to read the subtle signs of what is unfolding. This is the "Intuitive" approach to knowing the future.
>
> The third way to know the future is to be actively involved in creating it. This is the "Co-creative" approach to knowing the future. The key skills are to be able to have a vision of what you want to have unfold and to take action to begin to make it real.
>
> *(Neal, 2006, pp. 47–48)*

Those who are focused on the future often feel a sense of dissatisfaction about what is happening in the present. They have a drive to make things better. There is a concept called *preemptive transformation* that Freeland (2019) idiomatically defines in the subtitle of his article as, "even if it 'ain't broke,' you still ought to fix it." Leaders who are focused on the future are not satisfied with the status quo and are really drawn to the idea of continuous improvement. There is a restlessness and an excitement about them. They enjoy thinking of themselves as disrupters. They are easily bored and can fall into the trap of creating something new just for the thrill of it rather than being strategically creative.

Just as some organizations are focused on the past, there are other organizations such as high-tech companies as well as many cutting-edge financial firms whose time orientation is fixed on the future. Silicon Valley, as a region, is famous for its futuristic orientation. This time orientation can also be healthy or unhealthy. A healthy focus on the future builds on what is best in the past, particularly on core values. An unhealthy focus on the future can lead to pushing ethical boundaries as the organization treads into uncharted territories with products and services that have never been offered before. The economic crash of 2008 provides many examples of an unhealthy approach to the future. The corporate landscape is littered with organizations that went too far over the edge, often driven by leadership ego and chutzpah. Too much of a focus on the future can lead to missing cues in the environment about what is so in the present. A healthy focus on the future encourages experimentation, calculated risk-taking, and a little bit of craziness.

For organizations in turbulent times, which is almost all organizations, it is essential to have an interest in the future and to have methodologies or practices for developing a healthy relationship with the future.

Focused on the Present

At workshops on the Archetypes of Change, there are usually some participants who are committed to Eastern contemplative traditions that teach being in the present moment. These participants can sometimes be uncomfortable with the idea that there are benefits to focusing on the past or the future. They are correct about focusing on the present moment when we are working on our mindfulness, equanimity, and consciousness. Leaders who have some form of mindfulness or contemplative practice tend to be more effective leaders (Tsao & Laszlo, 2019). However, that's not what is being discussed in this section. It is possible to be mindful and in present-moment-awareness when you are focusing on the past, present, or future regarding organizational action.

A focus on the present has an action-oriented quality to it. It holds questions such as: What is right here in front of us that we need to pay attention to right now? What is the squeaky wheel here? What is mine to do? What are today's priorities? Leaders who have a time orientation that is present-focused are likely to care about execution and to be skilled at it. They value efficiency, often feeling that time is short and deadlines are looming.

An organization that is present-focused is likely to be a younger organization—one that does not have as much of a past to refer to. It has the tendency to be highly responsive to rapid changes in the environment. If it is a healthy organization, it can adapt quickly to opportunities and is not blocked by tradition, history, or "the way we've always done things." The shadow side of an organization that is primarily focused on the present is that it can feel chaotic as it lurches from one project or market to the next, perhaps never fully realizing the investment in what it had recently been working on. It may not value relationships and or building long-term trust with employees, vendors, and customers, and may treat its stakeholders only in instrumental terms.

Orientation to Change

For simplification, orientation to change is defined as a continuum with three variables (1) closed to change, (2) neutral about change, and (3) open to change.

Closed to Change

For some leaders and organizations, change is uncomfortable and can be fear-provoking. It takes time and energy to deal with changes, and that time and energy take away from productivity. Change can be stressful. It is common to resist change that has been imposed on you, but people can also have mixed feelings about changes they have chosen. They may not have the skills or experience to be resilient in the face of change (Hoopes & Kelly, 2004). Or they may have a history of traumatic changes that have led to loss and suffering. In this case, their relationship to change has been historically negative and they may find it hard to believe that new changes could be positive. Some leaders are just more comfortable and operate more effectively when things are stable and predictable. They can focus on what is important to them, and even develop a sense of mastery from doing something well over a long period of time.

If an organization is in a stable and predictable environment, it has probably been rewarded by the marketplace for doing something very well. That is hard to let go of, and there may be no reason to change. Another reason an organization might be closed to change is that the organization provides a product or service that no other organization can provide, so it is able to keep doing what it has always done. Some organizations are closed to change because the charismatic founder or owner is still in charge, and no one wants to confront them.

There is no judgment about individuals and organizations that are generally closed to change. This orientation to change may be a perfect fit for the circumstances. But as mentioned earlier, these kinds of circumstances are rare, and most of us find ourselves periodically confronted with the need to change. Having some resilience in the face of change (Hoopes & Kelly, 2004) tends to provide more adaptability and growth for both individuals and organizations. We will now explore the other end of the change continuum, open to change.

Open to Change

Openness to change results in less burnout and is positively associated with work engagement, job satisfaction, and quality of work (Sinval et al., 2021). There are levels of openness to change. Some leaders and organizations may accept change with little resistance. Other leaders and organizations actively embrace and take pride in change and innovation.

A leader who is open to change tends to have an optimistic view of people and of the world (Seligman, 2002). They have a spiritual sense of trust that things are likely to work and self-confidence that can help them to figure out how to get where they want to go, even if the road is not clear. They have an intuitive sense of what the next step is and a willingness to experiment. Some may even talk about feeling guided by something greater than themselves. These leaders know that when systems are in flux from one state to another, there are more opportunities to take chances and to intervene. When an organizational change process is occurring, they are likely to volunteer for the design team or to take leadership on new initiatives. They want to be involved in helping change to happen.

An organization that is open to change has leaders at the top who are open to change. These leaders set the tone for the culture. They tend to have an entrepreneurial streak. They may also be comfortable with, and encourage, calculated risk-taking. Some industries by nature require an openness to change. For example, fashion, entertainment, and technology are industries that require rapid alignment with customer preferences. Some industries—such as technology—work hard to influence customer preferences by creating products and services people did not even know they needed. A case in point is the rapid adoption of artificial intelligence and chatbots.

If we observe organizations over time that are open to change, an interesting distinction arises. They are generally more adaptive to rapidly changing environments, but the ones that have financial and reputational stability are the ones that are spiritually based or values-centered (Pruzan et al., 2007; Sisodia et al., 2007). The organizations that play fast and loose with ethics often achieve temporary superstar status but then crash and burn in scandal, with huge financial losses to stakeholders.

The level of openness to change can vary depending on the situation. An individual may be more open to change in some circumstances and closed to change in others. It is the same for organizations. The important thing is whether the openness to change is a fit for the environment the individual or organization is in. The more turbulent and unpredictable the environment, the more openness to change is required.

Neutral about Change

In the middle of the change continuum is a neutral space. Leaders and organizations that are neutral to change take the attitude of, "well, it depends." They are neither as rigid as those who are closed to change nor as enthusiastic as those who are open to change. Instead, they take a wait-and-see stance.

At the individual level, those who are neutral about change are most likely to be concerned about how the change will affect their work efficiency. Some organizational change processes in their past probably made things worse, and some made them better. Their willingness to accept a change also depends on how much learning is required, and how comfortable they are with learning new things.

At the organizational level, the neutral response to change is often predicated on their strategy of being neither first nor last with an innovation or a strategic decision. The organization waits and watches the actions and outcomes when their competitors stick their neck out and try something new. These organizations don't want to be the last ones on the train, and at the same time, they have some level of caution about moving into areas that have never been tried before.

In some ways, this neutral zone is a temporary place to dwell. Eventually, the individual or organization must decide either to adopt change or to reject it, to move towards openness or to become closed to this particular change.

Summary of the Archetypes of Change Model Dimensions

Individuals, leaders, and organizations tend to have a place along the time continuum and the change continuum that feels natural to them. Certain professions also have a common orientation to time and to change. The level of leadership in the organization can also have an impact on time orientation as well as change orientation. In my decades of experience as an organizational consultant, the higher a leader is in the organization hierarchy, the more future-oriented and change-oriented he or she is. The lower a leader is in the organization, the more past or present-oriented they are, and the more likely they are to be closed to or neutral about change. Finally, it should be noted that there are many other factors that can influence these continua, and these factors change depending on circumstances.

The Five Archetypes of Change at the Organizational Level

I have written elsewhere about the five archetypes of change at the individual level (Neal, 2006, 2011). In this section, each of the archetypes will be described at the organizational level.

To lay the groundwork for understanding the organizational archetypes, here is a brief definition of the individual archetypes.

- Referring to Figure 10.1, the upper right-hand corner is the quadrant that is high on openness to change and is focused on the present. This quadrant is labeled "Edgewalkers," defined as leaders who walk between worlds and have the ability to build bridges between different worlds. They have a strong spiritual life and are also very grounded and effective in the everyday material world (Neal, 2006). This archetype is the

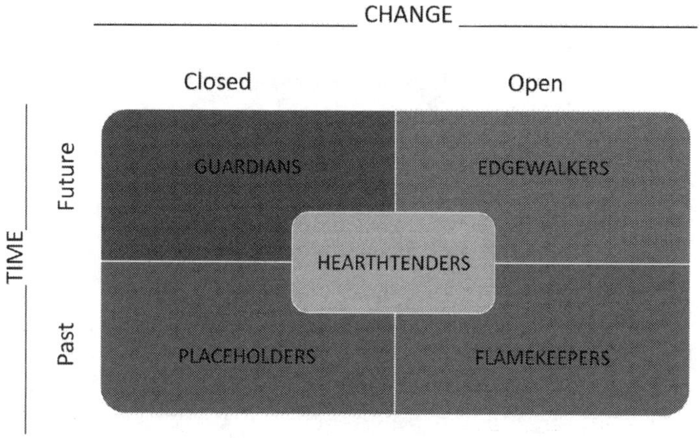

FIGURE 10.1 The Five Archetypes of Change

Note: Adapted from "Organizational Orientation" by Neal (2006).

leadership archetype that is most intentional and open about spiritual approaches to organizational change. The integration of spiritual values and practices in all aspects of leadership is important to them.

- The lower right-hand corner is the area where people are open to change but focused on the past. This is the quadrant of the "Flamekeepers," defined as leaders who keep the original vision and values of the organization alive (Neal, 2006). From a spiritual leadership perspective, this archetype might not speak or act openly about the integration of spirituality in organizational change. However, the leader is likely guided internally by their faith or spiritual tradition's values, which might be expressed in more secular ways.
- The lower left-hand corner is the quadrant representing those who are closed to change and focused on the past. This is the worldview of the "Placeholders," defined as leaders who can provide stability and predictability to the organization. They are the keepers of the boundaries and can keep an organization from going over the edge. They tend to resist change made just for the sake of change and are comfortable with routine (Neal, 2006). While I do not have any research to back this up, I hypothesize that leaders with a strong Placeholder archetype are more likely to be religious in a traditional or conservative faith.
- The upper left-hand corner is the area representing being closed to change with a focus on the future. This quadrant represents "Guardians" (originally called "Doomsayers") who are defined as leaders who tend to see all the things that could potentially be a future problem. They

have a gift for analyzing and/or sensing what could go wrong before it happens. They are committed to protecting people and the organization from potential harm (Neal, 2006). In most spiritual and religious traditions, there are those who have the gift of prophesy or divination. The prophet or shaman is the spiritual equivalent of the "Guardian" archetype in leadership.
- The box in the center represents the area that is neutral about change and focused on the present. This is the "Hearthtender" domain and is defined as leaders who get the day-to-day work of the organization done and who are focused on serving others (Neal, 2006). From a leadership perspective, I hypothesize that the Hearthtender archetype is likely to draw clear boundaries between their professional, personal, and spiritual lives. The primary way a Hearthtender leader expresses his or her spirituality at work is likely to be through creating a sense of fellowship or family in the workplace.

When I was creating this model, I thought these archetypes were personality characteristics and therefore not easily changed. I discovered that this is incorrect. The archetypes are worldviews or orientations—certain ways of seeing the world. They are easily changed through experience, self-awareness, coaching, and training, and they may vary due to circumstances. We can come from an Edgewalker perspective when leading our teams, for instance, and then come from a Placeholder perspective when working with our faith community. Most people have one orientation that is their usual, comfortable default. We all have the seeds of each archetype within us, and personal and leadership mastery comes from understanding the usefulness of each archetype in various situations. Awareness of these archetypes is also very useful in helping us understand others who may not respond to organizational change in the same ways we ourselves do. This awareness can be gained through a research-based assessment tool called the *Archetypes of Change–Individual* and is available to help individuals and teams to manage change more effectively. (Visit: https://edgewalkers.org/the-five-orientations-surveys/). The key thing to remember about any survey result is that the quantitative results are not *The Truth*. They are only a summary of employee perceptions and opinions, and a clearer sense of the truth can emerge with a generative conversation about the survey results, which can be followed by a conversation for action.

Next are descriptions of each of the five Archetypes of Change at the organizational level. What does it mean to be an Edgewalker organization or a Placeholder organization? Once leaders have a sense of the primary archetype that is expressed in their organizational culture, they can assess whether it is the most effective archetype for the challenges and opportunities faced by the organization. The descriptions below describe the characteristics and strengths of each of the five organizational archetypes. Each archetype may also have potential downfalls or shadow sides that may arise from carrying that worldview to an extreme. (For a detailed discussion on shadow work, see Chapter 13).

The Edgewalker Organization Archetype

The Edgewalker Organization seeks to be on the leading edge, is curious about what is emerging just over the horizon, supports creativity and innovation, and nurtures the human spirit. Leaders support team member spiritual development and may encourage shared spiritual practices such as opening meetings with a moment of silence. They develop collective methods of knowing the future such as forecasting and visioning. Risk-taking is encouraged and rewarded. The leaders understand how to use values, imagery, and inspiration to paint a picture of a desired future. Employees are imaginative, empowered, and know how to create what has never been created before. The Edgewalker organization archetype typically values great diversity in its leaders and employees. Differences are valued to a much greater degree than in a traditional organization, simply because Edgewalkers are curious and always wanting to learn about other people's worldviews. In time orientation, the organization primarily focuses on the future. The Edgewalker organization archetype not only embraces change, but it also seeks to create change and enjoys disturbing equilibrium. It tends to be a pioneer in workplace spirituality initiatives (Neal, 2018). The leaders in Edgewalker organizations are more likely to be in alignment with Allen and Fry's (2023) framework for leader, spiritual, and moral development. (For a more in-depth description of models of leadership and spiritual development, see Chapter 1).

The shadow side of an Edgewalker organization is that it may value newness, creativity, and risk so much that it does not put enough time and energy into systems that can help the organization to be stable and sustainable. The organization may ignore wisdom and experience from the past and could get so caught up in creating new rules for the game that it crosses over into actions that could be inappropriate or even lacking in integrity and ethics. It may also be so caught up in its vision of creating the future that it ignores external signs of events or trends that could be threatening to the ability to flourish in the future. Leaders in an Edgewalker organization may develop a collective egotistical sense of spiritual superiority over organizations that are not as explicitly spiritual, leading to a cult-like organizational culture that can blind it toward external realities. (Chapter 4 describes a "spiritually-structured organization" which has many similarities to the Edgewalker Organization described here).

The Flamekeeper Organization Archetype

A Flamekeeper organization is values centered. These values usually come from the founding values of the organization and may have been modified and refined over time. A Flamekeeper organization is one that considers its values when making major business decisions and is willing to take a stand for its core values, even when it may not make short-term bottom-line sense. There is a strong correlation between being a values-centered organization and having higher employee and customer loyalty, greater market share, and higher profit (Sisodia et al., 2007). The Flamekeeper organization is very clear about having a larger sense of mission and purpose in the world, which is typically attractive to high-talent employees. All members of the organization are likely to be very familiar with the organizational values. They can easily describe how the values are lived every day in the workplace. In time orientation, the Flamekeeper Organization focuses on the past, particularly the founding values. The Flamekeeper Organization welcomes change if the changes are in alignment with organizational values and vision. In some Flamekeeper organizations, the founders instilled their religious values into the culture from the beginning with enduring positive effects (Mitroff & Denton, 1999; Neal & Vallejo, 2008).

The shadow side of a Flamekeeper organization can emerge when the focus on core values becomes so central to how decisions and actions are undertaken that the organization becomes bogged down in values analysis and second-guessing its actions. If the Flamekeeper organization was founded on religious principles, it may have diversity, equity, and inclusion (DEI) challenges in an environment that has grown more litigious (Sullivan, 2013). It may also focus so much on the past that it does not scan the environment for new opportunities or possibilities. In general, the Flamekeeper organization is open to change, but it tends to run decisions and choices through the filter of the past, which can make the organization less nimble.

The Hearthtender Organizational Archetype

The Hearthtender organization is focused on efficiency, task orientation, and process. The organization is likely to have a strong interest in creating systems and controls so that things run smoothly. Leaders and their followers have clear expectations of what they are supposed to be doing in their work. Leaders emphasize process and procedures, although they also consider employee needs and responses. In fact, there are probably procedures and policies in place about tending to employee needs. Hearthtender organizations often have a core focus on service: they *tend the hearth*. This focus on service may either come from a core spiritual value around being of service, or it may be more instrumentally driven. Customers can sense when the service is from the heart or is by rote (Bayighomog & Arash, 2019). The Hearthtender organization focuses on the short-term needs of customers and employees and other stakeholders. This can allow leaders to be nimble if stakeholder needs change, but they tend not to think ahead and anticipate longer-term needs and possibilities. At the same time, they do not get stuck in the past. Leaders just want to do what works. In time orientation, the Hearthtender organization archetype is focused on the present time and the short-term. The Hearthtender organization typically prefers to avoid change because change can negatively impact efficiency and systems, but its leaders welcome changes that make the system more effective.

The shadow side of Hearthtender organizational archetype is that it may place too much emphasis on procedures and policies. In my experience, this can create a rigid bureaucracy and can reduce the slack that is needed to respond to situations in a spontaneous and unique way. An organization of this type can get so fixated on predictability and reliability that it becomes machine-like and loses a sense of aliveness and creativity. In general, the Hearthtender organization is not interested in creating or responding to change unless it is clear that the change is going to make work easier. However, too much reliance on proof of success can get in the way of taking calculated risks that could have a high payoff. If the organization becomes too rules-bound and process-focused, leaders who are more spiritually focused may reduce their commitment or even leave.

The Placeholder Organizational Archetype of Change

The Placeholder organization is focused on the past and more interested in stability than change. This organizational archetype focuses on tradition and loyalty and long-term relationships with employees, vendors, and other stakeholders. Leaders and employees in the organization may long for the past, which seems better to them than the current situation, and they may be right that the past was better. Some leaders may refer to the past for guidance in current and future actions. It is common to hear leaders in Placeholder organizations say, "This is the way we've always done things." The Placeholder organization is not likely to look outside itself for competitive ideas, and in fact may even see itself as immune from competition. The culture of the organization may be referred to as family-like because of the long-term relationships and strong sense of loyalty. The traditions of the organization may be based on the religious or spiritual practices of the founder(s) and are unlikely to be questioned. Placeholder organizations can be successful in stable environments where there is little or no competition. In time orientation, the Placeholder organization focuses on the past and it tends to resist change, unless the changes are going back to the way things used to be. A Placeholder organization may have experienced success in the past and may have an attachment to continuing to do what has always worked.

The shadow side of a Placeholder organization can come from too much emphasis on the past and on the way, things used to be. This can blind the organization to current and future problems and opportunities. The focus on the past and on stability can also keep the organization from taking risks that could lead to entrepreneurial gain. The leadership may use its authority to preserve its power rather than to serve the mission of the organization, which can lead to a highly politicized working environment. People may spend more time protecting their turf than helping the organization be effective.

The Guardian Organizational Archetype of Change

The Guardian organization is focused on problem prevention and protecting what is important to the organization: thinking about what could go wrong and then creating an action plan so that potentially harmful things do not occur. The products and services may be those that offer peace of mind or protection to customers. Guardian organizations tend to rely on analytical tools and approaches to decision-making and forecasting that allow them to predict and prepare for an uncertain future, such as scenario planning, risk assessment, and linear forecasting. In time orientation, the Guardian organization is focused on the future and on thinking through contingencies for responding to an uncertain future. Paradoxically, leaders in Guardian organizations are also likely to be intuitive or to have a gut sense of what might unfold in the future. This intuition and/or sensing can be enhanced by spiritual and contemplative practices (Tsao & Laszlo, 2019). Guardian organizations tend to be slow in initiating change because they are afraid something will go wrong and things will get worse. On the other hand, Guardian organizations are willing to implement organizational changes to avoid potential threats to organizational well-being.

The shadow side of a Guardian organization is that it may put too much emphasis on problem prevention and on what could go wrong. This can create a culture that is based on fear. Just as the problem-solving rational part of the human brain shuts down when individuals become fearful making them unable to think as clearly in a crisis, the same thing can happen in an organization's culture (Cooperrider & Srivastva, 2017). Collectively, people will have less of an ability to respond effectively if they are fearful. Leadership in a Guardian organization is likely to be hierarchical and even parental, ranging from benevolent parental leadership ("Let us take care of you") to autocratic dictator ("It's a scary world, and I know what's best for you"). Employees who belong to patriarchal or autocratic religious organizations will probably find the Guardian organizational archetype familiar and maybe even comfortable. If the workforce is young and inexperienced, this kind of Guardian archetype leadership can be effective, but in a mature organization, leading through fear will drive out the organization's creative talent.

Practical Leadership Applications in Utilizing the Archetypes of Change Model

Here are several principles to keep in mind when leaders are working with the Archetypes of Change model:

- Remember that each archetype is not a personality or cultural characteristic and that a person's worldview or orientation to change can shift in different situations and even in different stages of life.
- When an organization is experiencing significant change, honor that each archetype brings a valuable perspective. Listen for the wisdom of each archetype.
- As leaders of change, focus on amplifying the strengths of each archetype. At the same time, be aware of your own shadows or blind spots.
- When contemplating an organizational change, leadership or the planning team can take time to contemplate, "How would an Edgewalker see this? How would a Flamekeeper see this?" and so on.
- Consider creating an organizational map of archetypes. As a simple exercise, the leadership can take a large sheet of paper and colored markers and draw a symbolic representation of their organization. Then each person fills in which subsections of the organization (departments, teams, functions, and so on) are more likely to hold the energy of each of the archetypes. Where are you most likely to find Flamekeepers or Placeholders, for example? Then compare maps and explore how these perceptions fit with what archetypes are needed for ongoing organizational success.
- Use the Archetypes Circle exercise found in the appendix of this chapter (Appendix A). This exercise invites leaders or change agents to take on the mindset of each of the archetypes, one at a time.

A systemic approach to bringing in the Archetypes of Change model into an organizational change process is to have each member of the organization take the Archetypes of Change-Individual survey so that they each know their own archetype profile. Then, have all employees take the Archetypes of Change-Organization survey (https://edgewalkers.org/the-five-orientations-surveys/) that provides an assessment of how the employees perceive the leadership culture of the organization. By taking these two assessments, individuals can get a sense of where their individual archetype can contribute to organizational efforts, and the leaders of the organization can get a picture of how employees in various parts of the organization perceive the organization's response to change. As with any assessment tools, the real power is in the conversation that follows the reporting of the data and the action items that result from that conversation.

Summary

This chapter has presented the theoretical underpinnings of the Archetypes of Change model, described the five archetypes of change at the leadership cultural level, and offered several practical ways to work with the Archetypes of Change so that the leader can guide the organization to be more resilient to change, more in alignment with its values, and can understand where the resistance might be so that it can be transformed to higher engagement, meaning, and purpose. Leadership at the spiritual edge is a commitment to individual and collective evolution, and the more we understand about our ways of seeing the world and seeing each other, the more we grow toward our individual and collective spiritual edges. The Archetypes of Change model is a research-based approach to supporting this growth.

References

Allen, S., & Fry, L.W. (2023). A framework for leader, spiritual, and moral development. *Journal of Business Ethics, 184*(3), 649–663. https://doi.org/10.1007/s10551-022-05116-y

Bayighomog, S. W., & Araslı, H. (2019). Workplace spirituality–customer engagement Nexus: The mediated role of spiritual leadership on customer–oriented boundary–spanning behaviors. *The Service Industries Journal, 39*(7–8), 637–661. https://doi.org/10.1080/02642069.2019.1570153

Cooperrider, D., & Srivastva, S. (2017). The gift of new eyes: Personal reflections after 30 years of Appreciative Inquiry in organizational life. In D. A. Moumair, A. B. Shani, & D. P. Zandee (Eds.) *Research in organizational change and development*, 25, pp. 81–142. Emerald Publishing Limited.

Freeland, G. (2019, July 22). Preemptive transformations: Even if it ain't broke, you still oughta fix it. *Forbes.* https://www.forbes.com/sites/grantfreeland/2019/07/22/preemptive-transformations-even-if-it-aint-broke-you-still-oughta-fix-it/?sh=41cbe33c6313

Freinacht, H. (2017). *The listening society: A metamodern guide to politics book one.* Metamoderna.

Hoopes, L., & Kelly, M. (2004). *Managing change with personal resilience: 21 keys for bouncing back and staying on top turbulent organizations.* MK Books.

Mitroff, I., & Denton, L. (1999). *A spiritual audit of corporate America: Multiple designs for fostering spirituality in the workplace.* Jossey-Bass.

Neal, J. (2006). *Edgewalkers: People and organizations that take risks, build bridges, and break new ground.* Praeger.

Neal, J. (2011). Edgewalker organizations. In L. Bouckaert & L. Zsolnai (Eds.) *Handbook of spirituality and business*, pp. 369–377. Palgrave.

Neal, J. (2018). Overview of workplace spirituality research: A literature review. In S. Dhiman (Ed.) *Palgrave Handbook of Workplace Spirituality and Fulfillment*, pp. 1–56. Palgrave.

Neal, J., & Hoopes, L. (2013). Edgewalker assessment for spiritual leadership and resilience. In J. Neal (Ed.) *Handbook of faith and spirituality in the workplace: Emerging research and practice*, pp. 429–439. Springer.

Neal, J., & Vallejo. M. (2008). Family firms as incubators for spirituality in the workplace: Factors that nurture spiritual businesses. *Journal of Management, Spirituality and Religion, 5*(2), 115–159. https://doi.org/10.1080/14766080809518697

Pruzan, P., & Mikkelsen, K. P., Miller, D., & Miller, W. (2007). *Leading with wisdom: Spiritual-based leadership in business.* Greenleaf Publishing.

Seligman, M. (2002). *Authentic happiness: Using the new positive psychology to realize your potential for lasting fulfillment.* Free Press.

Sinval, J., Miller, V., & Maroco, J. (2021). Openness Toward Organizational Change Scale (OTOCS): Validity evidence from Brazil and Portugal. *Plos One, 16*(4): e0249986. https://doi.org/10.1371/journal.pone.0249986

Sisodia, R., Sheth, J., & Wolfe, D. (2007). *Firms of endearment: How world-class companies profit from passion and purpose.* Pearson Prentice Hall.

Sullivan, P. (2013). EEOC best practices support best practices for spirit and religion at work. In J. Neal (Ed.) *Handbook of faith and spirituality in the workplace: Emerging research and practices.* Springer.

Tsao, F. (2023). *One choice, one world: The rise of the well-being and happiness economy.* SelectBooks.

Tsao, F., & Laszlo, C. (2019). *Quantum leadership: New consciousness in business.* Stanford Business Books.

APPENDIX A

Archetypes Circle Exercise

Purpose

- To expand team perspectives on a particular change or challenge.
- To increase empathy for perspectives different from your own.
- To open up new possibilities for problem solving and generative ideas.
- To help the team feel more aligned in co-creating the future.

Roles

- Facilitator
- Five members of the change team to represent the five archetypes
- Scribe
- Stakeholders of the change as observers

The facilitator describes the steps of this exercise and asks all participants to pay attention to their own internal reactions to what they hear, and to pay attention to when the group energy increases and when it declines. Note-taking can be encouraged.

Step 1

All members of the team take the **Archetypes of Change – Individual** Survey at: https://edgewalkers.org/the-five-orientations-surveys/

The facilitator provides a brief overview/reminder of each of the five archetypes.

Step 2

Each team member shares their dominant Archetype and talks about what gift this archetype might bring a change initiative. Depending on the group size, you might want to break people up into groups of three or four people for this.

Step 3

The team creates a shared statement about the change they are facing. The scribe writes this on a whiteboard or flip chart where everyone can see.

Step 4

Select five people to represent each Archetype of Change. This could be based on their survey or self-assessment results, but it doesn't have to be.

Step 5

Create an Archetypes of Change circle of five chairs in the middle of the room. Put a paper or post-it sign on the back of each chair for each Archetype of Change. In other words, there is a chair for the Edgewalker perspective, a chair for the Flamekeeper perspective, and so on. Set up chairs around the Archetypes of Change circle for other stakeholders in the change. This will be in fishbowl style. The five members of the change team sit in the five chairs.

Step 6

The facilitator reads the shared statement of the change to the group and then asks each representative of an Archetype of Change to comment on the change from that particular perspective. For example, the Edgewalker Archetype might talk about how he or she is excited about the change and what they can envision. The Guardian might talk about his or her perspective on what could go wrong and how they want to protect the organization from harm. Each person should speak for about two minutes.

Step 7

Each person moves one chair to the right and now gives voice to the new archetype perspective he or she represents. About one minute each. Continue this process until everyone has had the chance to speak from all five of the Archetypes of Change. The facilitator encourages each person in the circle of five to really get into the role of each archetype and to resist falling back into the archetype that is most comfortable for them unless they happen to be sitting in that particular archetype's chair. Much learning can come from embodying a perspective that is different from your own.

Step 8

The facilitator leads a discussion with the following questions; first asking the members of the circle of five about their experience and then asking the stakeholder/observers for what they noticed. The scribe captures key points as people debrief.

Potential discussion questions:

For circle of five:

- What did you notice about yourself and your energy as you took on each Archetype of Change role? What was easiest? What was the hardest?
- What did you hear from others in the circle that inspired you?
- What surprised you?
- Where is the resistance, and how can it be honored? Can it be transformed? If so, how?
- How might these insights lead to action to move the change forward?

For stakeholder/observers:

- What did you notice about yourself and your energy as you listened to Archetype of Change sharing? Which did you resonate with the most? The least? Why?
- What did you hear from members in the circle of five that inspired you?
- What surprised you?
- Where is the resistance, and how can it be honored? Can it be transformed? If so, how?
- How might these insights lead to action to move the change forward?

For everyone

- What did I learn that changed my perception of how we might go about this change?
- What are our next steps in planning/implementing this change?
- Other comments, ideas, suggestions?

11

INNER ECONOMY

A Leadership Tool for Peace, Transformation, and Well-Being

Lisa A. Berkley

Introduction

Throughout this book, spirituality has been defined in multiple ways. Specifically, Indigenous, African, and Buddhist perspectives all point to a universal, unitive dimension of spirit which transcends and interconnects all life. It is this perspective I will use to define spirit and spirituality throughout this chapter: a fundamental aspect of all life which flows through Earth and all her animate and inanimate beings. Therefore, spirit is an inherent or intrinsic and foundational—almost unspoken—aspect of being human and, by default, the way in which we lead.

There is a growing recognition that spirituality plays an effective role in leadership (Dean, 2008; Phipps, 2012). Leaders who cultivate spiritual practices are often more resilient, act with integrity, and build meaningful relationships (Giacalone & Jurkiewicz, 2010). Additionally, engaging in introspective spiritual practices such as meditation and journaling allows leaders to develop self-awareness, reflect on their values, and enhance their moral reasoning abilities (Gonçalves, 2018). When leaders focus upon spiritual themes such as service, humility, and purpose, their leadership styles become focused upon stakeholder well-being and create more ethical and servant-oriented practices (Reave, 2005). Within this context, fostering spiritual competence between leaders and followers generates high-trust environments where organizations thrive (Bousa et al., 2022). Ultimately, spirituality cultivated among leaders seems to promote ethical behavior, transparency, purpose, and stakeholder consideration (Dean, 2008)

DOI: 10.4324/9781003396741-15

enabling organizations and communities to be characterized by integrity, fulfillment, and human dignity (Kauanui et al., 2010).

This chapter will lay the spiritual framework of the Law of Correspondence as a way of understanding the impact the individual can have on the collective and discuss the challenges of defining national well-being through the lens of gross domestic product (GDP). It will then introduce the term inner economy, a three-stage model for transformation based upon nine intelligences, which provides a framework for understanding the impact between an individual and their society. The chapter concludes with a worksheet for leaders to begin working with the inner economy model.

From Individual to the Collective: The Spiritual Framework of the Law of Correspondence

Almost all religions, or spiritual truths, at some point recognize the need to take personal responsibility for our thoughts, attitudes, and behaviors to positively affect the external world: the communities in which we live, and their inhabitants. Even if one is not a "believer," for centuries, moral values across cultures have reflected the Law of Reciprocity. This "Law" is often correlated with the Golden Rule: "Do unto others, as you would have done unto you." It suggests we should treat others as we would like to be treated, because how we treat others will correspond to how we are treated in return.

The phrase "as above, so below" expresses the core Hermetic principle that the universe reflects on itself from the heavenly realms down to earth (Dennis, 2002; Fowden, 1993). What is interesting to note is that the original text "does not say that what is below is like what is above, rather it says what is below comes from what is above" (von Balthasar, 1984, p. 130) indicating a more nuanced understanding of how reality is created.

Additionally, correlation between the macrocosm and the microcosm is repeatedly referred to in the Upanishads, the Vedic texts containing the foundational concepts of Buddhism, Hinduism, and Jainism. In particular, Chandogya, Chapter 6 of the Upanishads, refers specifically and in detail to the relationship between the Atman and Brahman or inner-self and the outer-self (the world, or cosmos) (Easwaran, 2007). Within human consciousness, there exists a "knowing" of personal responsibility and interconnectedness—that is, what is happening within a microcosm is happening in a macrocosm and vice versa.

GDP Fail: Not Defining Well-Being or Building a Peaceful World

The responsibility of creating a peaceful world ultimately relies upon the thoughts and behaviors of each individual working collectively. As the collective becomes more peaceful, the individual is supported in developing their own inner peace. This relationship is one of correspondence and an evolution of growth and development. Therefore, we must examine the definition and assessment of collective well-being.

For generations, we have based the assessment of progress, health, and the well-being of nations—and by default, the standard of living and well-being of individuals—on GDP. GDP is the total monetary or market value of a country's goods and services produced in a specific period of time. It provides a broad measure of overall domestic production and serves as a comprehensive scorecard of a country's economic health (Fernando, 2023). Simon Kuznets first developed GDP for a U.S. Congress report in 1934; in it, he made it clear that the welfare of a nation can be not inferred from a measurement of the national income (Kuznets, 1934).

The shortcomings of GDP are vast. It does not include what some refer to as the "core economy," the network of relationships and activities outside the market which create the social fabric and serve as the undergirding of societal well-being. It is much of the core economy, which is unpaid but makes life worthwhile: child rearing, running a household, helping friends and neighbors, volunteering, and local political participation. GDP does not account for the social and environmental costs of economic development. The "most pressing example [being] the long-term costs of climate change... Economist Nicholas Stern has [referred to climate change as] 'the greatest and widest-ranging market failure ever.' GDP entirely ignores our contributions to destroying our habitat and our children's futures" (Marks, 2010, p. 27). Yet, this is the very tool which has become the global standard for assessing the standard of living of people and nations. By maintaining this understanding of our collective state of being, we deny our most profound truths. What is most sacred to us—relationships, personal responsibility, and the deep knowledge of interconnectedness written about throughout the ages—has been negated. People are not concerned about GDP. They are concerned with living standards and want to measure well-being.

Defining Inner Economy

With GDP as the prevalent framework for collective well-being and considering the law of correspondence, incorporating, or applying nine key intelligences (emotional, spiritual/perceptional, ecological, ethical, somatic, cultural, creative, cognitive, and social) would be beneficial as each plays a significant role in being human. Yet for many, incorporating them into policy analysis and creation would be taboo, considered too "soft," and/or irrelevant. To integrate them easily into a national well-being assessment framework, the use of economic sounding language would be best.

TABLE 11.1 Economy and Inner Economy Definition Comparisons

Economy *(American Oxford English Dictionary, n.d.)*	**Inner Economy** *(Berkley, 2017)*
1 The wealth and resources of a country or region, esp. in terms of the production and consumption of goods and services.	1 The inner resources one gains, uses, and loses in the exchanges of daily life. Our personal inner resources draw from nine primary intelligences: somatic, spiritual/ perceptional, ecological, ethical, emotional, social, cultural, and creative.
2 Careful management of available resources.	2 Wise management of available inner resources.

In Table 11.1, a nation's economy is defined by the exchange of its wealth and resources. If we apply this concept to an individual, we can define their Inner Economy, that is the inner resources one gains, uses, and loses in the exchanges of daily life (Berkley, 2017). This is a term which was initially created by Nicole Moen, an award-winning poet, intuitive, healer, and activist who has produced and managed events which, among other areas, highlight new economic models and Indigenous language reawakening. Inner Economy also defines:

- the lens from which to view the internal well-being of an individual or community; and
- a three-stage model of nine intelligences which illustrates the relationship between an individual and society and the way in which they influence and impact one another.

By using an economic transactional term to define a relational aspect of being human, a non-threatening space is created; the individual and their well-being can be drawn into the conversation about global events. Through "economic language" we can access mainstream thinking and thus contextualize the need of the individual to develop these nine intelligences, so our species and planet can thrive.

Inner economy is relevant to well-being and peacemaking. It defines a person's internal resources, which are separate from any external valuation based upon financial or material wealth or other people's perceptions of that individual. Inner economy is about the relationship between the internal and external perspectives of an individual in which they recognize they are responsible for their emotional reality and cognitive interpretation of each situation in which they live. Resiliency, inner peace, integrity, lessons learned from failure, self-actualization, and dignity are all significant aspects of an individual's healthy or positive inner economy. Possessing a healthy inner economy brings one into a non-static sense of peace in which one has integrated their shadow side; feelings of anger, fear, rage, grief, and sadness are as accepted and valued as feelings of joy, love, compassion, and stillness (Berkley, 2017). (For more discussion on the shadow side, see Chapters 13 and 14; for more about the role of compassion, joy, love, and stillness, see Chapters 2, 3, and 13). Inner economy is that part of the person which is spiritually grounded and abundant no matter what their financial situation. Having a strong inner economy provides a perspective of value and meaning in life regardless of if the "outer economy" is in a bust or boom. An individual's inner economy is measured by their health and peace of mind. When one is grounded in this way of thinking, they do not fall prey to the shadow side of competition and material resources in which scarcity and fear-based human made rules govern (Hodges, 2010).

The Underpinnings of Inner Economy: Nine Intelligences

As mentioned earlier, inner economy is a three stage model made up of nine intelligences: somatic, spiritual/perceptional, ecological, cognitive, ethical, emotional, social, cultural, and creative. None of these intelligences are new, although, in Western cultures, cognitive intelligence has overshadowed any others for centuries and still does. Some, such as emotional (Côté, & Miners, 2006; Goleman, 2012), somatic (Kaparo, 2012; Levine, 1997) and cultural intelligences (Ang et al., 2006; Earley & Ang, 2003) have been recognized or re-claimed as relevant only recently. Each of the nine intelligences has been discussed or studied in the literature, often in isolation and with respect to a specific purpose. The relevance of the inner economy model is, first, the absence of hierarchical evaluation of any intelligence, and second, the emphasis on understanding the simultaneous and interconnected relationship between the individual and the collective defining both the whole person and the whole system (see Figure 11.1).

The inner economy model can contribute to the overall betterment of an individual and their society. When used by psychologists, academics, business consultants, and educators, the model and corresponding exercises for developing each intelligence provide an understanding of how an individual interacts with their environment and how they can affect change (e.g., developmental questions, see Table 11.2).

Moreover, it has been shown to help relieve individuals from stress and anxiety as well as creates a framework for mediation and conflict resolution. Below is a further discussion of each intelligence and how it contributes to inner economy.

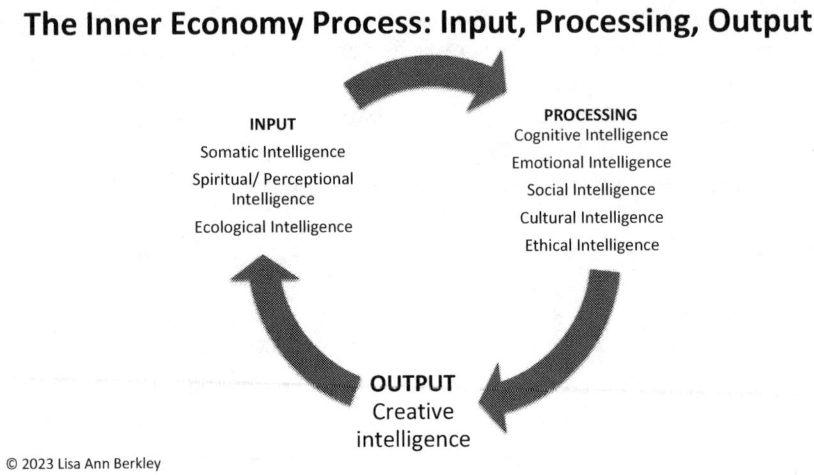

FIGURE 11.1 Three-Stage Nine Intelligence Model of Inner Economy

Note: The responsibility of creating a peaceful world ultimately relies upon the thoughts and behaviors of each individual working collectively. By default, as the collective becomes more peaceful, the individual is supported in developing their own inner peace. If we support individuals in having a meaningful life, in turn, it will support national well-being and vice versa. The relationship between the individual and society is one of correspondence and an evolution of growth and development. Each individual (person or community)'s output/creative intelligence affects all other intelligences. An individual's input is what they take in through somatic (body), spiritual/perceptional (extra-sensory senses), and ecological (environmental) intelligences; that information is processed through their cognitive intelligence as influenced by their ethical, emotional, social, and cultural intelligences. What they put out in the world reflects their creative intelligence—what they think, say, do, and create in the physical world.

Input: Sensing the World through Spiritual/Perceptional, Somatic, and Ecological Intelligences

Spiritual/Perceptional Intelligence

The dictionary defines spirit as the soul, true self, and seat of emotions (American Oxford Dictionary, n.d.). Spiritual/perceptional intelligence involves exploring deeper meaning and purpose in life (Emmons, 2000; Zohar & Marshall, 2000). It relates to contemplating identity, relationships, suffering and connections to the sacred (Vaughan, 2002). It reflects exploring human potential and consciousness expansion beyond the five senses (Radin, 1997). Joseph and Lakshmi (2011) define it as commitment to wisdom. Zohar and Marshall (2000) see this type of intelligence as exploring meaning, contextualizing actions and assessing life paths. Overall, this intelligence points to extraordinary capacities beyond logic for contemplating deeper meaning, purpose, and human potential.

TABLE 11.2 Developing Your Nine Intelligences: Who Are You?

	INPUT	
Intelligence	*Reflections*	*Exercise/Practice*
Somatic Intelligence	What is the story your body is telling right now?	Take a moment and breath into your body. This is an invitation to notice what is alive. What are the feelings, experiences, sensations, and thoughts as you scan your body?
Spiritual/ Perceptional Intelligence	What is your experience with your intuition, extra-sensory experiences? Connection with the divine? What do you believe in that you cannot see, taste, touch, or hear? When you believe in these things, how do you feel? Do you trust your sense of interconnectedness? Your inner voices, knowing, and wisdom? Please explain.	This is an invitation to breath into your whole body and extra-sensory skill sets. Notice where there is peace or calm in your body
Ecological Intelligence	What is your connection to the natural world? In what way does it nourish/support you?	Take a moment and go outside or look out your window-what you do you notice when you allow all parts of your body to relax, slow down, and breathe it in? What do you feel?

(*Continued*)

TABLE 11.2 (Continued)

	PROCESSING	
Intelligence	*Reflections*	*Exercise/Practice*
Cognitive Intelligence	How do your thoughts, feelings, and perceptions create your experiences and expectations?	This in an invitation to notice how when you change your thoughts, your feelings, and experiences, and even your expectations, your reality changes. As Nobel Prize-Winning, Theoretical Physicist, Max Planck, the originator of Quantum Theory stated: "If you change the way you look at things, the things you look at change." (Clements, 2018, para. 1)
Emotional Intelligence	What are you feeling in this moment? In what way is this impacting your mood and state of being? Can you change it?	This in an invitation to drop into your heart center and notice what you are feeling in this moment. Are you feeling happy? Sad? Angry? Joyful? Melancholic? Grief? Contentment? Peaceful?
Social Intelligence	In what way do the people in your life—friends, family, colleagues—impact you?	Take a moment, think-feel about your social environment; notice how your thoughts and feelings respond and reflect your relationship to those around you. Do you need to improve communications? Do you need to set more boundaries? Say "no" more? Drop some boundaries? Say "yes" more?

Cultural Intelligence	Who are you based upon your lineage and ancestorial stories? In what way do your ancestors influence who you are today?	This is an invitation to explore your "Blood Memory" an Indigenous term which conflates social and cultural norms such as storytelling, imagination, memory, interconnectedness, and genealogy into one term (Allen, 2002).
Ethical Intelligence	In what way do ethics guide or influence your life and behavior? Have you ever behaved unethically? If so, why? What was the motivation?	This is an invitation to explore your morals and ethics. In what way are they different or the same? Rosen (2021) stated, "Many people think of morality as something that is personal and normative, whereas ethics are the standards of 'good and bad' distinguished by a certain community or social setting."
	OUTPUT	
Intelligence	*Reflections*	*Exercise/Practice*
Creative Intelligence	Describe the world which you want to see. In what way are you contributing to it becoming a reality?	This is an invitation to dream the world you wish to live in and consider ways in making that happen, knowing you can contribute in both big and small ways. And knowing we are all in this together.

Note: Answer each Question under the Reflections column by any of the following: (1) Write: Free Thought/Stream of Consciousness; (2) draw or paint; (3) write a poem or story; (4) meditate on the intelligence, reflection, and exercise prompts and journal or create your inspiration; (5) express any type of creative response: Photography, Dance, Movement….

A key capacity of spiritual/perceptional intelligence is transcendence, perceiving deeper connections between self, others, nature, and the cosmos (Emmons, 2000) (for a greater discussion on transcendence, see Chapter 1). This promotes empathy, wisdom, and compassion. Studies link higher levels to satisfaction, resilience, and leadership (Emmons, 2000). Quantifying something so subjective presents challenges and remains controversial (Emmons, 2000; Sisk & Torrance, 2001). Some propose expanded awareness beyond the senses (Radin, 1997) with skills like telepathy. Small effects have been seen, but replication failures spark debates on methods and interpretation (Kennedy, 2013), making defining these intelligences difficult. Overall, while controversial, they point to extraordinary human capacities and meaning making.

People view spirituality as experiential rather than conceptual and transrational (Forman, 1997; Vaughan, 2002). Spiritual/perceptional intelligence is often associated with intuition or sensitivity to subtle energy currents in the body. Practices such as meditation, yoga, and martial arts, that quiet the mind can expand awareness cultivate sensory, rational, and contemplative ways of knowing, and refine perceptional sensitivity to energy, sound, light, and subtle levels of consciousness (Vaughan, 2002). Though subjective, these practices can cultivate spiritual/perceptional intelligence for a more meaningful living (Joseph & Lakshmi, 2011). These kinesthetic (experiencing through the body) experiences occur individually and reflect universal types of experiences; many of which are often referred to as inner knowing. This is where somatic intelligence enters the picture.

Somatic Intelligence

Somatic intelligence refers to the innate knowledge acquired through our body and physical experiences (Levine, 2010). Researchers study the "embodied mind"— how physical experiences shape thinking and behavior, viewing cognition not as abstract computation but emerging from body-world connections (Gibbs, 2006). Our cognition is profoundly shaped by embodied actions rather than separate internal thinking. Thus, cognition should be studied by looking at body-environment interactions rather than as internal thinking divorced from bodily contexts ("How the body shapes the way we think," 2022). This challenges notions of cognition as purely abstract.

Every cell within our body has what can be referred to as cellular memory. This is not just DNA—this is the premise that the experiences one's familial lineage, as well as their day-to-day experiences imprint within the "memory" of the cells of the body (Hurley, 2013); it is what Indigenous cultures refer to as Blood Memory (Allen, 2002) and what shapes our thought patterns and realities (Hay, 1998). By changing thoughts, we change our body and way of being. Through emotional and spiritual/perceptional intelligences, we can expand and reframe our reality. Through greater self-reflection and awareness, we can unlearn negative patterns such as criticism, anger, resentment, and guilt (Hay, 1998; Levine, 1997, 2005, 2010) which—when internalized (that is, turned against the self)—cause most dis-ease (Kubzansky et al., 2006; Sarno, 2007; Thomas et al., 2000). Ultimately, "thoughts impact the cells of our body allowing us to completely change it" (Chasse & Arntz, 2004, p. 69) so that we can thrive.

Somatic practices facilitate this. Levine's Somatic Experiencing explores how the body holds traumatic memories as frozen survival responses (Levine, 2010). Bringing mindful attention to these areas through breath, movement, and touch can "thaw" stuck energies, restoring the body's natural healing. As sensations shift, associated thoughts and emotions also shift, bringing new clarity. Leaning into feelings and the wisdom of the body reconnects us to inner peace, freedom and responsibility (Jampolsky & Cirincione, 1990).

Ecological Intelligence

Ecological intelligence refers to humankind's capacity to learn and adapt to environmental challenges in a sustainable manner (Reyers et al., 2018). As Goleman (2009) defined it, ecological intelligence represents "knowing what nature has to teach" and "learning how to live in harmony with natural systems" (p. 47). Developing ecological intelligence is critical as humanity faces escalating crises like climate change, biodiversity loss, and ecological degradation. Scholars argue that cultivating ecological intelligence can help foster the shift toward more sustainable societies (Barth et al., 2020; Wahl, 2016).

Fundamentally, ecological intelligence requires recognizing the interconnectedness of all living systems and having reverence for nature (Goleman, 2009). Indigenous cultures have long understood this, seeing the human spirit as linked to all aspects of the Earth (Deloria, 2003). (For a deeper discussion of the interdependence between humans and Earth from an Indigenous perspective, see Chapter 6). Ecological intelligence embraces this spiritual view, expanding ethical consideration and empathy to non-human entities and future generations. As Orr (1994) contends, ecological intelligence means "knowing, caring, and acting" to protect the Earth's systems and resources that sustain all life (p. 5). In developing compassion and wisdom about human-environment interdependence, ecological intelligence can guide humanity toward a more ethical, conscious, and spiritually-attuned relationship with nature.

Ecological intelligence ties into the spiritual understanding of our interconnectedness. When combined with ethical intelligence and spiritual/

perceptional intelligence—that is, as awareness of the divine or transcendent, and somatic intelligence—personal growth, a sense of interconnectedness, dignity, and peace, becomes likely.

Processing: Cognitive Intelligence through the Lens of Emotional, Social, Cultural, and Ethical Intelligences

Cognitive Intelligence

Loosely defined, cognitive intelligence is the brain's ability to assess and solve problems. "Cognitive ability is a latent trait that is assessed by psychometric tests" (Brody, 2004, p. 234) and has numerous aspects to it, most of which are out of the scope of this chapter. Within the context of the inner economy model, cognitive intelligence is how we process all the information we take in, regardless of if it is from our five senses (somatic intelligence) or any form of extrasensory input (spiritual/perceptional intelligence) or from the world around us (ecological intelligence).

Cognitive intelligence represents a deeper aptitude for understanding the world around us, grasping new information quickly, making sense of things, and figuring out solutions. In short, it refers to overall mental acuity and flexibility in perception, analysis, and decision-making (Gottfredson, 1997). In the context of inner economy, cognitive intelligence processing is how cognition interprets and works through, the lenses of emotional, social, cultural, and ethical intelligences, each of which is discussed below.

Emotional Intelligence

Emotional intelligence, or the ability to perceive, control and evaluate emotions (Cherry, 2006) is at the core of inner economy. Often abbreviated as EQ, emotional intelligence has many definitions which can be found in the mainstream media and popular books. However, per Mayer et al. (2004)—arguably the pioneers of emotional intelligence—a clear and scientifically useful definition of emotional intelligence is recognizable because it takes the terms *emotion* and *intelligence* seriously. *Emotion* refers to a "feeling state (including physiological responses and cognitions) that conveys information about the world around us including, about relationships" (p. 197) and *intelligence* refers to the "capacity to reason validly about information" (Mayer et al., 2004, p. 197).

This use of the term *emotional intelligence* in this fashion is consistent with scientific literature in the fields of intelligence, personality psychology, and emotions (Ashkanasy & Humphrey, 2011; Mayer & Salovey, 1997; Mayer & Salovey et al., 1999). Emotional intelligence enables perceiving, accessing, understanding and managing feelings to enhance thinking; it means applying reasoning to comprehend emotions and using emotion skills to enrich cognition and promote growth (Mayer et al., 2004). It is an ability to "recognize the meanings of emotion and their relationships, and to reason and problem-solve based upon them" (Mayer et al., 2000, p. 267).

The concept of emotional intelligence was brought into mainstream consciousness by Daniel Goleman's 1995 book: *Emotional Intelligence.* Goleman (2012)'s additional work highlighted the fact that those who manage their emotional lives more calmly and with greater self-awareness seem to have a distinct and measurable health advantages.

In the inner economy model, emotional intelligence and cognitive intelligence provide the bedrock to heal the self and, by default, the relational self, which extends to community.

Social Intelligence

If emotional intelligence is about learning about feelings and understanding emotions (as far as self-awareness and in relation to others), social intelligence is about the ability to understand human beings and their relations in a complex social and societal context and to build constructive relationships. Social intelligence describes the exclusively human capacity to use very large brains to connect with others and to navigate and negotiate complex social relationships—politics, romance, family relationships, collaboration, reciprocity, etc.—and environments (Social Intelligence Lab, 2014). Lewis et al. (2000) suggest: "people cannot be stable on their own—not should or shouldn't be but *can't* be…Total self-sufficiency turns out to be a daydream whose bubble is burst by the sharp edge of the limbic brain" (p. 86). The need for connection—for social relationships—is biologically anchored, which is why the experience of love and interdependency can be seen as a basic human need (Sayer, 2011; Seligman, 2011).

Modern neuroscience reveals humans possess an innate capacity for empathy through mirror neurons, which activate when observing others as if experiencing their actions directly (Decety & Ickes, 2009). This reflects humans' tendency for imitation and socialization (Lewis et al., 2000). The amygdala (part of the brain) plays a key role by rapidly perceiving nonverbal cues and eliciting corresponding feelings through emotional contagion, even before awareness (Goleman, 2006). While adept at sensing emotions, the amygdala lacks verbal pathways, so it reproduces others' feelings through physical reactions rather than descriptions. This serves as empathetic wiring to understand others.

Humans are biologically programmed to be highly social creatures who need connections with others to understand ourselves as individuals and communities (de Waal, 2009; Lerner, 2000). When we become self-absorbed, empathy and compassion are eroded and our world contracts as our problems seem potentially insurmountable. However, "when we focus on others, our world expands. Our own problems drift to the periphery of the mind and so seem smaller, and we increase our capacity for connection—or compassionate action" (Goleman, 2006, p. 54).

Social intelligence is strengthened by somatic, spiritual, and ecological awareness (Eisenstein, 2011; Lerner, 2000; Lewis et al., 2000). As mindful attention to the body and the natural world grows, the brain's structure changes enhancing self-awareness and empathy. Feelings of inner warmth and closeness to others which often arise during meditation practices develop and correlate with an increase in oxytocin. This chemical enhances love, bonding, and prosocial behaviors (Kaparo, 2012), which increases our awareness and sense of interconnectedness and assists in understanding our cultural intelligence.

Cultural Intelligence

The more we learn about ourselves, the better we are able to understand the "other." When referring to social intelligence, the role of the amygdala plays a very crucial part; it enables us to process who or what is around us and determine if we are in danger. Therefore, when entering another culture, some discordance is inevitable. How we process this information can depend on our cultural intelligence—our ability to adjust and effectively adapt to diverse cultural situations (Ang et al., 2006; Crowne, 2013; Ng & Earley, 2006).

Cultural intelligence builds on emotional intelligence (Earley & Mosakowski, 2004). High emotional intelligence means understanding universal human qualities as well as differences between individuals. High cultural intelligence means analyzing a person's or group's behavior to identify traits which are universal, peculiar to that culture, or neither. It involves discerning cultural influences—such as natural environment, food, language, and customs—which shape individuals or groups (Earley & Mosakowski, 2004) as well as recognizing one's own biases and positionality. Without self-awareness, we risk what Thomas and Inkson (2004) refer to as "cultural cruise control"-relying on our cultural assumptions and ignoring others (p. 42). This way of being can cause problems in cross-cultural interactions as holding cultural biases may lead to misjudging others and unnecessary conflict.

Cultural intelligence can be developed in several ways, including through formal education and training (Earley & Ang, 2003; Ferdman & Brody, 1996). However, experiential learning is critical. To counteract "cultural cruise control," the practice of self-reflection and mindfulness can be invaluable as it can serve as a critical link between self-awareness and knowledge about culture and appropriate behavior in cross-cultural situations (Thomas & Inkson, 2004).

Ethical Intelligence

Social, cultural, and ethical intelligences share a focus on relating to others and behaving with integrity. Social intelligence involves effectively navigating interpersonal relationships and social settings through awareness of norms, roles, and group dynamics (Goleman, 2006). Cultural intelligence relates to appropriately interacting with diverse groups based on cross-cultural understanding (Ng et al., 2012). Ethical intelligence integrates these by emphasizing moral values in conduct and decision-making (see Chapter 4 for a corresponding discussion on morality and spirituality).

Ethical intelligence is the ability to apply ethical reasoning to align choices with moral principles (Lennick & Kiel, 2005). Key capacities include moral awareness, sound judgment, and principled behavior even in difficult situations (Treviño et al., 2006). Developing it requires self-reflection on values and biases. Additionally, learning from role models provides guidance (Jordan, 2007). While formal ethics training builds skills in analysis and decision-making (Mihelič et al., 2010), practicing empathy, anticipating consequences, and overcoming self-serving rationalizations strengthens ethical intelligence. Ethical intelligence guides conscience and provides meaning, enabling wise navigation of complexity beyond self-interest. Those who cultivate it often describe living with greater authenticity, self-actualization, and inner peace.

Ethical intelligence has profound impacts on leadership and organizations by fostering trust, fairness, and corporate social responsibility. Leaders with strong ethical intelligence shape ethical organizational cultures and exemplify moral courage even at personal cost (Kalshoven et al., 2011). They prioritize the greater good in decisions rather than self-interest, championing transparency, accountability, and integrity within institutions; their behavior exhibits positive and care-based moral judgment and conduct, and benefits individuals, organizations, and society. As technology progresses and complexity increases, ethical intelligence becomes imperative.

Within the context of the inner economy model, ethical intelligence serves as a grounding rod for leaders as they examine the foundation of their behaviors and decision-making processes through the other intelligences. In an otherwise morally neutral model, or system of leadership development and change, it provides a framework and language for discussing what is morally responsible and is used to support positive human potential and growth.

Output: Creative Intelligence—Our Thoughts, Words, Actions, and Creations

Recent research highlights the benefits of creative activities for cognitive, emotional, and social well-being (Hunter et al., 2023). Additionally, the more one develops each of above discussed intelligences, the higher will be the level of their creativity and creative intelligence, and the greater contribution they will be for the overall good of society. "Creative intelligence is a way of expressing our humanity, our unique power to create, connect, and inspire" (Nussbaum, 2013, p. 39). The word creative means "relating to or involving the imagination or original ideas, especially in the production of an artistic work" (Oxford Dictionary, n.d.).

A central source of meaning in our lives, creativity is what sets us apart from other living species on this planet. It is reflected through our language, values, artistic expression, scientific understanding, and technology. One of its most unique aspects is that it does not happen inside people's heads; rather, it is revealed in the interaction between a person's thoughts and their sociocultural context (Csikszentmihalyi, 1996). Creativity represents a convergence of capacities that together allow for transcending traditional ideas, rules, patterns, relationships, or the production of meaningful new ideas, forms, methods, and interpretations (Magsamen & Ross, 2023). As Magsamen and Ross (2019) state in *Your Brain on Art*, "Creativity takes work. It takes curiosity, openness to explore concepts, flexibility, and problem solving" (p. 97).

Creative intelligence is the foundation for envisioning, innovation, transformation, and healing on both individual and societal levels; often its development requires risk-taking (a key component in change). In the context of inner economy, creative intelligence is the way in which we shape our individual and collective reality based upon our thoughts, communications, expressions, actions, or what we create in the physical world (Burr, 2015; Schwartz, 2022). It emerges at the intersection of knowledge, imagination, and evaluation. By integrating information across different domains and applying imaginative thinking, individuals can generate innovative ideas and solutions so that individuals and communities may thrive.

Conclusion

The intersection of leadership and spirituality is an emerging field recognizing leaders often act with greater integrity, resilience, and care when engaging in spiritual and self-awareness practices. The inner economy model provides a framework for leaders to develop critical spiritual capacities. By consciously cultivating the nine intelligences in an integrated way, leaders grow spiritually and become more effective. As they express their unique creativity, integrating the nine intelligences allows them to envision and build a more just, fulfilling, and spiritually-conscious world. Organizations and communities where leaders develop their inner economies become vibrant and people can thrive.

Developing spiritual/perceptional intelligence expands leaders' sense of meaning and connection to the sacred. Somatic intelligence teaches leaders to listen to inner wisdom through bodily awareness. Ecological intelligence fosters reverence for nature and sustainability. Together these inputs expand leaders' consciousness beyond the ego to perceive the interconnectedness of all life. Cognitive intelligence helps leaders analyze and solve problems. Ethical, emotional, social, and cultural intelligences shape how leaders apply cognition for the greater good. By grounding decisions in compassion, diverse perspectives and moral principles, leaders' choices uplift rather than exploit.

Within the inner economy model, spirituality is an animating life force interconnecting all existence. As leaders grow in respect for this spirit or lifeforce in themselves and others, their reverence extends beyond people to include nature and even inanimate objects. Leaders who cultivate inclusive spiritual perception through the inner economy framework often report an increased sense of inspiration, fulfillment, inner peace, and humility. In essence, consciously developing the nine intelligences creates more enlightened leaders who act from divine purpose rather than ego. Inner economy offers leaders a roadmap to profound spiritual maturation and a more enlightened leadership. Those who take this journey exemplify qualities such as integrity, compassion, courage, and wisdom. They can focus on supporting individuals to have a meaningful life, which in turn, will support national well-being and vice versa (Eisenstein, 2011; Nussbaum, 2011; Seligman, 2011; Stiglitz, 2012; Wheatley, 1999). The relationship between the individual and society is one of correspondence and reflects an evolution of growth and development and lays the foundation where the definition and assessment framework of national and international well-being is expanded so that organizations, communities, and the wider world are uplifted.

References

Allen, C. (2002). *Blood narrative: Indigenous identity in American Indian and Maori literary and activist texts.* Duke University Press. https://doi.org/10.1515/9780822383826

Ang, S. Van Dyne, L. & Koh, C. (2006). Personality correlates of the four factor model of cultural intelligence. *Group & Organizational Management, 31*: 100–123. Doi: 10.1177/1059601105275267

Ashkanasy, N., & Humphrey, R. (2011). Current emotion research in organizational behavior. *Emotion Review*, *3*(2): 214–224. https://doi.org/10.1177/1754073910391684

Barth, M., Jugert, P., Fritsche, I., & Reese, G. (2020). Ethical concerns about ecological intelligence: Pitfalls, challenges, and directions. *Perspectives on Psychological Science*, *15*(4), 1009–1018.

Berkley, L. A. (2017). *The Application of Inner Economy to the Peace and Security Sector* [Unpublished manuscript]. Institute for Inner Economy. https://innereconomy.com

Bousa, C., Kteily, N. S., & Fida, R. (2022). Integrating spirituality through workplace interactions: A social ecological framework for cultivating spiritual leader development. *Journal of Management, Spirituality & Religion*, *19*(1), 60–88. https://doi.org/10.1080/14766086.2021.1875999

Brody, N. (2004). What cognitive intelligence is and what emotional intelligence is not. *Psychological Inquiry*, *15*(3), 234–238.

Burr, V. (2015). *Social constructionism* (3rd ed.). Routledge.

Chasse, B., & Arntz, W. (Eds.) (2004). *Little book of bleeps: Quotations from the movie "What the Bleep Do We Know?"* Captured Light Distribution.

Cherry, K. (2006, September 8). How emotionally intelligent are you? Verywell mind. Retrieved November 5, 2023, from https://www.verywellmind.com/what-is-emotional-intelligence-2795423

Clements, E. (2018, July 12). *Notes from a small island - "If you change the way you look at things."* University of Buckingham. https://www.buckingham.ac.uk/latest-news/notes-from-a-small-island-series

Côté, S., & Miners, C. T. (2006). Emotional intelligence, cognitive intelligence, and job performance. *Administrative Science Quarterly*, *51*(1), 1–28. https://doi.org/10.2189/asqu.51.1.1

Crowne, K. (2013). An empirical analysis of three intelligences. *Canadian Journal of Behavioral Science*, *45*(2), 105–114.

Csikszentmihalyi, M. (1996). *Creativity: Flow and the psychology of discovery and invention*. Harper Collins.

Dean, K. L. (2008). Values-based leadership: How our personal values impact the workplace. *The Journal of Values-Based Leadership*, *1*(1). https://doi.org/10.22543/0733.61.1147

Decety, J., & Ickes, W. (Eds.) (2009). *The social neuroscience of empathy*. MIT Press.

Deloria, V., Jr. (2003). *God is red: A native view of religion* (3rd ed.). Fulcrum Publishing.

Dennis, G. (2002). *The encyclopedia of Jewish myth, magic and mysticism*. Llewellyn Publications.

De Waal, F. (2009). *The age of empathy: Nature's lessons for a kinder society*. Three Rivers Press.

Earley, P., & Ang, S. (2003). *Cultural intelligence: Individual actions across cultures*. Stanford Business Books.

Earley, P. C., & Mosakowski, E. (2004). Cultural intelligence. *Harvard Business Review*, *82*(10), 139–146.

Easwaran, E. (2007). *The upanishads* (Vol. 2). Nilgiri Press.

Economy. (n.d.). In *Online American Oxford Dictionary*. Retrieved from http://www.oxforddictionaries.com/us/definition/american_english/economy?q=economy

Eisenstein, C. (2011). *Sacred economics: Money, gift, and society in the age of transition*. Evolver Editions.

Emmons, R. A. (2000). Is spirituality an intelligence? Motivation, cognition, and the psychology of ultimate concern. *The International Journal for the Psychology of Religion*, *10*(1), 3–26. https://doi.org/10.1207/S15327582IJPR1001_2

Ferdman, B. M., & Brody, S. E. (1996). Models of diversity training. In D. Landis & R. Bhagat (Eds.), *Handbook of intercultural training* (2nd ed., pp. 282–303). Sage.

Fernando, J. (2023, March 30). *Gross domestic product (GDP): Formula and how to use it*. Investopedia. https://www.investopedia.com/terms/g/gdp.asp

Forman, R. (1997). *Grassroots spirituality*. Report prepared for the Fetzer Institute. Forge Institute.

Fowden, G. (1993). *The Egyptian Hermes: A historical approach to the late mind*. Cambridge University Press.

Giacalone, R. A., & Jurkiewicz, C. L. (2010). The science of workplace spirituality. In R. A. Giacalone & C. L. Jurkiewicz (Eds.), *Handbook of workplace spirituality and organizational performance* (2nd ed., pp. 3–26). Routledge.

Gibbs, R. (2006). *Embodiment and cognitive science*. Cambridge University Press.

Goleman, D. (2006). *Social intelligence: The new science of human relationships*. Bantam.

Goleman, D. (2009). *Ecological intelligence: How knowing the hidden impacts of what we buy can change everything*. Crown Business.

Goleman, D. (2012). *Emotional intelligence: 10th anniversary edition*. Random House.

Gonçalves, G. (2018). The effects of spirituality in the development of the moral reasoning of the leader. *Leadership and Organization Development Journal*, *39*(4), 519–532. https://doi.org/10.1108/LODJ-07-2017-0193

Gottfredson, L. S. (1997). Mainstream science on intelligence: An editorial with 52 signatories, history, and bibliography. *Intelligence*, *24*(1), 13–23. https://doi.org/10.1016/S0160-2896(97)90011-8

Hay, L. (1998). *Heal your body a-z: The mental causes for physical illness and the way to overcome them*. Hay House, Inc.

Hodges, P. (2010). *Inner economy: Redefining the meaning of wealth*. Sounds True.

How the body shapes the way we think. (2022, October 20). MIT Press. https://mitpress.mit.edu/9780262537421/how-the-body-shapes-the-way-we-think/

Hunter, S., d'Amato, A. L., Linnell, A. E., & Reiter-Palmon, R. (2023). Creativity in organizations macro perspectives: Leadership, interventions, and applications. In Handbook of *organizational creativity*: Leadership, *interventions, and macro level issues*, Second Edition (pp. 3–6). Elsevier. https://doi.org/10.1016/B978-0-323-91841-1.00028-2

Hurley, D. (May 2013). Grandma's experiences leave a mark on your genes. *Discover Magazine*. Retrieved 7 November 2023: https://www.discovermagazine.com/health/grandmas-experiences-leave-a-mark-on-your-genes

Jampolsky, G., & Cirincione, D. (1990). *Love is the Answer: Creating positive relationships.* Bantam Books.

Jordan, J. (2007). Dispositions and teacher assessment: The need for a more rigorous definition. *Journal of Teacher Education*, *58*(5), 365–369. https://doi.org/10.1177/0022487107308732

Joseph, M., & Lakshmi, S. S. (2011). Spiritual intelligence at work. *The IUP Journal of Soft Skills*, *5*(4), 21–30.

Kalshoven, K., Den Hartog, D. N., & De Hoogh, A. H. (2011). Ethical leadership at work questionnaire (ELW): Development and validation of a multidimensional measure. *The Leadership Quarterly*, *22*(1), 51–69.

Kaparo, R., (2012). *Awakening somatic intelligence: The art and practice of embodied mindfulness.* North Atlantic Books.

Kauanui, S., Thomas, K., Sherman, C., Waters, G., & Gilea, M. (2010). An exploration of entrepreneurship and play. *Journal of Organizational Change Management*, *23*(1), 51–70. https://doi.org/10.1108/09534811011017207

Kennedy, J. E. (2013). Can parapsychology move beyond the controversies of retrospective meta-analyses? *Journal of Parapsychology*, *77*(1), 21–35.

Kubzansky, L., Cole, S, Kawachi, I, Vokonas, P., & Sparrow, D. (2006). Shared and unique contributions of anger, anxiety, and depression to coronary heart disease: A prospective study in the normative aging study. *Annals of Behavioral Medicine*, *31*(1), 21–29.

Kuznets, S. (1934). "National Income, 1929–1932". 73rd US Congress, 2d session, Senate document no. 124.

Lennick, D., & Kiel, F. (2005). *Moral intelligence: Enhancing business performance and leadership success.* Wharton School Publishing.

Lerner, M. (2000, August 1). *Emancipatory spirituality.* Duke University Press. https://read.dukeupress.edu/tikkun/article-abstract/15/3/33/99050/Emancipatory-Spirituality

Levine, P. (1997). *Walking the tiger: Healing trauma.* North Atlantic Books.

Levine, P. (2005). *Healing trauma: A pioneering program for restoring the wisdom of your body.* Sounds True, Inc.

Levine, P. (2010). *In an unspoken voice: How the body releases trauma and restores goodness.* North Atlantic Books.

Lewis, T., Amini, F., & Lannon, R. (2000). *A general theory of love.* Vintage Books.

Magsamen, S., & Ross, I. (2023). *Your brain on art: How the arts transform us.* Random House.

Marks, N. (2010). GDP RIP (1933–2010). *Significance Magazine.* March 2010. The Royal Statistical Society.

Mayer, J., & Salovey, P. (1997). What is emotional intelligence. In P. Salovey & D. J. Sluyter (Ed.), *Emotional development and emotional intelligence* (pp. 3–34). BasicBooks, Inc.

Mayer, J. D., Salovey, P., & Caruso, D. R. (1999). Models of emotional intelligence. In R. J. Sternberg (Ed.), *Handbook of intelligence* (pp. 396–420). Cambridge University Press.

Mayer, J. D., Caruso, D., & Salovey, P. (2000). Emotional intelligence meets traditional standards for an intelligence. *Intelligence*, *27*(4), 267–298. https://doi.org/10.1016/s0160-2896(99)00016-1

Mayer, J., Salovey, P., &Caruso, D. (2004). Emotional Intelligence: theory, findings, and implications. *Psychological Inquiry*, *15*(3), 197–215.

Mihelič, K. K., Tekavcic, M., & Škerlavaj, M. (2010). Ethical leadership. *International Journal of Management & Information Systems (IJMIS)*, *14*(5), 31–41.

Ng, K. Y, & Earley, P. C. (2006). Culture +1 intelligence: Old Constructs, new frontiers. *Group & Organizational Management*, *31*(1), 4–19. https://doi.org/10.1177/1059601105275251

Nussbaum, M. (2011). *Creating capabilities: The human development approach.* Harvard University Press.

Nussbaum, B. (2013). *Creative intelligence: Harnessing the power to create, connect, and inspire.* Harper Collins.

Orr, D. W. (1994). *Earth in mind: On education, environment, and the human prospect.* Island Press.

Oxford Dictionary. (n.d.). Creative. In Oxfordlearnersdictionaries.com. Retrieved February 27, 2023, from https://www.oxfordlearnersdictionaries.com/us/definition/english/creative_1

Phipps, K. A. (2012). Spirituality and strategic leadership: The influence of spiritual beliefs on strategic decision making. *Journal of Business Ethics*, *106*(2), 177–189. http://www.jstor.org/stable/41476280

Radin, D. I. (1997). *The conscious universe: The scientific truth of psychic phenomena.* HarperEdge.

Reave, L. (2005). Spiritual values and practices related to leadership effectiveness. *The Leadership Quarterly*, *16*(5), 655–687. https://doi.org/10.1016/j.leaqua.2005.07.003

Reyers, B., Folke, C., Moore, M.-L., Biggs, R., & Galaz, V. (2018). Social-ecological systems insights for navigating the dynamics of the Anthropocene. *Annual Review of Environment and Resources*, *43*, 267–289. https://doi.org/10.1146/annurev-environ-110615-085947

Rosen, F. (2021, September 1). What's the difference between morality and ethics? *Encyclopedia Britannica.* https://www.britannica.com/story/whats-the-difference-between-morality-and-ethics

Sarno, J. (2007). *The divided mind.* HarperCollins.

Sayer, A. (2011). *Why things matter to people: Social science, values and ethical life.* Cambridge University Press.

Schwartz, J. M. (2022). *Living from the source: A guidebook for harmonic living and change agency.* NeuroAwareness.

Seligman, M. (2011). *Flourish: A visionary new understanding of happiness and well-being.* Atria Books.

Sisk, D. A., & Torrance, E. P. (2001). *Spiritual intelligence: Developing higher consciousness.* Creative Learning Press.

Social Intelligence Lab (2014). http://socialintelligencelab.com/social-intelligence/

Stiglitz, J. (2012). *The price of inequality: How today's divided society endangers Our Future.* W. W. Norton & Company.

Thomas, S., Groer, M., Davis, M., Droppleman, P., Mozingo, J., & Pierce, M. (2000). Anger and cancer: An analysis of the linkage. *Cancer Nursing: An International Journal for Cancer Care*, *23*(5), 344–349.

Thomas, D., & Inkson, K. (2004). *Cultural intelligence: People skills for global business.* Berrett-Koehler.

Treviño, L. K., Weaver, G. R., & Reynolds, S. J. (2006). Behavioral ethics in organizations: A review. *Journal of Management*, *32*(6), 951–990. https://doi.org/10.1177/0149206306294258

Vaughan, F. (2002). What is spiritual intelligence? *Journal of Humanistic Psychology*, *42*(2), 16–33. https://doi.org/10.1177/0022167802422003

von Balthasar, H. U. (1984). *Glory of the Lord: A theological aesthetics, Volume 2: Studies in theological style: Clerical styles.* Ignatius Press.

Wahl, D. C. (2016). *Designing regenerative cultures.* Triarchy Press.

Wheatley, M. (1999). *Leadership and the new science.* Berrett-Koehler Publishers.

Zohar, D., & Marshall, I. (2000). *SQ: Spiritual intelligence: The ultimate intelligence.* Bloomsbury Publishing.

12

LESSONS FROM ENTRAINMENT FOR SPIRITUAL LEADERSHIP DEVELOPMENT

Danny Sandra

Introduction

Entrainment is a phenomenon that we all have experienced in daily life, but perhaps not consciously. The outcome of entrainment is often coined as "being on the same wavelength," or "being in sync," and it typically brings forth an elevated emotion, energy, or feeling. Also, the adjustment of our bodies to the day/night rhythm due to jetlag is an example of entrainment. The word "entrainment" is derived from the French verb *entraîner*—to drag or to pull. The phenomenon was discovered by the Dutch mathematician, Christiaan Huygens (17th century), who noticed that pendulum clocks started to sync if they were placed on the same beam (Minorsky, 1962). Studies identified that cycles exist within individuals, groups, organizations, and environments; they entrain to one another (consciously and unconsciously), and there is a positive relationship between entrainment and outcomes, both at the personal (e.g., Childre & Cryer, 2000; McCraty et al., 2009) and organizational level (e.g., Dibrell et al., 2015; Khavul et al., 2010; Shi & Prescott, 2012). In other words, the entrainment lens is able to shed some light on personal and organizational challenges using distinct variables, such as, tempo, phase, duration, and intensity (Ancona et al., 2001; Ancona & Chong, 1996). Imagine now what the world would look like if we could benefit more from this natural phenomenon.

Spiritual leadership was first developed by Fry in 2003 and describes an organizational transformation process to build adaptability in response to the rapidly evolving environment (Fry, 2003, 2005; Fry & Slocum, 2008;

DOI: 10.4324/9781003396741-16

Fry & Whittington, 2005). The model is based on intrinsic motivation, incorporating vision, hope/faith, and altruistic love in such a way that it awakens a spiritual quest through calling and membership. The outcome is that life has meaning and makes a difference, and that one feels part of a greater whole, while being understood and valued (Fry, 2003). In 2008, the spiritual leadership theory was updated to highlight the importance of a spiritual or inner life practice as a crucial source of inspiration for its development, an inward journey of self-discovery and awareness (Fry, 2008; Fry et al., 2017). Furthermore, the spiritual leadership model can also be used at the personal level as a process for personal transformation (Fry, 2008; Sandra & Nandram, 2020; Sandra, 2021, 2022).

In this chapter, spirituality concerns "those qualities of the human spirit– such as love, and compassion, patience, tolerance, forgiveness, contentment, a sense of responsibility, a sense of harmony–which bring happiness to both self and others" (Dalai Lama XIV, 1999, p. 22). It is an invitation for being in touch with ourselves and, at the same time, with something larger while searching for meaning in life. A spiritual practice is any practice that nurtures these qualities of the human spirit or inner life, that is "a private space for imagination and reflection which nourishes one's creative spirit and a sense of well-being" (Naiman, 2018). Practices include meditation, mindfulness, yoga, journaling, art practice, and so on.

What lessons can be learned from the phenomenon of entrainment for these spiritual practices to enhance spiritual leadership development? Before providing an answer, first, I discuss entrainment and its integral entrainment matrix in more detail, followed by clarifying personal spiritual leadership and its development, and, finally, I discuss the impact of having a spiritual practice on spiritual leadership.

Entrainment

Bluedorn (2002) defines entrainment as:

> A process over time whereby two or more autonomous rhythmic processes interact with each other in such a way that they adjust towards and eventually lock-in to a common phase and/or periodicity, most often to the rhythm being more powerful or dominant. Afterwards, the processes maintain a consistent relationship.
>
> *(p. 149)*

This implies that, for entrainment to happen, three major components are necessary: autonomous rhythms, interaction, and adjustment. First, entrainment involves at least two rhythms. The completion of a phenomenon that is systematic and recurrent determines the cycle (Ancona & Chong, 1996; McGrath & Tschan, 2004). If the cycle is repeated over time, then a rhythm is established, based on the nature of the repetition. A cycle has three distinct features: (1) the pace, tempo, or periodicity at which an activity takes place; (2) the phase; and (3) the amplitude (Shankar, 2014).

Second, interaction between two or more rhythms is a prerequisite for rhythms to adjust. To facilitate this interaction, the periodicities of the rhythms need to be fairly close to one another (Aschoff, 1979). The interaction can be weak or strong. However, for entrainment to happen, interaction needs to be weak; otherwise, the rhythms would lose their autonomy and form a new coupled system. Rhythms can behave in a synchronized manner without interaction or adjustments. This phenomenon is called pseudo entrainment (Ancona & Chong, 1996).

Third, besides the autonomous rhythms and their interaction, adjustment of these rhythms to the more dominant rhythm (or *pacer*) needs to take place, leading to a consistent relationship. There are two possible adjustments: phase or tempo, leading to either phase or tempo entrainment. Phase entrainment refers to rhythms that are entrained by the phase or position in the cycle, while tempo entrainment refers to rhythms that are entrained by their tempo. For example, in organizations, the monthly production or sales cycles can be entrained to the quarterly reporting cycles. Holiday periods or specific marketing efforts can be scheduled to be in phase with the availability of additional work forces during holiday periods. Note that the organization is managing these ***induced*** rhythms. The rhythm of the seasons or day-night are examples of ***natural*** rhythms to which other rhythms may entrain, such as holiday periods, and/or work schedules.

There are a few terms closely related to entrainment: coherence, resonance, and flow. Coherence describes the degree of entrainment between rhythms, or, in other words, how many rhythms are entrained (in tempo and/or phase) to the more dominant rhythm. Resonance, on the other hand, involves the synchronization of ***dependent*** rhythms, while entrainment involves independent rhythms. Unlike coherence and resonance, the term "flow" refers to a mental state of an individual that is inherently enjoyable, motivating them to persist in the activity for the sake of the activity itself (Csikszentmihalyi, 1990).

Integral Entrainment Matrix

There are numerous rhythms, at every system or level (individual, group, organizational, societal, etc.), each with its own pace and phases. Different types of entrainment can be organized into three broad categories (Sandra, 2020; Sandra & Nandram, 2013):

1 *where* entrainment occurs (within or between systems);
2 *whereby* or by which rhythm (symmetrical or asymmetrical rhythms);
3 *how* rhythms eventually are entrained (tempo, phase, synchronic, harmonic, simultaneous, or sequential).

Because the latter category ("how") is independent of the other categories, a matrix can be created, defined as the integral entrainment matrix combining the first two categories: whether the entrainment occurs within a system (inner) or between systems (outer); and whether rhythms mutually entrain each other (symmetrical) or not (asymmetrical) (Sandra & Nandram, 2013). This results in intra-, extra-, inter-, and exter-entrainment (Figure 12.1). Note that this matrix is fractal, meaning that the intra-entrainment quadrant at one level represents another matrix at a more detailed level. For example, intra-entrainment within a group can be subdivided into four quadrants (matrix) at the individual level.

The integral entrainment matrix serves a number of purposes. First, it helps to make a better distinction between the different types of entrainment. Second, it highlights the integral nature of entrainment: entrainment within a system cannot be seen as standalone; it continuously entrains with other systems, but is also entrained by the environment of the system. Finally, it offers a framework for practitioners and researchers to identify the several rhythms to which they (personally) or their organizations entrain.

The following paragraphs discuss each quadrant of the matrix at the individual level using the human body as a reference system. As stated above, this matrix can be used at any other level.

	Inner entrainment (within a system)	**Outer entrainment** (between systems)
Symmetrical entrainment	Intra-entrainment	Inter-entrainment
Asymmetrical entrainment	Extra-entrainment	Exter-entrainment

FIGURE 12.1 Integral Entrainment Matrix

Note: Integral Entrainment Matrix. Adapted from Sandra and Nandram (2013). Copyright 2013 by the World Researchers Associations. Adapted with permission.

Intra-Entrainment

Intra-entrainment (upper left; Figure 12.1) is a type of entrainment describing the phenomenon where two or more autonomous rhythms *within* a system, like a human body, influence each other (i.e., *symmetrical*) and become entrained.

An example of intra-entrainment is entrainment of the human heart and brain, whereas the heart is the strongest dominant rhythm or pacer, entraining other rhythms in the human body, and, as a result, significantly influences how we perceive and react to ourself and our environment (Childre & Martin, 1999; Frysinger & Harper, 1990; Lacey & Lacey, 1970; McCraty et al., 1996). Studies show that holding elevated emotions—such as appreciation, care, nonjudgment, and forgiveness—influences intra-entrainment, which enhances cognitive performance, sensitivity, mental clarity, emotional stability, and well-being (Childre & Cryer, 2000; McCraty et al., 2009). In addition, meditative states are also known to foster entrainment (Tiller et al., 1996).

Inter-Entrainment

Looking at social interactions, individuals are able to entrain each other's rhythms (Kelly & Barsade, 2001; Waller, 1999). According to McCraty and Zayas (2014), "The smoothness of flow in any social interaction depends to a great extent on the establishment of spontaneous entrainment between individuals" (p. 61). This type of entrainment is defined as inter-entrainment (upper right; Figure 12.1), and also called *interpersonal* entrainment (individual level). It is symmetrical because rhythms are influencing and adjusting to each other.

Examples of inter-entrainment are emotional and behavioral entrainment. According to Goss (2007), individuals are attracted to some situations and blocked from others, based on their "emotional energy," and that sets the level of emotional entrainment. Furthermore, the structured and rhythmic nature of spiritual rituals and embodied performance, as described by Horan (see Chapter 8), serves as a potent catalyst for inter-entrainment, harmonizing participants' emotions and behaviors, and leading to collective resonance that enhances spiritual well-being. Following Kelly & Barsade (2001), behavioral entrainment refers to "the completely nonconscious processes by which one individual's behavior is adjusted or modified in order to coordinate or synchronize with another." (p. 109), including synchronization of body movements, affect, and attitudes. A curvilinear relationship between synchronicity and affect is hypothesized by Warner et al. (1986), "with moderately synchronous social interactions rated most positively" (p. 110).

The level of intra-entrainment plays an important role in the establishment of inter-entrainment. Sandra (2021) discovered a variation in inter-entrainment (measured via heart coherence) between client and therapists during craniosacral therapy sessions. Other forms of (deep) social interaction, such as personal coaching, may have a similar effect. Interestingly, people who develop a higher level of intra-entrainment will be able to connect or communicate more effectively with others (i.e., inter-entrainment) than people who do not have this higher level (McCraty & Zayas, 2014).

Extra- and Exter-Entrainment

Individuals being entrained by environmental rhythmic stimuli is a part of chronobiology (Chapple, 1970) and called asymmetrical entrainment (Sandra & Nandram, 2013), because the individual cannot influence the entraining rhythm (e.g., the cycle of light and dark). In such a situation, a human body is "forced" to adjust to external cycles without being able to influence them. When a human system as a whole is entrained by the environment, this is called exter-entrainment (lower right; Figure 12.1). When the environment entrains parts within a (human) system, then this is identified as extra-entrainment (lower left; Figure 12.1).

Within the human body, brainwaves undergo continuous fluctuations, overseeing the functioning of the nervous system and the level of consciousness. Meanwhile, these brainwaves remain open to entrainment by external rhythms during what is known as the "free-run" period, spanning from 5 to 25 seconds (Becker, 1990a, 1990b). An example of such an external rhythm is the Schumann resonance, having an average frequency of approximately 7–10 Hz (Balser & Wagner, 1960; Galejs, 1972; Schumann, 1952). According to Oschman (1997), such brainwave entrainment by the Schumann resonance during the "free-run" period typically happens when the individual is in a relaxed or meditative state (i.e., intra-entrainment). Moreover, Seto et al. (1992) discovered that the biomagnetic field projected from the hands in such a situation, of brainwave entrainment, is much stronger than without. This implies that extra-entrainment is positively influencing intra-, inter-entrainment. How the day-night cycle influences work-life balance or working rhythms is an example of exter-entrainment, because the behavior of individuals is influenced by an external pacer that cannot be changed.

Entrainment Coherence and Collective Resonance

Based on the learnings from physiological entrainment, Sandra (2020) posited that *entrainment coherence* is another variable to be added to the theory of entrainment, next to the notion of cycles, interaction, and adjustment. It is defined as "the degree of entrainment across all cycles, both in phase and in tempo. It is a measure of the degree of order, stability, and flexibility of these cycles" (p. 83). Furthermore, this concept of entrainment coherence aligns with Guenther's principle of oneness (see Chapter 3), emphasizing the interrelatedness with all beings and deepening the spiritual need for belonging and meaning in life. Such coherence is maximized, as described by Sandra & Nandram (2013, 2020), when entrainment occurs in all quadrants and levels of the integral entrainment matrix at the same time.

In her study, Levi (2003) collected and analyzed experiences of *collective resonance*, defined as "a felt sense of energy, rhythm, or intuitive knowing that occurs in a group of human beings and positively affects the way they interact toward a common purpose" (p. 3). She argued that this collective resonance could be a result of entrainment. Her study identified a number of factors that are able to influence the shift of a group into collective resonance. These factors are mapped onto the integral entrainment matrix in Figure 12.2. Some important shared factors were an acknowledged feeling of vulnerability (i.e., "a sense of not knowing"), and silence to connect with oneself, one another, and the environment (all quadrants).

	Inner entrainment	Outer entrainment
Symmetrical entrainment	**Intra-entrainment** - Vulnerability - Silence to connect with oneself	**Inter-entrainment** - Silence to connect with other - Silence/listening to acknowledge what is - Truth-telling (i.e., speak with own voice about own truth) - Container contraction (e.g., through human bodies sitting in a circle) - Shared intent
Asymmetrical entrainment	**Extra-entrainment** - Silence to connect with environment - Place or space (e.g., building, environment) - Sound or vibration (i.e., music, singing, speech)	**Exter-entrainment** - Silence to connect with environment - Container contraction through (e.g., darkness, movement)

Note: Factors in descending order of consensus

FIGURE 12.2 Factors that Influence Collective Resonance

Note: Factors that influence collective resonance. Reprinted from Sandra (2020). Copyright 2020 by Danny Sandra. Reprinted with permission.

Spiritual Leadership

Spiritual Leadership Defined

According to Kouzes & Posner (2023), the leadership challenge "has always been about how people go about mobilizing others to want to make extraordinary things happen" (p. xv). It is a complex interaction between the designated leader and the environment, both social and organizational (Fiedler, 1996), involving everyone in the community through a social process (Barker, 1997; Drath & Palus, 1994; Wenger & Snyder, 2000). Hence, everyone is considered a leader (Drath, 1998). Day (2001) argued that leader development emphasizes the building of intrapersonal competence (intra-entrainment), while leadership development focuses on building interpersonal competence (inter-entrainment).

Spiritual leadership is defined "as comprising the values, attitudes, and behaviors that are necessary to intrinsically motivate oneself and others so that they have a sense of spiritual survival through calling and membership" (Fry, 2003, pp. 694–695). It is based on intrinsic motivation, incorporating vision, hope/faith, and altruistic love, fueled by a spiritual practice or inner life (Fry, 2008). The vision depicts an image of the future created from the organization's reason for existence (i.e., culture and core values), while hope/faith is the source of believing that the organization's vision will be realized. Having faith is expressed through action and a willingness to do what it takes to realize the vision, in alignment with one's values, attitudes, and behaviors (Fry, 2003; MacArthur, 1998). Altruistic love is defined as "a sense of wholeness, harmony, and wellbeing produced through care, concern, and appreciation for both self and others" (Fry, 2003, p. 712). I should note that although the outcome of spiritual leadership is one's sense of spiritual well-being, this outcome cannot be pursued directly (Fry, 2005). Sandra and Nandram (2020) contended that spiritual well-being arises spontaneously through consciously aligning these three core elements (vision, hope/faith, altruistic love) into a coherent whole, also termed as "spiritual leadership coherence" (Sandra, 2022, p. 444). This implies that articulating an inspiring vision is just as important as the leader's actions, values, and attitudes in bringing that vision to life.

Spiritual Practice and Inner Life

Fry and Slocum (2008) posited that we all have spiritual needs (i.e., an inner life), in addition to the physical, mental, and emotional ones, both at work and at home. Moreover, they found that a spiritual practice is a crucial source for the development of vision, hope/faith, and altruistic love. According to Fry et al. (2017), having an inner life means embarking on a personal exploration of oneself and developing an understanding that genuine happiness does not come from selfishness and self-centeredness. Instead, it is achieved by shifting focus to others, cultivating a mindset of love and service for others. This transformation is the true nature of spiritual leadership.

Spiritual Leadership Development

Research shows that an inner life not only has a direct impact on one's own spiritual leadership, but also on one's followers (Fry & Slocum, 2008; Sandra, 2022). A spiritual practice thus influences the development of spiritual leadership in two independent but intertwined ways. First, the practice acts as a source of wisdom from which one can develop the vision, hope/faith, and altruistic love that make up spiritual leadership. Second, a spiritual practice positively influences the entrainment process, bringing these variables into better alignment.

How can spiritual leadership be developed concretely? A good starting point is nurturing one's inner life through a suitable practice. There are a variety of practices available these days. Organizations could start by providing a context and structure that welcome such a practice. One has to find a convenient space and time for these practices, for example, organizations can designate a certain area and provide guided meditations or yoga classes during lunch time. The lessons suggested below may help to enhance the use and organization of these practices. Typically, nurturing an inner life fosters intra-entrainment, which enhances cognitive and emotional performance, as well as the ability to communicate (Childre & Cryer, 2000; McCraty et al., 2009). Subsequently, this will foster the development of one's vision, the capacity to care (altruistic love), and put words into action. Moreover, intra-entrainment will also influence inter-entrainment, such as emotional and behavioral entrainment, connecting easier with other people.

Next, besides nurturing the inner life, one can spend (more) attention on how the personal vision, values (altruistic love), and actions (hope/faith) are aligned to one another. For example, is the personal vision sufficiently translated into appropriate action? Are the actions sufficient to realize the vision? Are the values lived in line with that vision? And do they support a caring life? Perhaps, only a small part of the vision has been translated into action.

Lessons for Spiritual Leadership Development

A spiritual practice is any practice that nurtures the qualities of the human spirit or inner life, which brings happiness to both self and others (Dalai Lama XIV, 1999). How can the learnings from entrainment enhance these practices and indirectly develop spiritual leadership?

First, an effective spiritual practice is a practice that enhances the level of entrainment in one or more quadrants of the integral entrainment matrix (i.e., entrainment coherence), because entrainment is a natural process of becoming synchronized with oneself (intra-entrainment), others (inter-entrainment), and the environment (extra- and exter-entrainment). As discussed earlier, the higher the level of entrainment, the higher the outcome in terms of cognitive performance, sensitivity, mental clarity, emotional stability, and well-being. For example, addressing challenging life issues becomes easier with greater clarity. Another example is the presence of calmness due to less inner "noise" caused by daily stress.

Second, a good starting point for increasing the effectiveness of a spiritual practice is to focus initially on improving intra-entrainment, which subsequently will raise the receptivity for extra-entrainment (cf. Schumann resonance) and the sensitivity for inter-entrainment. Breathing techniques that increase heart coherence are a good way to enhance intra-entrainment (Edwards, 2016), which deepens the connection with one's inner self beyond mind and body, as well as holding elevated emotions, such as appreciation, care, non-judgment, and forgiveness (Childre & Cryer, 2000; McCraty et al., 2009).

From her study mentioned earlier, Levi (2003) identified that silence to connect with oneself and to the environment as a key factor that influences the shift toward group resonance or inter-entrainment. Silence is a way to slow down one's own rhythm, getting more in touch with oneself and something larger at the same time, nurturing the human spirit through reflection and imagination. When used as a spiritual expression, silence is seen as a positive tool for enhancing one's overall experiences (Poland & Pederson, 1998; Poulos, 2004). The practice of silence in a work setting has multiple dimensions and can encourage reflective processes (Vu & Fan, 2022). However, it is important to note that silence is not solely individual-focused but instead derives meaning from the specific context in which it is used (Vu & Fan, 2022).

Third, spiritual practices are ideally done in a healthy natural environment of one's liking, such as a forest, sea, lake, or mountains. Similar to the Schumann resonance, these healthy natural environments have the ability to reinforce intra- and inter-entrainment and reduce entrainment to technological pacers that could be harmful. Moreover, honoring the wisdom and sacredness of nature with openness and humility, which includes recognizing the intrinsic value of all beings as highlighted in Chapter 6, positively influences intra- and inter-entrainment. If it is impossible to go to these environments, one can create a similar environment that resonates with them and fits their needs, noting that entrainment can only happen when periodicities of the rhythms are fairly close to one another.

Fourth, spend time with those people who really care about you, your environment, and others. One does not need to know these people; they just need to care. This elevated emotion enhances one's performance, sensitivity, clarity, stability, and well-being through intra-entrainment. Moreover, Levi (2003) identified that "an acknowledged feeling of vulnerability," "listening to acknowledge what is," and "speaking with own voice about own truth" are other shifting factors for inter-entrainment.

Fifth, pace the timing of the spiritual practice in terms of when to organize/attend. This implies establishing a repetitive action (or rhythm) that fits the person and their environment. For example, every other day, week, month, and so on. Over time, repetition creates a rhythm. Once a rhythm is in place, one can entrain it consciously to its environment (exter-entrainment), then it becomes easier to attend and participate.

Sixth, pace the spiritual practice itself to fit with one's self and environment. At the start, one takes time to connect with that environment. For example, meditating or doing yoga in silence early mornings outdoors; painting in the afternoon on one's favorite patio; journaling late evening while looking at the sea or along a slow rippling river; or doing a yogic sleep meditation before sleeping. These are forms of intra- and extra-entrainment (both tempo and phase), taking into account the wake-sleep cycle of human beings.

Seventh, select a spiritual practice that fits one's values to enhance emotional and behavior entrainment. Note that the setting, environment, and the people (if the practice is in a group) should fit these values too. Appreciation, care, love, non-judgment, and forgiveness are values known for enhancing entrainment (Childre & Cryer, 2000; McCraty et al., 2009).

Dark Side of Entrainment

Although entrainment is a natural process of adapting to one or more rhythms, human beings can be entrained to pacers that are artificial and harmful to mankind. Unlike pacers from nature, pacers can be generated on purpose by humans or through technology.

When individuals are entrained by environmental rhythmic stimuli, the human body is "forced" to adjust to these pacers without being able to influence them. Typically, this type of entrainment is beneficial and more efficient for the individual (Ancona & Chong, 1996). However, we can choose not to adapt to that pacer but that will take extra effort because it is less efficient. Consider, for example, the impact of night shift work on the human body and its biological clock.

When pacers are generated by humans, they can entrain others in a positive or negative way. As an illustration, studies indicate that the person who establishes an organization sets a rhythm during its founding period that endures as the most influential throughout its history (Schein, 1985). As an organization grows, numerous subcultures will grow too, which are smaller groups within the larger organization that share distinct values, norms, and beliefs. According to Schein (1996, 2009), subcultures influence how individuals within an organization perceive, interpret, and respond to events and experiences. The process of entrainment can put pressure on individuals to conform and align with the (sub)culture they are part of. This can lead to a loss of individuality and autonomy, where personal choices and decisions are strongly influenced by external forces rather than personal values or beliefs. Employees will perform (and feel) well if there is a fit between the (sub)culture and the rhythms generated from their own intra- and inter-entrainment. It becomes detrimental when individuals (unconsciously) adapt to cultures that do not fit.

Another example is the movement that government leaders can establish for certain causes, such as climate change or (seasonal) vaccination. The dark side of entrainment lies in the fact that influential individuals or organizations can exploit the process for their benefit. For example, specific leaders like Hitler and his Nazi party in Germany established numerous movements before and during the Second World War, manipulating public opinion, consumer behavior, or political ideologies through deliberately created entrainment patterns, all without considering the collective welfare.

In addition to human generated pacers, technology possesses the capability to generate potent pacers, a notion that becomes particularly evident when examining the rapid advancement of electronic information dissemination through mobile communication over the last two decades. This progression has given rise to a concerning outcome: electromagnetic radiation (EMR) emerging as a notable and novel form of pollution. This radiation interacts with human organs, with a particular emphasis on the brain and nervous system displaying heightened sensitivity to EMR. The degree of sensitivity is contingent upon the duration of exposure and the intensity of power density (Hu et al., 2021).

Overall, being mindful of the dark side of entrainment is crucial to avoid potential negative consequences. Striking a balance between being influenced by external factors (extra- and exter-entrainment) and maintaining critical thinking and individuality through spiritual leadership development (intra- and inter-entrainment) is essential for both personal and organizational growth.

Conclusion

The objective of this chapter was to draw lessons from the phenomenon of entrainment to enhance spiritual practices, because entrainment is a natural, influential process of becoming synchronized with oneself (intra-entrainment), others (inter-entrainment), and the environment (extra- and exter-entrainment). Spiritual practices affect spiritual leadership development in two distinct ways. First, they enhance cognitive and emotional performance, assisting in the development of an aspiring vision, actions (hope/faith), and corresponding values and attitudes (altruistic love). Second, they strengthen the coherence of these spiritual leadership elements, from which spiritual well-being can emerge. Moreover, entrainment could be considered as a natural force behind spirituality, bringing rhythms into harmony throughout all levels, and as a result, fostering well-being for self and others.

Seven lessons were drawn from the learnings of entrainment to enhance spiritual practices: (1) an effective spiritual practice is a practice that enhances the level of entrainment in one or more quadrants of the integral entrainment matrix; (2) a spiritual practice should focus initially on improving intra-entrainment, which will influence and enhance the other types of entrainment; (3) spiritual practices are ideally done in a healthy natural environment of one's liking; (4) spend spiritual practice time with those people that really care about themselves, their environment, and us; (5) pace the timing of the spiritual practice to establish a rhythm; (6) pace the spiritual practice itself to fit with one's own biological rhythm, likes, and environment; and finally (7) enhance emotional and behavior entrainment by selecting a spiritual practice that aligns with one's values. Implementing these lessons will not just elevate spiritual practices but also foster the development of spiritual leadership within oneself and among others.

References

Ancona, D. G., & Chong, C.-L. (1996). Entrainment: Pace, cycle and rhythm in organizational behavior. In B. M. Staw, & L. L. Cummings (Eds.), *Research in Organizational Behavior* (Vol. 18, pp. 251–284). Jai Press.

Ancona, D. G., Okhuysen, G. A., & Perlow, L. A. (2001). Taking time to integrate temporal research. *Academy of Management Review*, *26*(4), 512–529. https://doi.org/10.2307/3560239

Aschoff, J. (1979). Circadian rhythms: General features and endocrinological aspects. In D. T. Krieger (Ed.), *Endocrine rhythms* (pp. 1–61). Raven Press.

Balser, M., & Wagner, C. (1960). Observations of Earth–ionosphere cavity resonances. *Nature*, *188*, 638–641.

Barker, R. A. (1997). How can we train leaders if we do not know what leadership is? *Human Relations*, *50*(4), 343–362. https://doi.org/10.1177/001872679705000402

Becker, R. O. (1990a). The machine brain and properties of the mind. *Subtle Energies & Energy Medicine Journal Archives*, *1*(2), 79–87.

Becker, R. O. (1990b). *Cross currents: The perils of electropollution, the promise of electromedicine*. Penguin.

Bluedorn, A. C. (2002). *The human organization of time: Temporal realities and experience*. Stanford Business Books.

Chapple, E. D. (1970). *Culture and biological man: Explorations in behavioral anthropology*. Holt, Rinehart and Winston.

Childre, D., & Cryer, B. (2000). *From chaos to coherence: The power to change performance*. Planetary.

Childre, D., & Martin, H. (1999). *The heartmath solution*. Harper Collins.

Csikszentmihalyi, M. (1990). *Flow: The psychology of optimal experience*. Harper & Row.

Dalai Lama XIV. (1999). *Ethics for the new millennium*. The Putnam Publishing Group.

Day, D. V. 2001. Leadership development: A review in context. *The Leadership Quarterly*, *11*(4), 581–613. https://psycnet.apa.org/doi/10.1016/S1048-9843(00)00061-8

Dibrell, C., Fairclough, S., & Davis, P. S. (2015). The impact of external and internal entrainment on firm innovativeness: A test of moderation. *Journal of Business Research*, *68*(1), 19–26. https://doi.org/10.1016/j.jbusres.2014.05.012

Drath, W. H. (1998). Approaching the future of leadership development. In C. D. McCauley, R. S. Moxley, & E. Van Velsor (Eds.), *The Center for Creative Leadership handbook of leadership development* (pp. 403–432). Jossey-Bass.

Drath, W. H., & Palus, C. J. (1994). *Making common sense: Leadership as meaning-making in a community of practice*. Center for Creative Leadership.

Edwards, S. D. (2016). Influence of HeartMath quick coherence technique on psychophysiological coherence and feeling states. *African Journal for Physical Activity and Health Sciences*, *22*(4:1), 1006–1018.

Fiedler, F. E. (1996). Research on leadership selection and training: One view of the future. *Administrative Science Quarterly*, *41*(2), 241–250. https://doi.org/10.2307/2393716

Fry, L. W. (2003). Toward a theory of spiritual leadership. *The Leadership Quarterly*, *14*(6), 693–728. https://doi.org/10.1016/j.leaqua.2003.09.001

Fry, L. W. (2005). Toward a theory of ethical and spiritual well-being, and corporate social responsibility through spiritual leadership. In R. A. Giacalone, C. Dunn, & C. L. Jurkiewicz (Eds.), *Positive psychology in business ethics and corporate responsibility* (pp. 47–84). Information Age Publishing.

Fry, L. W. (2008). Spiritual leadership: State-of-the-art and future directions for theory, research, and practice. In J. Biberman, & L. Tishman (Eds.), *Spirituality in business: Theory, practice, and future directions* (pp. 106–124). Palgrave.

Fry, L. W., Latham, J. R., Clinebell, S. K., & Krahnke, K. (2017). Spiritual leadership as a model for performance excellence: A study of Baldrige award recipients. *Journal of Management, Spirituality & Religion*, *14*(1), 22–47. https://doi.org/10.1080/14766086.2016.1202130

Fry, L. W., & Slocum, J. W. (2008). Maximizing the triple bottom line through spiritual leadership. *Organizational Dynamics*, *37*(1), 86–96. https://doi.org/10.1016/j.orgdyn.2007.11.004

Fry, L. W., & Whittington, J. L. (2005, August 5–10). *Spiritual leadership as a paradigm for organizational transformation and development* [Paper presentation]. Academy of Management 2005 Annual Meeting, Honolulu, Hawaii.

Frysinger, R. C., & Harper, R. M. (1990). Cardiac and respiratory correlations with unit discharge in epileptic human temporal lobe. *Epilepsia, 31*(2), 162–171. https://doi.org/10.1111/j.1528-1167.1990.tb06301.x

Galejs, J. (1972). *Terrestrial propagation of long electromagnetic waves.* Pergamon Press.

Goss, D. (2007). Reconsidering Schumpeterian opportunities: The contribution of interaction ritual chain theory. *International Journal of Entrepreneurial Behavior & Research, 13*(1), 3–18. https://doi.org/10.1108/13552550710725156

Hu, C., Zuo, H., & Li, Y. (2021). Effects of radiofrequency electromagnetic radiation on neurotransmitters in the brain. *Frontiers in Public Health, 9*(691880). https://doi.org/10.3389/fpubh.2021.691880

Kelly, J. R., & Barsade, S. G. (2001). Mood and emotions in small groups and work teams. *Organizational Behavior & Human Decision Processes, 86*(1), 99–130. https://psycnet.apa.org/doi/10.1006/obhd.2001.2974

Khavul, S., Pérez-Nordtvedt, L., & Wood, E. (2010). Organizational entrainment and international new ventures from emerging markets. *Journal of Business Venturing, 25*(1), 104–119. https://doi.org/10.1016/j.jbusvent.2009.01.008

Kouzes, J. M., & B. Z. Posner, B. Z. (2023). *The leadership challenge: how to make extraordinary things happen.* Jossey-Bass.

Lacey, J. I., & Lacey, B. C. (1970). Some autonomic-central nervous system interrelationships. In P. Black (Ed.), *Physiological correlates of emotion* (pp. 205–227). Academic Press.

Levi, R. A. (2003). *Group magic: An inquiry into experiences of collective resonance* (Publication No. 3098829) [Doctoral dissertation, Saybrook Graduate School and Research Center]. PQDT Open. https://www.proquest.com/openview/e46064dfe5edeeffc605efffb7a3b8e5

MacArthur, J. F. (1998). *In the footsteps of faith.* Crossway Books.

McCraty, R., Atkinson, M., Tomasino, D., & Bradley, R. T. (2009). The coherent heart: Heart-brain interactions, psychophysiological coherence, and the emergence of system-wide order. *Integral Review, 5*(2), 10–115.

McCraty, R., Tiller, W. A., & Atkinson, M. (1996). *Head-heart entrainment: a preliminary survey.* [Conference presentation]. Key West Brain-Mind, Applied Neurophysiology, EEG Biofeedback 4th Annual Advanced Colloquium, Key West, FL, United States.

McCraty, R., & Zayas, M. A. (2014). Cardiac coherence, self-regulation, autonomic stability, and psychosocial well-being. *Frontiers in Psychology, 5*(1090), 1–13. https://doi.org/10.3389/fpsyg.2014.01090

McGrath, J. E., & Tschan, F. (2004). *Temporal matters of social psychology: Examining the role of time the lives of groups and individuals.* American Psychological Association.

Minorsky, N. (1962). *Nonlinear oscillations.* Van Nostrand.

Naiman, L. (2018, August 15). Want to be a better leader? Cultivate your inner life. *Inc.* https://inc.com/linda-naiman/want-to-be-a-better-leader-cultivate-your-inner-life.html

Oschman, J. L. (1997). Therapeutic entrainment. *Journal of Bodywork and Movement Therapies, 1*(3), 189–194. https://doi.org/10.1016/S1360-8592(97)80039-3

Poland, B., & Pederson, A. (1998). Reading between the lines: Interpreting silences in qualitative research. *Qualitative Inquiry*, *4*(2), 293–312. https://doi.org/10.1177/107780049800400209

Poulos C. N. (2004). Disruption, silence, and creation: The search for dialogic civility in the age of anxiety. *Qualitative Inquiry*, *10*(4), 534–547. http://dx.doi.org/10.1177/1077800403257679

Sandra, D. (2020). *Entrainment in organizations: An exploration at the individual and group level* [Doctoral dissertation, University of Antwerp, Belgium]. UA Repository. https://repository.uantwerpen.be/docstore/d:irua:1712

Sandra, D. (2021). Using digital technology to evaluate heart coherence in craniosacral therapy as an indicator of spiritual leadership. *European Journal of Integrative Medicine*, *44*(June), 101329. https://doi.org/10.1016/j.eujim.2021.101329

Sandra, D. (2022). Evaluating spiritual leadership coherence at a professional services company as a way to drive connectedness and well-being in organizations. *Humanistic Management Journal*. https://doi.org/10.1007/s41463-022-00140-6

Sandra, D., & Nandram, S. S. (2013). The role of entrainment in the context of integral leadership: Synchronizing consciousness. *Advances in Management*, *6*(12), 17–24.

Sandra, D., & Nandram, S. S. (2020). Driving organizational entrainment through spiritual leadership. *Journal of Management, Spirituality & Religion*, *17*(4), 316–332. https://doi.org/10.1080/14766086.2019.1585280

Schein, E. H. (1985). *Organizational culture and leadership*. Jossey-Bass.

Schein, E. H. (1996). Three cultures of management: The key to organizational learning. *Sloan Management Review*, *38*(1), 9–20.

Schein, E. H. (2009). *The corporate culture survival guide: Sense and nonsense about culture change*. Jossey-Bass.

Schumann, W. O. (1952). Über die strahlungslosen Eigenschwingungen einer leitenden Kugel, die von einer Luftschicht und einer Ionosphärenhülle umgeben ist. *Zeitschrift für Naturforschung A*, *7*(2), 149–154. https://doi.org/10.1515/zna-1952-0202

Seto, D., Kusaka, D., Nakazato, S., Huang, W. R., Sato, T., Hisamitsu, T., & Takashige, C. (1992). Detection of extraordinary large bio–magnetic field strength from human hand during external Qi emission. *Acupuncture and Electro–Therapeutics Research, the International Journal*, *17*(2), 75–94. https://doi.org/10.3727/036012992816357819

Shankar, R. (2014). *Fundamentals of physics: Mechanics, relativity, and thermodynamics*. Yale University Press.

Shi, W., & Prescott, J. E. (2012). Rhythm and entrainment of acquisition and alliance initiatives and firm performance: A temporal perspective. *Organization Studies*, *33*(10), 1281–1310. https://doi.org/10.1177/0170840612453530

Tiller, W., McCraty, R., & Atkinson, M. (1996). Cardiac coherence: A new, noninvasive measure of autonomic nervous system order. *Alternative Therapies in Health and Medicine*, *2*(1), 52–65. PMID: 8795873

Vu, M. C., & Fan, Z. (2022). Sounds of silence: The reflexivity, self-decentralization, and transformation dimensions of silence at work. *Journal of Management Inquiry*, *31*(3), 307–325. https://doi.org/10.1177/10564926211007942

Waller, M. J. (1999). The timing of adaptive group responses to nonroutine events. *The Academy of Management Journal*, *42*(2), 127–137. https://doi.org/10.2307/257088

Warner, R. M., Malloy, D., Schneider, K., Knoth, R., & Wilder, B. (1986). Rhythmic organization of social interaction and observer ratings of positive affect and involvement. *Journal of Nonverbal Behavior*, *11*(2), 57–74. http://dx.doi.org/10.1007/BF00990958

Wenger, E. C., & Snyder W. M. (2000). Communities of practice: The organizational frontier. *Harvard Business Review*, *78*(1), 139–145.

PART IV

The Shadow Side of Leadership and Spirituality

13

MAKING THE DARKNESS CONSCIOUS

Collective Shadow Work for the Spiritual Development of Leaders

Bianca Briciu and Amy K. MacDonald

Introduction

The multiple global crises we are facing today call attention to the urgent need for conscious, authentic leaders who can transform the worldviews and social structures that contribute to systemic problems. One important area of transformation is leaders' own inner worlds, which determine the quality of the conditions they create for others (Palmer, 1994; Scharmer & Kaufer, 2013). Many current leadership theories and development programs frame leadership practices into simplistic binaries of good versus bad (Chappell et al., 2019); they focus on developing desirable leadership traits (Kaiser et al., 2015; Vince & Mazen, 2014) or they propose idealized models of leadership that are ideologically appealing but difficult to attain in reality (Alvesson & Einola, 2019). These approaches ignore the complexity of human consciousness, which contains both positive and negative aspects. Accepting these false dichotomies without question not only "reinforces the great man myth," but also "serves as a defense mechanism" which turns these traits into the shadow (Chappell et al., 2019, p. 327).

In the last two decades, there has been an increased interest in the spiritual development of leaders in the Western world; a particular focus has been on exploring leadership as an inner journey to wholeness and an outer journey of interconnectedness and systems thinking (Anello et al., 2014; Fry, 2003; Scharmer & Kaufer, 2013). Research on spirituality and psychology offers frameworks for leadership development that transcend the dichotomy of good versus bad leaders and accounts for the complexity of consciousness including the dark or shadow side of the personality (Chappell et al., 2019;

DOI: 10.4324/9781003396741-18

Rozuel & Ketola, 2012). Understanding the shadow side makes it possible to move away from dualism, toxic positivity, and the myth of reason that pervades leadership approaches. Many leadership development programs reinforce the inner split leaders experience between desired positive traits and repression of undesirable traits that can lead to personal distress or the projection of undesirable traits on others (Ladkin et al., 2018).

This chapter analyzes the role of shadow work and its relationship to spirituality in leadership development. It describes three leadership shadows and their impact: the shadow of trauma, the shadow of power and hubris, and the shadow of spirituality. In the second half of the chapter, we propose five approaches for spiritual leadership development based on integration (wholeness) and interconnectedness. The five approaches invite leaders to explore collective shadow work based on Indigenous epistemologies, somatics, and psychospiritual practices. In doing so, they challenge the individualistic and dualistic Western paradigm, inviting leaders to step into "the leading edge of collective evolution" that Wilber (2000) called "integral consciousness" (p. 13).

The Shadow: Living a Divided Life

According to Jung (1967), the shadow contains all aspects of the self that are rejected and pushed into the unconscious because they do not fit the persona or because they are painful reminders of traumatic wounds. All individuals have an ideal self or persona shaped by the norms of their social and cultural environment (e.g., gender norms and religious norms) that represents the kind of person they want to be. They aim to behave in ways which are consistent with these norms (Masters, 2018).

Disowning aspects of the self creates inner division between the conscious and the unconscious (Ketola, 2007). This leads to a strong polarization between what is seen as good and evil, superior and inferior, what is desired and what is feared. Personal and collective elements seen as inferior are repressed and "coalesce into a relatively autonomous 'splinter personality' with contrary tendencies in the unconscious" (Jung, 1989, p. 398–399). Personality splitting is a defense mechanism that exposes "a painful gap between who we most truly are and the role we play in the so-called real world" (Palmer, 2008, p. 15).

The danger is that these denied aspects of the self do not disappear—they continue to exist and persist in the unconscious. These splinter personalities control the self, influencing thoughts and actions—through mechanisms of repression, projection, denial, trauma-re-enactment, and inner fragmentation—threatening authenticity, and well-being (Jung, 1989). Aspects of the unconscious mind take the driver's seat while remaining hidden from awareness. Leaders invested with power and influence over others, may be surprised to realize that their actions do not always reflect their conscious intentions (Kegan & Lahey, 2009).

Scharmer (2018) used the concept of "blind spot" to signal "the source from which leaders' actions and perceptions originate" (p. 33). The inner world is the space where leadership originates, but it remains unknown without practices of awareness, self-reflection, and dialogue that illuminate shadow elements. Awareness helps leaders understand why they make certain decisions or behave in certain ways, unmasking some habitual responses that are unconscious. The inner world is also seen as separate and unrelated to social reality, rendering invisible the contribution of human consciousness to it (Scharmer & Kaufer, 2013). The shadow remains hidden not only from one's consciousness but also from the social world, appearing only as a symptom without a trace. Symptoms of social pathology in organizational practices are the visible manifestations of inner pathologies from which they originate (Scharmer & Kaufer, 2013). One of these pathologies is the shadow as a mechanism of repression and projection.

Individuation: Shadow Work as Path to Hidden Wholeness

Carl Jung (2014) observed that "one does not become enlightened by imagining figures of light, but by making the darkness conscious" (p. 265). He called this process "individuation," a journey of self-realization that involves befriending and integrating the unwanted aspects of the unconscious shadow into the persona. This is a lifelong process of becoming whole and living with integrity as a more aware and spiritual self. Individuation is a movement toward reducing and overcoming the rigid split—between the conscious and the unconscious, between the person and the shadow—through a gradual increase in awareness and integration of the less desirable aspects of the self, which also reduces the boundaries between the individual self and the collective (Ladkin et al., 2018). There is a paradox in individuation: as one engages in a process of differentiation of the unique self, one also moves closer toward a sense of interconnectedness with others.

For Jung (1993), the goal of individuation is the authentic acceptance of one's individual uniqueness that increases awareness of one's collectively shared traits. Individuation happens through reflection, awareness, and collective engagement in processes of learning and discovery (Ladkin et al., 2018). The most difficult aspect of individuation is the encounter with the shadow, often referred to as "shadow work." For leaders brave enough to engage in shadow work, two transformative outcomes await: wholeness and interconnectedness, both of which relate to spiritual development. Palmer (1994) saw the individuation process as a spiritual journey to discover one's "hidden wholeness," the unified field of our shared humanity and unconditional care. According to Palmer (2000), leaders are "complicit" in world-making, which is an "awesome and sometimes painful responsibility" (p. 78). The inner journey to self-awareness and self-knowledge awakens leaders to understand how their unconscious beliefs influence their actions in ways that impact their work. For Palmer (2008), "wholeness does not mean perfection: it means embracing brokenness as an integral part of life" (p. 5). Dualism cannot be overcome by positive thinking: it is not about being "good," it is about becoming whole (Palmer, 2008). We can realize our hidden wholeness by embarking on the spiritual journey of shadow work.

Shadow Work and Spiritual Development

Shadow work and spirituality are two complementary approaches to leaders' inner development. Shadow work without spiritual practice is difficult and dangerous, and spiritual practice without shadow work can lead to spiritual bypassing, a way to take refuge in spirituality to avoid one's darkness and painful emotions (Masters, 2010). The goals of both shadow work and spiritual development are to increase integration within the self and a sense of interconnectedness with others.

Although there is no uniform definition of spirituality in leadership, many scholars refer to specific inner capacities: creativity, insight, openness (Levine, 1994); sense of collective humanity and shared truth (Kriger & Hanson, 1999); connections with self, others, environment, and a higher power (Koss & Holder, 2015); hope, faith, vision, and altruistic love (Fry, 2003); meaning, fulfillment, and belonging (Giacalone & Jurkiewicz, 2003). (For a detailed outline of the moral foundations of spirituality in leadership, see Chapter 4). We take our working definition of spirituality from Koss and Holder (2015), who provided a multi-dimensional view that includes connectedness at four levels of experience: "Spirituality is a feeling of connectedness to something greater experienced by cultivating a relationship with oneself, one's community, one's environment, and one's perception of the transcendent" (p. 207). Spiritual development means an increase of interconnectedness through the cultivation of a relationship with these four dimensions. This definition of spirituality reflects the Indigenous value of relationality, being in "'right relations,' a mode of being…characterized by relationality and reciprocity among both human and non-human relatives" (Gram-Hanssen et al., 2022, p. 675). Connectedness and relationality are essential to shadow work. Integrating the shadow can be a collective endeavor that grounds leaders in the value of care and responsibility toward the world.

Shadow work increases self-awareness and dismantles the dualism between good and evil, contributing to psychological integration that can expand ego-based consciousness to eco-centric consciousness (Irwin, 2006; Kass, 2017; Scharmer & Kaufer, 2013). Eco-centric consciousness is the capacity to hold a larger perspective, to see the system and understand one's role in it, to not cling to a certain identity or ideology (Scharmer & Kaufer, 2013). Developmental theories highlight an increasing level of complexity of consciousness through a process of differentiation and integration of different stages from ego-centric, to sociocentric, to world-centric (Wilber, 2000). Wilber (2000) saw psychospiritual development as a decline in egocentrism and moving toward integral consciousness, as the ability to inhabit deeper and wider perspectives with increased compassion. Wilber (2000) explained that as human consciousness grows into ever-expanding circles of compassion, it transcends and includes previous stages, moving from first-tier levels based on survival needs to second-tier consciousness that can integrate all other types, without seeing one as better than the other. He referred to this stage as integral consciousness, "the leading edge of human evolution that we are currently on the cusp of" (Wilber, 2000, p. 33).

Integral consciousness is the capacity to disidentify from the ego and become more open to complexity and transpersonal understanding, which is crucial for leaders today. Even though Jung's (1967) theory of individuation did not outline specific stages, it explains the process of expansion of consciousness through the integration of the shadow, coming close to developmental theories (Cook-Greuter, 2000). Integral consciousness is inclusive of diverse forms of knowledge and spirituality without seeing only one of them as the ultimate truth (Wilber, 2000). The processes of shadow work and the spiritual development of leaders both correlate with an interconnected perception of the outer world and a vision anchored in hope and compassion (Anello et al., 2014; Fry, 2003; Scharmer & Kaufer, 2013; Senge, 2006). In the following sections, we will explore manifestations of fragmented consciousness through the shadows of trauma, hubris, and spiritual bypassing, and their implications for leadership.

Shadow Typologies: Manifestations of a Divided Life

The Shadow of Trauma: Repressing Painful Emotions

Psychologist Richard Schwartz's (2013) framework of internal family systems (IFS) conceptualizes human consciousness as a family of different parts, governed by what he refers to as the "inner leader." Traumatic events can fragment the inner world, dividing it into repressed memories and protective parts that try to keep at bay the distressing emotions associated with those memories (Schwartz, 2013). He viewed the mind as a dynamic system of parts that are divided into two main categories: the "exiles" and the "protectors." Exiles are emotions and reactions associated with painful, distressing experiences (traumatic events) that have been repressed and are kept away from the conscious realm of experience. The exiles are a helpful way to examine the shadow of trauma.

The shadow of trauma leads to re-enactment of traumatic situations, dissociation, conflict triggers and reactivity, creating negative outcomes for leaders (Palmer, 2008; Walker & Kutsyuruba, 2016). Re-enactment of trauma is perpetuation of violence that can be direct (the person who suffered will make others suffer), structural (creating systems that perpetuate trauma), or attentional (denying other people's experiences and emotions because one has repressed them in oneself) (Hübl, 2020, p. 176). The most destructive effects of trauma are inner fragmentation and disconnection from one's spiritual core and the spiritual core of others (Maté, 2018).

Trauma adaptations may cause people to be strongly activated by triggers and stuck in flight, fight, freeze, or appease responses long after the stressful event happened, which influences their way of relating to the world (Haines, 2019). The freeze response leads to dissociation, a way of shutting down a part of themselves to prevent hurt (Haines, 2019, p. 118). Although all trauma adaptations can show up for leaders, the most common are fight response and dissociation. The fight response is a mechanism of protection through defensiveness and attack, when leaders may use power and aggression to hide vulnerability. Dissociation is a mechanism of protection from difficult emotions by denying all emotions and placing them in the shadow. The avoidance of emotions, "becoming mentally and spiritually hardened," is seen as one of the vices of leadership, whereas the shadow of anger begets leadership tyranny or even narcissism (Walker & Kutsyuruba, 2016, p. 215). Dissociation places the body and emotions in the shadow, excluding them from one's leadership, but this exclusion keeps at bay not only painful emotions but a person's overall emotional capacity to sense, attune, and resonate with others.

Experiences that threatened one's dignity, such as shame or marginalization, create trauma adaptations as fight responses that re-enact similar patterns through projecting one's pain onto others. In Padilla et al.'s (2007) examination of destructive leaders, they highlighted how negative life events, including unresolved childhood trauma and shame, contribute to leaders' ideologies of hate, which can be unconsciously projected onto others, creating enemies. Shadow work for trauma adaptations involves first a process of self-awareness and understanding of one's patterns in light of one's life story, and second, trauma integration, a re-tracing of painful events and the emotions they created, in a safe context, in order to bring back from exile the repressed parts of consciousness and reconnect to the inner leader, the spiritual core of the Self (Schwartz, 2013).

The Shadow of Leadership: Hubris, Power, and Projection

Leaders today face mounting pressures: they are expected to deliver high performance in increasingly complex and globalized contexts using ever-advancing technologies while navigating evolving relational dynamics (de Haan, 2016). These demands contribute to what de Haan and Kasozi (2014) called the "leadership shadow," an internal splitting phenomenon caused by assuming a leadership position and its accompanying expectations. Leaders are compelled to "bring to the foreground more 'positive,' 'leaderlike' characteristics of the self, and to cast aside the more 'negative,' 'denigrated' or 'follower-like' attributes" (de Haan, 2016, p. 508), relegating them to their leadership shadow.

The reality is that even so-called positive traits (such as drive, charisma, and confidence) which enable leaders to meet unrealistic expectations can shift into overdrive, marked by hubris, "a sense of overbearing pride, defiance, or presumption not justified by the circumstances or the perceptions of others" (de Haan & Kasozi, 2014, p. 20). Palmer (2000) called this "functional atheism" (p. 88), when leaders believe everything depends on them alone and that they are the only ones who can do the job right. There is an over-inflation of self (hubris) that is not willing to cede power and control, because they distrust the contributions of others; they must always dominate and never cease working. Hubris and overdrive can lead to "perceptual and cognitive biases," "increased stress and burnout," loss of resiliency to cope with stress, and eventually "physical and psychological illness, derailment, or collapse" (de Haan, 2016, p. 506). (For a contrasting view of the positive effects of surrender, see Chapter 2).

Chappell et al. (2019) stressed that the danger of leaders denying and suppressing their undesirable traits is that they can unknowingly project their unwanted parts onto others instead of facing and transforming them. Vince and Mazen (2014) used the construct of "violent innocence" to describe this psychological mechanism of denying and defending against negative feelings and aspects of the self by projecting them onto others. They argued that violent innocence is a means of domination that leads to "excessive positivity" which maintains and upholds unequal and destructive power dynamics by silencing alternative and critical voices (p. 191).

The denial of the shadow and its projection are amplified for leaders because they hold socially sanctioned positions of power and authority over others. This means leadership itself as a social position increases the split between one's positive traits and the shadow, thus leaders' projection of the shadow has a broader reach and collective impact. Projection increases leaders' sense of power as they place their undesirable traits on others, hiding their own vulnerability and creating an inflated sense of self-importance and infallibility. This is the shadow of hubris at work. A leader's shadow projections can also be replicated at the collective/organizational level, creating toxic work environments. When leaders with the shadow of hubris project it on others, they create conditions of "collective frenzy" or toxic workaholism that shapes organizational culture (Palmer, 2000, p. 89). This phenomenon is particularly pernicious in the Anglo-Saxon cultures, contributing to a "hubris of consciousness" that can derail leaders and organizations (Jung, 1991, p. 170).

The Shadow of Spirituality: Spiritual Bypassing

As more organizations become aware of the salience of spirituality in leadership, we can learn a few lessons from exploring the shadow of spirituality. We differentiate here between spiritual leadership (leaders of religious/denominational institutions), and spirituality in leadership, the latter being about the inclusion of spirituality as a leadership trait in general. The spiritual development of leaders is considered a way to humanize and bring the soul back into organizations threatened by the profit-driven machinery of efficiency (Bolman & Deal, 2011) (For a different perspective on the soul and spirituality as it relates to consciousness in leadership, see Chapter 5). Spirituality orients leadership toward serving the common good, an ethical concern with justice, and a compassionate commitment to well-being (Fry, 2003).

Spiritual practices can take leadership development to new dimensions of creativity, openness, connection, hope, complexity, and transcendence (Fry, 2003; Howard, 2002; Koss & Holder, 2015), but they can only do so if they include practices for integrating the shadow. Although spirituality is a rich domain of development, it has its own shadow side manifested through *spiritual bypassing*, the avoidance of psychological pain by relying on spiritual practice as a way to rise above the suffering created by unresolved issues (Welwood, 1984). These issues are entrusted to an omnipotent, divine figure, while pushing what is seen as negative into the unconscious and eventually projecting it on others. Spiritual bypassing is a form of premature transcendence that skips necessary developmental stages and avoids one's existential pain (Welwood, 1984). Spiritual practice is at its very core a way to become free from attachment, suffering and delusion, but the denial of real-world pain and vulnerability can lead to a toxic illusion of freedom and transcendence.

Masters (2010) differentiated between the kind of spiritual transcendence that leads to growth and spiritual bypassing. The former is a way to see pain mindfully and clearly without becoming overwhelmed or overly attached to it, whereas the latter is a dissociation in which pain remains unconscious, affecting one's actions from the hidden place of the shadow. In spiritual bypassing, spirituality is commodified and used as an instrument to alleviate existential pain, which is repressed as the shadow (Sherrell & Simmer-Brown, 2017). This dissociation or premature transcendence cultivates a false spiritual persona or a higher self that may become increasingly disconnected from the real self, creating a delusional omnipotence and hubris. The concerns of real, embodied life are devalued and relegated to the shadow, which creates dualism between what is seen as human and what is seen as spiritual. Masters (2018) cautioned that transcendence should not mean "turning away" from the vulnerability of embodied experience but "including it in the circle of our being" (p. 60). Shadow work is difficult because it requires engagement with one's suffering. Spiritual practices help develop mindfulness and compassion to attend to suffering.

Repression of the shadow can be undone by compassion and courage to engage with our disowned elements, increasing a sense of intimacy with and integration of all that we are (Masters, 2010). The development of leaders is well served by replacing spirituality as transcendence and denial of the body, with an embodied spirituality based on integration of the shadow and engagement with existential suffering. Spiritual practices that include shadow work can help leaders become aware of their pain, discover their deep humanity, and engage in leadership from a more caring and complex (integral) understanding of reality.

Five Strategies for Collective Shadow Work in Leadership Development

Shadow work is an ongoing process of moving toward wholeness and individuation that involves three dimensions: (1) Awareness: recognizing its symptoms, understanding how it works, connecting the dots between shadow elements and one's personal history (Masters, 2018); (2) a collective space for holding the shadow: safe circles, story sharing, heart-based listening (Hübl, 2020); and (3) transformation and integration of the shadow (Masters, 2018; Scharmer & Kaufer, 2013). The result of an unintegrated shadow-side is a divided life that alienates leaders from themselves and others (Palmer, 2008). This is reflected in the common manifestations of the dominant Western worldview of individualism, intellectualism (head over heart), dualistic thinking, hierarchy, lack of empathy, competition, and supremacist thinking (Rimanoczy, 2021). Although we acknowledge the importance of traditional psychotherapy, we also recognize the need to think beyond Western individualization and professionalization of psychospiritual development. There is value in bringing this conversation out of the therapist's office and into communal dialogue with others.

We see potential in a collective practice of shadow work for leadership development that reflects Indigenous worldviews and epistemologies, that is experiential and prioritizes relationality, holism, interconnectedness, spirituality, and embodiment (Gram-Hanssen et al., 2022; Graveline, 2000; Hanson & Danyluk, 2022; Wagamese, 2019; Woodley, 2022). Indigenous ways of knowing and being do not subscribe to dualistic ways of thinking that create disconnection and instead value interdependence, harmony, and balance in all things (Celeste, 2023; Solomon, 2022).

In the remainder of this chapter, we will outline five strategies for collective shadow work in leadership development. They are (1) relational, (2) self-aware, (3) embodied, (4) creative, and (5) spiritual. These practices aim to create inner conditions of awareness, compassion, and connection, which make shadow work possible in imaginative and safe ways. Working together they form a collective process that aims to empower leaders to move toward wholeness and interconnectedness, as they experience compassion for their shadows and those of others (For a further exploration of individual and collective practices to develop non-dual leadership that promotes interbeing, wholeness, and oneness, see Chapter 3).

Relationality: The Circle of Storytelling

As discussed earlier, shadow suppression, dualism, and projections can alienate us from ourselves and others. The purpose of shadow work is to reconnect us with self and other. That is why we propose a practice of collective shadow work. Palmer (1994, 2000) and Masters (2010) emphasized the relational nature of shadow work. It fosters wholeness, acceptance of self, and compassion for others by helping us embrace the aspects we reject in ourselves and others. Vulnerably confronting one's shadow in community counters the Western tendency toward individualism and the myth of positivity. By bringing the non-perfect parts of ourselves into the light of others, we can practice both compassion for others and experience compassion from others for our shadow. This increases the ability to integrate the shadow and overcome the shame and alienation that accompany it (Metzger, 1991).

Relationality is foundational to Indigenous worldviews. Ojibwe author Richard Wagamese (2019) explained that the common Indigenous spiritual salutation "all my relations" (***indinawemaaginadog*** in Ojibwe) referred to "everybody, everywhere, in all times" including "everything present in Creation," human and non-human, recognizing that we are all related (p. 43). Indigenous worldviews see everyone and everything as interconnected: well-being is a state of harmony between body, mind, and spirit; disharmony creates unwellness (Garrett & Wilbur, 1999), and medicine (healing potential) resides within all of us—and all of creation (Mehl-Madrona, 2010).

The circle is a powerful symbol of dynamic interconnectedness in Indigenous traditions, as reflected in the cycles of nature (Garrett & Wilbur, 1999; Stevenson, 1999). Gathering in the form of a circle is a helpful practice to counter Western tendencies toward hierarchy and dualism of teacher/student, or leader/follower, which contributes to the leadership shadow. There is equity in the circle—everyone is the same height and same distance from the center (Stevenson, 1999), and everyone is valued as both learner and contributor. Indigenous approaches do not position teacher above student or facilitator above participant but increase relationality by establishing all as collaborative learners who contribute to knowledge by sharing their truth (Woodley, 2022). Being equal among others in the circle is a practical way to counter the leadership shadow of hubris.

The circle provides a safe place for sharing, which allows healing to happen. In traditional Indigenous healing circles, participants see each other as therapists; circles are spaces where they can achieve self-understanding and self-acceptance for both the desirable and undesirable aspects of their personality (Stevenson, 1999). The Indigenous practice of talking circles is a powerful way to foster interconnectedness, as it is rooted in Indigenous knowledge systems that are grounded in "collective learning and being-in-relation with others" (Hanson & Danyluk, 2022, p. 7).

Oral and spoken word in the form of narratives and storytelling are vital elements of Indigenous epistemologies (Woodley, 2022). The story is a "powerful commonality" for interrelationship and connectedness (Wagamese, 2019, p. 32). Gathering in a circle to hear a story, akin to gathering around the warm flame of a campfire, taps into something fundamental about our humanity—"a spiritual feeling of togetherness, safety, and belonging" (p. 31). According to Woodley (2022), people see themselves in stories, not propositions (a pillar of Western pedagogies). Leaders could reflect on stories, identifying where they recognize themselves and their shadows or craft their own stories that express the nature of their shadow.

Self-Awareness: Mindfulness and Self-Reflection

Existing in the unconscious, the shadow is a blind spot that is unknown to self but influences the self's way of being, and is experienced by others through one's actions and ways of relating. Integrating one's shadow requires self-awareness, which is the ability to see all aspects of the self with clarity, understanding who we are and how we are experienced by others. Self-awareness develops through mindfulness and self-reflection practices. Mindfulness is not a practice that engages directly with the unconscious and there is the danger of its appropriation as an instrument for detachment and a quick fix to daily stressors, which leads to spiritual bypassing (Sherrell & Simmer-Brown, 2017).

Mindfulness is focused openness to present experience, awareness, and acceptance (Kabat-Zinn, 2004). It is a quality of focused attention to what happens in the moment, suspending judgment and immediate reactions that help leaders develop open presence through meditative practices. It is a way of engaging with the world that returns leaders to the body, to the present moment, and to the quality of being; increasing the capacity to tolerate the discomfort of shadow work and creating the capacity to witness one's own mind and body. Mindfulness reduces the tendencies both to categorize experiences into positive and negative and to repress or resist the negative ones, thus helping to prevent the mechanism of repression that creates the shadow side (Kabat-Zinn, 2004). It increases leaders' awareness of their thoughts and emotions and enhances their capacity to self-regulate. It is thus a foundational practice for the challenging work of witnessing one's shadow side. The calming effect and the reduction of judgment brought by mindfulness lay the foundation for expanding awareness of one's inner world. However, mindfulness can only reveal the inner mechanisms of the shadow when accompanied by self-reflection and critical insight (Sherrell & Simmer-Brown, 2017, p. 80). (For a detailed discussion of the role of awareness in leadership as well as the corporate misuses of mindfulness see Chapter 2).

Self-reflection is an intentional process of exploring the patterns of one's experience in greater depth. It generates learning about one's experiences, examining one's behavior in context, understanding one's impact on others, and their contribution to relational dynamics. It means taking a step back from the rhythm of doing and understanding the assumptions underlying patterns of work, interactions, and experiences; it is "thinking about thinking" (Raelin, 2002, p. 66).

Raelin (2002) highlighted the difficulties of engaging in reflective practice in workplaces with frenzied rhythms and overburdened leaders, some of whom are invested in maintaining the status quo. In a culture that overvalues doing and achieving results, there is not enough time for reflection, which means that the shadow remains unconscious, and persists in influencing leaders' actions. Self-reflection can bring freedom from the mental structures that hold leaders prisoners, while also enabling an examination of the gap between their "espoused theory (what I say I do) versus theory in use (what I actually do)" (Argyris, 1982, as cited in Senge, 2006, p. 164).

It can be an unfolding process of awareness and conscientization of one's inner world and the way it interacts with the outer world.

Building collective spaces and practices for mindfulness and self-reflection are essential strategies for shadow work. Mindfulness increases attention to and awareness of what usually remains unconscious, giving access to previously repressed shadow material. It also creates more complexity of consciousness as a process of individuation that reduces the separation between conscious and unconscious. Self-reflection done collectively builds cognitive complexity to critically reflect on thoughts and behaviors emerging from the shadow.

Embodiment: Healing the Mind/Body Divide

Shadow suppression involves dissociation from certain parts of the self, which can include the body as a site of trauma and shame (Burstow, 2003; Haines, 2019). This is why reconnecting with our own bodies and to other people in an embodied way fosters integration. Embodied practices involve developing bodily awareness, sensing, and expression. These practices may include yoga, dance, martial arts, somatic therapy, and other similar activities that include movement and physical sensation. They liberate our sensing capacities from the repression and constriction that accompanies the shadow (van der Kolk, 2014).

One somatic practice to engage with the shadow is called "blending with shame," which comes from the method of generative somatics developed by Haines (2019). Generative somatics is an approach that creates lasting transformation by working with habitual, embodied patterns that reflect unconscious reactions to harmful social relations. It works with embodied practices to heal trauma and liberate the self to live a life aligned with one's values, reclaiming love and hope (Haines, 2019). It has an important dimension of social justice, increasing awareness of the ways social power shapes our embodied system and our relational capacities (Burstow, 2003).

Experiences of humiliation lead to the shadow of shame that creates hiding, repression, and a sense of being fundamentally flawed (Haines, 2019). Blending with shame means creating a safe, connected, and curious dialogue about what is shameful, turning toward it, not away from it, and tracking it through body sensations. It starts with the question: "What is bad or wrong about you?" The answers are accompanied by an acknowledgment of a facilitator who repeats back what they hear, inviting the person to track their body sensations (Haines, 2019, p. 306). This dialogue allows the shadow to reach the surface, be seen in the safe and empathic company of another person, while moving through the body. This vulnerable exercise needs to be accompanied by a resourcing practice of allyship, where the person places other people around them in meaningful positions and creates a sense of allyship, inviting them to say meaningful phrases that convey connectedness and belonging (Haines, 2019).

Embodied practice counters Western dualisms between mind and body and creates a sense of wholeness by reconnecting mind and body, self and other, expanding the range of perception. (For an exploration of "embodied social change," as a non-Western approach to collective transformation, healing, and wholeness, see Chapter 8). Embodied practices, although potentially uncomfortable at first, can open a new door of understanding and help participants bring the body back from the shadow.

Creativity: Arts-Based Practices

Studies have found evidence for the use of arts-based methods (visual arts, drama, music, dance) in leadership development, particularly in increasing leaders' self-awareness, deepening their understanding of others' perspectives, enhancing their knowledge of the relationality of leadership, and exposing the power and associated responsibility inherent in leadership (Garavan et al., 2015; Romanowska et al., 2014; Sutherland & Jelinek, 2015). Arts-based methods provide an opportunity for leaders to confront and express their shadow in creative and symbolic ways, which is helpful when dealing with difficult thoughts and feelings.

A simple arts-based practice for a collective setting is representing one's shadow by drawing it or creating a collage. Sharing and discussing these images in a circle is a powerful opportunity to give and experience empathy for these uncomfortable unconscious feelings, tempering the critical inner voice, and amplifying the collective voice of compassion. Chappell et al. (2019) recommended building a character out of the shadow, called "Who am I." Participants describe five of their positive qualities and write down their opposite. They are then invited to imagine a person with these opposite qualities, giving them a name, appearance, and description, and engaging in a dialogue with them. Arts-based exercises tap into creative imagination as a safe way to explore the shadow collectively.

Spirituality: Compassion for Self and Others

Spiritual practices that cultivate certain qualities and ways of being—such as the practices of self-compassion and compassion—can be pathways to access the shadow. Self-compassion is a way of relating to oneself with mindfulness and kindness, which allows shadow work to unfold by taming the discomfort caused by shadow elements (Neff, 2015). Self-compassion is an attitude of caring and curiosity toward the self in all its positive and negative aspects

(Briciu, 2021). Psychologist Krystin Neff (2015) defined self-compassion as mindfulness of personal suffering, kindness toward oneself, and recognition of our shared human condition. Highlighting the difference between self-esteem and self-compassion, she argued that the former contributes to hubris (when succeeding) or despair (when failing) (Neff, 2015), whereas self-compassion implies radical acceptance of one's weaknesses and dark aspects, thus reducing the dualism that creates the shadow. Self-compassion is an attitude of accepting the full range of human emotions, rather than repressing and shaming certain emotions as negative. It holds vulnerability in awareness not as a personal flaw, but as an aspect of the human condition. It embraces both the light and the shadow, reducing the shame and self-criticism that accompany a perfectionistic relationship to oneself (Briciu, 2021). Self-compassion can be cultivated through exercises of journaling, dialogue, changing perfectionism-based critical self-talk, meditation, and awareness of one's needs (Neff, 2015). The cultivation of self-compassion creates a caring, less judgmental attitude toward oneself that tames the resistance and shame accompanying shadow work.

Compassion is defined as genuine concern about the suffering of others and the desire to alleviate it (Halifax, 2018). One exercise for cultivating compassion is the compassion meditation, or loving-kindness meditation with origins in the Buddhist tradition, a guided meditation that enhances love and care for all beings (Halifax, 2018). Compassion creates a bridge to the shadow in oneself and others. It is an essential capacity for leaders today, because the experience of compassion opens the self to the other and leads to a heart-based ethical approach to life and work (Halifax, 2018). Compassion counteracts the shame created by the division of consciousness between light and darkness and the division between self and others. It increases with the awareness of our common vulnerabilities and existential suffering as a profound lesson that "our own liberation is bound up with the liberation of others" (Halifax, 2018, p. 221). The practices of self-compassion and compassion contribute to the spiritual development of leaders by cultivating an attitude of open and loving curiosity toward the self and other that reduces the repression producing the shadow and enhances connection and resonance with others.

Conclusion

The journey of individuation through shadow work is a lifelong journey that is by no means easy or linear. It happens gradually with reflection, experience, and learning. It involves awareness, community, and transformation. Why would leaders engage in difficult shadow work, especially if some shadows are rewarded in our current social system (i.e., the shadow of hubris)? We proposed two worthwhile outcomes of shadow work as a crucial leadership development practice: wholeness and interconnectedness. Shadow work involves inner integration as a movement toward wholeness and individuation, undoing the dualism within the self between conscious and unconscious. This integration supports more authentic connections to other people and increases awareness of the interconnectedness of life.

The shadow-integrating spiritual development of leaders can inaugurate a paradigm shift from a technocratic, patriarchal, and hierarchical style of leadership to one that is more relational, holistic, and process-oriented (de Haan & Kasozy, 2014). Integration of the shadow means being aware of its presence and making choices that are aligned with one's core, authentic self, rather than being under the unconscious influence of the shadow. Shadow work helps leaders do the leap of transformation to the stage of integral consciousness, with major consequences for the way they lead. Leaders who operate from their higher self instead of the shadow can start making decisions that take into consideration the well-being of all and the interdependence of systems. Studies show that leaders with awareness of their shadow exhibit more ethical responsibility (Ketola, 2007), more awareness of the self and social systems (Scharmer & Kaufer, 2013), more courage (Palmer, 2008), and a strong sense of vision and purpose (Laloux, 2014).

In this chapter, we highlighted the dualism between the conscious and the unconscious, leading to the formation of the shadow as a source of repressed, denied, and unwanted aspects of the self, and demonstrated the psychological, interpersonal, and leadership issues caused by shadow suppression and projection. We offered three typologies of the shadow: (1) the shadow of trauma, created by repressing distressing memories and experiences; (2) the shadow of the leadership role, marked by hubris, overdrive, and projections that create toxic workplace cultures; and (3) the shadow of spiritual bypassing, as an avoidance of painful or "negative" aspects of reality in order to inhabit a (false) idealized persona.

We looked to the spiritual wisdom of Indigenous and Eastern practices, psychology, somatics, and spirituality, to reveal the potential of a collective practice of shadow work that is relational, self-reflective, embodied, creative, and spiritual. Taking shadow work out of the therapists' office and into collective relationships, valuing it as an essential aspect of psychospiritual integration in leadership development, holds potential not only for the well-being and wholeness of leaders themselves, but also for the well-being and interconnectedness of organizations, communities, and systems. Moving across the edge of human evolution suggested by Wilber (2000), means creating more public spaces that embrace the shadow and uphold a spirituality that is compassionate and integral; a spirituality of arrival and descent into embodied life and the complexity of the world. Holding the tension of opposites without rejecting any of them can help us heal the painful divisions between the inner and outer world, enabling us to respond to today's chaos, complexity, and uncertainty with a sense of collective hope and possibility.

References

Alvesson, M., & Einola, K. (2019). Warning for excessive positivity: Authentic leadership and other traps in leadership studies, *The Leadership Quarterly*, *30*(4), 383–395. https://doi.org/10.1016/j.leaqua.2019.04.001

Anello, E., Hernandez, J., & Khadem, M. (2014). *Transformative leadership: Developing the hidden dimension*. Harmony Equity Press.

Argyris, C. (1982). *Reasoning, learning and action: Individual and organizational*. Jossey-Bass.

Bolman, L. G., & Deal, T. (2011). *Leading with soul: An uncommon journey of spirit* (Rev. 3rd ed.). Jossey-Bass.

Briciu, B. (2021). *The revolutionary art of love: From romantic love to global compassion*. Academica Press.

Burstow, B. (2003). Toward a radical understanding of trauma and trauma work. *Violence against Women*, *9*(11), 1293–1317. https://doi.org/10.1177/1077801203255555

Celeste, K. (2023). *The colonial shadow: A Jungian investigation of settler psychology*. Routledge. https://doi.org/10.4324/9781003296546

Chappell, S., Cooper, E., & Trippe, G. (2019). Shadow work for leadership development. *The Journal of Management Development*, *38*(5), 326–335. https://doi.org/10.1108/JMD-08-2018-0216

Cook-Greuter, S. R. (2000). Mature ego development: A gateway to ego transcendence? *Journal of Adult Development*, *7*(4), 227–240. https://doi.org/10.1023/A:1009511411421

de Haan, E. (2016). The leadership shadow: How to recognise and avoid derailment, hubris and overdrive. *Leadership*, *12*(4), 504–512. https://doi.org/10.1177/1742715015572526

de Haan, E., & Kasozi, A. (2014). *The leadership shadow: How to recognise and avoid derailment, hubris and overdrive*. Kogan Page.

Fry, L. W. (2003). Toward a theory of spiritual leadership. *The Leadership Quarterly*, *14*(6), 693–727. https://doi.org/10.1016/j.leaqua.2003.09.001

Garavan, T. N., McGarry, A., Watson, S., D'Annunzio-Green, N., & O' Brien, F. (2015). The impact of arts-based leadership development on leader mind-set: A field experiment. *Advances in Developing Human Resources*, *17*(3), 391–407. https://doi.org/10.1177/1523422315588358

Garrett, M. T., & Wilbur, M. P. (1999). Does the worm live in the ground? Reflections on Native American spirituality. *Journal of Multicultural Counseling and Development*, *27*(4), 193–206. https://doi.org/10.1002/j.2161-1912.1999.tb00335.x

Giacalone, R. A., & Jurkiewicz, C. L. (Eds.). (2003). *Handbook of workplace spirituality and organizational performance*. M.E. Sharpe.

Gram-Hanssen, I., Schafenacker, N., & Bentz, J. (2022). Decolonizing transformations through 'right relations'. *Sustainability Science*, *17*(2), 673–685. https://doi.org/10.1007/s11625-021-00960-9

Graveline, F. J. (2000). Circle as methodology: Enacting an Aboriginal paradigm. *International Journal of Qualitative Studies in Education*, *13*(4), 361–370. https://doi.org/10.1080/095183900413304

Haines, S. (2019). *The politics of trauma: Somatics, healing, and social justice*. North Atlantic Books.

Halifax, J. (2018). *Standing at the edge: Finding freedom where fear and courage meet*. Flatiron Books.

Hanson, A., & Danyluk, P. (2022). Talking circles as Indigenous pedagogy in online learning. *Teaching and Teacher Education*, *115*, 103715. https://doi.org/10.1016/j.tate.2022.103715

Howard, S. (2002). A spiritual perspective on learning in the workplace. *Journal of Managerial Psychology*, *17*(3), 230–242. https://doi.org/10.1108/02683940210423132

Hübl, T. (2020). *Healing collective trauma: A process for integrating our intergenerational and cultural wounds*. Sounds True.

Irwin, R. (2006). Spiritual development in adulthood: Key concepts and models. In C.H. Hoare (Ed.), *Handbook of adult development and learning* (pp. 326–362). Oxford University Press.

Jung, C. G. (1967). *Collected works of C.G. Jung, volume 7, Two essays in analytical psychology*. Princeton University Press.

Jung, C. G. (1989). *Memories, dreams, reflections* (Rev. ed.). Vintage Books.

Jung, C. G. (1991). The problem of evil today. In J. Abrams & C. Zweig (Eds.), *Meeting the shadow: The hidden power of the dark side of human nature* (pp. 170–173). J.P. Tarcher/Penguin.

Jung, C. G. (1993). *The basic writings of C.G. Jung* (In V. S. De Laszlo, Ed.). (R. F. C. Hull, Trans.). Modern Library.

Jung, C. G. (2014). *The collected works of C.G. Jung: Complete digital edition. Volumes 1–19* (In G. Adler et al., Eds.). (R. F. C. Hull, Trans.). Princeton University Press.

Kabat-Zinn, J. (2004). *Full catastrophe living: How to cope with stress, pain and illness using mindfulness meditation*. Piatkus.

Kaiser, R. B., LeBreton, J. M., & Hogan, J. (2015). The dark side of personality and extreme leader behavior. *Applied Psychology*, *64*(1), 55–92. https://doi.org/10.1111/apps.12024

Kass, J. D. (2017). *A person-centered approach to psychospiritual maturation: Mentoring psychological resilience and inclusive community in higher education*. Springer International Publishing. https://doi.org/10.1007/978-3-319-57919-1

Kegan, R., & Lahey, L. (2009). *Immunity to change: How to overcome it and unlock potential in yourself and your organization*. Harvard Business Press.

Ketola, T. (2007). Ten years later: Where is our common future now? *Business Strategy and the Environment*, *16*(3), 171–189. https://doi.org/10.1002/bse.477

Ketola, T. (2012). Losing your self: Managerial persona and shadow pressures killing responsible leadership. *The Journal of Management Development*, *31*(5), 470–487. https://doi.org/10.1108/02621711211226051

Koss, S. E., & Holder, M. (2015). Toward a global understanding of spirituality and religiosity: Definitions, assessments, and benefits. In E. C. Roberts (Ed.), *Spirituality: Global practices, societal attitudes, and effects on health* (pp. 203–229). Nova Publishers.

Kriger, M. P., & Hanson, B. J. (1999). A value-based paradigm for creating truly healthy organizations. *Journal of Organizational Change Management*, *12*(4), 302–317. https://doi.org/10.1108/09534819910282144

Ladkin, D., Spiller, C., & Craze, G. (2018). The journey of individuation: A Jungian alternative to the theory and practice of leading authentically. *Leadership*, *14*(4), 415–434. https://doi.org/10.1177/1742715016681942

Laloux, F. (2014). *Reinventing organizations: A guide to creating organizations inspired by the next stage of human consciousness.* Nelson Parker.

Levine, L. (1994). Listening with spirit and the art of team dialogue, *Journal of Organizational Change Management*, *7*(1), 61–73. https://doi.org/10.1108/09534819410050803

Masters, R. A. (2010). *Spiritual bypassing: When spirituality disconnects us from what really matters.* North Atlantic Books.

Masters, R. A. (2018). *Bringing your shadow out of the dark: Breaking free from the hidden forces that drive you.* Sounds True.

Maté, G. (2018). *In the realm of hungry ghosts: Close encounters with addiction* (Revised edition.). Vintage Canada.

Mehl-Madrona, L. (2010). *Healing the mind through the power of story: The promise of narrative psychiatry.* Bear & Company.

Metzger, D. (1991). Writing about the other. In J. Abrams & C. Zweig (Eds.), *Meeting the shadow: The hidden power of the dark side of human nature* (pp. 299–302). J.P. Tarcher/Penguin.

Neff, K. (2015). *Self-compassion: The proven power of being kind to yourself.* William Morrow Paperbacks.

Padilla, A., Hogan, R., & Kaiser, R. B. (2007). The toxic triangle: Destructive leaders, susceptible followers, and conducive environments. *The Leadership Quarterly*, *18*(3), 176–194. https://doi.org/10.1016/j.leaqua.2007.03.001

Palmer, P. (1994). Leading from within: Out of the shadow and into the light. In J. A. Conger (Ed.), *Spirit at work: Discovering the spirituality in leadership* (pp. 19–40). Jossey-Bass.

Palmer, P. (2000). *Let your life speak: Listening for the voice of vocation.* Jossey-Bass.

Palmer, P. (2008). *A hidden wholeness: The journey toward an undivided life.* Jossey-Bass.

Raelin, J. A. (2002). 'I don't have time to think!' Versus the art of reflective practice. *Reflections*, *4*(1), 66–79. https://doi.org/10.1162/152417302320467571

Rimanoczy, I. (2021). Anthropocene and the call for leaders with a new mindset. In A. A. Ritz & I. Rimanoczy (Eds.), *Sustainability mindset and transformative leadership: A multidisciplinary perspective* (pp. 117–139). Palgrave Macmillan. https://doi.org/10.1007/978-3-030-76069-4

Romanowska, J., Larsson, G., & Theorell, T. (2014). An art-based leadership intervention for enhancement of self-awareness, humility, and leader performance. *Journal of Personnel Psychology, 13*(2), 97–106. https://doi.org/10.1027/1866-5888/a000108

Rozuel, C., & Ketola, T. (2012). A view from within: Exploring the psychology of responsible leadership. *The Journal of Management Development, 31*(5), 444–448. https://doi.org/10.1108/02621711211226088

Scharmer, O. (2018). *The essentials of Theory U: Core principles and applications.* Berrett-Koehler Publishers, Incorporated.

Scharmer, O., & Kaufer, K. (2013). *Leading from the emerging future: From ego-system to eco-system economies.* Berrett-Koehler Publishers. http://ebookcentral.proquest.com/lib/ottawa/detail.action?docID=1207874

Schwartz, R. C. (2013). Moving from acceptance toward transformation with internal family systems therapy (IFS). *Journal of Clinical Psychology: In Session, 69*(8), 805–816. https://doi.org/10.1002/jclp.22016

Senge, P. (2006). *The fifth discipline: The art and practice of the learning organization.* Currency.

Sherrell, C., & Simmer-Brown, J. (2017). Spiritual bypassing in contemporary mindfulness movement. *ICEA Journal, 1*(1), 75–95. http://doi.org/10.1177/1541344603259311

Solomon, E. (2022). *Come dance with me: A medicine wheel practice of Anishinaabe Catholic interculturation of faith.* Novalis.

Stevenson, J. (1999). The circle of healing. *Native Social Work Journal, 2*(1), 8–21. https://zone.biblio.laurentian.ca/dspace/handle/10219/456

Sutherland, I., & Jelinek, J. (2015). From experiential learning to aesthetic knowing: The arts in leadership development. *Advances in Developing Human Resources, 17*(3), 289–306. https://doi.org/10.1177/1523422315587894

van der Kolk, B. (2014). *The body keeps the score: Brain, mind and body in the healing of trauma.* Penguin.

Vince, R., & Mazen, A. (2014). Violent innocence: A contradiction at the heart of leadership. *Organization Studies, 35*(2), 189–207. https://doi.org/10.1177/0170840613511924

Wagamese, R. (2019). *One drum: Stories and ceremonies for a planet.* Douglas & McIntyre.

Walker, K. D., & Kutsyuruba, B. (2016). The seven deadly narratives of leadership. In A. H. Normore & J. A. Brooks (Eds.), *The dark side of leadership: Identifying and overcoming unethical practice in organizations* (pp. 207–233). Emerald Publishing.

Welwood, J. (1984). Principles of inner work: Psychological and spiritual. *The Journal of Transpersonal Psychology, 16*(1), 63–73. https://psycnet.apa.org/record/1985-15194-001

Wilber, K. (2000). *Integral psychology: Consciousness, spirit, psychology, therapy.* Shambhala.

Woodley, R. (2022). *Indigenous theology and the western worldview: A decolonized approach to Christian doctrine.* Baker Academic.

14

PERMANENCE AND IMPERMANENCE

The Shadow Side of Leadership and Climate Change

Maxinne Rhea Leighton and Lisa A. Berkley

Introduction

Leadership and the Dark Night of the Soul

As climate and weather-related disasters surge, it becomes clear that humanity is facing a dark night of the soul with Mother Earth, a moment of personal, societal, and global reckoning. The dark night of the soul is a term used to describe a phase of spiritual crisis marked by a sense of intense loneliness, doubt, and despair before reaching a state of greater healing and spiritual awareness (Underhill, 2002). For generations, we have constructed a world which we have considered permanent: buildings and infrastructures which would last well past our lifetimes into the future for generations to come. Yet, in the face of climate change, the true fragility of both the built environment and our existence has been revealed, exposing the true impermanence of life itself. Permanence has revealed itself as an illusion.

This shift from permanence to impermanence confronts leaders with complex and complicated challenges. Even if they have an awareness or tacit knowledge of living from an interdependent and cyclical nature of life, when faced with personal upheaval or disorder, leaders may default to operating from a place of fear, dominance, and control (de Vries & Balazs, 2010) (see Chapter 6 for further discussion of an interdependent framework). At the same time, they may want to create a sense of safety and protect community members from the painful realities of change. However, this is an unrealistic expectation. To address the realities of climate change and help people make sense of a life of impermanence, leaders must first make the

DOI: 10.4324/9781003396741-19

unconscious conscious. They must become aware of their dark or shadow side (de Vries & Balazs, 2010) and address their personal fears. At the same time, they must hold a vision of positive potential (Korten, 2006) while leaning into their community's vulnerabilities such as whether one should stay and rebuild or leave. This process requires leaders to "help people move into a relationship with uncertainty and chaos" (Wheatley, 2005, p. 126) so that both the leader and their community can come to terms with climate unpredictability, or impermanence.

The Leaders' Role: Holding a Vision While Self-Healing

Almost all spiritual teachings indicate that change begins with the individual. From there, it spreads to the family, the village, and so on (Hanh, 2004; Kahane, 2010). As mentioned above, the person leading must hold the vision of positive potential for their community while leading them through facing their personal and collective pain and uncertainty of the future. In addition, when working with their community, leaders have the responsibility to move themselves from the illusory state of permanence to the reality of impermanence; it is essential they look inward, self-reflect, and engage with their shadow side while also confronting the transitory nature of life (e.g., loss, change, and being confronted with one's mortality). By undertaking such a process, leaders can embrace change while holding the space for those who cannot. They are laying the foundation for authentic, empowered, courageous, and creative leadership in the context of building our future. By looking inward and confronting the transitory, leaders model embracing change while holding space for those who cannot (Hanh, 2004).

In this chapter, we begin with personal reflections and hopes for the future from one of the authors, Maxinne Leighton. Dr. Leighton is an expert within the design community focusing on climate change. Following that is a discussion of the dark night of the soul in terms of what we are collectively experiencing in relationship to Mother Earth. We provide a high-level overview of the hero's journey, which includes a discussion of the Jungian interpretation of one's shadow side in the context of rebuilding communities which have been impacted by environmental crisis. This includes a discussion of permanence and impermanence as they pertain to the relationship between the built environment and nature. This is followed by an exploration of the human psyche, or the internal world, with a focus on how individuals confront these concepts. Permanence and impermanence are foundational to the discussion of rebuilding community post-climate disaster.

To grapple with human understanding of, and adaptation to, the illusions of stability (or permanence), which provide a perceived sense of security or foundation from which most people build their lives, we draw from the wisdoms and practices of theosophy, Eastern philosophical and spiritual traditions, Indigenous cultures, and Jungian psychology. Included is a discussion of how these concepts contribute to the shadow side of the human psyche and how embracing them provides a positive and necessary framework for leaders responsible for building a future of sustainable communities.

Personal Reflections of Permanence and Impermanence in the Built Environment

> Authors' note: In this section, lead author Maxinne Leighton, shares her story, one which serves as the underpinning for her life and work.

My childhood was largely spent living in the New York City Housing Authority (NYCHA) buildings in Coney Island in Brooklyn, New York, also known as "the Projects." From an internal and external, individual and collective perspective, permanence and impermanence were part of the fabric of my community. The ocean was our backyard and served as a constant reminder of impermanence. Sometimes the ocean's power was breathtakingly beautiful. Other times, the ocean's power created violent destruction; its rhythmic unpredictable nature is a reminder that "in Buddhism…the wave has its own temporary identity, seemingly distinct from the ocean from which it manifests. It exists, however, only as an expression of the ocean" (Korten, 2006, p. 43).

For me, permanence and impermanence were also defined by the smell of smoke from buildings that had been deliberately set on fire. Coney Island was impacted by the huge spread of arson in economically disadvantaged urban neighborhoods throughout America (notoriously across New York City in the 1970s) (The Arson Strike Force, Office of the Mayor, 1986). Feeling helpless and vulnerable in the face of these forces which I could not understand, predict, or control became foundational to my worldview.

My relationship to an impermanent world led me to establish my life within the space of perceived permanence by building a career in architecture and engineering in New York City. I could put trust and feel security in places that had inter-generational permanence: the Chrysler Building, Grand Central Terminal, the World Trade Center… Or so I thought.

On September 11, 2001, when the buildings at the World Trade Center site came down, so did my illusion of permanence. A massive structural symbol of New York's skyline was gone. Nearly 3,000 people were gone. Life was irrevocably changed. We were thrust abruptly into the reality of impermanence. And this was not to be the only drama in the new century that undermined faith in the constancy of the New York urban landscape.

Hurricane Sandy and its aftermath in 2012 became the reality of another kind of unreality. People were devastated. Lives and communities were upended. Unlike 9/11, nature's impact seemed random, utterly unpredictable. One block would be untouched, retaining its permanence, while the one right next to it would be wiped out.

Sandy was more than a decade ago. Balancing permanence and impermanence is a space I thought I had mastered, given my lived experience. That was, until the smoke from the fires in Canada blanketed New York City (Wallace-Wells, 2023) while writing this chapter. The sun was red, the sky yellow. Iconic buildings visible just the day before, disappeared behind a heavy wall of haze. Even wearing a double mask, I could taste the smoke. Panic set in. Deep grief overwhelmed me. Perceived permanence was once again impermanent.

How did I revert so quickly to being shocked and virtually paralyzed by the possibility of life without permanence? Was trickster casting light on the shadow of my own human grandiosity? Or was it a return to the Buddhist space of the beginner's mind (*shoshin*) where, one is always starting over (Suzuki, 2010). As I reflect on these questions, I think too on what it will take for humanity to address our VUCA (Volatile, Uncertain, Complex, and Ambiguous) challenges.

As all change begins within, I look to myself first. As one who has more than 20 years in leadership roles within the design community/built environment, a strong spiritual practice, and years of exploration within various psychological modalities, when personally confronted with challenging events to a community, city, or country, my trust in impermanence and life cycles has been seriously shaken. I see how easily one's foundation can be rattled. Will our leaders have the courage to embark on their personal Hero's Journey, while holding the vision of the positive potential and guiding us through the depths of the shadow? Can Buddhist or Indigenous philosophies provide a foundation for meeting the environmental challenges we must tackle together as individuals and as a global community?

Internal Worlds: The Path Within

Human beings often seek permanence to maintain control or avoid the reality of impermanence: the inevitable cycles of life, death, and rebirth; these aspects of impermanence are reflected in crises and change, decline and renewal. They are crucial to the natural world and to Earth herself and therefore must be embraced by all of humanity. As such, we can embody the reality that we "are always in transition, …the only time is now, and that the future is completely unpredictable and open" (Chodron, 2001, p. 122).

Permanence and Impermanence: Eastern Philosophical Perspective

The concepts of permanence and impermanence are important to several Eastern philosophical and spiritual traditions. In Hinduism, for example, the concepts of permanence and impermanence are explored through the notion of *maya*, the illusionary and ever-changing nature of the world, contrasted with that the unchanging ultimate reality (*Brahman*), which underlies all transient appearances (Mitra, 2020). Both Buddhism and Taoism use the concept of *Wu Wei* or non-doing, the principle of aligning with the natural flow of change instead of pushing against it (Goodman, 1980) (see Chapter 2 for a further discussion of the intersection of Taoism and Adaptive Leadership).

In Buddhist philosophy, which dates approximately 2,500 years ago, the concepts of permanence and impermanence are central to the understanding of the nature of reality and the human experience. In this framework, permanence serves as a moment of stability within the context of impermanence, the ordinary and ubiquitous state of reality. Understanding this relationship between permanence and impermanence can help to develop a more flexible and fluid approach to life, which is critical when the very nature of our planet's reality is shifting and changing. "The Buddha taught that everything is impermanent—flowers, tables, mountains, political regimes, bodies, feelings, perceptions, mental formations, and consciousness. We cannot find anything that is permanent" (Hanh, n.d., para. 1). The precepts are that life flows from birth to death, possessions do not last forever, nor do relationships, cultures, status, governments, or communities. Everything changes including our natural environment, whether incrementally or suddenly. However, from the perspective of some non-Western philosophies, permanence is an illusion created by attachment and desire. In permanence, things exist independently as fixed entities which continue to exist in the same form forever. The assumption of permanence causes human beings to cling to material possessions as well as their ways of everyday life. But trying to hold on to and control what is valued today, leads to frustration, disappointment, and suffering in the face of never-ending change (Gokhale, 2021).

Vietnamese Buddhist Zen Master Thich Nhat Hanh wrote, "It is not impermanence that makes us suffer. What makes us suffer is wanting things to be permanent when they are not" (Hạnh, 2017, p. 64). Learning to treasure impermanence means every moment is appreciated; it means respecting and valuing what we have and not taking anyone or anything for granted. Yet the prevailing consciousness within the world is to hold on to and maintain permanence, despite the historical fact that mass extinction has already happened five times on this planet (Elewa, 2012) with a sixth one now possibly in progress (Kolbert, 2014).

Historically, mainstream, or widely accepted social theories relied on concepts which suggest permanence. However, the influence of non-Western cultural traditions such as Buddhism has made the ideas of decay, loss, rupture, and ending become more prominent and accepted within Western social theoretical discourse (Geismar et al., 2022). One benefit of acknowledging and normalizing the concept of impermanence is the recognition of interdependency as suggested in Sogyal Rinpoche's (2008) interpretation of *The Tibetan Book of Living and Dying*: "If everything is impermanent, then everything is what we call 'empty,' which means lacking in any lasting, stable, and inherent existence, and all things, when seen and understood in their true relation, are not independent but interdependent" (p. 37).

The Dark Night of the Soul

This chapter began by stating that humanity is in its dark night of the soul with Mother Earth. The dark night of the soul provides a powerful framework for addressing our current global VUCA situation. The phrase, *dark night of the soul,* has its origins in the writings of St. John of the Cross (Coe, 2000), a Spanish mystic and poet, and has been used in many spiritual and psychological traditions to denote times of crisis. In Buddhism, the dark night is often called the *Dukkha nanas* or knowledge of suffering and refers to the impermanence of things (Tibetan Buddhist Encyclopedia, n.d.). In Hinduism, the shadow side is found in the terms *nirvana* and *moksha* (Mishra, 2013), and in Taoism, it is referred to as *Wu Wei* and non-action (Goodman, 1980). (It is worth it to also note that *Wu Wei* also addresses the issue of permanence and impermanence).

Indigenous cultures do not have one specific word that is related to the dark night of the soul; rather, shamanic initiations and ceremonial rites of passage serve to guide individuals through similar processes of death, rebirth, and transformation. This journey is similar to what is commonly referred to in the West as shadow work, based on the work of Jung (1951). According to Johnson (2013), "To honor and accept one's own shadow is a profound spiritual discipline. It is whole-making and thus holy and the most important experience of a lifetime" (p. x).

Jungian Psychology and the Shadow

The importance of the shadow side is expressed throughout countless cultures and mythologies and often shared through storytelling (Campbell, 1949). The stories reflect the hero's journey (Campbell, 2020), a transformative spiritual descent within which the shadow is met as one traverses the worlds of the divine and the human. The mastery of these two worlds is also aligned with the recognition and acceptance of impermanence, which is part of the hero's ability to meet and move through these very obstacles thereby overcoming the shadow and becoming more whole.

When embracing the shadow, one faces the hidden or unconscious aspects of themselves; this part has been repressed, denied, or ignored (Jung, 1951) and has been impacted by the collective unconscious, or "that aspect of the unconscious mind which manifests inherited, universal themes which run through all human life" (Jung, n.d.). The shadow is not to be feared or dismissed as it is a means to become a more whole and integrated human being (Jung, 1951). Jung's ideas about the collective unconscious as well as archetypes and the ownership or dismissal of the shadow sit at the intersectionality of permanence and impermanence: "In the realm of consciousness, we are our own masters ... But if we step through the door of the shadow, we discover with terror that we are the objects of unseen factors" (Jung, 1969, p. 23).

Meeting the Shadow

When one faces their deepest wounds and limitations and meets their shadow, they may enter the dark night of the soul. The dark night of the soul is a period of intense struggle, where everything one has valued as fundamental to their life and life's purpose is brought into question. Going through such a period challenges one's feeling of stability and brings them to the interstice between permanence and impermanence. There is profound loneliness, loss, isolation, confusion, terror, and even rage because one no longer feels connected to one's own life or to anything greater than the self (Fox, 2012). Jung (1963, 1969) described this process of passing through the dark night of the soul as the integration of conscious and unconscious aspects of oneself in which the shadow aspects of the psyche—the parts of us which are hidden and repressed—are encountered. This is where we face our inner demons and struggle with what has been hidden in our unconscious. Through meeting of the shadow, the unconscious too is brought to light and one becomes more authentically aligned with their true self and with the surrounding world.

Positive Potential within the Shadow

Within the shadow aspect of self lies not only negative qualities, but also "positive potential" (Korten, 2006, p. 41). Facing the shadow takes courage as it is a critical threshold for both individuals and society to cross in order to heal personal past, and often intergenerational, wounds. As Korten (2006) points out, working through the shadow is a necessary journey applicable to both the individual and the collective. On the collective level, individual healing is a crucial component for the growth and well-being of countries and nations; it requires critical examination and taking ownership of the gap between idealized national self-image and ownership of past transgressions so that healing and reconciliation can occur. This will require "a profound shift in the perception of reality... both as cognitive revolution and spiritual awakening" (Macy, 2009, para. 10) (see Chapter 11 for practices of individual healing in the context of healing society and Chapter 15 for a discussion of national healing).

When both the individual and the collective have the courage to confront the shadow, there is an opportunity to develop a deeper understanding of the interdependence between people and the planet. Engagement with Mother Earth can evolve from being transactional or opportunistic to being authentic, inclusive, and universal. Such frameworks as the Iroquois Confederacy's Seventh Generation Principle (Sargent, 2020), also known as the Haudenosaunee (Iroquois) philosophy, which states that "the decisions we make today should result in a sustainable world seven generations into the future" (Joseph, 2023) or, alternatively, the Buddhist Eastern Philosophy lens or continuum of permanence and impermanence can provide the groundwork for our collective way forward.

Between Permanence and Impermanence: Meeting the Trickster in the Shadow

Chodron (2001) suggested that true bravery means living without self-deception. In the context of impermanence and permanence, the shadow side presents as self-deception. When one believes there is an actual point of arrival, a place where the embodiment of the teachings has been realized, there is nothing else to do. But this belief is an illusion; it is where the archetype of the trickster lives. The very nature of "arriving" implies permanence, a final stopping point. But this runs contrary to the very nature of the impermanence of life, which is a journey, not a point of arrival.

Throughout history, the trickster has appeared in multiple cultures and spiritual world views using humor and deception to awaken both individuals and society. The trickster is at "one and the same time, creator and destroyer, giver and negator, he who dupes others and is always duped himself" (Radin, 1988, p. 5). In early Indian Buddhism, the Buddha was found using tricks to help people embrace their impermanence (McClintock, 2011). Indigenous cultures' Trickster Coyote possesses the ability to see through illusions and delusions (Ballinger, 1989). Trickster plays a significant role in the conversation around leadership, permanence and impermanence, spirituality, and climate change in that he is the reminder and awakener of self-deception.

Entering the Paradoxical Gateway: Bridging the Internal and External

Coming to terms with the paradoxical juncture between the finiteness of a life span and the infinite—which includes being part of something much bigger such as the Earth herself—is an existential passage in which humanity is brought to a moment of personal and societal reckoning. Theosophists have spoken of such extreme events in terms of the "dweller on the threshold" (Llewellyn, n.d.; Theosophy World, n.d.). Blavatsky (1993) and Bailey (1995) described the threshold as a frightening place where an individual must face the monstrous force (the Dweller) embodying accumulations of karmic wrongdoings. Anthroposophist Rudolph Steiner (1912a, 1912b) expanded upon this concept, referring to the "Guardians of the Threshold" (p. 1) connecting a very individual experience to the greater society (Sparby, 2023). This is the very precipice at which the global community stands today.

In the aftermath of a natural disaster, it can feel as if a threshold into another world is being crossed. For many, the devastating consequences of climate change have made life surreal and unrecognizable, leaving them feeling disoriented and terrified. From this state of being, the concept of the *dweller (or guardian) of the threshold* may resonate, providing a framework for understanding the feelings of individual disconnection from the collective. For others, this idea may weigh too heavily on the esoteric and thereby be less accessible.

Another way to embody the concept of the dweller on the threshold is by addressing the confluence between the spiritual and the psychological. Metzner (1995) described this climate caused separation as a "dissociative split" (p. 66), a break between the mental and the spiritual, which disassociates a person from their own innate nature and therefore from nature herself. This creates an oppositional pattern of projection, which focuses on separation. Conversely, cultures in which interdependence and impermanence are foundational "consider future generations and the future health of the ecosystem. Recognizing and respecting worldviews and spiritual practices different from our own is perhaps the best antidote to the West's fixation on the life-destroying dissociation between spirit and nature" (Metzner, 1995, p. 67).

Interdependency and Intergenerational: Storytelling and Indigenous Perspectives

In addition to considering Eastern philosophical perspectives on permanence and impermanence, leaders can learn from Indigenous communities whose worldview is that life is inextricable from nature and spirituality. This perspective was often passed from one generation to the next through storytelling. "For thousands of years prior to colonization, leadership in Indigenous communities was based upon the character of the land and the needs of the people in their traditional territories" (Kenny, 2012, p. 1). The power and centrality of storytelling achieves interconnected leadership and creates a reference point from which we can "manifest our solidarity and strengthen our people to take their next steps in encouraging good and healthy lives" (Kenny, 2012, p. 1). Stories in this context, "provide powerful bridges that connect our histories, our legends, our senses, our practices, our values, and, fundamentally, our sustainability as peoples" (Kenny, 2012, p. 4). They capture cultural and personal history and offer an intergenerational lens within an impermanent world. Stories provide grounding and stability. They establish a space of remembrance and reflection which can give one the courage to live within the reality of impermanence.

A well-known though seldom-honored Native American proverb states, "Treat the Earth well. It was not given to you by your parents, it was loaned to you by your children. We do not inherit the Earth from our ancestors, we borrow it from our children (SEANeighborhoods, 2023)." Gutiérrez (2012) underscored this perspective from the International Council of Thirteen Indigenous Grandmothers: "Ours is an alliance of prayer, education, and healing for our Mother Earth, all Her inhabitants, all the children, and for the next seven generations to come" (p. 105). This principle is rooted in the knowledge that everything is in a state of transformation and that the presence of one's ancestors as well as the land itself evolves. It reflects heart-based interdependency, which includes the cycles of life (death and birth, permanence and impermanence) and closely aligns with key and universal aspects of Indigenous cultures. Reflecting this, some Indigenous communities have begun to create community plans for sustainability and energy conservation based expressly on the seven generations perspective (Harjo, 2012; Brookshire & Kaza, 2013).

The External Reality of Environmental Crisis

With ongoing anthropogenic changes to the natural environment, there is growing awareness of the interdependency between the impermanence of the natural world and the perceived permanence of the human-scale built environment. The lack of recognized interdependency between the built environment and the natural world causes major disruptions in global economic and social systems. (Birch & Wachter, 2006). Whereas climate hazards such as hurricanes, droughts, flooding, and fires have historically been natural events in weather and planetary cycles, the number of worldwide climate-related disasters has tripled in the last 30 years (Oxfam International, 2023). As global climate events expand in scope to impact small town, countryside, rural communities and up to the scale of cities and wider regions, the interdependency between the natural environment and human communities continues to grow (Hallegatte et al., 2011).

Climate change disasters are highlighting the social inequities which have been inadequately addressed for many decades. It is a sad commonplace that when catastrophe strikes, those who are already living on the edge suffer the most (Gould & Lewis, 2021). Leaders have the responsibility of creating frameworks and policies which embrace the reality of environmental impermanence so that gaps of inequity do not become wider. This begins with a shift in consciousness, or, a coming to terms with the impermanence of one's external reality—the built environment and the natural world. Undoubtedly, this is a challenge.

Whereas some perceive these dramatic earth changes as a punishment or retribution either by an angry patriarchal God or a cruel matriarchal force of nature, they are neither. Quite the contrary, they are an opportunity to rethink how humans live with nature, themselves, and each other in a more sustainable and equitable manner. Some might consider this a "road to Damascus" moment (Rowlatt, 2022), which, though challenging, often frightening, and overwhelming, is part of the dark night of the soul's awakening. It provides a chance to reframe the way in which we address environmental changes. Within this context, it is an opportune time for leaders to self-reflect and come to terms with the impermanence of their own existence. Through this internal process, they are better prepared to initiate and lead the necessary conversations around permanence and impermanence and what it means to build community in the face of climate change.

Building Sustainable Communities

In the aftermath of many climate-impactful events such as hurricanes, wildfires, and sea level rise, the objective of many recovery and rebuilding initiatives is to develop communities which are sustainable when confronting climate impacts. The phrase, *sustainable communities,* has a variety of different meanings. The American Planning Association (2016) defined sustainability as "improving the quality of people's lives while living within the capacities of supporting natural and human systems" (p. 5). This common definition was developed by several nongovernmental organizations and United Nations agencies in 1991. In short, sustainable communities are being asked to embrace the impermanence of our human existence within the natural world. Each year since 2008, the number of people internally displaced by climate change-related disasters has risen to an annual average of 21.5 million (Internal Displacement Monitoring Centre & Norwegian Refugee Council, 2016). The Institute for Economics and Peace (2020) has estimated as many as 1.2 billion environmental migrants expected in the next 30 years. Climate change, environmental insecurity, and climate refugees are creating unprecedented challenges.

Permanence, Impermanence, and Rebuilding

A community that experiences a climate disaster understandably wants to "build it back," a slogan widely used after Hurricane Sandy (Leighton, 2020), meaning to restore and return to the life once known. The desire to recreate the sense of permanence is to be expected. Leaders, who are often impacted by the very same natural disasters as those they lead, are required to process their own lived experience. At the same time, they are tasked with helping those they serve navigate extreme loss and impermanence sustained during a natural disaster. The community members are often experiencing shock and grief saying such things as "I want *it* back. I want *it* back." This is not a response of just wanting their house or even their community back. Rather, it is a response of wanting their life—a feeling of permanence—back (Leighton, 2020). These community members do not want to face the reality of the impermanence of life amidst this level of duress. They are experiencing what can only be described as the reality of an unreality.

What was once considered permanent exists no longer. After a natural disaster, leaders try to apply their "relevant prior experiences" but are often overwhelmed with the "peculiarities of the situation" (Schön, 1983, pp. 128–129). Furthermore, they need to reflect more deeply on the nature and implications of the typically employed frameworks and approaches to rebuilding, which are rooted in the dream of permanence but do not consider the actuality of today. This reflection can lead to new thoughts and, more importantly, to *new questions* which enable both leaders and community to embrace the reality of impermanence. What happens when faced with the unthinkable—when permanence dissolves and nothing is left but impermanence? How does a leader lead? How do they face a traumatized community in need of a home and sense of security? How do they address questions of rebuilding?

Within a traumatized community, it is difficult to broach whether to rebuild (or not) and what considerations should be made for individuals to stay or leave the place which has been home. Such conversations can be further traumatizing for people who are in "deep shock as a result of exposure to death and devastation, [and are] left numb, afraid, vulnerable, and very alone" (Erikson, 1976, pp. 153–154). It is therefore incumbent on those leading the rebuilding effort to work with the individuals in the community with care and compassion, remaining aware of the trauma, shock, and possible sense of disempowerment they are experiencing.

In the context of climate change and environmental migration, solutions for rebuilding are complex. Leaders can pledge to develop the greenest and most resilient community on the planet, but when it comes to implementing the necessary changes, it is very difficult. Some leaders feel that society is not prepared to make these tough choices in the next 15 to 20 years unless something ultra-catastrophic happens (Leighton, 2020). What will this ultra-catastrophic event be? How many more communities, people, animals, and nature will be destroyed before we start making the tough decisions? Leaders initiating and fostering conversations about the built environment's illusion of permanence in the face of these environmental realities is a good first step. Human beings tend to look at modern life through the lens of permanence. But this is only until nature or a person-made disaster alters that reality.

In Partnership with Mother Earth

The concept of saving the world, often found in heroic narratives, has also translated specifically to climate change or "saving the earth." Mother Earth does not need a human savior. Rather, she needs advocacy and partnership. To build sustainable communities, a spiritual model of leadership which reflects the collective narrative and fosters interdependency and impermanence is needed. Leaders must develop self-awareness to embrace change while holding the space for those who cannot. This will require them to embrace intergenerational communities and strengthen "the locus of authentic personal power—not power over people and things, but rather the power of partnership with others, the power to cocreate life and to cooperate with an evolving universe" (Plotkin, 2008, p. 39).

For this vision to occur, leaders must courageously embark upon the hero's journey (integrating their shadow side and facing the trickster), so they may embody the ideas of interdependence and the Buddhist and Taoist- concept of *Wu Wei*. Drawing from the Indigenous wisdoms of multigenerational planning and storytelling, leaders can help people adapt to the concepts of permanence and impermanence in a more accessible and less threatening way. By embracing these perspectives, leaders can develop the spiritual foundation from which to guide communities in the face of the ongoing, and likely increasing challenges of climate change.

References

American Planning Association. (2016). *The sustainability policy framework: Revised draft final document—January 4, 2016.* https://planning-org-uploaded-media.s3.amazonaws.com/document/Sustainability-Policy-Framework.pdf

Bailey, A. A. (1995). *The seven rays of life.* Lucis Press. (Original work published 1948).

Ballinger, F. (1989). Living sideways: Social themes and social relationships in Native American trickster tales. *American Indian Quarterly, 13*(1), 15–30. https://doi.org/10.2307/1184084

Birch, E. L., & Wachter, S. M. (2006). Introduction: Rebuilding urban places after disaster. In E. L. Birch & S. M. Wachter (Eds.), *Rebuilding urban places after disaster: Lessons from Hurricane Katrina* (pp. 1–12). Counterpoint.

Blavatsky, H. P. (1993). *Collected writings,* Vol. XII. Theosophical Publishing House. (Original work published 1889).

Brookshire, D., & Kaza, N. (2013). Planning for seven generations: Energy planning of American Indian tribes. *Energy Policy, 62,* 1506–1514. https://doi.org/10.1016/j.enpol.2013.07.021

Campbell, J. (1949). *The hero with a thousand faces.* Princeton University Press.

Campbell, J. (2020). *The hero's journey: Joseph Campbell on his life and work.* Joseph Campbell Foundation.

Chodron, P. (2001). *The places that scare you: A guide to fearlessness in difficult times.* Shambhala Publications.

Coe, J. H. (2000). Musings on the dark night of the soul: Insights from St. John of the Cross on a developmental spirituality. *Journal of Psychology and Theology, 28*(4), 293–307. https://doi.org/10.1177/009164710002800408

de Vries, M. K., & Balazs, K. (2010). The shadow side of leadership. In F. Bournois, J. Duval-Hamel, S. Roussillon, & J. Scaringella (Eds.), *Handbook of top management teams.* (pp. 183–190). Palgrave Macmillan. https://doi.org/10.1057/9780230305335_19

Elewa, A. M. T. (2012). Mass extinction—A general review. In A. M. T. Elewha (Ed.), *Mass extinction* (pp. 1–4). Springer.

Erikson, K. T. (1976). *Everything in its path.* Simon & Schuster.

Fox, B. F. (2012). *The dark night of the soul: Conscious suffering, meaning, and transformation.* Pacifica Graduate Institute.

Geismar, H., Otto, T., & Warner, C. D. (Eds.). (2022). Introduction. In H. Geismar, T. Otto, T., & C. D. Warner (Eds.), *Impermanence: Exploring continuous change across cultures* (pp. 1–24). UCL Press.

Gokhale, P. P. (2021). Buddhist approaches to impermanence: Phenomenal and naumenal. *Religions, 12*(12), Article 1081. https://www.mdpi.com/2077-1444/12/12/1081

Goodman, R. (1980). Taoism and ecology. *Environmental Ethics, 2*(1), 73–80. https://doi.org/10.5840/enviroethics19802115

Gould, K. A., & Lewis, T. L. (2021). Resilience gentrification: Environmental privilege in an age of coastal climate disasters. *Frontiers in Sustainable Cities, 3.* https://doi.org/10.3389/frsc.2021.687670

Gutiérrez, R. D. (2012). Indigenous grandmas and the social justice movement. In. C. Kenny & T. N. Fraser (Eds.), *Living Indigenous leadership: Native narratives on building strong communities* (pp. 97–113). UBC Press.

Hanh, T. N. (n.d.). *Impermanence by Thich Nhat Hanh*. Great Mystery. (2019, September 7). https://greatmystery.org/perspectives-impermanence/

Hanh, T. N. (2004). *Peace begins here: Palestinians and Israelis listening to each other.* Parallax Press.

Hạnh, T. N. (2017). *The pocket Thich Nhat Hanh*. Shambhala Publications, Inc.

Hallegatte, S., Henriet, F., & Corfee-Morlot, J. (2011). The economics of climate change impacts and policy benefits at city scale: A conceptual framework. *Climatic Change, 104*(1), 51–87. https://doi.org/10.1007/s10584-010-9976-5

Harjo, L. L. (2012). *Muscogee (Creek) Nation: Blueprint for a seven generation plan.* (Publication No. 3513774) [Doctoral dissertation, University of Southern California]. ProQuest Dissertations and Theses Global.

Institute for Economics and Peace. (2020). *Over one billion people at threat of being displaced by 2050 due to environmental change, conflict and civil unrest.* https://www.economicsandpeace.org/wp-content/uploads/2020/09/Ecological-Threat-Register-Press-Release-27.08-FINAL.pdf

Internal Displacement Monitoring Centre & Norwegian Refugee Council (2016). *GRID 2016: Global report on internal displacement.* https://www.internal-displacement.org/sites/default/files/publications/documents/2016-global-report-internal-displacement-IDMC.pdf

Johnson, R. A. (2013). *Owning your own shadow: Understanding the dark side of the psyche.* Harper Collins.

Joseph, B. (2023, June 6). What is the seventh generation principle? *Indigenous Corporate Training Inc.* https://www.ictinc.ca/blog/seventh-generation-principle#:~:text=The%20Seventh%20Generation%20Principle%20is,seven%20generations%20into%20the%20future

Jung, C. G. (1951). *Aion: Researches into the phenomenology of the self* (Vol. 9, Part 2 of *The Collected Works of C. G. Jung*). Princeton University Press.

Jung. C. G. (1963). *Memories, dreams, reflections.* Random House.

Jung, C.G. (1969). *Archetypes of the collective unconscious* (2nd ed.). Princeton University Press.

Jung, C. (n.d.). *The concept of the collective unconscious* - baha'i studies. http://www.bahaistudies.net/asma/The-Concept-of-the-Collective-Unconscious.pdf

Kahane, A. M. (2010). *Power and Love.* Berrett-Koehler.

Kenny, C. (2012). Liberating leadership theory. In C. Kenny & T. N. Fraser (Eds.), *Living Indigenous leadership: Native narratives on building strong communities* (pp. 1–14). UBC Press.

Kolbert, E. (2014). *The sixth extinction: An unnatural history.* Picador.

Korten, D. C. (2006). *The great turning: From empire to earth community.* Berret-Koehler.

Leighton, M. R. (2020). *Arising: Hurricane (Superstorm) Sandy's impact on design/planning professionals* [Doctoral dissertation, Antioch University]. Antioch University Repository & Archive. https://aura.antioch.edu/cgi/viewcontent.cgi?article=1598&context=etds

Llewellyn. (n.d.). Term: Dweller on the threshold. In *Llewellyn* [Online encyclopedia]. Retrieved June 11, 2023, from https://www.llewellyn.com/encyclopedia/term/Dweller+on+the+Threshold

Macy, J. (2009). *The great turning.* Center for Ecoliteracy. https://www.ecoliteracy.org/article/great-turning

McClintock, S. L. (2011) Compassionate trickster: The Buddha as a literary character in the narratives of early Indian Buddhism. *Journal of the American Academy of Religion*, *79*(1), 90–112, https://doi.org/10.1093/jaarel/lfq061

Metzner, R. (1995). The psychopathology of the human-nature relationship. In T. Roszak, M. Gomes, & A. Kanner (Eds.), *Ecopsychology: Restoring the earth, healing the mind* (pp. 55–67). University of Pennsylvania Press.

Mishra, R. C. (2013). Moksha and the Hindu worldview. *Psychology and Developing Societies*, *25*(1), 21–42. https://doi.org/10.1177/0971333613477318

Mitra, A. (2020). Maya–A conceptual history. *Prabuddha Bharata*, *125*(1), 266–275.

Oxfam International. (2023). *5 natural disasters that beg for climate action*. https://www.oxfam.org/en/5-natural-disasters-beg-climate-action#:~:text=The%20number%20of%20climate%2Drelated,their%20homes%20by%20climate%20change

Plotkin, B. (2008). *Nature and the human soul. Cultivating wholeness and community in a fragmented world*. New World Library.

Radin, P. (1988). *The trickster: A study in American Indian mythology*. Schocken Books.

Rinpoche, S. (2008). *The Tibetan book of living and dying: A spiritual classic from one of the foremost interpreters of Tibetan Buddhism to the West* (Revised & Updated ed.). Random House.

Rowlatt, J. (2022, February 2). *Climate change: The science briefing that convinced Boris Johnson*. BBC News. https://www.bbc.com/news/science-environment-60203674

Sargent, K. (2020.). Clan Mothers and founding fathers: The impact of the Iroquois confederacy on American constitutionalism. *Scholars Crossing*. https://digitalcommons.liberty.edu/honors/963/

Schön, D. A. (1983). *The reflective practitioner: How professionals think in action*. Basic.

SEANeighborhoods. (2023, March 25). *Why I'm thankful for indigenous resistance*. Front Porch: Seattle Department of Neighborhoods. https://frontporch.seattle.gov/2021/11/10/why-im-thankful-for-indigenous-resistance/

Sparby, T. (2023). Rudolf Steiner and the 'Guardian of the Threshold,' Part I. *Steiner Studies. Internationale Zeitschrift für kritische Steiner*-Forschung, 3(1). https://www.steiner-studies.org/articles/10.12857/STS.951000340-12/print/

Steiner, R. (1912a). *Four mystery plays. GA14: The guardian of the threshold*. The Rudolf Steiner Archive. https://rsarchive.org/Books/GA014/English/APC1925/GA014-3_scene01.html

Steiner, R. (1912b). *The gates of knowledge*. Theosophical Publishing Society. https://ia601507.us.archive.org/34/items/b29011875/b29011875.pdf

Suzuki, S. (2010). *Zen mind, beginner's mind* (40th Anniversary ed.). Shambhala.

The Arson Strike Force. (1986, September). Arson in New York: 1985- Office of Justice Programs. https://www.ojp.gov/pdffiles1/Digitization/103200NCJRS.pdf

Theosophy World. (n.d.). Dwellers on the threshold. In *Theosophy World Resource Centre* [Online encyclopedia]. Retrieved June 11, 2023, from https://www.theosophy.world/encyclopedia/dweller-threshold

Tibetan Buddhist Encyclopedia. (n.d.). Dukkha. Dukkha - Tibetan Buddhist Encyclopedia. http://tibetanbuddhistencyclopedia.com/en/index.php?title=Dukkha

Underhill, E. (2002). *Mysticism: A study in the nature and development of spiritual consciousness*. Dover Publications.

Wallace-Wells, D. (2023, May 21). There's no escape from wildfire smoke. *The New York Times*. https://www.nytimes.com/2023/05/17/opinion/wildfires-smoke-pollution-distance.html?searchResultPosition=2

Wheatley, M. J. (2005). *Finding our way: Leadership for an uncertain time*. Berrett-Koehler.

15

LEADERSHIP AND SPIRITUALITY AT THE UNITED NATIONS

Moving from Realpolitik to an Ethics of Care

Lisa A. Berkley and Robert Zuber

Introduction

Inspiration

For many global leaders, Nelson Mandela, the first president of a new South Africa, served as an inspirational compass, inspiring international or national service and commitment to improving the state of humanity and the world (Urquhart et al., 2013). Such influence impacted former U.S. President Barack Obama, who claimed his political career was ignited by the South African leader. Stating he would continue to learn from Mandela's life until his last breath, Obama proclaimed, "I studied [Mandela's] words and his writings. The day that he was released from prison gave me a sense of what human beings can do when they're [*sic*] guided by their hopes and not by their fears" (Urquhart et al., 2013, para. 5). Hope then became the foundation for Obama's 2008 victorious campaign. However, from the beginning, the U.S. president recognized hard work would be required by all to maintain the vision which undergirded that hope (Barackobamadotcom, 2008; Phillips, 2009). Indeed, Mandela's inspirational life and message have motivated global leaders around the world, such that the United Nations (UN) General Assembly passed a resolution on November 10, 2009, which declared July 18 as Nelson Mandela International Day.

Honoring Mandela

In 2023, on Nelson Mandela International Day, UN Secretary-General António Guterres gave a brief speech remembering Mandela for his

DOI: 10.4324/9781003396741-20

incredible courage, conviction, achievements, and extraordinary humanity. Acknowledging the vast meta-crisis related to global economic debt, climate crisis, poverty, discrimination, hate, racism, and inequity, Guterres called on members of the General Assembly to honor Mandela's legacy by taking action to "expel the poison of racism, discrimination, and hate; extinguish the legacies of colonialism; [and]... promote equality, human rights and above all, justice" (United Nations, 2023, lines 4–6). Stating that everyone has the power within themselves to help solve these problems, he implored members to "commemorate Nelson Mandela's life and legacy, [...] be animated by his spirit of humanity, dignity, and justice...[and]...take action to build a better world" (United Nations, 2023, lines 12–14). Indeed, July 18, 2023, proved to be as inspirational as every other Nelson Mandela International Day since its inception in 2009. But then the question remains, what happens on July 19?

This chapter will examine that question; it will reflect upon the role of both unmet inspiration and idealism and the promises made and broken, which have helped to create a world characterized by cynicism, ambivalence, and inaction within the international community. Seeking to articulate how the UN can progress further as a force for global good, we will discuss the intersection of leadership and spirituality at the individual level as well as the UN's institutional ethical framework. Using broad brush strokes, we will explore the role of leaders within the UN—those charged with addressing both the global poly-crisis (Tooze, 2022), and meta-crisis (See the Introduction for a discussion on meta- and poly-crisis). We discuss the significance of leadership, which focuses on solving immediate crises within the context of creating longer-term and sustainable policies and solutions while recognizing the role of personal responsibility and that peacebuilding is "as much a spiritual journey as it is a political, social, and educational process. It is [first] an attitude of the heart and a principle by which we abide in our personal life" (Aram, 2013, p. 48). Keeping this in mind, we will examine ways to move forward so hope and care can be reawakened, allowing the UN to begin to move from a global, fear-based realpolitik stance into one rooted in compassion, equity, and honoring our interconnectivity amongst peoples and between people and planet.

As this chapter examines the intersectionality of leadership and spirituality, it is important we clearly define what we mean when we refer to spirituality. We define spirituality as an intrinsic life force or vital energy that flows through and interconnects all of existence, both animate and inanimate. It is an inherent, fundamental aspect woven into the fabric of being human that both consciously and unconsciously shapes thought and behavior. Spirituality represents an unspoken, almost taken-for-granted undercurrent that vitalizes and connects all existence. Yet, despite being such a profound and pervasive aspect of life, it is not always considered within decision-making processes by the UN and other major global institutions.

The Role of the United Nations

Comprised of 193 member nations (United Nations, n.d.-a) The UN is one of the most influential international organizations in the world with a critical mission to maintain international peace, promote human rights, foster social progress, and uplift lives across the globe. With such a charge, one would hope those in leadership positions prioritize practices consistent with servant leadership. Developed by Robert Greenleaf in 1970, servant leadership is, first and foremost, a commitment to serving the needs of others (Greenleaf, 1977). It also emphasizes the skills of openness and persuasion rather than control. It is a form of stewardship, or "holding something in trust for another" (Spears, 2004, p. 9), which reflects Greenleaf's outlook regarding all institutions: CEOs, staff, and trustees all played significant roles in holding their organizations "in trust for the greater good of society" (Spears, 2004, p. 9). Such stewardship is not created through formal rules. Rather, it is an organic, skills-based facilitation process rooted in a commitment to growth, healing, and wholeness driven by moral courage in service to the organization or cause and committed to the creation and generation of interpersonal and institutional trust (Hernandez, 2008). Inherent in stewardship, much like in servant leadership, is the understanding that the long-term best interest of the group or community gets placed ahead of personal goals that serve individual self-interests. Such a high charge necessitates high levels of multiple intelligences (see Chapter 11 on the use of the multiple intelligences as part of the inner economy framework), self-reflection, and personal accountability among leaders (see Chapters 5 and 12 for discussion on self-reflection and personal accountability). Also beneficial to leaders within an environment energized by servant leadership is the embodiment of holistic and interconnected philosophies found in the Indigenous and African worldviews (see Chapters 6 and 7, respectively). These qualities lay the foundation required to help humanity thrive in relationship to one another and Earth herself. Unfortunately, however, in recent years, the UN has faced criticism for intermittent ethical failures among its leadership, including abuse of power, deficits in promise-keeping to constituencies, and sexual misconduct scandals which have undermined trust in the institution (Bishara et al., 2020; Lynch, 2018). How is it that leaders in an organization that requires care and a commitment to the betterment of humanity can lose their way? Has the honoring of Spirit—the vitalizing force in all life—become lost in battles of personal will and exchange of force?

Power Dynamics

While UN leadership outwardly champions human rights, development, and peacebuilding, experts argue that real-world actions undermine these ideals due to geopolitics and inconsistent application of principles. Analysis indicates that the UN Security Council (UNSC) often responds robustly (if not always decisively) to violations affecting favored or powerful states while being hamstrung in addressing controversial actions by Council members and their allies (Hehir & Murray, 2017; UN News, 2022). For example, the UNSC was able to direct concerted policy attention on Russia's Ukraine invasion while facing critiques of being paralyzed on issues like the Israel-Palestine crisis for decades. This inconsistency signals double standards (Fabricius, 2022; Lundgren, et al., 2022). Additionally, issues of preparation and responsibility are reflected in the wide gap between the UN's pro-poor and pro-vulnerable rhetoric and the reality that global humanitarian crises (largely due to conflict and climate threats) have worsened post-2020 (International Rescue Committee, 2021).

This inconsistency reflects a cognitive dissonance, which some scholars believe is due to the outsized influence certain member states exert within UN decision-making and funding structures (Deen, 2020). Competing national interests, unilateral actions, and political showmanship often supersede collective responsibilities (Deen, 2020). While real budgetary, legal, and operational constraints exist, experts argue that leaders manipulate such limitations as a pretext for advancing state power over proclaimed global ideals of human rights and development (Lundgren, et al., 2022). Increased transparency regarding such limitations alongside equitable governance reforms would likely mitigate tendencies to privilege rhetoric over realities on the ground.

Without a doubt, power dynamics substantially shape and restrict UN leadership despite organizational commitments to uphold international peace and security (Hehir & Murray, 2013; UN News, 2022). According to Secretary-General Guterres, geopolitical divides are undermining the work of the Security Council (France 24, 2022). Council stalemates neither reflect the intended purpose of the UN nor demonstrate a holistic approach to resolving our global meta-crisis. At best, the results are in the form of temporary, short-term band-aids. Unfortunately, with these types of issues and dynamics center stage, the spirit of humanity that unites us all often gets overshadowed. Pursuing dominance and control often leads nations to lose sight of the spiritual values—compassion, care, and our shared essence—which lie at the foundation of the UN's intention. Making true and lasting peace requires recognizing that beneath our differences we are spiritual beings who must focus upon, and cultivate, the spirit of care and goodwill toward others. Structural changes are required to enable consistency between noble multilateral goals and practical capacity. But how do we get there?

Leadership and Spirituality

Within the context of the UN, spirituality and spiritual intelligence are important dimensions of creating an environment of collaboration, transparency, care, and dignity. Spiritual leadership motivates individuals by providing a vision and culture which gives people a sense of purpose, meaning, and interconnectedness. It does this by proposing a collective mission which allows members to feel their lives matter and that they make a positive difference (Fry, 2003). Additionally, spiritual leadership helps to foster an altruistic, compassionate environment where both leaders and followers authentically care for, understand, and appreciate each other as well as themselves (Fry, 2003). In turn, this produces a sense of community in which all people feel valued as an integral part of that community.

Academic research on leadership increasingly points to the relevance of spirituality, defined as one's search for meaning, purpose, morality, and self-transcendence (Benefiel et al., 2014; Cacioppe, 2000). Spirituality and religion have historically informed concepts of ethical leadership across cultures and faith traditions (Singh & Mishra, 2022). In the modern workplace, spirituality is consistent with servant leadership approaches emphasizing integrity, empathy, and concern for the greater good (van Dierendonck & Patterson, 2015).

UN leaders operate in a multi-faith context and are expected to uphold the organization's humanitarian ideals. However, recent scandals of policy and practice indicate that lofty spiritual principles have not always translated into ethical practices within the institution. Applying insights from transpersonal psychology, which examine spiritual growth and human potential, can help explain this discrepancy (Enright et al., 2022; Schwab, 2021). (See Chapter 1 for more on transpersonal psychology and leadership). In this context, a tendency toward spiritual bypassing is highly relevant.

Spiritual Bypassing and Lack of Responsibility

Spiritual bypassing refers to using spiritual practices and beliefs to avoid painful wounds, emotions, and experiences (Cashwell et al., 2004). At the UN, spiritual bypassing could take the form of leaders invoking humanitarian values or paying lip service to ideals of peace and human rights while failing in their responsibility to address ongoing political conflicts and power abuses occurring within the organization, abuses which impede the keeping of promises to both UN staff and its global constituents.

Welwood (1984) suggested that spiritual bypassing reflects impaired ego development as individuals seek self-transcendence before doing the necessary work of forming a healthy, integrated identity. Applied to UN leadership, this suggests that elaborate visions of world peace will lack moral authority if leaders have not done the basic psychological work of taking responsibility for their own ethical blind spots and destructive impulses, of committing to self-reflection, self-awareness, and improvement, and working toward the crafting of more impactful and context-appropriate policies (see Chapter 2 for a discussion on spiritual bypassing and leadership).

Recent examples indicate that spiritual bypassing has been used to justify unethical behaviors among UN leaders. A 2018 report found that some UN staff invoked their humanitarian commitments as a rationalization for paying for sexual services—a practice condemned by the UN as exploitation (Nichols, 2018). This hypocrisy reflects a disconnect between proclaimed values and actual conduct, stemming in part from a refusal to acknowledge our shadow side.

The Shadow Side of Leaders

Swiss psychiatrist Carl Gustav Jung coined the term "shadow" to describe the unknown or denied parts of oneself, containing repressed weaknesses, shortcomings, and instincts (Jung, 1959). The shadow manifests itself through uncontrolled or even violent outbursts or projections onto others. Importantly, Jung viewed the shadow as the seat of human creativity and an opportunity for growth—not just something to eliminate. However, shadow work involves seeking hidden truths about oneself, truths which are often at odds with more "surface" reputations and branding.

From a Jungian perspective (Sheets-Johnstone, 2017; Tallman, 2003), it could be said that UN officials accused of corruption and sexual misconduct can be seen as acting out their unrecognized shadow qualities and desires for power. Populist authoritarian political leaders also exemplify this dynamic, attracting followers with righteous exteriors while indulging their egos (Wayment & Bauer, 2008). However, it is important to recognize that facing one's shadow creates the possibility of redemption (see Chapters 13 and 14 for a discussion on facing the shadow). A leader who has fallen from grace can re-establish trust by taking accountability rather than making excuses. Reform at the UN similarly requires more than policies—it entails senior officials courageously confronting their own limitations and encouraging others to do likewise.

The dangers of spiritual bypassing arise when leaders disown their shadows, instead projecting their dark impulses onto others while presenting themselves as doing high value humanitarian work or being spiritually enlightened (Welwood, 1984). These tendencies are enabled in organizational cultures where open discussion of ethics and spirituality is discouraged. For the UN to cultivate and sustain the trust needed to address its recent crises, leaders must cultivate reflective practices and advisors to help them see their blind spots before they lead to misconduct.

Creating Change: Individual to Collective

How we perceive and function in the world vis-à-vis meaning, vision, and value is often rooted within a spiritual context (Zohar, 1997). Vaughan (1995, 2002) suggested that wisdom rooted in spirituality is "[a path that] requires commitment and integrity [and] can lead from the bondage of unconsciousness to spiritual freedom, from fear and defensiveness to love and compassion…" (2002, p. 23). If the UN system is going to change for the good, the development of greater self-awareness, strategies for individual personal growth, and moral and ethical development among its leaders are required. Affirming the intersection of leadership and spirituality provides insight into how leaders can cultivate greater integrity and take ownership of all aspects of themselves. This integration includes the parts of themselves they are proud of and show to the public, as well as those parts from which they hide or of which they are ashamed.

Socrates famously argued that "the unexamined life is not worth living" (Famakinwa, 2012). Part of the process of moving toward more spirituality-based leadership is the need for studying spiritual bypassing tendencies as well as the Jungian concept of shadow work. Leaders committed to facing their shadows are more able to honestly meet the darker parts of themselves rather than avoiding or denying those parts (Cashwell et al., 2004; Schwab, 2021). National representatives who do not understand themselves or each other can create dysfunctional relationships, agreements, and decisions (Kets de Vries & Balazs, 2009). Denying their shadow side can easily lead to greater harm to the collective. Childhood patterns rooted in pain, fear, or anger will likely lead to destructive and repetitive cycles of decision-making in which leaders lose their sense of purpose and direction (Kets de Vries, 2009). It could then be argued that doing self-reflective work is a moral and ethical requirement within the arena of human rights, conflict resolution, peacemaking, and care for people and planet. Ultimately, responsible leadership requires courage, humility, and commitment to ongoing self-reflection.

Humility and Jungian Shadow Work

How can UN leaders engage in the self-examination required for moral development and avoid spiritual bypassing? An important starting point involves developing humility: the ability to acknowledge gaps in one's knowledge, awareness, and character (Owens et al., 2013). Humility paves the way for honest self-appraisal and reflection. Facing one's shadow side while also leading (see Chapter 14 for a discussion on this) is a skill set that requires profound courage and a willingness to be wrong.

Specifically, applying the framework of Jung's shadow work is another constructive approach. This application of shadow involves noticing one's tendencies to project negative aspects of the self onto others, owning undesirable traits, and integrating contrasts within oneself (Schwartz, 2021). Projections refer to the tendency to see one's own flaws in others. For instance, a UN leader who berates a country for corruption may project their hidden, financially unethical dealings onto that nation. Owning the shadow means recognizing one's complex humanity and not simply identifying with an idealized version of oneself. Integrating contrasts implies resolving inner conflicts—accepting that one can be both generous and selfish, indifferent, and compassionate depending on context and levels of reinforcement.

Reflective Practices

Engaging in the abovementioned practices will likely lead to more effective and ethical decision making as well as fewer counterproductive work behaviors, better listening, and an ability to provide clearer directives (Kets de Vries, 2009). Additionally, reflective practices focused inward can reveal difficult truths about oneself. Such efforts can also help leaders to understand their role and contribution to difficulties in reaching agreements and decisions. Often, these revelatory practices are best done either in solitude or with the guidance of experienced experts. Such practices as centering prayer and mindfulness meditation create spaces for self-reflection by suspending conventional or self-justifying thoughts (Keating, 2006). Journaling and speaking honestly with a counselor or peer mentor can also provide pathways into the shadow self. Ultimately, like most people, UN leaders seek meaning and purpose in their work (Dhiman, 2017). They often have a profound desire to connect with one another and to contribute to making the world a better place—to return to the original call to service and to the spiritual undergirding of interconnectedness, wholeness, and unity. These practices can support them in following their internal compass so they may remain faithful to the high ideals that they believe guide their purposes and principles (see Chapter 12 on how to use entrainment to optimize the use of spiritual practice).

Moving from Realpolitik to an Ethics of Care

When we move the focus from the individual to the collective and consider the ways in which individual leaders can better "clarify" themselves, we must also examine the foundations on which organizations such as the UN function as a whole. In addition to moral development, the UN as an institution needs to evolve beyond outdated realpolitik approaches and toward a leadership framework that fully embodies its humanitarian vision. Realpolitik refers to politics based on practical and material factors like military and economic power rather than ethical ideals (Mandry, 2022). This model has dominated international relations for centuries. However, the meta-crisis and poly-crisis we currently face today call for an evolution to an "ethics of care" paradigm in global governance. Such a paradigm would enable the UN to reorient its priorities around inter-dependency, and human flourishing, as opposed to political expediency across its peacebuilding, sustainable development, climate change, and human rights initiatives (Conway, 2022; Peters, 2021).

Of course, the role the UN plays in the arena of international peace and security remains central. A primary goal in this endeavor is focused on protection and the need to think, plan, and prepare for worst-case national and international conflicts and disasters. Subsequently, fear can often become the default starting point for strategy and tactics which in turn, influences international decision-making and governance. By default, fear—sometimes referred to by psychologists as self-protection or self-preservation—becomes the cornerstone of the realist perspective which governs most nations, and certainly many communities in the Western world (Moisi, 2010). Within the field of International Relations, the realist perspective defines the interactions between sovereign states pursuing power and self-interest; it is grounded in a fear-based view of the world where conflict between competing interests is inevitable. As such, all nations must gauge the threats they face, decide how best to protect their land and people, and "choose the sacrifices that they will make and the risks they will accept in the name of national security" (Spiegel et al., 2012, p. 290). However, there is a cost. Often, political and historical contexts are ignored, and the economic, cultural, and psychological aspects of security are given insufficient attention (Nye & Lynn-Jones, 1988, p. 7).

Between 1945 and 1990, during the period defined in large measure by the Cold War, national security issues were centered around traditional topics and concerns such as deterrence, military power, and arms control (Spiegel et al., 2012). More recently, however, the events of 9/11, perhaps more than any other single event (post-World War II and post-Cold War), showed us how globally interconnected we are (Smith & Baylis, 2005). For example, the conflicts between Russia and Ukraine, Israel and Palestine, and within states such as Sudan and Yemen have been clear examples of what it means to think of our present, often-troubled era as a globalized one. These events reflect the major issues of the post-Cold War era yet are more amorphous as they include arms proliferation, terrorism, and organized crime, issues which are at the center of these conflicts and reflect what political scientist John Mueller terms, "the remnants of war" (Spiegel et al., 2012, p. 293).

The line between conflict and cooperation, or war and peace, is a delicate one. We face it every day, not just between countries and nations, but also through the actions of non-state actors, such as Hamas, ISIS, Boko Haram, and other extremist groups. It is the task of members of the peace and security sector to weigh the complicated and ever-changing factors that contribute to maintaining balance and, hopefully, over time, move us toward peace. As an integral part of the peace and security sector, The UN provides an example of the limitations of realpolitik. Historically, UN peacekeeping missions were often authorized based on political bargaining between powerful member states rather than a careful and caring assessment of needs on the ground (Aoi et al., 2007). Critics argue that this lack of care contributed to some catastrophic failures to protect civilians, such as in Rwanda and Bosnia (Dorn, 2022). A care-based approach, now finding some expression in such missions, defines security in human rather than nationalistic terms and ensures that peacekeeping operations can continue to prioritize the protection of human life over political expediency (Peters, 2021). This type of approach can provide a small sense of hope. As human security moves to the forefront of discussions, care is invited back into negotiations, by default, so too is the spiritual thread which weaves us together from person to person and people to planet.

Ethics of Care

Scholars argue that an ethics of care could transform the field of international relations by making care and responsibility for human welfare the central concern guiding policy and actions between states and global governance institutions (Held, 2006). As nations recognize their interconnectedness and affirm their obligations to citizens worldwide, an ethics of care lens could prioritize human rights, development, peacebuilding, and global public goods over national interests alone. It would entail nurturing caring relationships among nations, listening closely to needs, and crafting mutually supportive policies that promote human dignity and better ensure that communities can thrive within and across borders. Some even see the ethics of care as providing a unifying foundation for reconceiving global cooperation.

The ethics of care is posited as a normative ethical framework emphasizing the importance of relationships, interdependence, and care for others in moral decision-making and actions (Held, 2006). Some key aspects of an ethics of care include:

- Focusing on responsibility and attentiveness to relationships rather than rigid rules. Care ethics considers the contextual elements of relationships and caring responsibilities when determining moral obligations.
- Valuing emotion and attentiveness to need. An ethics of care framework views emotional intelligence as informative in discerning and responding to others' needs. Caring depends on noticing, understanding, and meeting needs.
- Highlighting human interconnectedness and interdependency rather than independence. Care ethics recognizes that people are embedded within social relationships and dependent on others to thrive.
- Promoting the moral development of caring persons and relationships, specifically among leadership. The goal is cultivating caring dispositions and shaping relationships and institutions guided by attentiveness, responsibility, competence, and responsiveness.

Ultimately, the Ethics of Care framework provides an undergirding rooted in spirituality. It is the fabric of being human that both consciously and unconsciously shapes thought and behavior and provides the memory and knowledge of an intrinsic life force or vital energy that flows through and interconnects all of existence, both animate and inanimate.

SDGs: Ethics of Care in Practice

The UN's Sustainable Development Goals (SDGs), also known as the Global Goals, are 17 international goals adopted by the UN in 2015 (United Nations, n.d.-b). They represent a call to action to end poverty, protect the planet, and ensure that by 2030, all people can enjoy peace, dignity, and prosperity (United Nations, n.d.-b). The SDGs present an opportunity to move from realism to an ethics of care. Though lauded as a shared blueprint for humanity, the framework has been critiqued from an ethics of care perspective (Conway, 2022; Robbins, 2020). Specifically, the broad indicators and targets are believed by some to focus too much on rational technocratic solutions versus responding concretely to vulnerable people's lived experiences. However, they could be transformed, even at this relatively late date, by centering on an ethic of care that prioritizes those most marginalized and integrates holistic values of solidarity and relationships.

Additionally, climate change negotiations reveal tensions between realpolitik national self-interest and a care orientation. Developing nations justifiably demand increased climate financing from richer polluting countries, which have caused the most environmental damage (Dorsch & Flachsland, 2017). Yet, binding financial commitments stall under realist zero-sum assumptions, that is, where states compete for power and resources and one state's gain is another state's loss. Feminist and care theorists propose alternative frameworks of ethics, empathy, and mutual sharing to break the impasse (Sherman & Biermann, 2021). This is merely one example of how care-based principles could guide and transform collective problem-solving while at the same time, providing a spiritual-based lens.

Finally, centering an ethic of care could help revolutionize the UN's human rights institutions and approaches. Critics argue that the dominant rights paradigm excessively focuses on legal procedures versus human needs and relationships (Engster, 2015). Ethicists whose work centers around the Ethics of Care contend that authentic progress stems from compassionate dialogue, not legalistically-defined duties alone. For instance, truth and reconciliation processes aim to heal atrocities through voluntary confession and forgiveness, a care-based form of justice (Lambourne, 2021). This model could expand beyond transitional contexts into tangible reforms within the UN human rights bodies.

In summary, realist frameworks have long become ingrained across UN sectors, obscuring in some measure its original humanitarian vision. Transitioning in part, or in whole, to an Ethics of Care paradigm would entail reimagining global governance as a collaborative project of human flourishing and spirituality—the unifying thread which vitalizes all life and reflects our interconnectedness—beyond state interests. Such a shift could well enable the UN to better live up to its ideals in promoting holistic and ethical security, sustainable development, climate action, and human rights globally.

Conclusion

The field of international peace and security, of which the UN is a key player, is where critical decisions are made every day. These decisions have significant ramifications for the daily lives and security of whole communities if not countries. Increasingly, the global and national challenges that leaders in this field face are complex, multi-dimensional, and community-impacting. Recent scandals and policy missteps at the UN point to the need for greater self-awareness and moral development among organizational leaders. Insights from transpersonal psychology reveal the pitfalls of spiritual bypassing, which allow leaders to hide destructive impulses behind moral facades. It is evident that shadow material stands in the way of the body's work, which may reflect the world as it is today. However, Jung's shadow work continues to suggest a relevant framework for honestly facing and integrating the denied parts of oneself. Leadership grounded in humility (see Chapter 9 for lessons of humility drawn from Sufism and how they can be applied to leadership development) and ongoing self-reflection can help the UN move forward and regain lost trust. At an individual level, leaders must summon the courage to know their shadows rather than projecting them onto others. As well, they must remember and return to their original call of service and honor the conscious or unconscious recognition of our connection, the spiritual thread which enables us to create the peaceful world toward which we envision and create.

The UN requires institutional-wide ethical growth beyond outdated realpolitik approaches. An ethics of care paradigm focused on human welfare and flourishing could help guide urgent reforms across peace and security, sustainable development, climate change, and human rights sectors. This wisdom holds relevance far beyond the UN and across contexts which require complex, ethical decision-making in an interconnected world.

This chapter may well seem a bit idealistic or naïve given that the large and powerful UN members control much of the UN's priorities and practices and that UN diplomats are tasked with representing positions rather than crafting them with little real responsibility for implementing the consensus documents they help to create. Many in the UN's diplomatic missions and secretariat offices feel that something is amiss, that they are failing those who look to the UN for relief from the meta- and poly-crisis, the horrors of war and the deprivations of climate change, for tangible signs of hope that the vast inequalities of our world can narrow rather than expand. (See Chapter 3 for a discussion on the role of coherence in establishing healthy leadership).

The annual Mandela event noted at the beginning of this chapter is but one example of how much the wider UN community remains open to incarnations of inspiration and wisdom, courage and hope from those who lead its processes and promote its ideals. It is moving each year to hear diplomats speak in tones rarely replicated during the rest of the year, speaking less of what they want and more of what has inspired them and more of what led them once upon a time to serve in UN policy spaces. If only we could capture and/or recover more of those commitments to self-reflection, service, and idealism, and if only we could inspire more determination to keep policy promises and not just make them, then the UN system we need and want could flourish in new and inspiring ways. It remains, to a significant degree, the responsibility of its leadership to encourage and enable those transformations.

References

Aoi, C., De Coning, C., & Thakur, R. (2007). *Unintended consequences of peacekeeping operations.* United Nations University Press.

Aram, K. (2013). Faith-inspired work for societal change and peaceful co-existence: The Gandhian experience. In H. Moksnes & M. Melin (Eds.), *Faith in civil society religious actors as drivers of change* (pp. 45–54). Uppsala Centre for Sustainable Development, Uppsala University.

Barackobamadotcom (2008, November 3). *Barack Obama: "We have a lot of work to do"* [video]. YouTube. https://www.youtube.com/watch?v=cfjQujYrfEk

Benefiel, M., Fry, L. W., & Geigle, D. (2014). Spirituality and religion in the workplace: History, theory, and research. *Psychology of Religion and Spirituality, 6*(3), 175–187. https://doi.org/10.1037/a0036597

Bishara, A. J., DeFrancisco, V. P., & Palihapitiya, M. (2020). Sexual exploitation and abuse in UN peacekeeping operations: A case study of Haiti and Liberia. *International Peacekeeping, 27*(2), 277–307. https://doi.org/10.1080/13533312.2020.1729463

Cacioppe, R. (2000). Creating spirit at work: Re-visioning organization development and leadership: Part II. *Leadership & Organization Development Journal, 21*(2), 110–119. https://doi.org/10.1108/01437730010318205

Cashwell, C. S., Myers, J. E., & Shurts, W. M. (2004). Using the developmental counseling and therapy model to work with a client in spiritual bypass: Some preliminary considerations. *Journal of Counseling and Development, 82*(4), 403–409. https://doi.org/10.1002/j.1556-6678.2004.tb00327.x

Conway, G. (2022). An ethic of care critique of the sustainable development goals. *Journal of Global Ethics, 18*(1), 70–86. https://doi.org/10.1080/17449626.2022.2035680

Deen, T. (2020). *UN's 75th anniversary shadowed by multiple crises.* Inter Press Service News Agency. https://www.ipsnews.net/2019/10/uns-75th-anniversary-shadowed-right-wing-nationalism-widespread-authoritarianism-budgetary-cuts/

Dhiman, S. (2017). *Holistic leadership.* Palgrave Macmillan. https://doi.org/10.1057/978-1-137-55571-7_7

Dorn, W. (2022). *Keeping watch: Monitoring, technology and innovation in UN peace operations.* United Nations University Press.

Dorsch, M., & Flachsland, C. (2017). A polycentric approach to global climate governance. *Global Environmental Politics, 17*(2), 45–64. https://doi.org/10.1162/GLEP_a_00400

Engster, D. (2015). Care ethics, dependency, and vulnerability. *Ethics and Social Welfare, 9*(2), 100–114. https://doi.org/10.1080/17496535.2015.1010786

Enright, D., Knights, J., Grant, D., & Young, G. (Eds.). (2022). *Transpersonal leadership in action how to lead beyond the ego.* Routledge. https://doi.org/10.4324/9781003150626

Fabricius, P. (2022, October 4). *Russia's war in Ukraine revives calls for Security Council expansion.* Elect The Council. https://electthecouncil.org/russias-war-in-ukraine-revives-calls-for-security-council-expansion/

Famakinwa, J. O. (2012). Is the unexamined life worth living or not? *Think, 11*(31), 97–103. https://doi.org/doi:10.1017/S1477175612000073

France 24. (2022, September 20). Guterres warns U.N. Security Council that world is 'in great peril'. *France 24*. https://www.france24.com/en/diplomacy/20220920-un-chief-warns-that-world-is-in-great-peril-as-leaders-arrive-for-general-assembly

Fry, L. W. (2003). Toward a theory of spiritual leadership. *The Leadership Quarterly, 14*(2003), 693–727. https://doi.org/10.1016/j.leaqua.2003.09.001

Greenleaf, R. K. (1977). *Servant leadership: A journey into the nature of legitimate power and greatness*. Paulist Press.

Hehir, A., & Murray, R. W. (Eds.). (2013). *Libya, the responsibility to protect and the future of humanitarian intervention*. Palgrave MacMillian. https://doi.org/10.1057/9781137273956

Hehir, A., & Murray, R.W. (Eds.). (2017). *Protecting human rights in the 21st century (1st ed.)*. Routledge. https://doi.org/10.4324/9781315436692

Held, V. (2006). *The ethics of care: Personal, political, and global*. Oxford University Press.

Hernandez, M. (2008). Promoting stewardship behavior in organizations: A leadership model. *Journal of Business Ethics, 80*, 121–128. https://doi.org/10.1007/s10551-007-9440-2

International Rescue Committee. (2021, April 22). How climate change drives humanitarian crises. *International Rescue Committee*. https://www.rescue.org/article/how-climate-change-drives-humanitarian-crises

Jung, C. G. (1959). *Collected Works of C.G. Jung, Volume 9 (Part 2): Aion: Researches into the Phenomenology of the Self* (G. Alder & R. F. C. Hull, Eds.). Princeton University Press. http://www.jstor.org/stable/j.ctt5hhqh6

Keating, T. (2006). *Open mind, open heart 20th anniversary edition*. Continuum.

Kets de Vries, M., & Balazs, K. (2009, September). *The shadow side of leadership*. https://www.researchgate.net/profile/Manfred-Kets-De-Vries/publication/304681824_The_Shadow_Side_of_Leadership/links/586bbfee08aebf17d3a5ad62/The-Shadow-Side-of-Leadership.pdf

Lambourne, W. (2021). *Transitional justice and peacebuilding after mass violence*. Routledge.

Lundgren, M., Oksamytna, K., & Bove, V. (2022). Politics or performance? Leadership accountability in UN peacekeeping. *Journal of Conflict Resolution, 66*(1), 32–60. https://doi.org/10.1177/00220027211028989

Lynch, C. (2018). The imperative of moral leadership in international humanitarian and development work. *Center for Strategic and International Studies*. https://www.jstor.org/stable/resrep20156

Mandry, C. (2022). Practicing policy, practicing care: Care ethics as critical approach to international relations theory and practice. *International Feminist Journal of Politics, 24*(2), 211–231. https://doi.org/10.1080/14616742.2020.1846391

Moisi, D. (2010). *The geopolitics of emotion: How cultures of fear, humiliation, and hope are reshaping the world*. Doubleday.

Nichols, M. (2018). *Misconduct by UN staff 'impunity' unacceptable, says Sec-Gen's envoy victims*. Thomson Reuters Foundation. https://news.trust.org/item/20180620121056-twdyu/

Nye, J. S., & Lynn-Jones, S. M. (1988). International security studies: A report of a conference on the state of the field. *International Security, 12*(4), 5–27.

Owens, B. P., Johnson, M. D., & Mitchell, T. R. (2013). Expressed humility in organizations: Implications for performance, teams, and leadership. *Organization Science*, *24*(5), 1517–1538. https://doi.org/10.1287/orsc.1120.0795

Peters, D. (2021). Reimagining refugee protection through a gender lens: An ethics of care perspective. *International Journal of Refugee Law*, *33*(4), 621–644. https://doi.org/10.1093/ijrl/eeab003

Phillips, M. (2009, January 21). *President Barack Obama's inaugural address*. The White House Archives. https://obamawhitehouse.archives.gov/blog/2009/01/21/president-Barack-obamas-inaugural-address

Robbins, M. J. (2020). Evaluating the sustainable development goals from the perspective of ecofeminist ethics of care. *Journal of Global Ethics*, *16*(2), 243–256. https://doi.org/10.1080/17449626.2020.1775342

Schwab, K. A. (2021). The challenges of shadow integration in the individuation process. *Journal of Humanistic Psychology*, *61*(4), 484–501. https://doi.org/10.1177/0022167817739728

Schwartz, R. C. (2021). Embracing your demons: An overview of acceptance and commitment therapy. *Psychotherapy*, *58*(1), 116–120. https://doi.org/10.1037/pst0000272

Sheets-Johnstone M. (2017). The body politic: A Jungian perspective. *Psychotherapy and Politics International*, *15*(3), e1426. https://doi.org/10.1002/ppi.1426

Sherman, J. G. A., & Biermann, F. (2021). Re-engaging ethics for planetary stewardship: An ethics of care approach to the sustainable development goals. *Journal of Global Ethics*, *17*(3), 371–385. https://doi.org/10.1080/17449626.2021.1976211

Singh, S. K., & Mishra, P. (2022). Influence of religiosity and spirituality on ethical leadership. In *Connecting ethical leadership to total responsibility management* (pp. 130–144). Emerald Publishing Limited. https://doi.org/10.1108/S2058-880120220000021009

Smith, S., & Baylis, J. (2005). Introduction. In S. Smith & J. Baylis (Eds.), *The globalization of world politics: An introduction to international relations* (3rd ed., pp. 1–14). Oxford University Press.

Spears, L. (2004). Practicing servant leadership. *Leader to Leader*, *2003*(34), 7–11. https://doi.org/10.1002/ltl.94

Spiegel, S., Matthews, E., Taw, J. M., & Williams, K. P. (2012). *World politics in a new era* (5th ed.). Oxford University Press.

Tallman, B. (2003). The organization leader as king, warrior, magician and lover: How Jungian archetypes affect the way men lead organizations. *Organization Development Journal*, *21*(3), 19–30.

Tooze, A. (2022, October 22). Welcome to the world of the polycrisis. *Financial Times*.

UN News. (2022, February 26). *Russia Blocks Security Council Action on Ukraine | UN news*. United Nations. https://news.un.org/en/story/2022/02/1112802

United Nations. (2023, July 20). *Nelson Mandela international day, July 18, for freedom, justice and democracy*. United Nations. https://www.un.org/en/events/mandeladay/events_2023_SG.shtml

United Nations. (n.d.-a). *Who are the current members of the United Nations? – ask dag!* United Nations. https://ask.un.org/faq/14345#:~:text=There%20are%20currently%20193%20UN,UN%20organs%20is%20provided%20below

United Nations. (n.d.-b). *The 17 goals | sustainable development.* United Nations. https://sdgs.un.org/goals

Urquhart, C., Roberts, D, Lewis, P, & Willsher, K. (2013, December 6). Nelson Mandela: World leaders mourn inspirational figure. *The Guardian*. https://www.theguardian.com/world/2013/dec/05/nelson-mandela-death-world-reaction

van Dierendonck, D., & Patterson, K. (2015). Compassionate love as a cornerstone of servant leadership: An integration of previous theorizing and research. *Journal of Business Ethics, 128*(1), 119–131. https://doi.org/10.1007/s10551-014-2085-z

Vaughan, F. (1995). *Shadows of the sacred: Seeing through spiritual illusions.* Quest Books.

Vaughn, F. (2002). What is spiritual intelligence? *Journal of Humanistic Psychology, 42*(2), 16–33.

Wayment, H. A., & Bauer, J. J. (Eds.). (2008). *Transcending self-interest: Psychological explorations of the quiet ego.* American Psychological Association.

Welwood, J. (1984). Principles of inner work: Psychological and spiritual. *The Journal of Transpersonal Psychology, 16*(1), 63–73.

Zohar, D. (1997). *Rewiring the corporate brain: Using the new science to rethink how we structure and lead organizations.* Berett-Koehler.

INDEX

Note: **Bold** page numbers refer to tables.

Made in the USA
Monee, IL
14 September 2026

62978587R00188